People and Empires in African History

People and Empires in African History:
Essays in Memory of Michael Crowder

Edited by
J.F. Ade Ajayi
and
J.D.Y. Peel

LONGMAN
London and New York

LONGMAN GROUP UK LIMITED,
Longman House, Burnt Mill, Harlow,
Essex CM20 2JE, England
and Associated Companies throughout the World

Published in the United States of America
by Longman Inc., New York

First published 1992

British Library Cataloguing-in-Publication Data
People and empires in African history: Essays in memory of Michael Crowder.
  I. Ajayi, J. F. Ade   II. Peel, J. D. Y.
  960

  ISBN 0–582–08997–2

Set in Linotron 202 10/12pt Bembo

Produced by Longman Singapore Publishers (Pte) Ltd.
Printed in Singapore

Contents

The Contributors

J.F. Ade Ajayi is Emeritus Professor of History, University of Ibadan.

Bawuro M. Barkindo is Senior Lecturer in History, Bayero University, Kano.

Louis Brenner is Lecturer in African Religious Studies, SOAS, London.

Mavis C. Campbell is Professor of History, Amherst College, Massachusetts.

Augustus Casely-Hayford is a research student in African History, SOAS, London.

La Ray Denzer is Professor of History, University of Ibadan.

Toyin Falola, formerly Senior Lecturer in History, Obafemi Awolowo University, Ife, is now Visiting Professor of History, York University, Ontario.

Eldred D. Jones is Professor of English, Fourah Bay College, Sierra Leone.

Murray Last is Reader in Anthropology, University College London.

B.T. Mokopakgosi is Lecturer in History, University of Botswana.

Neil Parsons is Honorary Research Fellow, Institute of Commonwealth Studies, London.

J.D.Y. Peel is Professor of Anthropology and Sociology with reference to Africa, SOAS, London.

Richard Rathbone is Senior Lecturer in the Contemporary History of Africa, SOAS, London.

Paul Richards is Reader in Anthropology, University College, London.

Amanda Sackur, who once worked as Michael Crowder's research assistant, recently completed her Ph.D. in African History at London University.

Akintola J.G. Wyse is Professor of History, Fourah Bay College, Sierra Leone.

List of Maps

Publications

Academic works

1959 *Pagans and Politicians*, Hutchinson.

1962 *The Story of Nigeria*, Faber (published in the USA as *A Short History of Nigeria*, Praeger); rev. edn 1966; third edn 1973; fourth edn 1977.

   Senegal: a study in French assimilation policy, Oxford University Press; rev. edn 1967, Methuen.

1964 with Lalage Bown (eds.), *Proceedings of the First International Congress of Africanists*, Longman (published in USA by Northwestern University Press).

1967 with David Brokensha (eds.), *Africa in the Wider World; the interrelationship of area and comparative studies*, Pergamon.

1968 *West Africa under Colonial Rule*, Hutchinson & Northwestern University Press; new edn 1981.

1970 with Obaro Ikime (eds.), *West African Chiefs: their changing status under colonial rule and independence*, University of Ife Press.

1971 (ed.), *West African Resistance: the military response to colonial occupation*, Hutchinson; new edn 1978.

1971 with J.F. Ade Ajayi (eds.), *History of West Africa*, vol. I, Longman; second edn 1976, third (rev.) edn 1985.

1973 *Revolt in Bussa: a study in British 'native administration' in Nigerian Borgu 1902-1935*, Faber.

1974 with J.F. Ade Ajayi (eds.), *History of West Africa*, vol II, Longman; second (rev.) edn 1987.

1978 *Colonial West Africa: collected essays*, Cass.

1981 with Roland Oliver (eds.), *Encyclopaedia of Africa*, Cambridge University Press.

1983 (ed.), *Stepping Stones: memoirs of colonial Nigeria 1907–1960*,

	(the posthumous memoirs of Sylvia Leith-Ross) Peter Owen.
1984	(ed.), *Education for Development in Botswana,* Macmillan and the Botswana Society.
	(ed.), *Cambridge History of Africa*, vol VIII, *c.1940–c.1975*, Cambridge University Press.
1985	with J. F. Ade Ajayi (eds.), *Historical Atlas of Africa*, Longman (published in the USA by Cambridge University Press).
1988	with Neil Parsons (eds), *'Monarch of all I survey': Bechuanaland diaries 1929–1937* (diaries of Sir Charles Rey) Botswana Society and James Currey.
	The Flogging of Phenehas McIntosh: a tale of colonial folly and injustice, Bechuanaland, 1933, Yale University Press.

In preparation Biography of Tshekedi Khama, Regent of the Bangwato, 1925–50.

Articles and book chapters

1964	'Indirect rule: French and British style', *Africa*, 34 (3): 197–205; republished in P.J.M. McEwan (ed.), *Nineteenth-Century Africa*, Oxford University Press, 1965, and in Irving Leonard Markovits (ed.), *African Politics and Society*, Free Press, 1970; and numerous other symposia.
	'Colonial rule in West Africa: factor for division or unity', *Civilisations* 4; republished in Marion Doro and Newell M. Stultz (eds.), *Governing in Black Africa: perspectives on new states*, Prentice-Hall, 1970.
1965	'Independence as a goal in French West Africa 1944–1960', in William H. Lewis (ed.), *French-Speaking Africa: the search for identity*, New York, pp. 15–51.
1966	'Tradition and change in Nigerian literature', *Triquarterly*, Evanston, 1966.
1968	'West Africa and the 1914–18 war', *Bulletin of IFAN*, 20 (1), series B.
1969	Guest Editor of *Tarikh*, 2 (4), 'France in Africa', with article on 'The administration of French West Africa', pp. 59–71.
1970	with La Ray Denzer, 'Bai Bureh and the Sierra Leone hut tax war of 1898', in Robert I. Rotberg and Ali Mazrui (eds.), *Protest and Power in Black Africa*, Oxford University Press, pp. 169–212.
	'The white chiefs of tropical Africa', in L. H. Gann and Peter Duignan (eds.), *History of Colonialism in Africa*, vol. II, Cambridge University Press.
	'The impact of colonialism', in John Paden and Edward Soja (eds.), *The African Experience*, vol. 1, Northwestern University Press.
	'Vichy and Free France in French West Africa during the

Second World War', *Afro-Asia*, 10–11: 67–78.

1971   'French-speaking West Africa', *International Yearbook*, Europa Publishing Corporation, pp. 161–5 (and all subsequent editions).

1974   'West Africa and the First World War', in J. F. Ade Ajayi and M. Crowder (eds.), *History of West Africa*, vol. 11, pp. 484–513.

With J. F. Ade Ajayi, 'The colonial situation: West Africa 1919–1939', in J. F. Ade Ajayi and M. Crowder (eds.), *History of West Africa*, vol. II, pp 514–41.

'West Africa and the Second World War', in J. F. Ade Ajayi and M. Crowder (eds.), *History of West Africa*, vol. II, pp. 596–621.

With Donal Cruise O'Brien, 'French-speaking West Africa 1944–1960', in J. F. Ade Ajayi and M. Crowder (eds.), *History of West Africa*, vol. II, pp. 664–99.

'The use and abuse of symposia', *Journal of African History*, 15 (1).

1975   'The French suppression of the 1916–17 revolt in Dahomeyan Borgu', *Journal of the Historical Society of Nigeria*, 8 (1); longer version published in M. Crowder, *Colonial West Africa: collected essays*, Cass, 1978, pp. 179–97.

1976   with J. F. Ade Ajayi, 'Culture contact: Africa today and tomorrow', *Family of Man Encyclopedia*, 7 (88).

1977   'The Borgu revolts of 1915–1917', *Tarikh*, 5 (3): 181–30.

'The imposition of the native authority system in Bussa: the rebellion of 1915', paper presented to a seminar on the history of the Niger-Beauve Valleys, sponsored by the history departments of the universities of Ahmadu Bello and Ilorin, 1974, reprinted in *Colonial West Africa; Collected Essays*, Cass, 1978, pp. 151–78.

'West Africa and the Europeans: five hundred years of direct contact', paper written for the Conference of the Historical Society of Ghana, 1971, reprinted in *Colonial West Africa*, pp. 1–25.

'Blaise Diagne and the recruitment of African Troops for the 1914–18 war', paper given as a public lecture, Institute of African Studies, University Ibadan; 1967, reprinted in *Colonial West Africa*, pp. 104–21.

'The contemporary artist in Nigeria: his patrons, his audience and his critics', *Presence Africaine*, 105–106: 130–45.

1978   'African studies for the 1980s', in *Dynamic Processes in African Studies*, University of Bayreuth, pp. 34–40.

1981   'Patronage and audience in Nigeria', *Black Orpheus*, 4.

1982   'The outsider and African culture: the case of E. H. Duckworth and *Nigeria Magazine*', in Robert W. July and Peter Benson (eds.), *African Cultural and Intellectual Leaders and the Development of the New African Nations*, Rockefeller Foundation and Ibadan University Press.

	'"Classical" imperialism', in *Atlas of Mankind*, Mitchell Beazley.
1984	'The impact of two world wars on Africa', *History Today*, January: 11–18.
	'The Second World War: prelude to decolonisation', in M. Crowder (ed.), *The Cambridge History of Africa*, vol. VIII, pp. 8–51.
1985	'Tshekedi Khama and opposition to the British administration of the Bechuanaland Protectorate, 1926–36', *Journal of African History*, 26 (2): 193–215.
	'The First World War and its consequences', in A. Adu Boahen (ed.), *General History of Africa*, vol. VII, *Africa Under Colonial Domination, 1880–1935*, UNESCO and University of California Press/Heinemann, pp. 283–311.
1986	'Lugard and colonial Nigeria: towards an identity', *History Today*, 36 (February): 23–9.
	'Africa's other famine: the book crisis in Africa', in Hector Blackhurst (ed.), *Africa Bibliography*, 1985, Manchester University Press for the International African Institute.
1987	'"Us and them": the International African Institute and the current crisis of identity in African Studies', *Africa*, 57 (1): 109–22.
	'Whose dream was it anyway? Twenty-five years of African independence' *African Affairs*, 86 (342): 7–24.
	With 'Jide Osuntokun, 'The First World War and West Africa, 1914–1918', in J. F. Ade Ajayi and M. Crowder (eds.), *History of West Africa*, Vol. II, second (rev.) edition, Longman.
1988	'Botswana and the survival of liberal democracy in Africa', in Prosser Gifford and William Roger Louis (eds.), *Decolonization and African Independence 1960–80*, Yale University Press.
	'Tshekedi Khama and South West Africa', *Journal of Modern African Studies*, 25 (1), 25–42.
	With Suzanne Miers, 'The politics of slavery in Bechuanaland: power struggles and the plight of the Basarwa in the Bamangwato Reserve 1926–40', in Suzanne Miers and Richard Roberts (eds.), *The End of Slavery in Africa*, Madison, University of Wisconsin Press.
	'The succession crisis over the illness and death of Kgosi Sekgoma II of the Bangwato, 1925', in Jack Parson (ed.), *Succession to High Office in Botswana: Three Case Studies*, Athens, Ohio: Ohio University Press.
	With Jack Parson and Nick Parsons, *Legitimacy and Faction: Tswana Constitutionalism and Political Change*, in Jack Parson (ed.), *Succession to High Office in Botswana: Three Case Studies*.

In preparation
'Africa under British and Belgian domination, 1934–1945', in Ali Mazrui (ed.), *UNESCO General History of Africa*, vol. VIII, London: Heinemann/Berkeley; Los Angeles: University of California Press.
'Professor Macmillan goes on Safari: the British Government Observer Team and the crisis over the Seretse Khama marriage, 1951', in Shula Marks and Hugh Macmillan (eds.), *Essays to Mark the Centenary of the Birth of W. M. Macmillan* London: Institute of Commonwealth Studies.
'"Many questions—some answers": African resistance in West Africa—a general view', in Ronald Robinson and Stig Forster (eds.), *Proceedings of the Conference to Mark the Centenary of the Berlin West Africa Conference 1884–85* (provisional title), Oxford: Oxford University Press.
'Tshekedi Khama: statesman', in R. F. Morton and J. Ramsay (eds.), *The Birth of a Nation: the making of Botswana*, Longman.
'Resistance and accommodation to the penetration of the capitalist economy in Southern Africa: Tshekedi Khama and mining in Botswana, 1929–1959', in Alan Mabin (ed.), *Essays on Southern Africa* (provisional title), Johannesburg: Ravan Press.

School textbooks

1966   with Rex Akpofure, *Nigeria; a modern history for schools*, Faber.
1970   with R. J. Cootes and L. E. Snellgrove, *Ancient Times: a junior history for Africa*, Longman.
1977   *West Africa: an introduction to its history*, Longman.
1979   with Guda Abdullahi, *Nigeria: an introduction to its history*, Longman.
1980   *West Africa: 1000 AD to the present day*, Longman.
1983–85 *Longman Social Studies for Junior Secondary Schools*, 3 vols., Longman, Nigeria.
1986–87 with Elizabeth Paren, *Macmillan Social Studies for Botswana*, 2 vols., Macmillan, Botswana.

Books for children

1963   with Onuora Nzekwu, *Eze Goes to School*, African Universities Press.
1976   with Umaru Ladan, *Sani Goes to School*, African Universities Press.
1978   with Christine Ajayi, *Akin Goes to School*, African Universities Press.

Introduction

It was in 1952 that Michael Crowder, aged 19 and fresh from school at Mill Hill, first came to West Africa. He was a second lieutenant in the Nigeria Regiment, to which he had been seconded for his national service, and was stationed first at Enugu, later at Kaduna. He returned to Britain to read Philosophy, Politics and Economics at Hertford College, Oxford, where he took a First in 1956. During two long vacations at Oxford, he found sponsorship from publishers to enable him to return to Africa, travelling by local transport from Bissau through Guinea, Sierra Leone, Senegal and Gambia. This apprenticeship in travel and writing prepared him for his even more extensive travels of 1956–7. Now he went accompanied by a Sierra Leonian Creole friend, whose extended family connections gained them entry to homes as far as Accra, Lagos and Cameroon. Armed with letters of introduction and his own journalist's skills, he was able to meet many prominent African figures of the British and French colonial establishments, and the most prominent African politicians aspiring to take their places.

He told the story in his first book, *Pagans and Politicians* (1959). 'For me', he wrote, 'the attraction of West Africa is the attraction of its people, largely unrestricted by the straightjacket of Western religion and social behaviour, with very little past but with everything in the future; of an exciting life that since the Second World War has been moving at a rate unprecedented in history. It is an excitement of revolution . . . a revolution in the social, economic and cultural patterns of a people . . .' Crowder belonged to that generation of Englishmen that grew up during the 1940s and matured in the 1950s, who supported reform at home and decolonization abroad. They were inspired by all the hopes and aspirations symbolized in Nkrumah's Ghana and the projected 'development decade' in Africa.

His precocious knowledge of people and places in West Africa soon landed him with what he considered a marvellous job. In 1959 he was appointed editor of *Nigeria Magazine*, responsible directly to the Chief Secretary of Nigeria, with a lovely house on the Lagos Marina. He was also Director of the Exhibition Centre, a publicly-financed gallery for displaying the whole range of Nigerian art, from the traditional to the most contemporary, in all media. Above all he was charged with organizing the cultural aspects of Nigeria's Independence celebrations in 1960. In that post Crowder was able to read all there was to read about Nigeria, and to speak to anyone who had anything to say about Nigerian culture. The Independence issue of *Nigeria Magazine* reflects something of his achievements, but it was in *The Story of Nigeria* (1962) that he set out a synthesis of what he had learnt. His view of Africa's past had now altered radically: he wrote *The Story of Nigeria* 'to dispel the assumption of which I was once guilty and which is still often made, that before the colonial period, Africans had very little history'.

Michael Crowder had little of the conventional training of the academic historian. He had neither a first degree nor a Ph.D in history. But beyond his first degree in PPE – an excellent preparation for understanding current social and economic realities – he had a practised skill in lucid writing, extensive knowledge and contacts in West Africa, and above all a tremendous zest for the region and its people. Nevertheless, he was aware of criticisms of his unconventional background, and he approached academic life with both diffidence and a determination to show a mastery of the genres of academic historiography.

From *Nigeria Magazine* Crowder was invited in 1962 to apply for the post of Executive Secretary of the newly-established Institute of African Studies at the University of Ibadan. Here he worked directly to a superior, the Director of the Institute, but as that was also the Vice-Chancellor of the University, K.O. Dike, he enjoyed a fairly free hand in running the Institute, and enjoyed full academic status as a member of Senate. Here he served as Secretary of the Organizing Committee of the First International Congress of Africanists and was, with Lalage Bown, co-editor of its *Proceedings* (1964). At Ibadan he chose to live off campus, in a splendid house on Mokola Hill, whose decoration he organized himself.

From the start he made it his policy to identify and groom probable local successors, so that he need not remain in the same job for longer than a few years. By June 1964 he had trained a successor to his Ibadan post and was ready to move on. He now felt committed to a career as an academic historian, and wanted to achieve the substantial work that alone would justify a full professorship. From his early travels in Upper

Guinea and Senegambia, where he had observed the differential impact of the colonial systems of France, Britain and Portugal on related peoples, he derived a fascination with the study of colonial policy. A short study of French assimilation policy in the *quatre communes* of Senegal was published for the Institute of Race Relations in 1962, and in 1964 there appeared in *Africa* his classic paper 'Indirect Rule: French and British Style'. After two summers teaching at Columbia University, he was invited to spend 1964–5 as Visiting Professor at Berkeley, teaching West African colonial history. Here he planned and started work on his first major book, *West Africa under Colonial Rule*, which appeared in 1968.

From Berkeley, Crowder went to Fourah Bay College as Director of the Institute of African Studies and Dean of the Faculty of Social Studies. Though he found life in Freetown very agreeable, the scope of his post was narrower than he had been used to in Nigeria, and resources were tight. He scandalized the British community in Freetown, but won much local respect, when he chose to march with the students in protest at British inaction at UDI in Rhodesia. Here he began to develop an interest in the relevance of pre-colonial history and in patterns of African resistance to colonial rule, undertaking with LaRay Denzer a study of Bai Bureh and the rebellion against hut-tax in the Sierra Leone Protectorate.

1967 brought him back to Nigeria, first to a term as Visiting Professor at the Institute of African Studies at Ibadan, to plan, with Ajayi as co-editor, the two volumes of the *History of West Africa* (1971 and 1974); and then on to the University of Ife, as Director of African Studies. This marked another high point in his career. He enjoyed the full support of a powerful and enlightened Vice-Chancellor, H.A. Oluwasanmi, who ensured he had a free hand to develop his ideas. Picking up a theme from his first Nigerian post, he established the Ori Olokun Centre, off campus in Ile-Ife town, to relate directly to working artists and the general public. The Ife Annual Festivals of Art and Culture became national events and models of what universities might do to foster the cultural renaissance of an independent nation. Several of Ola Rotimi's best-known plays – *The Gods are not to Blame*, *Kurunmi* and *Overami Nongbasi* – had their premiers here. In fact Crowder played the role of the missionary, Adolphus Mann, in the first performance of *Kurunmi*. Alongside this, the Institute sponsored a programme of collecting and recording Yoruba oral traditions, and their study from various perspectives – linguistic, literary, religio-philosophical and historical. Crowder himself convened two conferences whose proceedings became major books: *West African Chiefs* and *West African Resistance*. He revived *Odu: a Journal of African Studies*. For several years he was active on the Council of the Historical Society of Nigeria, and a major force in the establishment of *Tarikh*, the Society's journal of African history for schools and colleges.

By 1971 Michael Crowder was again ready to move. Because of the concentration of universities, publishing and the modern media in the south of Nigeria, the cultures of Northern Nigeria had tended to be neglected in the post-independence cultural renaissance to which Crowder had notably contributed. He now responded to an invitation from the Vice-Chancellor of Ahmadu Bello University to attempt, for Hausa studies, what he had been doing at Ife for Yoruba. He chose to go to Abdullahi Bayero at Kano, a college of Arabic and Islamic studies which ABU was developing into a modern institution of higher education. He loved Kano, and had a house just outside the old city walls. Here for the first time he was appointed as a professor of history, and many graduates of Bayero remember him as an inspiring teacher. He was also to supervise the establishment of a new Centre for Nigerian Cultural Studies, which would specialize in Hausa language, literature and theatre, at the main ABU campus at Zaria. When this was ready in 1974, he moved to Zaria.

The change in political climate after 1975, which also led to an abrupt change in the management of the University, made Crowder feel that Ahmadu Bello had become a less agreeable place in which to work. Nevertheless, as he moved south again in 1977 to a Research Professorship in the Centre for Cultural Studies at the University of Lagos, he could feel that the cultures of Northern Nigeria had a higher national profile than before. During the World Festival of Black and African Arts (FESTAC), held at Lagos in 1977, ABU made an impressive contribution with the spectacular staging of Tafawa Balewa's Hausa story *Shehu Umar*. Lagos, however, turned into something of an anti-climax. He could not but compare his cramped flat at Alagbon Close with the fine house he had occupied on the Marina nearly twenty years before. Lagos itself was tense and stressful with the effects of the oil boom. The growing government intervention in university affairs made the academic environment less congenial. Perhaps too he began to feel that the time for his particular kind of contribution to academic and cultural life in West Africa was passing. So for the first time in his life, he found attractions in the idea of moving back to live in Britain; and he slipped quietly back to London in 1978.

If we have several times mentioned the houses Michael Crowder lived in, it is not accidental. He always strove to choose and furnish his houses very carefully, since the quality of the ambience in which he worked at home was essential to his serenity of mind and a condition for his formidable work energy. Moving as frequently as he did, he was often constrained in where he could live, and came to feel the need for a permanent retreat. With this thought he had bought a house in the mid-1970s in the Casbah at Tangier, a place of cultural diversity and tolerance, overlooking both the Atlantic and the Mediterranean. It was generously made available to his friends, both African and European. Now on his return to London he sold his small *pied-à-terre* in North Kensington and bought an early nineteenth-century semi-detached house in Addington Square, Camberwell, a mile or so south of the river. Inside it glowed with traditional West African textiles and artefacts, as well as with the works of many of the Nigerian artists whom he had encouraged and promoted for over two decades.

In London, Longman the publishers offered him the editorship of *History Today*, that organ for the '*haute vulgarisation*' of the best historical research, to freshen it up and broaden its range. Crowder was ideal for the job, and he threw himself into it with characteristic vigour. He also found time to serve for a year as Co-Director of the International African Institute and to reorganize its publications activities, to join the editorial board of the *Journal of African History* and to edit the final volume, dealing with Africa since 1940, of the *Cambridge History of Africa*. But this new pattern of work was not to last long. Once *History Today* had been relaunched in its new format, it began to build up its subscriptions steadily; and by 1981 it was sufficiently sturdy for control of the journal to be transferred from Longman to an independent consortium. With the change of control, in which he took a very active and initiatory part, the editorship passed from Michael Crowder to his successors; though he retained his association with the journal as Consultant Editor. The successful journal of today still bears ready witness, in character and in physical format, to the new version that Crowder and his team had made of it in those key transitional years. He was in the unaccustomed position of having to change jobs before he himself had decided to move. He decided to return to Africa. West Africa had lost much of its old appeal. Instead he turned to the South, and accepted the Chair of History at the University of Botswana.

He was in Botswana from 1982 to 1986. He found the Tswana an urbane people, and appreciated living in one of the few relaxed, democratic countries left in Africa. His fears of unwanted involvement with South Africa, where he had an uncle living, proved unfounded. He enjoyed teaching, and participated fully in university committee life. From Gaborone, he made his influence felt in the history departments in Zimbabwe, Malawi and Lesotho. Above all, these were years of intense research, writing and publication. He was fascinated with the comparison of Botswana and Northern Nigeria as regards the position of chiefs under colonial rule, and with the relations between Botswana and the expansionist Union of South Africa. The projected (and at his death half-written) biography of Tshekedi Khama touched on both themes. He also became more concerned with problems of development, and of the relevance of pre-colonial and colonial history to the problems of post-colonial Africa. Major works in which he had a guiding hand were published in these years: Volume VIII of the *Cambridge History* (1984) and the *Historical Atlas of Africa* (1985). After extending his initial three-year Botswana contract for a further year, he returned to Britain as the best base from which to pursue his various writing projects. With a base at the Institute of Commonwealth Studies, he arranged to spend a semester a year teaching African history at Amherst College. He was preparing to spend six months at the Woodrow Wilson International Center for Scholars in Washington DC when in April 1988 he was struck down by the illness from which he died four months later.

Michael Crowder's death left a large rent in the international fabric of African studies. Over the three decades of his active life as an Africanist his achievement was astonishing above all in its range. Of the more formally academic part of his output – his scholarly writings and the many symposia, conference proceedings, journals and collective volumes which he edited, and of his role in the establishment of institutes and centres of African or cultural studies – much has already been said. There was also his energetic commitment to establish a two-way cultural interplay between the campus and the wider society – of which Ori Olokun at Ife was the finest product – and his continuous efforts to seek out and promote local artists. He was always sustained by a vision of what Africa was at its best and might become in the future, and he laboured for this end. There was something of the crusader in his youthful writings, and though he outgrew this, he managed to express commitment without didacticism in his more mature work. Unusually for a serious scholar, he did not disdain to write for young people, simple tales where his earlier idealism still showed, and introductory texts in history and social science. In his last few years he recovered his earlier interest in contemporary issues – evident in his mainstream historical writing. Some of his latest published lectures, such as 'Us and Them: the International African Institute and the current crisis of identity in African Studies' (1986), or 'Twenty-five years of African Independence: Whose dream was it anyway?' (1987), took on a new voice of authority, even vision, concerning Africa's current predicament. But in the end, Michael Crowder will be best remembered for the generosity and human concern that he showed to so many students, scholars, artists, writers and others whom he identified, inspired, befriended, supported, encouraged or pushed along; for the writing and teaching which opened to so many a new understanding of Africa and of humanity; and above all for his unforced and abiding love of Africa.

☆　☆　☆

The contributors to this volume have all been colleagues of Michael Crowder's, particularly at the various universities in Africa where he left his mark as teacher, researcher and administrator, and they have all addressed themes pertinent to his achievements as a historian of Africa. Crowder's work was focussed on the colonial period in West Africa, with the exception of the last six years of his life, when he moved to the South but retained his focus on the workings of European colonialism and the responses of African people to it. As is often the case, the dialectic of difference (in region) and similarity (in period and theme) proved stimulating; his vigour as a historian was renewed, and we looked forward to a major biography of that pivotal figure of colonial Botswana, Tshekedi Khama. Yet both in his vision and in his practice, Crowder was always much more than just a historian of colonialism. For him the history of the colonial period needed both to be set in relation to the much longer span of pre-colonial history, and made relevant to contemporary issues of decolonization and cultural development.

Our contributors evoke all these aspects of Crowder's work. At a more substantive level, the thread which is most continuous through the different periods touched on, is the relationship between large-scale systems of rule ('empires') and diverse populations. This diversity is as much the product as the antecedent of empire, and has several dimensions: of language, culture, race, historical experience, occupation, political status, class.

The first three contributions may be read as a tribute to Crowder's most notable work of long-term historical synthesis, *The Story of Nigeria*, whose very ease and lucidity almost belies its originality. They deal with the pre-colonial history of large-scale polities in an area largely co-terminous with northern Nigeria, an area where we can go back further and in greater detail than for most other areas of Africa. These states faced problems of legitimation and control that bear comparison with those of their European colonial successors. The pilgrimages made by the Saifawa rulers of Borno-Kanem over many centuries were not just expressions of Islamic piety but served also to confirm the Saifawa, in their own eyes as in the eyes of politically-significant others, as legitimate rulers. Bawuro Barkindo makes one of his most telling points in relating heightened pilgrimage activity to the ascendancy of the Mai in the internal relations of the state. The issue of the rulers' legitimacy is also at the heart of Louis Brenner's examination of a famous diplomatic corespondence, between Muhammed Bello of Sokoto and al-Kanemi of Borno. Again external relations were intimately tied in with the internal constitution of states that embraced a population that was heterogeneous both ethnically and religiously, through the vital issue of whether particular rulers and subjects were by their practices to be considered true Muslims. In Murray Last's paper on 'corruption' in Sokoto, the issue of legitimacy focusses more exclusively on relations between rulers and subjects, and the parallel between colonial European and pre-colonial Islamic rule is explicitly made. His theme is the specific ways in which subjects might turn the ideology of rule to *their* advantage – a possibility that can outlive the political defeat which, here, befell the subjects.

With Eldred Jones's essay on Shakespeare's *The Tempest* we move to the earliest formation of British colonial attitudes, at a time when Britain's involvement with West Africa had barely begun. Race – as such, in its later sense – does not come in. It is more a matter of 'the problem of government' faced by colonizers when their subjects are culturally distinct and refractory to alien rule. Jones sees the play as an imaginative anticipation of colonial relationships, and draws our attention to a matrix of ideas about savagery and civility which would play a central role in the legitimation of colonial rule. The denial of mutuality between ruler and ruled – or one might add, between Muslim and *Kafir* in the Islamic empires – and the use of force and/or magical coercion – which we might read in modern terms as culture – to sustain it, is as evident in Shakespeare's scenario as in the later realities of empire.

It was Crowder's own experience as a junior army officer in the colonial twilight of Nigeria which opened his understanding of African colonialism. From it he retained a vivid sense of colonialism as essentially a system of *rule* – always more pertinent to him than its character as a system of *exploitation* – racially organized and dependent on the military control of the population. His writing was at its liveliest when dealing with soldiers and administrators, and always rested on a solid appreciation of their professional cultures, as well as of the constraints under which they operated. At the same time – and this is what distanced him from any whiff of 'imperial history' – he gave at least an equal measure of regard to the African military leaders who had to be defeated for colonial rule to be established, and to African rulers who did not accede complaisantly to imperial demands and remained a powerful constituent of colonial realities. His two edited collections – *West African Resistance* (1971) and, with Obaro Ikime, *West African Chiefs* (1970) – are among the very best things of their kind, and show his flair as a catalyst and impresario of others' research. He liked to write about strong, even preposterous, characters, such as Colonel Rey of the Bechuanaland Protectorate – of whom Parsons writes below – especially when they faced a doughty African opponent, such as Tshekedi Khama. Nor was he at all loath to document the sheer ineptitude which colonial administration could attain, when it rested on a complex of local political forces which it only dimly comprehended. His own monograph *Revolt in Bussa* (1973), which documents such a case, remains one of the most nuanced accounts of all sides of 'native administration' in Nigeria.

African resistance to colonial rule, in its various forms, is a theme of several of the papers here. In Mokopakgosi's study of the Nama of south-eastern Namibia it took the form of open war, provoked by the loss of their lands to mining companies. Mavis Campbell tells the extraordinary story of Montague James, who led the Maroons over many decades from the original site of their resistance in Jamaica through their sojourn in Nova Scotia to their eventual settlement in Sierra Leone. James's life was full of ambivalences: the struggles he led were against the British power from which he held a series of commissions, and they involved an artful mix of compromise and defiance. The resistance of the Ikale and Ilaje, the two south-eastern Yoruba groups considered by Richards, was rather against the attempts of outsiders – whether the British, missionaries, or more conventional Yoruba – to impose their own cultural and economic scenarios on these distinctively organized farmers and fishermen. Finally, as if to remind us that resistance was not just a matter for men and the public spheres of war and politics, Amanda Sackur shows (*inter alia*) how vigorously the mulatto women of early nineteenth-century Senegal might rebut a European's racial slur.

Colonialism rested on several contradictions. But the most fateful one was not primarily political or economic but cultural (though it also served to encode political and economic divisions). This was the contradiction between the professed principles of the colonizing powers, which were universalist (variously liberal, Christian, humanitarian, developmentalist), and their institutional practices, which were pervasively racialist. As a young officer commanding West African troops, Michael Crowder knew at first hand, and deeply deplored, that white was the colour of command.

A general model of colonialism as a racialist system of rule requires to be modified in two directions. Firstly, there were variations between the policies and practices of different colonial powers. Crowder's own study of French assimilation policy in Senegal is the starting-point for Sackur's examination of the impact of the universalist ideology of the French Revolution on race relations in the French coastal settlements of Senegal. She finds that the impact of Revolutionary ideas on French practice has been exaggerated, and documents the force of racial prejudice on the ground.

Secondly, though Europeans often appeared to Africans as a solidary, dominant racial 'caste' – the Oyinbo, Turawa etc. – they typically comprised a number of segments whose outlook and interests often pulled in different directions. In this volume such tensions are most fully explored in the two papers on southern Africa: by Parsons on the conflict between what he calls the 'missionary' and the 'mercenary' traditions of Bechuanaland administration, and by Mokopakgosi on tensions between the administration, the mining companies and the missionaries in relation to the Nama. Crowder's own treatment of missionaries in *West Africa under Colonial Rule* shows marked ambivalences. Himself 'religiously unmusical', Crowder was unsympathetic to the evangelistic project of the missionaries and understated their religious impact on West African society. Yet he gave full weight to their provision of the greater part of the Western education available to Africans in the colonial period. And the interstitial or mediating groups who emerged from the missionary encounter – the Creoles, the Christianized populations of the coast, independent churchmen, educated Africans generally and eventually, of course, the core constituency of nationalism – engaged him greatly. It was their physical and psychic mobility, their betwixt-and-betweenness, which was the key to their cultural creativity, and he saw a good deal of himself in their situation.

Several contributors examine groups, or individuals, of this kind. Working on a broader canvas than Sackur or Campbell, Akintola Wyse reviews the remarkable spread of Sierra Leonians (particularly Krio) since the mid-nineteenth century. As teachers, pastors, clerks, traders, planters, craftsmen and much else, they moved all down the West African coast, even as far as Namibia and the Cape, and in places such as Nigeria well into the interior. Themselves a people forged in Sierra Leone from diverse origins, they mediated European culture as well as their own cultural synthesis to other populations. They exploited opportunities given by the colonial expansion, but also made critical contributions to the politics of the black diaspora. Parallel in some ways but also in marked contrast stand the Lebanese, whose history becomes most intensely entwined with the Krio in Sierra Leone. Toyin Falola, taking his lead from Crowder's concise account of them in *West Africa under Colonial Rule*, presents an overview of the Lebanese achievement, his central theme being that 'they were foreigners, but they operated as local merchants'. Though their consequent relations with their hosts were often strained, they lacked neither flexibility in exploiting new commercial opportunities nor acumen in adapting to local political circumstances.

Crowder's account of West African colonialism was thinnest as regards the *social* history of the African population. This is, indeed, still a thinness in the field as a whole, and it is easy to see why: the material for it is enormously diverse, local, fragmented, and not to be found in official or standard documentary forms. Several of the authors – Last, Sackur, Wyse, Falola, Richards and Denzer, particularly – contribute something towards making up the shortfall, but none address the problem more squarely than Augustus Casely-Hayford and Richard Rathbone. They too write about a group of cultural mediators, the educated elite of the southern Gold Coast, and specifically about the intersection of family and politics in the masonic lodges which were such a noteworthy feature of their social life. Nothing is more refractory of study than secret societies, yet Casely-Hayford and Rathbone with great prosopographical flair succeed in giving a persuasive account of their social significance up to the

1930s. This was precisely the milieu from which one of La Ray Denzer's three subjects, Mabel Dove, emerged. Taking us on from colonialism, Denzer presents a comparative study of the contribution of public life of three women – Wuraola Esan, an Ibadan Yoruba, and Aoua Keita of French Sudan (Mali) being the other – over the period of decolonization. Though all of 'elite' background, their gender itself produced a kind of marginality in the political sphere. Her account focusses on the social context of their careers, and particularly the importance of their relations, whether positive or strained, with their fathers and husbands as well as with other women.

In moving beyond the immediate focus of Michael Crowder's work or in addressing topics – such as several of the social dimensions of African history – which he underplayed, the contributors are continuously mindful of what they have learned from him, in personal as well as in scholarly terms. Crowder wrote with peerless lucidity about what engaged him and seemed especially important in that thirty-year period of decolonization and new independence, when he was active as a scholar. It is a mark of his distinction as an editor that he was so generously receptive to the best work of those who opened topics or essayed styles of historiography different from those in which he worked himself. He never sought to make disciples or to establish an orthodoxy but to facilitate the emergence of a scholarship in which the forces that have shaped modern African history and the concerns of Africans themselves would receive full and due treatment. In seeking to build on the foundations he laid, our contributors are being most faithful to his memory. We would like, in conclusion, to express our appreciation to two particular friends and sometime colleagues of Michael Crowder's, namely Robin Horton and Lalage Bown. Though neither has been able to contribute a paper, we have greatly valued their support for the project of bringing out this volume in Michael's memory. Murray Last is owed our thanks for his help on the Arabic orthography of several papers. Finally, we should acknowledge the particular commitment on the part of our publisher, Longman, to the appearance of this volume. Lester Crook and Andrew MacLennan have given much more than a routine editorial contribution, which stands as a tribute to Michael Crowder's long association with Longman and his own excellence as an editor.

J. F. Ade Ajayi
J. D. Y. Peel

Chapter One

The Royal Pilgrimage Tradition of the Saifawa of Kanem and Borno

BAWURO M. BARKINDO

H ajj or pilgrimage must be performed between the eighth and the thirteenth day of the month of Dhul-al-Hajjah in Mecca and within an explicitly limited geographical area between Mina-Muzdalfah and Arafat. Though not mandatory, almost all pilgrims also travel to Medina to visit the tomb of the Prophet Muhammed and pray at his mosque. Pilgrimage is a true indication of a Muslim's dedication to his religion, involving personal, physical and financial burdens. It is one of the five pillars of Islam which all Muslims who have physical and financial ability (istitaa) to do so, are mandated to undertake once in their lifetime. The Holy Quran and traditions (Sunna) of the Prophet Muhammad are explicit about this injunction.[1]

In its interpretation of ability (istitaa) the Maliki school of law does not place much emphasis on provisions (zad) and means of transport (rahila) as pre-conditions for undertaking the pilgrimage. Lack of provisions could be compensated for by any lawful occupation *en route* to Mecca.[2] If the intending pilgrim did not own or could not hire the means of transport, he or she had to walk all the way to the Holy Land if physically able to do so. The Maliki interpretation of istitaa, as rightly pointed out by Dr. Ahmed Mohammed Kani, partly explains why pilgrimage occupies such a central position in the life of the West African Muslims. They are predominantly Malikite, and so strong in their adherence that many came to believe that without the pilgrimage their faith (iman) was incomplete.[3] Thus from the beginnings of Islam in the region until today every year thousands of Muslims leave their homes with the intention of making the pilgrimage.

The journey to the Holy Land, even for the rich and the powerful, was

---

difficult and dangerous. It was made on horses, camels or on foot. It took a long time, and went through difficult or hostile areas. Many pilgrims never returned to their homes, dying, or being forced by circumstances beyond their control, to settle down permanently far away from home. However, all these dangers and difficulties were considered a small price to pay for the opportunity to perform the pilgrimage, considered the nearest spiritual contact with God. It is also the best opportunity the Muslim has of witnessing a practical demonstration of the universality of the Muslim community (umma) in addition to reaping the great reward in the hereafter. Thus after a successful pilgrimage not only does the pilgrim come to feel that all the dangers and the difficulties were worth the undertaking but many yearn to repeat the exercise over and over again, though well aware that all subsequent performances of the pilgrimage are not obligatory but supererogatory acts of devotion to Allah.

Hence one can understand why Muslims should consider their governments constitutionally obliged to provide all the means necessary to enable citizens to undertake the pilgrimage.[4] There is no Quranic injunction which explicitly says so, but the Prophet Muhammad himself organized and led the first Muslim pilgrimage to Mecca, thereby making it binding on all subsequent rulers of Muslims to do the same. According to al-Mawardi, the organization of the pilgrimage is an obligation which must be discharged by a Muslim state.[5] All members of the Muslim community who want to perform the pilgrimage, he contends, must be catered for by the state.

Leading the pilgrimage to the Holy Land, therefore, is considered one of the most important Islamic obligations of the head of a Muslim state. When he is unable to do so the Muslim sovereign is expected to appoint his representative in the person of the Amir al-Hajj who will lead the pilgrimage on his behalf. The Muslim sovereign, whether he personally leads the pilgrimage or not, is obliged to ensure the security of pilgrims from his state to and from the Holy Land. In the Holy Land and all along the way, the sovereign is required to see that the pilgrims do not suffer destitution. From early times, therefore, the tradition grew of African Muslim states building hostels and schools in the Holy Land and at important stopping places, especially in Egypt, where pilgrims could sojourn during the pilgrimage.[6] To date very little is known of the organization of the pilgrimage in the early Muslim states of West Africa. This paper is an attempt to show that, despite our fragmentary sources, the tradition of the pilgrimage in the Saifawa states of Kanem and later Borno fits in well with practices in the early Middle-Eastern and North African states.

Pilgrimage can be divided into two forms: the organized pilgrimage, which itself can be sub-divided into royal and non-royal, and the private pilgrimage. This paper is concerned with the organized royal pilgrimage tradition of Kanem and Borno from the latter part of the eleventh century when it appears the Saifawa Mais started to perform the pilgrimage to the end of the first half of the eighteenth century when the tradition came to an end (see map 1).

The place of the Saifawa Mais in the royal pilgrimage traditions of West Africa

Several early Muslim rulers from West Africa are known to have performed the pilgrimage. A certain Baramandana, reputed to have been the first Muslim king of ancient Mali, was said to have gone on pilgrimage in the eleventh century.[7] He was followed by three more kings of Mali. Mansa Uli was said to have performed the pilgrimage in the second half of the thirteenth century. Sakura, a freed slave who usurped the Malian throne, performed the pilgrimage in the first decade of the fourteenth century.[8] However, on his return journey, Sakura was said to have died at Tajura on the North African coast.[9] The throne of ancient Mali thereafter reverted to its legitimate heirs. We still know very little about these pilgrimages.

The fourth and the last king of ancient Mali known to have performed the pilgrimage was Mansa Musa (*c.* 1312–37) whose pilgrimage in 1324[10] is the most famous hajj to have been performed by any West African ruler. In fact a later historian, Ibn al-Iyas who died in 1524, described Mansa Musa's pilgrimage as the most outstanding event of the year 724 AH/1324 AD.[11] Mansa Musa is said to have left home with an entourage of about 8,000 comprising scholars, courtiers and slaves.[12] By the time he arrived in the Holy Land, Mansa Musa's caravan was said to have swelled to about 60,000 souls.[13] All along the pilgrimage route, and especially Egypt, Musa was said to have spent lavishly to the extent that the 100 loads of gold which he carried with him were exhausted.[14] On his return he had to borrow money from Egyptian merchants. While on his pilgrimage Mansa Musa entered into friendly diplomatic relations with several of the North African rulers and the Sultan of Egypt.[15] The scholars whom he brought with him contributed greatly to the spread of Islam in Mali and one of them, Abu Ishaq, was said to have built for the king a new palace with a central dome the like of which was never seen before in Mali.

I have described the pilgrimage of Mansa Musa at length because, with the exception of the one later performed by Askia Muhammad of Songhai, it is the only pilgrimage from early Muslim West Africa on which we have detailed information. I suggest, however, though less extravagant, the pilgrimages of the Saifawa Mais[16] were conducted on the same lines, aiming to achieve the same religious and political goals even if none of them were able to 'hit the headlines' in the annals of the Muslim geographers in the same way. Mansa Musa, of course, was the last king of ancient Mali known to have performed the pilgrimage.

In Songhay, Askia Muhammad (*c.* 1493–1528) was, like Sakura of Mali, a usurper to the throne, and, also like Sakura, went on the pilgrimage as soon as he came to power. This may have been in an attempt to legitimize his hold on the throne. He went in 1495, returning two years later. His caravan included an escort of 500 cavalry and 1,000 infantry. He carried with him 300,000 pieces of gold, a third of which was set aside for the charitable foundations of the Holy Cities, and bought a hostel in Cairo for the Sudanese pilgrims. While in Cairo Askia Muhammad was said to have established a close relationship with Sheikh Jalal Al-Din Al-Suyuti and in Mecca he was said to have been formally invested, at his own request, as the Caliph of Takrur by the Sharif of Mecca.[17]

Returning home as a pilgrim-king and as an invested caliph, the sovereignty of the Askia and his successors was not only recognized at Gao but throughout the Southern Sahara from Walata to Tadmekka without, it seems, campaigning in those parts.[18] Again, the pilgrimages of the Saifawa Mais seem to have followed the same pattern. Mai Ali Gaji of Borno, as I shall discuss further below, appears to have been invested a caliph of Takrur about ten years before the royal pilgrimage of the great Askia.

In Hausaland the pilgrimage tradition was maintained by scholars and later by the common people.[19] During the period under study there is no definite report of royal pilgrimage from any Hausa state. Admittedly, in the *Kano Chronicle* two kings of Kano, Alhajj son of Kutumbi (*c.* 1648–9) and Al-Hajj Kabe son of Kumbaru (*c.* 1743–53), are given the title 'Alhajj'.[20] However, since we have not any information of their having performed the pilgrimage during the period of their rule – and certainly this would not have escaped record of the meticulous compiler(s) of the *Chronicle* – it seems most likely that they performed the pilgrimage, if at all, either before their accession or after they had been deposed.

In the Saifawa state of Kanem, and later in Borno, royal pilgrimage started in the latter part of the eleventh century. This was also the period when proper Islam was adopted in Kanem, a move which was definitely associated with the emergence of the Saifawa as the undisputed rulers of Kanem. Thus, the attempt to perform the pilgrimage by Mai Hume (*c.* 1086) and especially the multiple pilgrimages of his son and successor Dunama (*c.* 1086–1140) were undertaken at the same period as that of Baramandana of Mali. However, unlike all other West African states, royal pilgrimage became an established tradition of the Saifawa government first at Kanem and later at Borno. Indeed, more Saifawa rulers performed the pilgrimage than all other Muslim rulers of West Africa put together.

We know few details of the royal pilgrimages of the Saifawa, and cannot even list all those Saifawa Mais who performed the pilgrimage. The *Diwan* which is our most important primary source names only three Mais who performed the pilgrimage: Dunama b. Hume, Umar b. Idris and Hamdun b. Dunama.[21] Of the three, only Dunama's pilgrimages are discussed, perhaps because of their political implication, the others merely being given the title al-hajj without any explanation. Thus even the famous pilgrimage of Idris Aloma, or the five pilgrimages of Ali b. Umar, three of which he made as Mai, are not mentioned in the *Diwan*.

We are, however, lucky to have contemporary or near-contemporary Arabic and European sources which give information on the pilgrimages of Saifawa rulers. These together with internal Borno sources like the various *Mahrams*, works of Imam Ahmad b. Fartua and others, yield valuable information on the pilgrimages of the Saifawa.

The first royal pilgrimages of the Saifawa

Mai Hume (*c.* 1075–86), under whose rule proper Islam was adopted in Kanem, appears to have performed the pilgrimage, since the sources say he died in Egypt.[22]

Hume's son and successor, Dunama (*c.* 1086–1140) is said to have performed the pilgrimage twice and was allegedly murdered by the Egyptians while going on a third. According to the author(s) of the *Diwan*,

> On his (i.e. Dunama's) first pilgrimage he left in Misr (Egypt) 300 slaves and on his second occasion a like number. When he was on his third pilgrimage and took his ship the people of Misr said to themselves 'If this king returns from Mecca to his country he will take from us our land and our country without doubt.' So they took counsel to destroy him. They opened a sea-cock in his ship, so that the sea drowned him by command of God.[23]

This information in the *Diwan* is not corroborated by any other source, leading some scholars to doubt the claim that Dunama was murdered by the rulers of Egypt because they considered him politically dangerous. However, some of the activities of the Mai could have easily aroused the suspicion of the Egyptian rulers. As I have explained elsewhere, the final movement of the Fatimids from Ifriqiyya to Egypt in *c.* 973 contributed to several developments.[24] The Almoravid religious reform movement marched out of the Sahara to overrun North-West Africa and Spain; and the impulse to their religious reform came when Yahya b. Ibrahim, the Chief of the Gudala and the initiator of the movement, went on pilgrimage in 1035.[25]

Even before the rule of Dunama b. Hume the Mais had already started to react to the new developments in North Africa and the Sahara, especially after the arrival in 1052 of the Banu Hilal and Sulayman Arab nomads. Mai Arku (*c.* 1026–67) is said to have owned a number of slaves of whom he settled 300 each at Dirki, Kawar and Fezzan where he died.[26] This may mean that the Kanem ruler was reacting to the chaos by embarking on raids in order to ensure the safety of the southern section of the trans-Saharan trade (and later pilgrimage) route. That Mai Dunama appears to have been acting almost in the same manner could easily have given the impression that the attention of the Saifawa was being drawn to the political instability of Egypt.

Certainly, Egypt during the period of Dunama's last pilgrimage was already bedevilled with civil dissension and violent intrigues amongst the leading members of its ruling class.[27] In addition to all these, Mai Dunama was already renowned as a warrior-king and, after his first pilgrimage, a jihadist. He was said to have possessed a strong force of 100,000 mounted troops and 120,000 foot-soldiers which he had already deployed on several expeditions within Kanem and probably also in Borno.[28] In the light of this, it would not have been surprising that Mai Dunama felt the urge to extend his jihad northwards into Egypt. Alternatively, he may have been drawn into supporting one of the competing factions in Egypt. Either way, Dunama would have appeared as a dangerous person, and thus he invited his elimination.[29]

After the death of Mai Hajj Dunama b. Hume there appears to have followed a period of Islamic backsliding in Kanem. Although the sources emphasize continuing Islamic developments – for example Mai Biri b. Dunama (*c.* 1140–66) was noted as a *faqih* (great scholar) and Abd Allah (*c.* 1166–82) as a builder of mosques and a patron of learning — there seems to have been at the same time a gradual re-introduction of some pre-Islamic customs which had probably been suppressed under Mai Hume and Dunama. These include the re-emergence of the office of the Magira or Queen Mother as a very important post in the Saifawa government, the tradition of the ruler holding audience behind a screen and probably some of the activities associated with the enthronment of the Mai.[30] There was no report of any royal pilgrimage during this period.

The Pilgrimage of Mai Dunama Dibalami

It was during the rule of Mai Dunama b. Abd Allah (*c.* 1210–48) surnamed Dibalami that the Saifawa made an attempt to re-establish proper Islam. In fact Dunama Dibalami appears to have been the first Mai to have attempted an Islamic reform in Kanem. This is reflected in the writings of Al-Maqrizi which declare Dunama Dibalami to have been the first Muslim king of Kanem.[31] Dibalami is said to have modelled himself on his ancestor and namesake Dunama b. Hume. Like him he built a cavalry force which is said to have numbered 41,000.[32]

Mai Dunama Dibalami certainly performed the pilgrimage as is stated in the *Mahram* of Ngalma Duku. The *Mahram* is said to have been given to Ngalma Duku by Mai Salma b. Bikuru (*c.* 1182–1210), Dunama Dibalami's brother and predecessor. Dibalami who ratified the *Mahram* during his reign is addressed as:

> Our Lord the Commander of the Faithful, Sultan of the Muslims,
> Al-Hajj Dunama b. Dabale.[33]

We are not, however, certain whether this was the same pilgrimage from Kanem which took place in 1242–3 AD and which was reported by Al-Maqrizi in the fourteenth century, but borrowing materials from the earlier works of Ibn Said, Ibn Khaldun and Al-Umeri, Al-Maqrizi stated of the Madrasa Ibn Rashiq that it:

> belongs to the Malikites and is situated in the Hamman al-Rih quarter [Khutt] in old Cairo. When the Kanim [one of the communities of Takrur] reached Cairo in 640s/1240s proposing to make the pilgrimage they paid to the *qadi* Alam al-Din Ibn Rashiq money with which he built it. He taught there and so it took its name from him. It acquired a great reputation in the land of Takrur and in most years they used to send money to it.[34]

Al-Umeri who wrote earlier, in *c.* 1337–38, says that the school was also used as a hostel where students and pilgrims from Kanem resided. Both Dr. Ahmed Kani and Dr. Abubakar Mustafa feel that the hostel (Riwaq Borno) was different from the school.[35] This may have been so although al-Umeri was specific:

> They have built at Fustat, in Cairo, a Malikite Madrasa where their companies of travellers lodge.[36]

It is possible that Dunama Dibalami did not make the pilgrimage in 1243 AD but at some other time during his reign. However, the pilgrimage of 1243, even it it was not personally led by the mai, nevertheless was organized on royal orders.

The giving of money to build the school/hostel, and regularly sending money from Kanem for maintenance smacks of power and wealth which could only emanate from royalty. It is possible that one of the scholars who are mentioned in the sources was appointed the Amir al-Hajj (or in the Kanuri terminology Zanna Makkama) to lead the famous pilgrimage which was accompanied by several other scholars. Al-Umeri mentioned two such scholars and either might have led the pilgrimage: the 'virtuous and ascetic shaykh Uthman al-Kanimi, who is related to their kings' or 'Abu Ishaq Ibrahim al-Kanimi the poet and a man of letters'.[37]

Palmer asserts that Dunama Dibalami was the first Mai to bear the title 'Caliph', a usage which was continued by his successors. This is not improbable; but his further assertion that Dunama's caliphate was 'apparently recognized at Mecca and some say in Syria and Spain as well'[38] is difficult to accept for this early period of Saifawa history.

After his pilgrimage, Dunama modelled himself as a 'pilgrim-king', 'a warrior prince' and a 'patron of learning'. He entered into diplomatic relations with the rulers of Egypt and the Hafsids of Tunisia, and this served to spread his fame in North Africa and the Middle East.

Thus validated, the Mai must have now felt strong enough to bring in further Islamic reforms in government. He attempted to cut back all the pre-Islamic rites and traditions which seem to have been making a comeback since the death of Dunama b. Hume. We are told that Mai Dunama Dibalami opened the Mune, probably a venerated object wrapped in skins believed to have been a protection of the Saifawa dynasty and by extension the whole kingdom.[39] He also undertook several military expeditions, now termed jihad, against many areas in both Kanem and in Borno. It must have been during this time that the forces of the Saifawa occupied Fezzan and established control with a capital at Traghan.[40] The Mai's pilgrimage must have convinced him that Fezzan was an important link in the pilgrimage and commercial traffic between Kanem and the countries to the north.[41]

Royal pilgrimage during the period of decline in Kanem

Dunama Dibalami's immediate successors Kadai (*c.* 1248–77) and Biri (*c.* 1277–96) seem to have continued with his reforms despite mounting crisis, though neither undertook the pilgrimage. Kadai not only brought Fezzan effectively under the rule of the Saifawa, thereby strengthening Kanem control over the pilgrim and trade route, but by the end of his reign the Saifawa had implanted themselves firmly in Borno. Two Mais were said to have performed the pilgrimage during this period. They were Ibrahim b. Biri (*c.* 1296–1315) who performed the pilgrimage in about 1300, and his son Idris b. Ibrahim (*c.* 1342–66), probably in about 1351.[42] These pilgrimages show the commitment of the Mais to the Hajj even in the face of very difficult conditions. Mai Ibrahim is said to have been the first Saifawa king to have ordered the killing of one of his sons,[43] which may have meant that the son attempted to supplant him while he was on pilgrimage.[44] In fact the Mai himself was soon afterwards assassinated by the Yerima (the governor of the northern province).[45]

After the death of Mai Ibrahim b. Biri, the Saifawa were involved in a political crisis in Borno, where his four successors, who ruled an average of one year each, were said to have died while fighting the So. It is of interest to note that as soon as temporary stability was achieved during his rule, Idris b. Ibrahim embarked on the pilgrimage in 1351. This was despite the problems at home and the fact that Fezzan, the important entrepôt to the pilgrimage and trade route had been lost to Kanem soon after his father's pilgrimage in *c.* 1300.[46]

The pilgrimage of Mai Idris b. Ibrahim appears to have been the last to be performed by the Saifawa while in Kanem. During the rule of Mai Umar b. Idris (*c.* 1382–7) the problems in Kanem became so unsurmountable that the Mai, on the advice of the ulama, abandoned Kanem and together with his family and partisans migrated to Kaga in Borno.

The early decades of the Saifawa in Borno

The problems of the Saifawa were not over when they migrated to Borno. Their Bulala rivals took over Kanem and outstripped them in the diplomatic contacts with Egypt. Aided by the Judham Arabs, the Bulala also kept up raids on Borno with the intention of dislodging the Saifawa. Mai Umar b. Idris and two of his successors were said to have died in the fighting.

We are not informed of any royal pilgrimage during this period although in *c.* 1391 Mai Uthman b. Idris (*c.* 1389–1421), during whose reign the Bulala incursions into Borno subsided, sent an embassy to the Mamluk Sultan of Egypt, al-Zahir Barquq (*c.* 1389–1421) accusing the Judham Arabs of aiding the Bulala and soliciting for the help of the Sultan. The letter was said to have been taken to Egypt by an ambassador who arrived there in the company of pilgrims, so it is possible that the 1391 embassy was part of an organized pilgrimage led by a state official.[47]

After the embassy of *c.* 1391 the Saifawa faced more problems. The Bulala incursions into Borno were renewed with vigour, and there were also dynastic conflicts. The Mais were forced to move with their followers from one part of Borno to another. Economic and cultural relations with the north became very difficult indeed. It must have been their inability to maintain regular contacts with Egypt and the Hijaz that led Mai Kaday b. Uthman (*c.* 1439–40) in *c.* 1440 to write to some prominent scholars in the Tuat oasis requesting them to send scholarly missions (bithat) to Borno.[48]

Did Mai Ali Gaji (c.1465–97) perform the Pilgrimage?

Mai Ali b. Dunama (*c.* 1465–97) surnamed Gaji is, according to Borno traditions, one of the three most celebrated rulers of the second Saifawa empire.[49] He ended the dynastic crisis and the Bulala incursions into Borno. In about 1472 he founded Birni Gazargamu which remained the capital of the Saifawa until the demise of their power. With a secure and permanent capital, Ali Gaji began to reorganize the structure of the state. The over-powerful title holders had their powers reduced and like his predecessors, Ali Gaji surrounded himself with the ulama whose advice he always sought in running his government. It was on their advice that Mai Ali Gaji adopted the title Amir al-Muminin or 'Commander of the Faithful', a claim which was widely accepted not only in Borno but also in Hausaland.[50]

Did Ali Gaji perform the pilgrimage during his tenure as mai? With the exception of the *Mahrams* of the Ngalma Duku and Idris Katagarmabe [51] (Katakarmabe), there is no source which specifically says that Ali Gaji had performed the pilgrimage. Yet, circumstantial evidence suggests that he either performed the pilgrimage or at least organized one with a political mission just as did Mai Dunama Dibalami in *c.* 1242–43 or Mai Uthman b. Idris in *c.* 1391. Ali's reform seems to parallel those of Dibalami and Idris Aloma. In fact, it appears the Saifawa Mais felt most emboldened to undertake difficult political and religious reforms after they had returned from the pilgrimage.

Mai Ali Gaji's political achievements were undoubtedly boosted by his success, while on pilgrimage, in getting himself invested as the Caliph of Takrur. Al-Suyuti recorded in his autobiography:

> Then in the year eighty-nine [889 AH/1484 AD] the pilgrim caravan of Takrur arrived and in it were the Sultan, the qadi, and a group of students. They all came to me, and acquired knowledge and traditions of me . . . A eunuch servant came in the company of the qadi as a present from his cousin. The Sultan of Takrur asked me to speak to the Commander of the Faithful [the nominal Abbasid Caliph in Cairo, Abd al-Aziz] about his delegating to him authority over the affairs of his country, so that his rule would be legitimate according to the Holy Law. I sent to the Commander of the Faithful about this, and he did it.[52]

We have already observed that Kanem was considered 'one of the communities of Takrur', so the said Sultan could have come from any part of the bilad-as-Sudan including Kanem.[53]

Contrary to the thinking of some earlier writers, the above quotation cannot refer to the pilgrimage of Askia Muhammad Gao of Songhay, since he came to power only in *c.* 1493, went on the pilgrimage two years later and returned in 1497. It must therefore refer to another Sudanese ruler; and the date and the contents of the quotation fit in well with Mai Ali Gaji. Some scholars like Professors Harry Norris and John Lavers also conclude that the quotation referred to him.[54] We therefore conclude that, unless new evidence proves the contrary, Mai Ali Gaji performed the pilgrimage in *c.* 1484 and that it was after his return that he started to bear the title Amir al-Muminin. This would make him the first Mai of the second Saifawa empire to have performed the pilgrimage.

The royal pilgrimage of Mai Idris Aloma

Mai Idris b. Ali (*c.* 1564–96), posthumously surnamed Aloma, is certainly one of the most celebrated Sultans of Borno. Most scholars agree that Borno reached its apogee during his reign, the first twelve years of which have been described and panegyrized by his Chief Imam, Ahmad b. Fartua.[55] At home Idris Aloma was described as a military and administrative innovator and Islamizer while in foreign affairs he was recognized as a skilled diplomat who corresponded with the major Muslim potentates of his day.

Idris Aloma seems to have performed the pilgrimage during the ninth year of his rule, *c.* 1571. This is how Imam b.Fartua described the event:

> Thus leaving the kingdom he loved and an envied pomp, he went east, turning his back on delights and paying his debts to God . . . So he made the pilgrimage and visited . . . the tayiba of the Prophet . . . and he bought in the noble city a house and date grove, settled some slaves yearning after a plenteous reward from the Great Master. Then he prepared to return to the kingdom of Bornu.[56]

Thus like his predecessors, Idris Aloma not only made the pilgrimage but also provided accommodation for pilgrims from Borno at Medina.

After his return from the pilgrimage, Idris Aloma attempted a number of reforms aimed at bringing Borno in line with other Islamic states. Before this time most disputes were settled not by the ulama but by the tribal heads and other members of the nobility. Although his attempt to separate the judiciary from the administration was not entirely successful, nevertheless much improvement was made in the dispensation of justice. Most of the old mosques in the capital and other major towns, which were formerly made of reeds, were pulled down and in their places structures built with burnt bricks were erected. Numerous Middle-Eastern, Egyptian, North African and central Sudanese scholars were attracted to the court of the Mai, which earned him the added title of Patron of Scholars.

One of the fruits of Idris Aloma's pilgrimage was the acquisition of Turkish musketeers and slaves trained to fire the muskets. This corps of Turkish musketeers enabled the Mai to conquer areas which hitherto were thought of as impregnable and enhanced his reputation as a powerful protector. After his pilgrimage all his battles were seen as jihad.

The diplomatic relations between Idris Aloma and the Ottomans and the Saadians do not need to be discussed at any great length here. What has, however, been less noted is that Idris Aloma's experiences during his pilgrimage contributed greatly to the diplomatic relations. Let us examine his relations with the Ottomans.

Ottoman-Borno relations [57] had been cordial since the establishment of the Ottoman rule in North Africa in the early sixteenth century. In c. 1556, for example, Mai Dunama b. Dunama (c. 1539–57) entered into a treaty of 'friendship and commerce' with Turghut Pasha, the Ottoman governor-general of Tripolitania. The treaty was continuously renewed by successive rulers on both sides of the Sahara. Even when the Ottomans took control of Fezzan in c. 1549 relations between them and Borno continued to be cordial until about 1570.

In 1571, the annual tribute of Fezzan to the Ottomans was suddenly raised from 1140 to 3000 mithqals of gold.[58] This coincided with a period of great famine in Fezzan and the other central Saharan settlements; and the combination of these hardships forced many people to migrate to Borno and Hausaland. But rather than scale down their demands, the Ottoman officials forced those who were left to make up the difference in the annual tribute; marauding expeditions were sent out to exact tax payments. Moreover even those normal pilgrims and travellers from Borno and other areas of West Africa were forced to pay taxes, and the properties of those who died on the road to or from the Holy Land were confiscated.

It was in the same year, 1571, that Mai Idris Aloma performed the pilgrimage and on his way obtained first-hand information of the situation at Fezzan and the other central Saharan oases; at Kawar he received the submission and complaints of the people of Jado who were probably among the Ottoman victims.[59]

It must have been these pressing demands – not the need to secure arms as has been emphasized by most scholars – which forced Idris Aloma in c. 1574 to despatch a six-man embassy to Turkey with three specific demands: the guarantee of security of life and property of all pilgrims and other travellers from Borno while passing through Ottoman territory;

the proper management or, failing which, the cession to Borno, of all the recently-acquired Saharan fortresses including Guran; and co-operation between Borno and the Ottoman powers in dealing with the Tuaregs and any others who might disturb peace in the region.[60]

The reply of the Ottoman Sultan Murad III dated 5 May 1577 agreed with all the requests of Mai Idris Aloma except the ceding of the Guran fortress which, however, he promised would henceforth be properly managed. Edicts were sent to the governors-general of Tripolitania and Egypt as well as the district officer of Fezzan, telling them of Idris's demands and ordering them to comply. In one of the edicts sent on 14 of August 1579, to the governor-general of Egypt, the question of the pilgrimage was the main subject matter:

> Idris, the ruler of the blacks . . . sent a letter asking that the goods
> of individuals dying on pilgrimage be given to their sons if any or,
> if there were no sons, to their heirs according to the Holy Shariah
> without interference from anybody else. For this reason I give you
> my noble command that whenever a pilgrim from those lands dies,
> his goods are to be given to his sons . . . [61]

Ten days later another edict gave a fuller explanation:

> Now that the letter sent by the ruler of the state of Bornu, His
> Highness Prince Idris has come to my court with his messenger, the
> exalted and most eminent and noble Yusuf, seeking as is proper, to
> confirm the petition with our good . . . authority, according to the
> aforementioned prince and to the people of his territory freedom
> to travel along the roads and trails and to rest at the hostels and
> stations in security and contentment whether as merchants or as
> pilgrims desiring to circumvubulate the Holy House of God and
> visit the tomb of the Holy Lord of the Believers. My noble order
> is to accord with the request . . .[62]

On the same date a similar edict went to the district officer of Fezzan.[63]

Royal pilgrimage traditions during Borno's classical period

The seventeenth and the first half of the eighteenth centuries are regarded as the Golden Age of the Borno Empire. The conquests of Idris Aloma were consolidated by his successors who attempted further administrative reforms. Despite the antiquity of the state-organized pilgrimage in the Saifawa states, it seems to have been only during this period that the office of the Zanna Makkama or the Amir al-Hajj emerged as a permanent office with clearly spelled-out responsibilities. Dr. Abubakar Mustafa on the authority of the *Idara* (written in the second half of the eighteenth century) says the Zanna Makkama had the responsibility to:

i   arrange transport and safe passage of the Muslims from Borno on the journey;
ii give guidance on routes and on all other matters relating to Hajj and Umrah;
iii provide the animals to be sacrificed during the Hajj;
iv arrange for the pilgrims' feeding, accommodation, protection and security during the Hajj. [64]

More Mais performed the pilgrimage during this period than at any other. About five Mais are said to have either performed or attempted the pilgrimage and they did so against many odds: rising dynastic rivalries, mounting opposition from the non-court ulama, increasing Tuareg and Kwararafa attacks on Borno, and at times the hostility of the North African and Saharan rulers through whose territories lay the way to Hijaz.

The first Mai who performed the pilgrimage during this period was Umar b. Idris (*c.* 1619–1639) who was already at an advanced age of fifty years when he became the Mai. [65] He went in about 1634 in the company of a large band of pilgrims and merchants, as well as Ali his son and immediate successor. [66] The pilgrimage of Mai Umar is said to have contributed greatly to the cementing of diplomatic relations between Borno and the Barbary states, especially Tripolitania and Tunis. [67]

It was, however, from the rule of Umar b. Idris that disaffection started to be noticed between the Mais and the court ulama on one side and the non-court ulama on the other. Mai Ali was said to have ordered the killing of one Sheikh al-Jarmiyu, a prominent Tuareg scholar, when he and the prominent Fulani Sheikh Waldede were found to have been engaged in spreading sedition against the Mai. [68] It was because of his iron discipline that Mai Umar was praised as 'The Mai who made men like a ball of chaff'.

Mai Ali b. Umar (*c.* 1639–77) was a young man when he succeeded his father but already well-experienced in international affairs. The serious challenges he faced during his reign did not prevent him from performing three more pilgrimages in 1648, 1656 and 1667 and dying in *c.* 1677 while coming back from his fifth. [69]

Ali came to power amid intense dynastic rivalry and is said to have ordered the elimination of four of his brothers and rivals[70]; but this did not deter other ambitious princes from attempting to oust him. On Ali's return from one of his pilgrimages he found that his brother

Kashim Biri, who acted as regent during his absence, was plotting to supplant him; he ordered Kashim Biri to be blinded and exiled to Tolaram.[71]

During his second pilgrimage Mai Ali was received in Cairo with much pomp.[72] However, during his return there was an abortive attempt by agents of the Ottoman governor of Tripoli to seize him. Ali escaped safely to Borno and relations between Tripolitania and Borno were strained for a number of years.[73] In 1668, after returning from his fourth pilgrimage, Mai Ali had to defend the capital against attacks by Tuaregs and Kwararafa.[74]

Despite all the challenges, including a protracted famine in Borno, Mai Ali made his fifth and last pilgrimage in about 1677 and on his return journey died at Aqaba. After his death it was reported that his tomb became the scene of local pilgrimage. Ali's reign was looked upon as the apogee of Borno history. His piety and scholarship led many of his contemporaries to regard him as a saint, with miraculous powers. His frequent pilgrimages earned him the Arabic sobriquet, Tahr, the 'bird' for 'to him the journey to Mecca was but a night ride'.[75]

One contemporary seventeenth century source reports that a Sultan of Borno had purchased houses in Cairo, Mecca and Medina for use as lodgings for pilgrims from Borno, and also acquired ships to generate the income needed to maintain them.[76] We assume that the Sultan in question was either Mai Umar or his son Mai Ali, most probably the latter.

Mai Idris (*c.* 1677–96), Ali's son and successor, also attempted to perform the pilgrimage during the last year of his rule. He, however, died at Fezzan where his tomb is still venerated.[77]

The only Mai who appears to have broken the chain of continuous royal pilgrimages during this period was Dunama b. Ali (*c.* 1696-1715) who must have been prevented by the mounting problems of his reign, especially seven years of severe famine. Even during this reign, however, there was a royal pilgrimage although not led by the Mai in person, for it was reported, in 1707 that two sons of the Sultan of Borno arrived in Cairo on the pilgrimage.[78]

The last Mai clearly indicated in the sources to have performed the pilgrimage was Hajj Hamdun b. Dunama (*c.* 1715-29)[79] although some sources suggest that the latter's successor Muhammad b. Hamdun (*c.* 1729-44) may also have performed the pilgrimage.[80]

After the rule of Muhammad b. Hamdun, the Saifawa Mais faced a mounting sequence of crises which culminated in the jihad of Shehu Usman dan Fodio and the collapse of the Saifawa dynasty in the early nineteenth century. There is no direct evidence, but we can strongly surmise that it was their struggle to maintain their state against growing difficulties which prevented the Saifawa rulers after Muhammad b. Hamdun from going on pilgrimage.

Conclusion

The above survey gives us clear evidence of the importance of the royal pilgrimage to the Saifawa rulers of Kanem and Borno. The Mais not only performed the pilgrimage themselves as a fulfilment of Islamic obligation but they also took their responsibility to lead it very seriously indeed. They strove to see that pilgrims from Kanem or Borno were given the most favourable conditions to perform the Hajj, and especially that travellers of all kinds whether accompanied by their rulers or not should enjoy security during their journeys. To this end, efforts were made to occupy the major Saharan oases which lay on the pilgrim and trade routes. This was why the Kawar oasis and Fezzan featured prominently in the military and diplomatic affairs of Kanem and later Borno. In addition, peaceful treaties were made with all those powers who controlled the areas through which travellers from the Saifawa state passed. In the case of Mai Idris Aloma, for example, the question of security for travellers from Borno formed one of the most important aspects of his diplomatic missions. From the time of Dunama Dibalami in the thirteenth century to that of Mai Ali b. Umar in the eighteenth century several Mais bought houses at Cairo, Mecca and Medina and turned them into schools/hostels for pilgrims and students from their kingdom, setting up endowments for their maintenance.

Throughout its history the Saifawa government based itself on Islamic principles, and the Mais, especially after they came to be seen as Khalifa, sought a specifically Islamic legitimacy. The Mais surrounded themselves with learned scholars, many of whom had come from North Africa and the Middle East or at least had ben partly educated there. To hold their own in this Islamic atmosphere, the Khalifa had to be learned men, which most of the Saifawa Mais strove to be. Completion of the pilgrimage endowed them with baraka or efficacious blessings; with their moral authority thus enhanced, the Mais were able to rule their people with little fear of disapproval from the learned ulama. This is why, it seems, many of the Mais undertook difficult reforms after their return from pilgrimage.

Their journeys to the Holy Land afforded the mais first-hand information on socio-political and religious developments in the older Islamic countries. Many of the Mais, on their return from the pilgrimage attempted to bring developments at home up to the level of those which they had seen abroad. The pilgrimage enabled the Mais to establish friendly relations with the rulers through whose territories they passed and to patronize scholars, especially in Cairo, a place which by the thirteenth century was one of the leading centres of the Muslim world. In addition to the resultant political and economic benefits, they also helped to enhance the standing of the Saifawa rulers in the eyes of the Muslims throughout the world.

Finally, it appears the pilgrimage route favoured by the Saifawa Mais, which went through Kawar, Fezzan and Egypt, was the same route favoured by merchants between West and North Africa. The brisk commercial relations which flourished across the Sahara, especially from the mid-sixteenth century to the end of the eighteenth century, was of great benefit to the rulers of both sides. Trade and travel of all kinds benefitted from the efforts of the Mais to protect the pilgrimage routes.

Certainly, the royal pilgrimage tradition of the Saifawa merits consideration by all West African governments which would like to get the respect and recognition of their Muslim subjects.

Notes

1. Quran, 3:97; *Sahih Bukhari*, trans. Muhammad Mukhsini Khan, Vol.II, 1976, Hadith No.584; Sahih Muslim, trans. Abdul Hamid Siddiq; Vol.II, New Delhi 1977 p. 577.

2. Umar Al-Naqqar, *The Pilgrimage Tradition in West Africa*, (Khartoum 1972), p. XVII.

3. A. Moh.Kani, 'Pilgrimage in time's perspective: the West African experience', Seminar paper, Department of History, ABU, Zaria, Not dated, pp. 1–2.

4. Y.T.Gella, 'The Making of a policy: Some consideration of the conditions that influenced the Hajj Policy of the caliphate of Muhammad Bello (1817–1837), Seminar paper, Department of History, ABU, Zaria, 3 July 1985, pp. 4–5.

5. Al-Mawardi, *Al-Ahkam al-Sultaniyya*, (Cairo, 1880) 1973, p. 103.

6. For details see Al-Naqqar, *The Pilgrimage Tradition*, pp. XXI – XXII.

7. Ibn Khaldun, 'Kitab al-Ibar' in N. Levtzion and J.F.P. Hopkins, *Corpus of Early Arabic Sources for West African History*, (Cambridge, 1981), p. 322.

8. Ibid. pp. 323, 334.

9. Ibid. p. 334

10. Ibid. pp. 323, 334–5.

11. Ibn al-Iyas (died in 1524) cited in N. Levtzion, 'The Early States of the Western Sudan to 1500' in J.F.A. Ajayi, and M. Crowder, (eds.) *History of West Africa*, Vol.I, third edition (London, 1985), p. 142.

12. Muhammad Kati, *Tarikh al-Fattash*, ed. and trans. O. Houdas (Paris, 1913) p. 34.

13. Abd al-Rahman b. Abdullah, Al-Sadi, *Tarikh al-Sudan*, ed. and trans. O. Houdas (Paris, 1898–1900).

14. Al-Umeri 'Masalik al-absar fi mamalik al-amsar' in *Arabic Sources*, p. 269.

15. Ibn Khaldun, 'Kitab al-Ibar' in *Arabic Sources*, p. 335.

16. Mai is the Kanem and Borno title for 'king'. The Saifawa were known under various titles, like *Sultan* and, especially after 1484, also Khalifa. The term *Mai* will be retained here throughout the work because it is peculiar to the Saifawa rulers.

17. For discussions on the Askia's pilgrimage and his investiture as the 'Caliph of Takrur' see, for example, J. Hunwick, 'Songhay, Borno and the Hausa States' in *History of West Africa*, Vol.I 3rd edition, pp. 342–3; and *Sharia in Songhay: the replies of Al-Maghili to the questions of Askia Al-Hajj Muhammad*, (London, 1985), pp. 26–7; E.M. Sa'ad, *Social History of Timbuktu* (Cambridge, 1983), pp. 47–8.

18. Ibid. refer E.M. Sa'ad, p. 48.

19. See re-constructions in, e.g. J.E. Lavers. 'The adventures of a Kano Pilgrim, 1892–1893', in *Kano Studies*, I (1968); John A. Weeks, *Pilgrims in a Strange Land; Hausa communities in Chad*, (New York, 1976).

20. 'Kano Chronicle' trans. H.R. Palmer in *Sudanese Memoires*, (1928), 1967, Vol.3, pp. 119, 125.

21. 'Diwan al-Salatin Bornu' in various versions. Unless otherwise stated the version used here is the one in D. Lange *Contribution a L'histoire dynastique du Kanem-Bornu*, (thesis,) Paris, Vol.I, 1974, and the published version: *Le Diwan des Sultans du Kanem-Bornu: Chronologie et histoire d'un royaume Africaine*, (Wiesbaden, 1977) both of which have been consulted.

22. 'Diwan' in Lange, *Contribution a L'histoire*, p. 76; Dr. Abubakar Mustafa based on his iterpretation of written traditions (*Girgam*) of Borno suggests that Mai Hume built a mosque in Cairo: 'The contribution of the Saifawa 'Ulama to the Study of Islam *c*. 1086–1846 AD, Ph.D. Thesis, Bayero University, Kano, 1987 p. 43.

23. *Diwan* in H.R. Palmer, *Bornu Sahara and Sudan* (London 1936), p. 19.

24. B.M. Barkindo, 'Early States of the central Sudan: Kanem, Borno and some of their Neighbours to *c*. 1500 AD' in J.F.A. Ajayi and M. Crowder, *History of West Africa*, p. 233.

25. Al-Bakri, 'Kitab al-Masalik wa-'l mamalik' in *Arabic* Sources, p. 71.

26. 'Diwan' in Lange, *Chronologie et Histoire*, p. 67.

27. H. Barth, 'Chronological table of the History of Bornu' in his *Travels and Discoveries in North and Central Africa*, (London [1857] centenary edition, 1965) Vol.II, pp. 582–3; Palmer, *Bornu Sahara and Sudan*, p. 164.

28. 'Diwan' in Lange, *Chronologie et Histoire*, pp. 68–9.

29. Professor Muhammad Nur Alkali feels that the traditional rivalry between the Saifawa Mais of Kanem and Egypt dates from this period. See his 'Power game and Diplomacy in the Sixteenth Century: Borno – Ottoman – Saadi Confrontation', Workshop on Studies in Borno history, Maiduguri, 12–13 August 1987, p. 1.

30. Barkindo, 'The Early States of Central Sudan', p. 236.

31. Al-Maqrizi, 'Al-Khitat' in *Arabic Sources*, p. 353.

32. 'Diwan' in Lange, 'Chronologie et Histoire', pp. 71–2; Al-Maqrizi on the other hand estimated Dunama's troops at 100,000 men: 'al-Khitat' in *Arabic Sources* p. 353 while Imam Ahmad b. Fartua put it around 30,000 men: 'Kanem wars' in H.R. Palmer, *Sudanese Memoires*, Vol.1, p. 50.

33. *Mahram* of the 'Ngalma Duku' in Palmer, *Bornu, Sahara and Sudan*, p. 19. *Mahrams* are certificates of privileges and tax exemptions bestowed on scholars and certain individuals by the mais for certain services. They were normally ratified by the succeeding Mais, as long as the recipient remained in the royal favour. For problems associated with using the *mahrams* as sources for history see O'Fahey, R.S. 'The Mahrams of Borno', *Fontes d'Histoire Africaine*, 1981, *Bulletin of Information*, No.6, International Academy Union Commission, XXII, pp. 19–25.

34. Al-Maqrizi, 'Al-Khitat' in *Arabic Sources*, p. 353

35. A. Moh. Kani, 'Aspects of Cultural and intellectual relations between Northern Africa andCentral Sudan, *c*. 700–1900 AD with special reference to Kanem-Bornu and Hausaland: A Survey, Post graduate seminar, Department of History, ABU, Zaria, November 1979, p. 4; A. Mustafa, 'The Contribution of the Sayfawa Ulama', p. 113.

18

36. Al-Umeri, 'Masalik al-Absar' in *Arabic Sources*, p. 261.

37. Ibid. pp. 260, 261.

38. Palmer, *Bornu, Sahara and Sudan*, p. 19

39. Barkindo, 'Early States of the Central Sudan', pp. 238–9. For a different interpretation on the subject of the *Mune* see A. Mustafa, 'The Contribution of the Sayfawa Ulama', especially pp. 48–53.

40. J.E. Lavers, 'Kanem and Borno under three dynasties' in J.F.A. Ajayi and Bashir Ikara (ed.) *Evolution of Political Culture in Nigeria* (Lagos, 1985) p. 22.

41. Ibid.

42. Al-Maqrizi, 'Al-Khitat' in *Arabic Sources*, pp. 354, 356; Al-Qalqashandi, 'Subh al-aᶜsha' in ibid. p. 347. See also the '*Mahram of Ngalma Duku*' in Palmer, *Borno, Sahara and Sudan*, p. 19.

43. 'Diwan' in Lange, *Chronologie et Histoire*, p. 87.

44. Barth, 'Chronological table of the History of Bornu' p. 385.

45. 'Diwan' in Palmer, *Bornu, Sahara and Sudan*, p. 195.

46. B.G. Martin, 'Mai Idris of Bornu and the Ottoman Turks 1576–78' in *International Journal of Middle-East Studies*, 3,1, 1972, p. 484.

47. Al-Qalqashandi, 'Subh al-asha' in *Arabic Sources*, p. 344

48. The letter is reproduced in A. Martin, *Les Oasis Sahariennes d'Algiers*, 1908, 1, pp. 122–3. See also A.M. Kani, 'Aspects of Cultural and Intellectual relations'. p. 5.

49. A. Smith, 'The Early States of the Central Sudan' in J.F.A. Ajayi and M. Crowder, *History of West Africa*, p. 181.

50. For a more detailed discussion on the Caliphship in Borno see M.N. Alkali, 'Kanem-Borno under the Saifawa. A Study of Origin, Growth and Collapse of a Dynasty', Ph.D. Thesis, ABU, 1978; A. Mustafa, 'The Contribution of the Sayfawa Ulama'

51. Both *Mahrams* title Mai Ali Gaji *Al-Hajj*. See Palmer, *Sudanese Memoires*, pp. 14,24.

52. Jalal al-Din al-Suyuti *Ala - Tahadduth bi - Nimat Allah* (Autobiography), ed. E.M. Sartain, 2 vols (Cambridge University Press, Vol.2, 1975),p. 158.

53. See Al-Maqrizi as we have quoted above (footnote 34) where Kanem was referred to as 'one of the communities of Takrur'.

54. A.T. Norris, *Saharan Myth and Saga* (Oxford, 1972), pp. 50–60; Lavers, 'Kanem and Borno under three dynasties', p. 25. See also Saad, *Social History of Timbuktu*, p. 47.

55. Imam Ahmad Ibn Fartua, 'Tarikh Mai Idris wa Ghazwatihi lil Imam Ahmad Burnuwi', J.R. Redhouse, as 'Translation from the original Arabic of an account of many expeditions conducted by the Sultan of Burnu Idris the Pilgrim, son of Ali, against various tribes his neighbours, other than the Bulala, etc., inhabitants of Kanim', in *Journal of Royal Anthropological Society*, 1, XIX, 1862; and by Sir H.R. Palmer as *History of the First Twelve Year reign of Idris Aloma of Bornu* (London/Lagos, 1926). Both translations are used in this work.

56. Ibid. Redhouse's trans. p. 203. See also Palmer, *Bornu, Sahara and Sudan*, p. 227.

57. The diplomatic relations of Idris Aloma have been re-examined in B.M. Barkindo. 'The Borno Caliphate – Its relations with its Neighbours and the areas of the Mediteranean Littoral: 1500 – 1800' in UNESCO *General History of Africa*, Vol.VII (Oxford, forthcoming).

58. C. Orhonlu, 'Osmani-Bornu Munasebetine al-belger' in *Tarikh Dergisi*, 23, Istambul, 1969. Trans. S.E. Brown as 'Documents relating to Ottoman – Borno relations.' Document 1, pp. 2–3. I am grateful to Professor John Lavers for the English translation.

59. Ibn Fartua, 'Tarikh' in Redhouse, p. 203.

60. Unfortunately the original letter sent by Idris has not yet come to light. Its contents could, therefore, only be worked out from the reply of the Ottoman Sultan.

61. Orhonlu in Brown, 'Document'7, p. 10.

62. Ibid. 'Document' 8, pp. 10–11.

63. Ibid. 'Document' 9, p. 11.

64. A. Mustafa, 'Contribution of the Sayfawa 'Ulama', pp. 300–1. 'The Idarah fi nizzam Mulk Kanem-Borno' was written by Amir of Alage in about 1771 AD. The full Arabic text of the Idara is contained in pp. 425–63 of Abubakar Mustafa's Thesis. See also M.N. Alkali, 'Some contributions to the study of pilgrimage tradition in Nigeria,' in *Annals of Borno*, II (1985) pp. 131–34.

65. Palmer, *Bornu, Sahara and Sudan*, p. 245.

66. J.E. Lavers, 'Kanem and Bornu to 1800' in O. Ikime (ed.) *Groundwork of Nigerian History* (Ibadan, 1980), p. 199.

67. Girard, *L'histoire Chronologie du Royaume de Tripoli*, Vol.2, Bibl. Nat. Paris, 1685 MS. Francaise (ancient Fonds) MS. 12219.

68. Muhammad Bello, 'Infaq al-Maysur' paraphrased and translated by E.J. Arnett as *The Rise of the Sokoto Fulani* (Kano, 1922), p. 5.

69. J.E. Lavers, 'Trans-Saharan trade before 1800. Towards quantification'. Postgraduate history seminar, Bayero University, Kano, 1979, p. 13. Palmer is, however, of the view that Mai Hajj Ali died at Manan in Kanem, *Bornu, Sahara and Sudan*, p. 247. E. Celebi said he died at Aqaba: 'Seyahatname', cited in Hopkin, T. *Nigerian Perspectives*, London, 1969, p. 136.

70. Girard, *Histoire de Tripoli*, 11, MS 321. For the discussion on 'fratricide' in Bornu during this period see B.M. Barkindo, 'Islam in Mandara: Its introduction and impact upon the state and people' in *Kano Studies* (New Series) I, (1979) pp. 41–42.

71. Palmer, *Bornu, Sahara and Sudan*, p. 248.

72. T. Walt, 'Trade between Egypt and Bilad al-Takrur in the XVIIIth century', paper for the Economic History of West African Savanna, Kano, 1976, p. 15.

73. Lavers, 'Kanem and Bornu to 1800', p. 137.

74. Barth, 'Chronological table of the History of Bornu', p. 589; Palmer, *Bornu, Sahara and Sudan*, p. 246; Lavers, 'Kanem and Borno under three dynasties', p. 26.

75. Palmer, *Bornu, Sahara and Sudan, op. cit.* p. 248

76. 'Letter from the Maillet' in C. Beccari (ed.) *Rerum Aethiopicarum Scriptores Occidantales*, Vol.IV, (Rome, 1914), p. 384.

77. Mai Idris is ommitted by mistake in the *Diwan* but he is mentioned in the kinglists recovered by G. Nachtigal *Sahara und Sudan*, Berlin, Vol.2, 1879, p. 396 and M.A. Landeroin, 'Notice historiques' in M.Tilho (ed.) *Documents Scientifiques de la Mission Tilho*, (Paris, 1909) Vol.II, p. 350. Idris's tomb in Fezzan and its veneration in the nineteenth century was reported by Duveyries, *Les Toaregs* p. 277 and Nachtigal, *Sahara und Sudan*, I, p. 384.

78. 'Letter from the Maillet' in C. Beccari, p. 384.

79. '*Diwan*' in Lange, *Contribution a L'histoire*, p. 106.

80. Walt, 'Trade between Egypt and Bilad al-Takrur', p. 15.

Chapter Two

The Jihad Debate between Sokoto and Borno: an Historical Analysis of Islamic Political Discourse in Nigeria

LOUIS BRENNER[1]

Shaikh Uthman dan Fodio, the caliphate which he inspired, and the jihad which he led, have become powerful symbols and points of reference in contemporary Nigerian political debate. This development is hardly surprising when one considers that the jihad, which commenced in 1804 in the far northwest of what is today Nigeria, was one of the most important manifestations of Islamic resurgence to have occurred in the nineteenth-century Muslim world. Recent studies have suggested that this movement, like others during the same period, resulted from pressures of renewal and reform which had been germinating within the umma throughout the eighteenth century.[2] Whatever its historical antecedents in the context of the wider Muslim community (and these have by no means been adequately studied), the political reverberations of the jihad were deeply felt throughout Sudanic Africa, from the Atlantic coast in the west to the upper Nile valley in the east. The Sokoto Caliphate became the dominant political and economic force in the central Sudan during the nineteenth century, and although it was never completely unified within itself, there is no doubt that the Islamic identity of present-day Northern Nigeria is a direct heritage of the pre-colonial Sokoto polity. Indeed, one could argue that the far north of Nigeria has become one of the most profoundly Islamized societies of the late twentieth century.

Perceptions and expressions of Islam in Nigeria today are not identical to those which were current in the nineteenth century, but the Caliphate, and especially Shaikh Uthman himself, are consistently evoked in order to justify and legitimate one or another position or interpretation in contemporary Nigerian Islamic discourse. Nowhere is this more evident

---

This chapter © Louis Brenner 1992

21

than in Nigerian academic writing; students in Nigerian universities have in recent decades produced a veritable explosion of theses and long essays on Islamic topics in which the authors refer to the Caliphate and its founders for guidance in the resolution of Nigeria's contemporary problems.[3] The preponderant weight of argument is that Nigeria is suffering a moral crisis for which Islamic principles offer the most promising and perhaps the only solution. In the more historically-orientated theses, Shaikh Uthman, his brother Abdullahi, or his son Muhammad Bello, are held up as ideal Muslim leaders whose ideas and actions remain forcefully relevant to contemporary political and social issues. In the context of recent Nigerian historiography, and of Nigerian politics, each of these leaders has come to represent a different political inclination.

This kind of writing derives directly from Nigeria's heritage of Islamic discourse, not simply because the jihad and its leaders are the preferred focus of this genre of history, but methodologically, in the conceptualization of relevant themes, the selection of evidence and the form of analysis. Historically, Islamic discourse in the western Sudan has been characterized by two dominant conceptual tendencies. The first was an emphasis on the legal and normative aspects of Islam and its history, with the corollary that the analysis of the socio-political context of actual events was often considered of only secondary import in any dispute. Debate, or analysis, tended to centre on the interpretation of the legal implications of incidents or behaviour in the light of both religious texts and historical models, and only secondarily on actual events. The second conceptual tendency was an emphasis on individual personalities, as models either of upright Muslim behaviour or its opposite, unbelief, tyranny or apostasy. The sources of this preoccupation with individual leadership are deeply embedded in the history of Muslim Africa, for example, in the devotional focus on the Prophet Muhammad as Insan al-kamil, the perfected human being, and derivative ideas of Sufi shaikhs and awliya as persons who had moved closer to God and who could intercede on behalf of other less accomplished Muslims. These kinds of ideas have produced the concept of 'religious persona' among African Muslims and led to a personalization of the analysis of legal and political disputes; the most striking example of such personalization in the context of the jihad is to be found in one of Shaikh Uthman's most fundamental legal arguments, that the religion of the ruler of a polity determines the religion of his subjects.

These themes in the Islamic discourse will be explored with reference to a specific historical event: the debate about the legitimacy of extending Shaikh Uthman's jihad into Borno. It is well-known that the intellectual, as well as military, defence of Borno was taken up by Al-Hajj Muhammad al-Amin al-Kanami. A lengthy correspondence ensued between al-Kanami and the Sokoto leadership which extended over a period of about five years (1808–12). A total of more than twenty letters were probably exchanged between the disputing parties during this period, when the 'Borno question' was a major preoccupation in Sokoto. Of these letters, only eleven are extant (see Appendix I), preserved because Muhammad Bello published them in his history and justification of the jihad, *Infaq al-Maisur*, which he completed in 1812.[4] Another relevant work is Shaikh Uthman's *Taꞌlim al-Ikhwan*, completed in 1813, in which he reiterates his own arguments on the Borno question.[5] The Sokoto-Borno debate therefore provides an excellent opportunity to examine the elements of Islamic political discourse, because it is a well-documented exchange among disputing scholars which was expressed within a completely Islamic idiom.

The legal debate

The purpose of this essay is not to attempt an 'objective' reconstruction of the events of the jihad in Borno, but to examine the internal development of the debate among the antagonists in the dispute in order better to understand the principles which informed their discourse. Bello's *Infaq al-Maisur* was a systematic contemporary account of these events as well as a contribution to the debate.[6] Approximately one quarter of this text was devoted to events in Borno and to the accompanying correspondence, reflecting the great import which the Sokoto leadership placed upon them.[7] Although our presentation of the debate will follow the evolution of the dispute as presented in *Infaq al-Maisur*, it must be recalled that Bello had a vested interest in how he portrayed these conflicts, as will become evident in the course of this essay.

Bello's account of the jihad in Borno begins in the following manner:

> When the [Muslim] communities began to press against the amirs of Daura, Katsina, and Kano, [these amirs] sought the assistance of the amir of Borno, who sent word to his wazir to go to their aid and assistance . . . He began to make preparations to march to the aid of the amirs of Daura, Kano and Katsina, following the commands of his own amir.[8]

As a result of the hostilities which ensued, the Borno Fulbe (Fulani) began to unite around several different leaders, who eventually managed to defeat the 'wazir' and to drive him from his capital.[9] At this point Mai Borno sent an envoy, one al-Hajj Adam, to Shaikh Uthman to enquire about the cause of hostilities. Al-Hajj Adam explained that Mai Borno

23

was Amir al-muminin, and that the Shaikh should 'prevent the Fulbe
from continuing their flight (hijra) from his country.'[10] In his first letter
to al-Kanami, Bello wrote:

> As for your country, we do not know how warfare broke out there
> except for what we heard in past years from a man called Adam
> al-Hajj who claimed he was sent by the imam of Borno, Ahmad b.
> Ali, to the Shaikh in order to ask about the cause of this affair.[11]

In response to this envoy, the Shaikh ordered Bello to write to the
Mai to explain the causes of their jihad: 'I explained the conditions of
the amirs of Hausa, that they were unbelievers, and that support of them
by a Muslim constituted apostasy.' The Mai was invited to join the jihad,
and another letter was sent to the Borno Fulbe 'warning them against
aggression in [the Mai's] country.[12] The messenger who delivered this
letter received an extremely hostile reception, and only barely managed
to escape with his life. By now the Mai himself was personally involved
in hostilities with the Fulbe in Borno's western territories. His campaign
went disastrously wrong; the 'wazir' and commander of the armies were
both killed, and the Mai fled back to his capital.

Although the precise dates of these events are uncertain, it was at this
stage that Sokoto recognized the jihad in Borno to have commenced.
There is no mention in Bello's account of any official permissions or
flags given to the Borno Fulbe, but the text clearly recognizes certain
scholars in southern Borno as the leaders of the Borno jihad: al-Mahir al-
Mukhtar, al-Bukhari, Hamid, and Buba Yero. These men were described
collectively as 'emulating the Shaikh.' Warfare between this group and
the Mai's armies became intense, and it was under the leadership of
al-Mukhtar (known locally as Goni Mukhtar) that the Mai was driven
from his capital for the first time.

> Al-Mahir al-Mukhtar . . . embarked on the jihad against the people
> of Borno until he drove Amir Borno from the capital of his
> kingdom. He fled to Kanem, and al-Mukhtar took up residence
> in his capital.[13]

During his flight to eastern Borno (and not to Kanem), the Mai brought
al-Kanami into his entourage. Together they eventually drove the Fulbe
from the capital. It was now that al-Kanami wrote his first letter to
Sokoto, about which Bello remarked, 'Nothing alarmed us so much as
a letter from al-Hajj al-Amin [al-Kanami].[14]

Before examining al-Kanami's letter, several remarks about the pre-
ceding account are in order. This historical reconstruction was put
together after the events took place. Bello readily admits, on more

than one occasion, that Sokoto was not informed about political affairs in Borno, nor about the nature of Islam there, at the time of the outbreak of hostilities. Upon sending his envoy, the Mai, like the Hausa rulers, was invited to join the jihad; his hostile rejection of this invitation was interpreted by Sokoto as a rejection of the Shaikh and his community. In spite of this lack of information, Bello opens his account of the jihad with the assertion that the Mai had sent military assistance to Daura, Kano and Katsina against the attacks of Muslim communities who were supporting Shaikh Uthman's jihad. This claim became the key point of fact in Sokoto's legal argument to justify their jihad in Borno.

Before writing to Sokoto, al-Kanami had already corresponded with the Borno Fulbe. Only one letter survives from this exchange (published in Appendix II to this paper). Written in May 1808,[15] it represents the earliest document available to us from the subsequent lengthy debate. This letter is significant because it illustrates the conceptual approach adopted by a gifted and learned scholar who is seeking to resolve a dispute among Muslims. However, caution is also in order in interpreting the letter, because we do not know to what extent al-Kanami may have already been involved in the rapidly developing events in Borno. It would seem that he was not yet openly allied with the Mai, who was not mentioned in the letter, but he may well have been involved in hostilities with certain Fulbe.

Al-Kanami adopts the classical role of mediating scholar. His letter is generally neutral in tone and requests the Borno Fulbe leadership to justify their behaviour in a situation which al-Kanami views as fitna, or conflict within the Muslim community, and which he seeks to resolve. He offers his own legal views of the matter, which seem to foreclose almost any possibility of a response which might convince him of the justification of the Fulbe actions. He suggests only one: 'If you are the whip of punishment, and God has given you his authority over the people of this region due to their arrogance . . . then there is no disavowal [of you].' In other words, the only acceptable justification would be for the Fulbe to prove that God had directly charged them to carry out His will, and in this way to transcend the ordinary and mundane application of divine law among men. This point takes on particular significance when one recalls that one of the pillars of the legitimacy of the jihad was Shaikh Uthman's claim that he had received permission for it in a vision, an incident which he recorded in one of his own books,[16] and that the historical sub-text of Bello's treatment of Borno, as will be demonstrated below, is that the Mai was an anti-Islamic tyrant.

The text of this letter certainly demonstrates that as late as May 1808, the Borno Fulbe had not made public their allegiance to Shaikh Uthman, or if they had, al-Kanami had not received the news. Between the time that this letter was despatched to the Borno Fulbe, and al-Kanami's first letter to Sokoto, hostilities in Borno intensified. Al-Mukhtar and his companions had responded to al-Kanami with, according to him, 'a weak answer, not such as comes from an intelligent man, much less from a learned person, let alone a reformer.'[17] The Fulbe attacked the Borno capital, and al-Kanami wrote yet again, and this time the only response seems to have been further attacks. It was in this context that al-Kanami wrote his first letter to Sokoto; by now, the Borno Fulbe had made clear their association with Sokoto, because in this letter al-Kanami addressed the Sokoto leadership directly: 'Tell us . . . why you are fighting us and enslaving our free people.'

For al-Kanami the conflict had shifted from a local affair to a confrontation between Borno and Sokoto, and his own position had changed from that of mediator to an interested party. Apparently, the Borno Fulbe had justified their jihad on the basis of alleged paganism or unbelief, and al-Kanami confronted Sokoto on this basis:

> Among the biggest of your arguments for the paganism of the believers generally is the practice of the amirs of riding to certain places for the purpose of making alms-giving sacrifices there; the uncovering of the heads of free women; the taking of bribes; embezzlement of the property of orphans; and oppression in the courts.[18]

Al-Kanami categorically denied that paganism existed among the peoples of Borno, and he went on to argue that although the five mentioned acts were 'sinful' and reprehensible, they did not constitute unbelief, and therefore did not justify jihad.

In Bello's response, he agreed that these five acts did not justify jihad: 'I am surprised that it is said we are fighting people for these five things for they are happening among us now quite a bit, so if we were fighting for these reasons we would be fighting our own people.'[19] In fact, he must have been more than surprised, because he also asserted that 'the person who gave you your information slandered us if he said we were waging the jihad against Borno and others because of the unbelief [contained in these five acts].'[20] As we have suggested, al-Kanami's information presumably came from the Borno Fulbe.

But Bello continued, in separate passages, to expound the basic Sokoto argument for the jihad, both in Hausaland and in Borno. Indeed, the general thrust of the letter is to justify the jihad in Hausaland; at this early date, information about Borno was rather sparse in Sokoto.

> Know, al-Kanami, that we did not war against the people [of Hausaland] for the reasons you have been told. Rather we warred against them in order to protect ourselves, our religion and our

people, when they molested us and provoked us and tried to force us to return to that which was forbidden to us. . .

As for your country [Borno], we have no knowledge of the state of its faith or its sultans except that your amir rose up in order to harm your Fulbe neighbours who were emulating the Shaikh. He coerced them to take flight, allying himself with the kings of Hausa and helping them. It is known that unbelievers help one another and believers do likewise.[21]

This argument was repeated on every possible occasion:

Know that the cause of our fighting you was because of your giving assistance to the Hausa unbelievers against us without being coerced. You know that whoever in the absence of coercion assists unbelievers against believers is like them, according to the Book, the sunna, and consensus. It was also due to your rising up to harm your neighbours of the jamaa [community] that they were forced to emigrate; [that occurred] when you began fighting them on behalf of and in aid of the kings of Hausa. It is obvious that you assisted them against the believers only because of your good will toward their religion. Surely good will towards unbelief constitutes unbelief, and you know this if you have studied religion. And the saying of prayers, payment of tax, fasting during Ramadan and the construction of mosques does not prohibit fighting you and are of no use to you in this world nor in the next due to the certainty of your apostasy.[22]

For Sokoto, the central legal question in the entire affair was the apostasy of the Mai of Borno due to his alleged assistance to the Hausa rulers. The argument that association with unbelievers constituted unbelief had been developed by Shaikh Uthman based upon the opinions of al-Maghili, a sixteenth-century Algerian scholar.[23] As late as 1813, the Shaikh was still presenting the Borno events as if the Mai had without provocation initiated attacks against local Fulbe in support of the Hausa enemies of his jamaa.[24] But no matter how appropriate the views of al-Maghili might have been to conditions in Hausaland, their applicability to Borno rested upon an assessment of the facts of that specific situation. Late in the correspondence, al-Kanami gave his version of the relevant facts: that it was the Borno Fulbe who had commenced the hostilities by raiding the border regions of Borno, burning villages and enslaving free people, and that the Mai's attacks had been in reaction to this. And, he added, even if the Shaikh was following the sunna in his own affairs, the Borno Fulbe were ignorant, and their actions did not conform with the sunna.[25]

However, the debate was not going to hinge on the collection and evaluation of actual facts in Borno. Other principles were brought to the fore, such as the concepts of 'emulation' and 'association.' Sokoto was prepared to embrace the Borno Fulbe because they were 'emulating the Shaikh.' 'Unbelievers help one another and believers do likewise.' Al-Kanami had anticipated some of these arguments in his first letter to Sokoto:

> Is it not forbidden for followers of the sunna to revolt against the king after having paid him allegiance, even if the king is guilty of serious sins? This matter is as clear as the sun at midday. . . Let us admit for the sake of argument that these [five] deeds render a person an unbeliever. How will the unbelief spread to others? The Almighty has said, 'No burdened soul can bear another's burden.' [XXXV, 18] And the Almighty also said, 'Whoso doeth right it is for his soul, and whoso doeth wrong it is against it.' [XLI, 46]
> Let us admit for the sake of argument that unbelief can spread from one person to another. That would bring about the negation of the law and the apostasy of the entire community (God forbid!) since there has never been a time in any country when sinfulness and misdeeds have not been widespread. . . Do not pretend that there is an era or a country without its share of innovation and misdeeds. If all these persons are infidels, then all the great writings and traditions [of Islam] are null and void. Thus, how can you follow their writings when according to your own claims the authors of these writings were unbelievers?[26]

Bello rejected these claims, arguing firstly that allegiance to the imam was not relevant in Hausaland, because the rulers of Hausaland were unbelievers, not imams:

> We have no doubts about the unbelief [of the Hausa rulers] due to their ignorance of religious principles, their sacrifice to stones and trees, their denial of the Day of Resurrection, and their failure to enter Islam at all, as well as their abuse, rejection and ridicule of it. We know this to be the case in these countries of ours.[27]

Al-Kanami's attack on the validity of the argument of unbelief by association was rejected as having been made in bad faith. Indeed, the general tone of the two letters quoted here was extremely hostile.

These early letters were exchanged during a period of intense warfare in Borno. The Mai's capital of Birni Gazargamu was occupied four times by the Fulbe before it was finally and definitively abandoned in favour of a new capital in eastern Borno. By then, much of Borno's former western territory had fallen into the hands of the Fulbe, although Al-Kanami and his armies managed to regain some of it. During this time, Bello was trying unsuccessfully to keep in touch with the Borno Fulbe. And then, a shift in attitude took place between al-Kanami and Sokoto. Bello's future wazir, Gidaado dan Layma, wrote a conciliatory letter to al-Kanami, which elicited a similar response. Bello replied in a very friendly fashion, addressing al-Kanami as 'brother,' and ending his letter with a prayer that God might 'take you and us by the hand and lead us in the straight path; that He reconcile us in the manner He wishes and will please Him, and that he bind us together and create understanding and friendship between us.'[28]

Bello's conciliatory letter never reached al-Kanami, who may have been willing to make a settlement with Sokoto during this period in order to bring peace to Borno's western frontiers. However, the Borno Fulbe do not seem to have been interested in any such settlement, and Sokoto was in no position to control their activities. Al-Kanami had nothing but contempt for his Fulbe antagonists in Borno, referring to them as 'worthless people' who, far from spreading Islam, were diverting Muslims from 'the religion of God' with their constant raiding and endless palavers. 'Whenever there is an exchange of letters between us and you,' he complained to Shaikh Uthman, 'and we hope for an end to this fitna, they return to their attacks on Borno.'[29] The nub of the problem was that although Sokoto could not control the Borno Fulbe, neither were they willing to denounce them, and there was no way that al-Kanami would recognize the legitimacy of their actions. In his opinion, the Borno Fulbe were seeking political power, not the renewal of Islam.

And so, the correspondents resumed their previous postures of mutual hostility, precipitated by another angry letter from al-Kanami to the Borno Fulbe. Bello's response to this letter, which was forwarded to him by its Fulbe recipients, opened the final phase of the debate.[30] The six final letters which were exchanged basically restated and elaborated points which had already been put forward, but they were slightly different in tone from the earlier ones. Slender hopes for reconciliation are still reflected in these texts, based perhaps on the fact that by now al-Kanami and the Sokoto leadership had found some degree of mutual respect among themselves as learned scholars. Al-Kanami was willing to accept Shaikh Uthman's religious and scholarly stature, but he continued vehemently to condemn the local manifestations of jihad in Borno. And Shaikh Uthman argued in his final letter to him that al-Kanami's only proper legal recourse, as a good Muslim, was to emigrate from Borno to a true Muslim community.[31]

Al-Kanami's letter to the Borno Fulbe directly challenged the legitimacy of their actions and restated themes expressed in his earlier correspondence. When had God authorized them to punish and discipline the people of Borno?[32] How could they be so arrogant as to compare what they were doing with the deeds of the most venerated scholars of the sunna?[33] Bello's response to this letter was largely a historical exegesis on early Islamic history and on the history of Songhay under Askia Muhammad, again using al-Maghili as his primary legal source for justifying the jihad. Bello's basic line of argument was to demonstrate that contemporary conditions in Hausaland, as regards unbelief and the practice of Islam, were similar to those at the time of Askia Muhammad, and that jihad was justified in both instances.

The final letter in this lengthy correspondence was a lucid summary of Sokoto's argument written by Shaikh Uthman himself. The letter opens with an explanation of the jihad in Hausaland, upon which the case against Borno was constructed. The causes of war in Borno had nothing to do with sinful acts, or various manifestations of unbelief (for which much evidence had now been produced); jihad was declared because the Mai of Borno had aided the unbelieving Hausa rulers who were enemies of the jihad. To assist unbelievers makes one an unbeliever. The Borno Fulbe, who were emulating the shaikh, were therefore justified in their military activities, and al-Kanami should abandon Borno for a Muslim country.

Al-Kanami was never convinced by the arguments for jihad; he consistently referred to the conflicts as fitna. His own conservative inclinations are evident throughout the correspondence, suggesting that he was unable to accept the radical enterprise upon which the Sokoto leadership had embarked.[34] His own legal position was based upon the concept of obligatory allegiance to the legitimate Muslim ruler and the danger of killing Muslims in the kinds of wars which were spreading in the region. He revealed a growing respect for the scholarly and religious stature of Shaikh Uthman, but this was balanced by a deep contempt for the Borno Fulbe leadership. He accepted that the radicalism of jihad could be authorized directly by God, a point on which he and Shaikh Uthman agreed, but he never accepted that the Borno Fulbe could claim such an authorization simply by emulating the Shaikh.

'Religious persona' and legitimate leadership

The entire debate centered on a single issue: the question of legitimate Islamic leadership. The legitimacy of the jihad ultimately rested upon the personal and religious integrity of Shaikh Uthman, upon his 'religious persona'. From this premise, all else followed: the religious exhortations and the various legal interpretations about belief and unbelief by association. To 'emulate the Shaikh' was to be in the right; to attack persons claiming to be 'emulating the Shaikh' was equivalent to unbelief. Rulers who refused to join the jihad were unbelievers, and the subjects of unbelieving rulers were themselves unbelievers:

> . . . the law of a country is the law of its sultan. If he is a Muslim, then the country is dar al-Islam; if he is a pagan, then the country is dar kufr. Only those ignorant of the words of the ulama will deny this.[35]

This kind of elitism was at the core of contemporary Islamic religious culture in the western Sudan, and Shaikh Uthman's legal argument, based on the ideas of al-Maghili, was designed to reinforce it. On one occasion, Bello cites al-Maghili's advice that good Muslim rulers must be advised by one of the 'scholars of the Reminder . . .who are like the prophets of former communities'.[36] The scholars of the Reminder were 'godly and learned men' according to al-Maghili, and Shaikh Uthman was one of them, according to his supporters.[37]

But this kind of thinking also evokes its opposite. If the legitimacy of a movement depends on the integrity of its leader, then one way to disparage the movement is to disparage its leader. This is precisely how the Sokoto leadership was justifying warfare all over Hausaland, by arguing (in legal terms, of course) that the Hausa kings were not Muslims. Part of the strategy of argument was therefore to attack, either explicitly or implicitly, the personal integrity of the opposition. This dimension of confrontation began in the debate in al-Kanami's first letter to Sokoto, which included a direct challenge to the sincerity of Shaikh Uthman's intentions:

> We have been surprised at you, after having gained great fame in religious learning, that you love the worldly kingdom so much and that you desire it to such an extent that you have allowed yourself to be seduced and you have come to imagining things. You are being guided by appearances which you should disregard. We have heard of the conduct of Shaikh Uthman b. Fodiyo and we know his writings are contrary to your deeds. If this affair stems from his opinion then, there is no power nor strength except in God, we must say we thought better of him. As has been said, 'I love the Shaikh and the truth as long as they agree, but when they differ, the truth must prevail.'[38]

Bello retorted angrily to this passage. 'How can you arrive at such evil conclusions about someone whose good deeds have been spread to all quarters and who is praised by the elite and common people alike?'[39] Al-Kanami's judgment had been marred, Bello asserted, and he was speaking in contradictions. He had been misled by enemies of Sokoto; or if he had been told the truth, he was intentionally distorting it for his own purposes. In a subsequent letter, Bello lashed out more vehemently, asserting that al-Kanami was either ignorant or had taken leave of his sanity, and his allegations were

> . . .either confused or the words of someone whom Satan has struck with madness. First you acknowledge that we are good, then you charge us with evils. That suffices to demonstrate your feeble-mindedness or your madness. And how can you claim that we love power when you know that love is one of the deeds of the heart? Did you penetrate our hearts so that you can see what is within them? Are you acquainted with what is unseen? That suffices to demonstrate that what comes from you is lies and falsehoods. Similarly with your words about Shaikh Uthman b. Fodiyo. First you acknowledge his goodness, then you accuse him of evil. This madness and feeblemindedness in your heart suffices to reveal your deceitfulness.[40]

These kinds of angry exchanges were not simply emotional outbursts in an otherwise reasoned debate; they were important elements of a strategy to discredit the opposition. This is why al-Kanami's questioning of the sincere intentions of Shaikh Uthman was greeted with such vituperative anger. If the Shaikh could be shown to be either inadequately godly or inadequately learned, then the entire jihad movement risked being discredited. And so, Bello turned these same kinds of arguments and accusations back on al-Kanami.

A similar strategy was adopted in Sokoto in order to discredit the Mai of Borno. Gradually the Sokoto leadership built up a multi-faceted argument, designed to demonstrate that not only had the incumbent Mai become an apostate because of his attacks in aid of the unbelievers and against a community which was emulating the Shaikh, but also that the institution of kingship in Borno was itself deeply corrupted by un-Islamic practice. This argument slowly takes shape in the correspondence itself. The fundamental justification for declaring jihad against Borno remained consistently the allegation that they had aided the Hausa unbelievers against the jihad community. But over the years, an increasing number of allegations surfaced in Sokoto about the non-Islamic practices of the Borno people, which then appear regularly in the letters. These are claims about sacrifices to rocks and trees, the existence of shrines with idols in them, and certain ritual practices at the river similar to those performed by the Copts in the 'Nile in the days of the *Jāhiliyya*.'[41]

It was Shaikh Uthman himself who developed the most detailed argument about these kinds of practices, in his *Taᶜlīm al-Ikhwān*, written in 1813. This book must be read as an integral part of the Sokoto-Borno debate; although the text addresses the question of unbelief throughout the central Sudan, there is a specific section on Borno, and there is an extensive discussion about rituals which centre on trees.[42] Shaikh Uthman's concern about the ritual significance of trees was most certainly in response to an observation by al-Kanami in his first letter to Sokoto:

> Consider Damietta, a great Islamic city between Egypt and Syria, a place of learning and Islam: in it there is a tree, and the common people do to this tree as did the non-Arabs. But not one of the ulama rises to fight them or has spoken of their paganism.[43]

Shaikh Uthman demonstrated in his text that in the past quite a number of ulama had interfered with various rituals associated with trees; he did not, however, produce any evidence to show that jihad had been fought over such practices. And indeed, he clearly stated that the jihad in Borno was not declared because of these kinds of practices.

> All the same, we did not fight with them over those things by which they have gradually come to deserve designation as unbelievers, such as the sacrifices previously mentioned. We fought them only because they began to attack us; they were the first to commit aggression against us. What led them to commit such aggression was their cooperation with the unbelievers.[44]

There is a strong dose of propaganda in this kind of argument. On the one hand, the kings of Hausaland and Borno deserved to be condemned as unbelievers because of a wide range of practices and behaviours which were clearly unbelief and which they tolerated or participated in themselves. However, jihad was not declared against them because of this, but because they associated with and aided other unbelievers. Presumably, Shaikh Uthman did not consider the argument for jihad on the basis of these kinds of practices to be very strong, which was al-Kanami's contention from the beginning of the correspondence. The original jihad against Gobir had been declared in defence of the Muslim community; the kings of Gobir were unbelievers because they had attacked the community. The subsequent jihads against the kings of Hausa and Borno were similarly legitimate because they were in defense of the Muslims. As Shaikh Uthman said in the previous quotation: 'We fought [Borno] only because they began to attack us.'

This kind of propaganda was most fully developed in *Infāq al-Maisūr* in the historical sections about Borno. The book is organized geographically, beginning with Baghirmi in the east and moving to Futa

Toro in the far west. The history of the jihad, which constitutes the bulk of the book, falls within the section on Hausaland. In the sections on both Baghirmi and Borno, Bello paints a picture of the Mai, of several different Mais, as oppressive and particularly harsh toward certain Muslim scholars resident in the country. These historical sketches, brief as they are, must be seen as part of a general propaganda campaign mounted by Bello against Borno; they were carefully constructed to portray the Mai in the worst possible light.

In his account of Baghirmi, for example, Bello includes a discussion of a certain Shaikh Waldede, a seventeenth-century scholar who was forced to flee for his life from Borno to Baghirmi in order to escape the wrath of the Mai.[45] According to Bello, this shaikh subsequently predicted that 'one of the friends of God would appear in these countries in order to renew religion, to revivify the sunna and to correct religious practice.'[46]

In his account of Borno, Bello devotes considerable space to Muhammad al-Tahir, an eighteenth-century scholar who enjoyed some influence in the court of the Mai Ali b. Hamdun (1747–92).[47] At some point, al-Tahir became embroiled in conflict at the court, and Bello claims that he, too, predicted the appearance of a mujaddid or rejuvenator of religion in Borno. Of course, the prediction of the appearance of a mujaddid at the beginning of a new Islamic century was not unusual; it was widely accepted in West Africa that each Islamic century was blessed by the appearance of such a mujaddid. But Bello was implying that these predictions referred directly to his own father,[48] and to the fact that the jihad would drive the Mai of Borno from his capital due to his infidelity and oppression of Islam.

Enough is now known about Muhammad al-Tahir to state categorically that Bello presented a distorted view of the man, and even quoted his poetry out of context in order to support the jihad's case against the Mai. Al-Tahir certainly experienced difficulties at the Borno court, and at one time he was estranged from the Mai. But the overall picture is of a scholar who was not only a member of the court, and therefore embroiled in court politics, but a firm and loyal supporter of the Mai.[49] Judging from his own writings, he advised the Mai on the religiously proper conduct of affairs of state, encouraged him in his military campaigns, and wrote eulogies to him as an upstanding Muslim, a view of Mai Ali which is confirmed in the *Diwān*, or king-list of Bornu, which recognized him as a mujaddid in his own right.[50]

The portrayal of the Mai presented by Bello in *Infāq al-Maisūr* could not have been in greater contrast, and he distorts al-Tahir's words to make his point. He introduces the Mais of Borno in the following passage:

> Their sultans are in a category of their own as to violence, deceit, ignominy, lack of charity, bloodshed, tyranny and immorality.

The professor al-Tahir b. Ibrahim said about them in his poem:
[1]Verily the Kanuri [of old]
    Were a people of conquest and dominance.
[2]Alarming rumour was to them
    Like the jingling rajaz metres of eulogy.
[3]The legends which they possess
    Constitute the very pillar of their building.
[4]According to them, lies are
    Among the most marvellous of misdeeds.
[5]The legends are jingling metres
    Of the gardens of transient [pride].
[6]O children of Kanur,
    This is [a product] of the arts of scorn.'[51]

These six verses were selected by Bello from a total of 189; fifteen verses intercede between the first two quoted by him. When the poem is read in full, it is evident that the object of vilification in verses [2] through [6] was not the Mais of Borno, but slanderers. The poem was composed to condemn certain unnamed courtiers for their slander and rumour-mongering in the court.

The original poem communicates a very different attitude toward the Mai to that evoked by Bello.

Truly Mai Ali is a high-minded man, unimpaired in his
    uprightness.
If a slanderer comes to him with a libelous and malignant
    report,
He shuts his eyes and closes his ears in order to shun such
    unkind behaviour.
He weighs their remarks on the balance of his innermost heart
    with careful consideration.
He weighs the truth upon a correct and trustworthy scale.
    Then he discards all that which is uncouth,
      And he ostracizes the slanderer as blameworthy, even as one
    banished in nakedness.
He never ceases to be guided by the Book in every matter.

Al-Tahir's intention in this poem was to praise the Mai for his resistance to the slanderous activities of some of his courtiers, presumably directed against al-Tahir's own person. But even that conclusion is not directly supported by the content of the poem, and is only arrived at by associating it with a specific occasion on which al-Tahir was excluded from the court.[52]

Bello's intention was to communicate that al-Tahir's difficulties at court resulted from his defense of Islam against an unbelieving tyrant. But a broader reading of al-Tahir's verse strongly suggests another interpretation: of a religious scholar who was profoundly implicated in court politics. Indeed, careful study of al-Tahir's career may reward us with some rarely documented insights into the complex role of Islamic scholarship in the pre-jihad courts of the central Sudan. Al-Tahir was certainly a learned scholar, and a considerable proportion of his writing was devoted to the religious sciences. But he was also politically ambitious, and much of his writing was addressed to the Mai, either as praise or advice, inevitably couched in the appropriate Islamic idiom. But there were also exhortations to encourage military campaigns, or to praise those already concluded. In other words, the overwhelming weight of his poetic compositions was to support the policies and the person of Mai Ali.

Concluding remarks

Bello's interpretation of Muhammad al-Tahir has entered the historical (and political) discourse in Nigeria, where he is consistently presented as a prime example of the pre-jihad Muslim reformer, critic of non-Islamic government, and victim of the tyranny of those unjust rulers whom the jihad replaced.[53] Maigari even goes so far as to credit al-Tahir with epitomizing the 'religious and reformist' zeal of such leaders as Sulaiman al-Futi of Senegal, Ahmad Lobbo of Masina and Shaikh Uthman himself, although none of the evidence which Maigari musters in his own paper suggests that al-Tahir ever acted against incumbent authority in any way, or ever considered the establishment of a government which would be 'more Islamic' than the one he was serving.

Bello's presentation of al-Tahir as an oppressed scholar was of course related to his need to portray the Mai as an anti-Islamic tyrant. And this strategem was dictated in turn by the elitism which was fundamental to jihadist argument. The principle, repeated many times by Shaikh Uthman in his writings, was that Muslims were to be guided in the proper practice of their religion by learned scholars whose expert command of legal texts qualified them for leadership of the community. The structure of the Muslim community which he proposed was very simple; ideally, it was composed of three groups:

> the ulama whose belief is sound;
> the talaba whose belief is sound;
> those who listen to what the ulama say and follow the example of the above two groups[54]

The followers of Shaikh Uthman saw him as a peerless Muslim leader, not only in terms of his scholarship, but his spiritual accomplishments

36

as well, which together led to his receiving divine authorization for the jihad in a vision. These characteristics constituted the 'religious persona' upon which his legitimacy as an Islamic leader was based.[55]

If the Mai of Borno, who already considered himself Amir al-muminin, was also perceived as an ideal Muslim leader, then any conflict between Borno and Sokoto would be fitna, as al-Kanami had perceived it. No jihad would have been legitimate in such a situation, no matter what other political differences were at play. It is therefore extremely significant that throughout the entire lengthy correspondence, very little attention was paid to exploring what precisely led to hostilities between the Borno Fulbe and the Borno administration. From the first, and well before they had any detailed knowledge of the local events, Sokoto claimed that the Mai's actions had been in aid of the Hausa kings. This conclusion logically emerged from the tenets upon which the Sokoto leadership based its thinking. Since his hijra, Shaikh Uthman had become the imam (and Amir al-muminin) of the Muslim community; he should now be emulated, and all local Muslims should affiliate with his community. All subsequent political and legal issues then became extremely simple to resolve: either one joined the Shaikh, and submitted to his leadership, or one apostasized from Islam by rejecting affiliation with the true Muslim community. All other issues about former political associations, about the legitimacy of local complaints and hostilities (such as in western Borno), became subsumed under this central question of acceptance of the Shaikh as leader of Muslims.

The numerous legal arguments about sunna and illegal innovations, and about who was or was not a Muslim, were all subsumed under the fundamental concept of taqlid: of emulation of the ideal Muslim leader. However, the Mai also considered himself Amir al-muminin, and his cause was defended by a scholar who was capable of debating the issues with the Sokoto leadership. Al-Kanami shared the same elitist perceptions as Sokoto, except that he based his arguments on an acceptance of the Mai as a legitimate Muslim ruler. According to him, the Borno Fulbe had initiated hostilities, and the Mai had moved to discipline them; these Fulbe were resident in the Mai's territories, and he had every right to respond to their attacks in kind. This was the argument of obligatory allegiance to the legitimate ruler. According to Sokoto, these same Fulbe were emulating the Shaikh, and an attack against them was an attack against the Muslim community. With time, al-Kanami conceded that the Shaikh personally may have been defending and renewing the sunna in Hausaland, but that the Borno Fulbe were not worthy of being followed, or emulated, by anyone. Having said this, al-Kanami never offered his allegiance to Sokoto, and the issues in Borno were finally resolved, not by legal argument, but by military force.

Appendix I

Outline of correspondence between Sokoto and Borno

The correspondence which Muhammad Bello published in *Infāq al-Maisūr* was written between 1808, the date of al-Kanami's first letter to the Borno Fulbe, and 1812, when *Infāq al-Maisūr* was completed. None of the letters published by Bello was dated; the numbers in the left hand column refer to their relative chronology as they appear in *Infāq al-Maisūr* (IM). Letters referred to as not extant are mentioned in *Infāq al-Maisūr* but not published there.

Not extant	Early correspondence between Mai Borno and Sokoto
Not extant	al-Kanami to Borno Fulbe, which never arrived
1808	al-Kanami to Borno Fulbe (University of Ibadan MS 82/237)
Not extant	Response from Borno Fulbe to al-Kanami
Not extant	al-Kanami to Borno Fulbe
IM no. 1	al-Kanami to Sokoto
Not extant	Abdullahi b. Fodiyo to al-Kanami
IM no. 2	Bello to al-Kanami, in response to IM no. 1
IM no. 3	Bello to al-Kanami, a second response to IM no. 1
Not extant	Bello writes regularly to Borno Fulbe for facts, but letters do not reach their destination
Not extant	Gidaado dan Layma [future wazir] to al-Kanami
Not extant	al-Kanami replies to Gidaado in a conciliatory manner
IM no. 4	Bello to al-Kanami, a conciliatory letter which never reaches al-Kanami
Not extant	Bello to al-Kanami, seeking a truce
Not extant	al-Kanami to Borno Fulbe, a hostile letter which is forwarded to Bello
IM no. 5	Bello to al-Kanami, in response to the preceding letter
IM no. 6	Shaikh Uthman to al-Kanami

IM no. 7   Bello to al-Kanami [nos. 6 and 7 seem to have been sent together]

IM no. 8   al-Kanami to Shaikh Uthman, in response to no. 6

IM no. 9   al-Kanami to Bello, in response to no. 7

IM no. 10   Shaikh Uthman to al-Kanami, described by Bello as the definitive response to al-Kanami

Appendix II

Letter from al-Kanami to the Borno Fulbe dated 17 Rabiᶜ al-Awwil 1223 (13 May 1808)

Praise be to God who has commanded his worshippers to pursue piety and the fear of God, and has prohibited obedience to worldly men and reliance upon the material world, and has prohibited the pursuit of [mundane] pleasures. Blessing and peace upon him who has pursued actively the noble love, and upon his family and companions who did not turn away from the true religion [leaving it] hidden and unknown.

After that, perfect peace, may the blessings and mercy of God be upon you. From the most humble of the creatures of mankind and the one most in need of the King, the Creator, the diminutive servant of God Almighty, Muhammad al-Amin b. Muhammad al-Kanami by origin, Fezzani by birth and residence, Maliki by legal school, Asharī by theological doctrine, and Junaidi by tariqa. To the brothers in the religion of God Almighty, al-Alim Hamid, al-Mahir Mukhtar, al-Alim Ali and al-al-Alim al-Bukhari, and the entire community in general and in particular.

After that, the reason for the writing of this letter is that when fate carried me to this country seeking the abundance of God, I found the fire of discord between you and the people of the country. Its spark was spreading and its wood was being affected. So I asked about the cause. One person said, 'A faction has been seeking the throne.' Another said, 'A faction has arisen which is gaining victory for the religion of God Almighty.' So I began to investigate, and I asked everyone who possessed knowledge about the situation of the members of these factions, but they could not expand on the question for me except by speculation, nor [assist in my] investigation except as unlettered persons [ajam] due to the difference of the languages. So I wrote this letter to you in order that the matter might become clear. If it is a good thing [which you are doing], then it is to be respected, but if it is a sin, it must be purified. So explain to us with an unequivocal statement, and may God have mercy upon you.

What is the cause of this discord? What do you seek from the people, and in which matter has a difference arisen between you and them? And inform us whether or not you have any connection with him whose fame has spread far and wide, the shaikh, my master, Uthman b. Fodio. Know that anyone who reaches us from you will receive good treatment and safe conduct.

But we condemn the evil of raids, and the authorization of blood-letting, and the enslavement of free persons, and the violation of lands lying outside what has been witnessed to be in your domain. And we do not know if this emanated from your own advice or not. If you are the persons who summon [people] to the religion of God, and if you are guides to the worshippers of God, then the matter of the raids has confused us. If you are the whip of punishment and God has given you his authority over the people of this region due to their arrogance, as when God gave authority to Nebuchadnezzar over the people of Jerusalem when they became proud, then there is no disavowal [of you].

But do not be surprized at our disavowal of these raids, because it has occurred to us in our limited understanding that the people of this country are of four types:

The first type is allowed in blood and wealth, as in your own opinion, as he is the one who has associated another deity with God, etc., according to what the authors have mentioned about this.

The second type is killed for unbelief, and his wealth is allowable but you may not capture his sons, for he is the one who has disclaimed what he has learned of religion through necessity, etc., according to what has been said of this.

The third type, and he is the majority of the people of this land, will have the Islamic Day of Judgment imposed upon him, and he will find his place among those who reside in hell for eternity, for he is the one who has pronounced the two Shahadahs, according to tradition, but he does not know anything about what God requires of him, and he is not fond of [religious] duties at all, or even a little, [and he avoids] the tradition or the emulation of those who were before him whether they were misguiding or guiding rightly.

The fourth type are those who believe in God and his Prophets, and they are completely immovable in their faith, and their external and internal spiritual dimensions are equal in belief. So one should carry forward their concepts with respect and determination. These will be saved by the grace of God in this world and in the next, God willing.

Every country in this region contains these four types. Anyone who gains a position over them by raids will inevitably have the difficulty of discrimination. And whenever the difficulty of discrimination has made all injury general, then the abandonment of the unbeliever is more acceptable than the killing of the Muslim, as is known to anyone who has experienced anything of the religious sciences.

May God pray for us and you, and may he guide and alert both us and you to that which was hidden from us. Consider this letter, may God guide you. Compose your answer well, may God assist you, in clear phrase and true resolution, in order that it display your design and dispel doubts from the heart. The Muslims in the religion of God, all of them, are equal, and the believers, as the Quran emphasizes, cling to [religion] mutually. If we had not heard that you were sympathetic to religion then we would not have attempted to write to you, nor would we have gone to all this trouble.

I have written a letter to you before this, and I sent it to you with some malams, but the letter was held up, so I wrote another. I do not know if my first letter reached you or not. Peace.

Notes

1. The first lectures on African history which I attended were delivered by Michael Crowder at Columbia University in the summer of 1963. Subsequently, he played a significant role in directing me toward a study of nineteenth-century Borno for my dissertation research. I am therefore very pleased to be able to contribute this essay to a volume dedicated to his memory.

2. See N. Levtzion and J. Voll, eds., *Eighteenth Century Renewal and Reform Movements in Islam* (Syracuse: Syracuse University Press, 1987). Of the many works dealing with Shaikh Uthman's jihad, the best introduction remains M. Last, *The Sokoto Caliphate* (London, 1967). See also, M. Last, 'Reform in West Africa: the jihad movements of the nineteenth century,' in J.F.A. Ajayi and M. Crowder (eds.), *History of West Africa*, revised second edition, (London, 1987).

3. Julie Lawson, 'Nigerian Historiography and the Sokoto Jihad,' (Unpublished MA dissertation, SOAS, University of London, 1989). See also Elizabeth Hodgkin, 'Islamism and Islamic Research in Africa,' *Islam et Sociétés au Sud du Sahara*, no. 4 (1990), pp. 73–130. During a research trip to Nigeria, Hodgkin compiled a list of well over 800 theses (Ph.D, MA, and BA) on Islamic subjects completed since independence; her survey did not include all of Nigeria's universities.

4. Muhammad Bello, *Infāq al-Maisūr*, ed. by C.E.J. Whitting (London, 1957). Referred to subsequently as IM. Ten of the eleven surviving letters appear in IM.

5. Translated by B.G. Martin in 'Unbelief in the Western Sudan: Uthman dan Fodio's '*Taʿlīm al-Ikhwān*', '*Middle East Studies*, 4(1976), pp. 50–97. Referred to below as TI.

6. For twentieth-century accounts, see L. Brenner, *The Shehus of Kukawa: a History of the al-Kanemi Dynasty of Bornu* (Oxford, 1973); K. Tijani, *The Dynamics of Administrative Development in pre-Colonial Borno*, Ph.D dissertation, Ahmadu Bello University, Zaria, 1980; L. Brenner and R. Cohen, 'Bornu in the Nineteenth Century,' in J.F.A. Ajayi and M. Crowder (eds.), *History of West Africa*, revised second edition,(London, 1987); M. Last, 'The Sokoto Caliphate and Borno,' in J.F. Ade Ajayi (ed), *Africa in the Nineteenth Century until the 1880s, General History of Africa*, vol. VI (Paris: UNESCO, 1989). For a discussion of the legal issues relevant to this debate, see M. Last and M.A. al-Hajj, 'Attempts at Defining a Muslim in 19th Century Hausaland and Bornu,' *Journal of the Historical Society of Nigeria*, III, 2 (1965), pp. 231–40.

7. The section on the jihad in Borno is found in IM, pp. 121-74.

8. IM, pp. 121–2. The 'wazir' referred to in the text is thought to have been the Galadima, administrator of Borno's western territories and resident in Nguru.

9. That is, the Fulbe drove the Galadima from Nguru. For further details, see Brenner, *Shehus*, pp. 26ff; V.N. Low, *Three Nigerian Emirates: A Study in Oral History* (Evanston, 1972); Muhammad Bose Ahmad, 'The Refugee Emirate: Misau's Bornoan Origins and its Relations with its Neighbours, circa 1805–1903 (unpublished Ph.D thesis, University of Birmingham, 1989).

10. IM, p. 122; reference to hijra in this context seems to refer to those Fulbe who were joining the various jamaa which were now forming around certain Muslim leaders

in the Borno provinces, especially in Deya. The hijra was therefore more a flight from the Mai's authority than from his 'country,' as he perceived it.

11. IM, Letter no. 2, IM, p. 131.

12. IM, pp. 122–3. These events are also recounted in Letter no. 2.

13. IM, p. 124.

14. Ibid.

15. University of Ibadan manuscript 82/237.

16. *Wird* (Zaria: Gaskiya Corporation, 1962).

17. IM, Letter no. 1, p. 124; this letter is translated in part by Abdullahi Smith in T. Hodgkin, *Nigerian Perspectives* (London, 1960), pp. 198–201. This quotation is taken from Smith's translation.

18. IM, Letter no. 1, p. 125; Hodgkin, p. 200.

19. IM, Letter no. 2, p. 132.

20. Ibid.

21. Ibid., pp. 129 and 133.

22. IM, Letter no. 3, p. 136.

23. For Al-Maghili, see J.O. Hunwick, *Sharīʿa in Songhai: the Replies of al-Maghili to the Questions of Askia al-Hajj Muhammad* (London: The British Academy, 1985). For a discussion of the role of al-Maghili's ideas in the thought of Shaikh Uthman, see L. Brenner, 'Muslim Thought in Eighteenth Century West Africa: the Case of Shaikh Uthman b. Fudi,' in Levtzion and Voll, op. cit.

24. In TI, pp. 89–90, Shaikh Uthman gave his account of the origins of hostilities in Borno.

25. IM, Letters nos. 8 and 9, pp. 162–6.

26. IM, Letter no. 1, pp. 126–7. It is interesting to note that these passages were not included in Abdullahi Smith's translation of this letter in Hodgkin, op. cit.

27. IM, Letter no. 2, p. 133.

28. IM, Letter no. 4, p. 141.

29. IM, Letter no. 8, pp. 163–4.

30. IM, Letter no. 5, pp. 142–60; about one-fifth of the contents of this letter is translated in Hodgkin, pp. 202–5.

31. IM, Letter no. 10, pp. 172–3.

32. IM, Letter no. 5, p. 157. Bello quotes passages from al-Kanami's letter in his response.

33. Ibid., p. 152; also p. 150, translated in Hodgkin p. 204.

34. It is impossible to know the extent to which al-Kanami's own political interests affected his arguments in the early stages of his exchanges with Sokoto.

35. IM, Letter no. 5, p. 143; Hodgkin, p. 203.

36. IM, Letter no. 5, p. 158.

37. For al-Maghili on the 'people of the Reminder', see Hunwick, *Sharīʿa in Songhay*, pp. 65ff. and 112–3.

38. IM, Letter no. 1, p. 127. Again, it should be noted that the first part of this quotation does not appear in Smith's translation of this letter in Hodgkin, op. cit.

39. IM, Letter no. 2, p. 135.

40. IM, Letter no. 3, p. 138.

41. IM, Letter no. 5, p. 143; Hodgkin, p. 203. The same claims are made by Shaikh Uthman in IM, Letter no. 11, p. 173.

42. TI, pp. 84–87.

43. IM, Letter no. 1, pp. 125–6; this translation is from Hodgkin, p. 200.

44. TI, p. 89.

45. See J.E. Lavers, 'Diversions on a Journey, or the Travels of Shaykh Ahmad al-Yamani (1630–1712) from Halfaya to Fez,' in Y.F. Hasan and P. Doornbos, *The*

Central Bilad al-Sudan, Tradition and Adaptation (Khartoum, n.d.); and 'Islam in the Borno Caliphate: a Survey,' *Odu*, no. 5 (April 1971), pp. 27–53.

46. IM, p. 7.

47. IM, pp. 11–13.

48. He states this specifically in IM, p. 29.

49. See Tahir Maigari al-Barnawi, 'Al-shaikh Tāhir Feroma ibn Ibrāhim al-Fallātī al-Barnāwī,' unpublished paper (in Arabic) presented in the Department of Islamic Studies, Bayero University Kano, n.d. The paper is an analysis of the writings and political activities of Muhammad al-Tahir, and quotes extensively from his poetry.

50. Dierk Lange, *Le Diwan des Sultans du [Kanem]-Bornu: Chronologie et Histoire d'un Royaume Africaine (de la fin du Xe siècle jusqu'à 1808)* (Wiesbaden, 1977), p. 87.

51. IM, p. 11; with the exception of verse [4], this translation is from A.D.H. Bivar and M. Hiskett, 'The Arabic Literature of Nigeria to 1804: a Provisional Account,' *Bulletin of the School of Oriental and African Studies*, XXV, Part 1 (1962), p. 138–39. The verses are taken from a poem entitled, '*Qasīda fī nuṣḥ li'l-salṭān min samīᶜ aqwāl al-washāh*' – 'Advice to the Sultan about listening to slanderous speech.' It is known in Kanuri as '*Fané Fané*', or 'Listen, Listen;' an allusion to gossip-mongering. A copy of this poem was made available to me by Dr. David Spain, University of Washington, and it is quoted extensively in Maigari, op. cit. The Arabic rendering of verse [4] in IM had been corrupted, which resulted in Bivar and Hiskett translating it as:

> The fables current amongst them
>
> Concern the 'Torture of the Henna'

The translation of verse [4] in the above text is my own.

52. Maigari presents evidence which suggests that al-Tahir was very much an advocate of Fulbe interests at court, and that some of the critical references to the Kanuri in the above poem were related to certain ethnic conflicts and competitions. These observations raise important historiographical questions about local perceptions of the jihad in Borno and its Fulbe leadership, but their analysis is beyond the scope of the present paper. Al-Tahir composed poetry in Arabic, Fulfulde and Kanuri.

53. For recent examples, see, M.B. Ahmad, 'The Refugee Emirate,' pp. 48–9, and Kiyari Tijani, op cit., pp. 543–4; 581.

54. Quoted from Shaikh Uthman's *Nūr al-albāb*; see Brenner, 'Muslim Thought in Eighteenth-Century West Africa,' p. 52. The talaba were students, those on the path to becoming ulama.

55. For a discussion of the personal, as opposed to institutional, basis of legitimacy in Muslim societies, see David D. Laitin, *Hegemony and Culture. Politics and Religious Change among the Yoruba* (London, 1986).

Chapter Three

'Injustice' and Legitimacy in the Early Sokoto Caliphate

MURRAY LAST

Introduction

The prophet Moses met Satan with five donkeys, laden with goods. Says Moses, 'Satan, where are you going to?' He answered that he was away hawking his hide-bags of stuff. Says Moses, 'What's in them?' Says Satan, 'The donkey in front has oppression [zalunci] in his – I'm taking that to the rulers; the second donkey has pride in his – that I'm taking to the sons of rulers; the third one has envy in, and I'm taking that to the ulama; the fourth donkey has hatred in, and I'm taking that to a rich merchant; while the fifth donkey has 'had-I-but-known' in – that I'm taking to women.'

The story, written down in Hausa by an alim in Sokoto *c.* 1905, affirms a commonplace; as the Hausa say, oppressive officials are *the* 'guests' of kings – just as ulama are 'God's guests'. 'Azzalumi', 'zalunci' – these are the usual terms in Hausa for the misuse of power, so usual that the terms are applied to a husband mistreating his wife, or to a chairman of a seminar shutting up a recalcitrant speaker. Though etymologically Arabic, the concept is now vernacular, thus adding one more to the stock of words implying 'harm' but one with the connotation of illegality; indeed, in translations from the Arabic, 'zalunci' is used in Hausa for a wide range of Arabic words implying forceful misappropriation of rights of many kinds. It is this concept that I have in mind when discussing in this essay the debates in early nineteenth-century Sokoto over the 'unjust ruler' and people's rights against him and his officials.

How the ruled fought the injustices and illegitimacy of their rulers was a central theme in Michael Crowder's writing, especially in his last

---

works on Botswana in the Protectorate period. He demonstrated the way the ruled could use against their rulers the very language of justice that the rulers themselves used to legitimate their own position. As a consequence, colonial bureaucracies were always liable (as he showed also in *Revolt in Bussa*) to escalate an initial error of judgment on their part into a major crisis that called in question the moral basis of their regime. Force, rather than success or social justice, was thus seen to sanction their right to rule. Yet the colonial regimes, if not the individuals involved, survived these crises; the struggle against rulers considered illegitimate went on. In this essay, the idiom is not that of the colonialist Europe that Michael Crowder studied, but the perhaps even stricter idiom of Islamic justice. At issue too is how the concept a government official may have of justice can differ fundamentally from that held by a local leader who is much less legally sophisticated yet nonetheless representative perhaps of ordinary opinion. This implicit clash of cultures, and the often disastrous misunderstandings that resulted, was the stuff of Michael Crowder's histories.

I wish to focus here on an extreme case, a peculiarity perhaps, where the case for action against an 'unjust ruler' appears at its weakest yet was nonetheless pressed hard. It shows how in a real incident if not in legal theory, the issues that inspire people to fight are muddy, emotional and, sadly for us historians, seldom text'd, even when they are put forward by ulama (albeit of a certain kind). For in the arguments under discussion, the issue of 'zalunci' runs through like a continuous but sometimes hidden thread. In Hausa popular thought oppression ('zalunci') justifies resistance, yet Islamic law apparently takes away that justification. In consequence, if resistance or even dissidence was to be 'properly' legitimated, it had to be so via concepts like takfir and jihad. In short, the incident to be described illustrates that problematic gap between what the scholarly-muslim alim thinks is Islamically 'right' and what the vernacular-Muslim alim prefers instead to emphasize.

The central figures in this essay are the dissident scholar Abd al-Salam and his Amir al-muminin at Sokoto, Muhammad Bello. Both the details of the incident and the arguments used are taken from a single manuscript text, the book, in Arabic, by the second Sokoto Caliph Muhammad Bello b. al-Shaikh Uthman dan Fodio called *Sard al-Kalām fī mā jarā baynī wa bayn ʿAbd al-Salām* (written *c.* 1818). In it are quoted some six letters by Muhammad Bello and three by Abd al-Salam. Although an alim (Muhammad Bello addresses him as 'Shaikh', but in other contexts gives him no title), Abd al-Salam was it seems more of a preacher than a literary scholar. Muhammad Bello implies as much, and indeed Abd al-Salam's longest letter, as quoted, is stylistically and linguistically awkward: its quotations of hadith and legal authorities are strung together in a manner that suits better an oral presentation.

We have, then, an example of the discrepancy between the preacher's style of Islam and the professional scholar's; yet the text preserved is, of course, compiled by the professional scholar. Abd al-Salam often did not reply in writing to Bello's letters, and Bello preserves only a few of Abd al-Salam's oral comments. As a result, some of the arguments Abd al-Salam will have used in his speeches or preaching have to be inferred from Bello's own letters. That Abd al-Salam was highly effective as a speaker, and persuasive in his arguments, is clear both from how Bello treats him and from the masses of people whom Bello says joined him. I want therefore to emphasize here that amidst all our discussions of the *textual* niceties of the Sharia we must nonetheless always be aware of the oral, preachers' 'chorus' that acts as a commentary and to which people listen, with perhaps more attention than they give to the protagonists' formal disputations.

Historical background

The jihad movement in north-western Hausaland (in Northern Nigeria) in the last two decades of the eighteenth century eventually brought about a very disparate coalition of interests, idealistic and opportunistic together. Support for jihad came from among both pastoralists and peasants; from freemen and slaves; urban princes and rural scholars; women and youths, all seeking greater access to Islam and the rights it promised; from Tuareg, Fulbe, Hausa of different regions – the pressure had already been such as to put into power, in most of the existing Hausa states, reforming Sultans. It was pressure, too, that had been felt during most of the eighteenth century throughout most of West Africa – from Futa Jallon and Futa Toro in the west to the Chad basin in the east. Yet when it came to the hardships of actual war (and the diseases that accompanied it), only a much smaller, closer-knit group survived to emerge as victors.

Not surprisingly, not all these disparate interests could be satisfied – any more than had the last reforming sultans before the jihad been able to satisfy the earlier conflicting demands or keep the lid on revolt. Dissidence within the ranks of the jihad movement started very early. One of the movement's chief architects and chroniclers, Abdullahi dan Fodio, himself temporarily abandoned the jihad out of disgust with the misconduct and oppression of his fellow mujahidun. The jihad commanders were more than once unable to control their soldiery, and on occasions even had to be rescued from being murdered by their own men when they interfered with the way their men took booty. Apparently the element within the jihad forces most identified (at least in the popular mind) with this 'oppression', the jihad's 'hard men', were the Fulbe pastoralists (Tuareg were the other 'hard men' of the area). They had always been somewhat outside the local state's law, and persons in dispute with the state had tended to find safe refuge with them – as indeed before the jihad had Abd al-Salam and his jamaa (which almost certainly included convert runaway slaves). As a conseqence, as the jihad wore on, with starvation widespread and the peasantry increasingly antagonistic to the plundering jihad armies, the 'Sudani' element in the jihad movement started to disassociate itself from the leadership. Princes who had studied under the jihad scholars and initially supported the jihad now left the movement; so too did certain village and town chiefs. In this context an alim like Abd al-Salam was but one dissident among many; but as a scholar rather than, say, a town chief (who would have to decide whether to open or close his town's gates to the mujahidun), he could express his dissidence by staying aloof from some campaigns: there was, after all, an old tradition that scholars did not fight. Whatever the reason, the reluctance to become further involved in the jihad reached such proportions that the jihad commanders often could not raise enough troops for a campaign.

Abd al-Salam, as Muhammad Bello points out, was a 'Sudani', a ba-Are from the Arewa qabila (between the Songhai and Hausa areas); his original name was Mikaila. Why his father Ibrahim called him Mikaila is not known, but it was not uncommon for West African scholars to identify themselves and their ancestors with Old Testament figures and peoples ('of the Book'), and therefore not as pagans. Certainly, Abd al-Salam claimed he was an 'old' Muslim; he had been, too, a student of the Shaikh Uthman's, whom he always treated as his shaikh and master; he settled his community near the shaikh at a place he called Dar al-Salam (and thus took the new name Abd al-Salam). He drew in large numbers of converts from his people and others (whom Bello refers to as al-Sudan to distinguish them from the people he calls 'Fillan'). The harassment of Abd al-Salam and his community was one of the immediate causes that precipitated the actual jihad fighting. There was, then, a symbolic quality to Abd al-Salam – symbolic of the jihad's defence of Sudani Muslims against their state's officials, of Fulbe-pastoralist readiness (as Bello specifically says) to take them into their settlements and hide them as 'brothers in Islam'.

What, then, occasioned the dispute specifically with Abd al-Salam? As Muhammad Bello tells it, following the final victory of the jihad forces in 1808, the conquered state territory had to be re-allocated, with a town and seven hamlets being given to Abd al-Salam and his jamaa under the overall supervision of Shaikh Uthman's brother Abdullahi dan Fodio. Abd al-Salam's district was in the western quadrant of the caliphate, but not in fact in his 'home' area. As a successful preacher and leader, Abd al-Salam continued to seek out and attract followers in the aftermath of the jihad, and to expand his area of authority. He apparently wanted to move out of his allocated area, but we are not told where to. He was refused permission by Abdullahi, who anyway objected to his expansionist methods which were causing considerable friction locally. He was accused of sedition. Eventually apologizing to Shaikh Uthman, Abd al-Salam was transferred finally, with much foreboding, to a very fertile valley site under the eye of Muhammad Bello at Sokoto. Here his settlement flourished and grew, and he got permission from Muhamad Bello (who asked Shaikh Uthman's permission) to wall his town.

When after a long illness Shaikh Uthman died in his house at Sokoto on a Sunday night in April 1817, the Caliphate itself became the centre of a crisis. Mahdist expectations, which the Shaikh and Bello had both (temporarily?) promoted were still unfulfilled; and there was no one of the Shaikh's reputation to take his place. Bello was in Sokoto at the time, and those there with him that very Monday paid him allegiance as his father's successor. His father's Vizier and brother, Abdullahi, was not there; and when he did reach Sokoto, he found the gates shut on him. Nor was Abd al-Salam there. As a consequence, Bello's rather hasty succession to the Caliphal position was disputed: traditionally, some four or five days might elapse before a new ruler was chosen – indeed the Friday following the Shaikh's death was used as the occasion for a second show of allegiance. In May Abdullahi dan Fodio issued a book implicitly questioning the succession, to which Bello towards the end of July replied; the breach between the two was not really healed for some two years, until the last remnants of Abd al-Salam's dissident jamaa were finally destroyed in a joint Bello-Abdullahi campaign.

For over ten years Abdullahi dan Fodio had been criticizing his colleagues' conduct in the jihad and the way they enjoyed their success. The manner of Bello's succession only seemed to confirm that what they had established was mulk, not imana. If so, asks Abdullahi indirectly, what should a true Muslim now do? Quotations he chooses to use in *Sabil al-Salama* (from the Imam Malik and al-Suyuti) suggest that if the incumbent ruler is not as just as Umar b. Abd al-Aziz, then he need not be supported; and if there are two claimants, and neither of them is just, then one should stay neutral and defend oneself. The textual basis for dissidence, then, had been laid out by the senior mujahid, the caliphate's Vizier himself.

The dispute

The nub of the dispute appears to be that Abd al-Salam and his people, though Muslims and long-time supporters of the Shaikh Uthman, had 'lost out' following the success of the jihad; to them, the jihad had been 'hijacked'. They felt they were victims of oppression, 'zalunci'.

But so long as the Shaikh Uthman was Amir al-muminin and Shaikh to the jamaa as a whole, Abd al-Salam merely complained, and in the meantime built up the prosperity and population of his community. Though the crisis did not come to a head until September as the rains ended, his campaign of dissidence really begins on Shaikh Uthman's death, when he challenges Muhammad Bello as the legitimate, 'just' ruler of the Shaikh's whole community.

A. Abd al-Salam's charges

A.1: Is Bello legitimately the Amir al-muminin? By his actions but not in his letters, Abd al-Salam disputed the way in which Bello succeeded to the Caliphate. He failed to come in straightaway and pay allegiance to Bello, and instead had to be summoned by Bello. Though some paid allegiance to Abd al-Salam, it is unlikely that he really expected to be accepted as Caliph – yet given the size and prosperity of his settlement (which was not a ribat like Sokoto or Wurno), and his title 'Shaikh', perhaps it was not then as fanciful a dream as it seems to us with hindsight. I think, however, he planned simply to be independent. Nonetheless Abd al-Salam did eventually come in on a Friday and publicly pay allegiance to Bello, who, while escorting him out of town, promised to increase his territory – and confirmed the promise in writing.

By querying Bello's election (and in doing so Abd al-Salam was doing no more than had the Shaikh's vizier himself done), Abd al-Salam was surely undermining Bello's argument that the emir must be obeyed at all costs, that the emir is 'right'. Whether Abd al-Salam ever claimed that when he finally made his baya he was acting under duress, out of taqiyya, we do not know: there is no such claim in the letters, but Bello in his account does stress incidents that would seem to be aimed at refuting an argument-from-duress.

Underlying this challenge to Bello's legitimacy is the charge that the Caliphate had become a family affair, the private property of a single household – and not a true 'community', with properly elected leaders and officials; that the 'family' of Muslims – symbolized by Bello's use of that telling phrase 'brother in Islam' (akh fil-Islam) – was no longer operative, and so Bello could scarcely claim to be its head.

A.2: Is the distribution of the spoils of war legitimate? The charge that the Caliphate was a family affair is made most explicitly in the dispute over the division of territorial authority. The Shaikh had divided up the new state into quadrants, allocating to members of his own family (including one son-in-law) responsibility for supervizing each quadrant. On a separate sheet of his letter, Abd al-Salam drew a diagram of the quadrants, pointedly showing who had got what (though Allah had given it to all the community of Muslims), and asked the question, what had he received? – no more than he had had before the jihad! In a famous phrase he called the division of power 'a hyenas' share-out' (qismat al-fahd, translated in Hausa as rabon kura) – famous, since Abd al-Salam ultimately died at a town called 'No Hyena', while his body, buried there in haste, was dug up, so the story goes, and eaten by hyenas.

Given the notorious difficulties the jihad leadership had had over dividing booty up according to the law, their record in dividing up conquered territories (whether declared waqf or not) was obviously liable to be disputed as further evidence of the fundamentally oppressive nature of their government. The implications were that there was to be now no hope of a senior place in the hierarchy for any scholar outside the family clique; and therefore that Abd al-Salam was right to run his own autonomous community of Muslims. For to be party to oppression or to cooperate with oppressors (azzalumai) in any way was, he says, to risk, hellfire. In consequence, Abd al-Salam started suborning the loyalties of ahl al-Sudan still under Bello, inviting them to join his more 'just' community.

A.3: Are the Emir and his officials acting oppressively? The unfairness of Abd al-Salam's share of the spoils of war – which Bello was willing to remedy as soon as he could – itself counted as zalunci, oppression. But Abd al-Salam's charges of zalunci against Bello's regime went further. In the general difficulties that always occur when peasants and pastoralists live side-by-side (and especially when grazing may be short, and safe fertile valley-bottom land is scarce), some of Abd al-Salam's people will have been hurt and their fields damaged. So too traders going to and from Abd al-Salam's town had been stopped by Bello's officials on the grounds they were trading with dar al-harb, and their goods sequestrated. Dhimmis were deemed to have broken their ahd (amana in Hausa) if they were in touch with areas and peoples now declared as dar al-harb. As there had been widespread 'revolt' (or non-recognition of Bello as the new rightful ruler) on the Shaikh's death, there was probably considerable confusion over who was and who was not a 'harbi'. The fact, too, that Abd al-Salam's settlement was overwhelmingly drawn from ahl al-Sudan, and it was ahl al-Sudan who comprised the bulk of both the Muslim rebels and the kuffar, made links between the two inevitable, if only at the fairly innocuous level of kinship exchanges.

Though the Shaikh Uthman and other jihad leaders had sought to subordinate kin and ethnic links within the wider Islamic brotherhood,

the charge that the caliphate had become merely a family affair showed how important those links were still considered to be. One issue, for example, in the various rows over the division of booty concerned the allocation of captured women and children – some of whom will have been the kin of those who supported Abd al-Salam and who may have sought to be set free and re-united with their own relatives. If the umma, then, was to take precedence over the family, it had to be more than just 'just'.

The problem was accentuated by the appointment of the Amir al-jaish (and Bello's brother-in-law) Ali Jedo as the governor of the northern quadrant where Abd al-Salam's people lived. Ali Jedo was notorious for his behaviour anyway, but though a thorn in the government's side, was apparently far too powerful or important a military leader to be sacked.

But it was not blood unjustly spilt, or property unjustly seized, that only constituted zalunci. It was also lack of respect. Abd al-Salam put forward the argument that where a 'zalimi' could not (for lack of power) spill blood or seize property but could only dishonour someone, he was no less at fault, given his intention to be oppressive. This marked insistence on respect or honour can only refer, I think, to the contempt often expressed by pastoralists such as the Fulbe and Tuareg for 'Sudani' peasants. Whether Abd al-Salam felt he was being patronized by the Shaikh's family and their friends, we do not know; he apparently felt excluded from the charmed circle that brought with it power. Certainly, if the quality of his Arabic as quoted is anything to go by, his scholarship was not on a par with that of the jihad leadership; indeed, Fulbe ulama especially are noted for their excellent command of Arabic. It is probable that Abd al-Salam was out of his depth academically, but interpreted his colleagues' awareness of this in ethnic terms. Thus Bello, in linking him with the raiya (usually translated as 'talakawa', the poor) and the 'Sudani' peoples may simply be reflecting Abd al-Salam's own view of things.

B. The tactics of dissidence

Abd al-Salam's tactics in his conflict with Bello mirror those that had been used by Bello and his father in their jihad against the Gobir authorities. Essentially this was to avoid direct conflict, forcing the state to be the first to act aggressively against them. They all the while maintained that they were Muslims, and that any attack on them was an attack upon Muslims. Abd al-Salam opens his letter by stressing this and spelling out the consequences for a Muslim who attacks another Muslim. As there was a story current in Sokoto that the shaikh in his last years had a nervous breakdown from his anxiety that through his jihad he had caused the death of innocent Muslims, this argument of Abd al-Salam's may have had a sharpness to it we now miss.

Secondly, Abd al-Salam's tactics included ignoring the orders of the state. He (and his Qadi and Muezzin) allowed people to go on trading or travelling where and with whom they wished, though they were explicitly told by Bello to put enemy territory out of bounds; and they allowed people to give aid to any one who was being 'oppressed' or harassed by state officials. Thus traders whose goods had been confiscated were freed on Abd al-Salam's orders. He thus set himself up as merely protecting the rights of 'his' Muslims vis-à-vis the oppressive agents of a now illegitimate state; in short, they were acting in self-defence.

Abd al-Salam's tactics, then, were to opt out as far as possible – but in doing so he was of course using the tactics of provocation, in which actions were more important than letters of complaint. Indeed his refusal to answer Bello's letters, like his delay in answering a summons, was itself provocative; furthermore, he took care that any action was mainly taken by 'hooligans' or 'hotheads' (sufaha; in Hausa, wawaye). This is the *same* term Bello uses for his own supporters when they, right at the outset of his jihad, set upon a column of the enemy and freed Abd al-Salam's people while they were being marched to captivity; in that context he was using it to excuse the jihad leadership of responsibility for the *casus belli*. Throughout the dispute, then, the language of both sides (and some of the incidents) echo and re-echo the events of twenty years earlier – one must assume quite deliberately.

C. Bello's response

The response of Muhammed Bello as Amir al-muminin to the challenge posed by Abd al-Salam was one of extreme caution, as befits someone who had successfully used these same tactics to justify his own jihad. In general, Abd al-Salam was treated as leniently as possible by Bello and his father (if not necessarily by their subordinates), who tried to give him no further ground for complaint. Thus they eventually allocated him good land, and promised him more; they allowed him to wall his town; they addressed him politely as Shaikh, and reiterated their goodwill towards him right up to the end – yet they never actually gave him the kind of official position or responsibilities that he sought.

Bello appears to have had two main tactics. First, to manoeuvre Abd al-Salam into overt acts of disobedience, and thus distance him from his officials, particularly the Qadi and the Muezzin. Secondly, he sought to make Abd al-Salam's acts of provocation appear as acts, instead, of oppression; and to provoke Abd al-Salam into further such acts. The most notable incident occurred when Bello was sending, presumably on the route past Abd al-Salam's town, a convoy carrying twenty million cowries (some texts read 20,000) to Tuareg to obtain salt and camels; the convoy was manned by Bello's servants, and must have been a very easy, tempting target. As the Tuareg from Agades were the allies Bello eventually called in to help crush Abd al-Salam, one can recognize that Abd al-Salam may have been suspicious of the possible uses of such a very large sum of money. But by seizing it, Abd al-Salam put himself clearly in the wrong. Bello also mentions incidents in which specifically Fulani villages and Fulani-owned crops etc. were attacked or damaged by hotheads from among Abd al-Salam's people; we are not, of course, given the details, and the rights or wrongs of the cases are unknown. In one instance, Fulbe are stopped from collecting wood to use as gates – again, an act that may itself have been intended to be deliberately provocative.

Bello's responses to Abd al-Salam's arguments are generally conciliatory. Bello readily admitted that there had been (and still were) cases of 'zalunci' – he could hardly do otherwise! – but pointed out that he recognized it and was trying to overcome the problem, and that zalunci did not in itself excuse one from fighting alongside a 'zalimi' in jihad. He also recognized that Abd al-Salam deserved more territory: Bello added, however, in his defence that he could only give Abd al-Salam more when he could – and that Abd al-Salam was not entitled to demand more of his emir than what was *possible*. Bello is arguing here that his own room for manoeuvre was limited, and hinting perhaps that his subordinates were in favour of taking a tougher line on Abd al-Salam than he (Bello) was.

A more forceful line of argument was that the dhimmis associated with Abd al-Salam were in breach of their ahd by going to dar al-harb. To prove it and create a test case, Bello arranged for the capture of two traders from dar al-harb going to Abd al-Salam's place, and two of Abd al-Salam's traders going to dar al-harb; and then Bello summoned Abd al-Salam's Qadi and Muezzin in order to quiz them on the case.

His final argument was to demonstrate that Abd al-Salam was himself in league with the enemy, that his people had paid him formal allegiance and that he had even pronounced the pagan shibboleth ('*tawaye*') that identified him with the rebel kuffar. Abd al-Salam and his people were thus murtaddun, renegades who had to be killed, All this was based on information received, from spies and others, which one must assume Bello believed (or was it merely excellent propaganda?). Nonetheless Bello still offered Abd al-Salam safe conduct out of the Sokoto area with his people. They were free, he said, to join the enemy in Zamfara. The legal rationale for this offer to murtaddun is not clear, but such an emigration would have proved exactly whom Abd al-Salam considered his real allies – which might explain why Abd al-Salam refused the offer.

Furthermore, Bello tried to isolate Abd al-Salam, by writing and urging (a) his wife and son; (b) the wives of Abd al-Salam's people; and (c) Abd al-Salam's community generally, to abandon Abd al-Salam and his ridda. Only a few, Bello says, took up the offer, while those who did try to arrange a truce were executed by Abd al-Salam.

While Bello's continuing generosity, with its determination not to shed Muslim blood unnecessarily, has a good legal rationale to it, another factor was that, as he says, his own resources were adequate only to harry but not defeat Abd al-Salam's community which at this stage apparently outnumbered Sokoto's two to one. For Abd al-Salam had by now successfully rallied both much of the local peasantry and several chiefs to his side.

Abd al-Salam's challenge was resolved finally in early January 1818 by war between him and the allied armies under Bello's Amir al-jaish Ali Jedo. Bello's victory was complete: Abd al-Salam was wounded and fled to Zamfara where he died. However, some of his people joined another Hausa-speaking ex-student, ex-mujahid – Dan Baiwa – who was resisting Abdullahi dan Fodio's attempt to bring him back into the caliphate. There, when the place was finally conquered, there was disagreement whether the 'rebels' were to be spared as Muslims (as Abdullahi reportedly wished), or were to be killed as apostates (as Bello argued). They were killed; but, so the story goes, the site of the sacked town had leaves from the Quran and other texts lying abandoned on the ground – thus invoking once more a symbol that recurs again and again in accounts of resistance to the jihad. Finally, Abd al-Salam's son was allocated a town to the south where the remnants of the Muslim dissidents settled and built a major trading town – and whose descendants today are still the butts of jokes about rebels, about being 'yan tawaye'.

In conclusion

The traditional method of protest (whether at home or in politics) is withdrawal – physically by emigration, or, if that is not feasible, by studiedly ignoring those claiming power. A personal sense of grievance has to win public sympathy to transform it into an effective protest. Open conflict and bad temper are undignified and only lose one both one's superiority over the 'oppressor' and also people's sympathy. Abd al-Salam turned to his kin and then more widely to the ahl al-Sudan for the required sympathy and support against what he initially saw, I think, as a calculated insult. For Muhammad Bello, Abd al-Salam's challenge became a test case: if he lost the loyalty of ahl al-Sudan, if they saw themselves as mazlumun, victims of zalunci, then the caliphate's wider legitimacy was in jeopardy. Historically, Bello won both the military and the propaganda war – in the record Abd al-Salam's protest has been branded as ridda (probably rightly so!), and the test case became just another incident.

In law, Abd al-Salam had a difficult task to justify his challenge to Bello – more difficult than Abdullahi dan Fodio, who simply retired increasingly from public affairs. Not only was Muhammad Bello a much abler, more learned and, it seems to me, more obviously dedicated a Muslim than Abd al-Salam, but he also had the constitutional position of Imam of the community. Nonetheless Abd al-Salam felt aggrieved enough, as did many others, to risk opposing Bello, by attempting to opt out of Bello's caliphate. He was not, I think, seeking to fight Bello militarily; instead, more to protect himself from attack than to substantiate his case, he appealed, above all, to the sanctity of Muslim life, property and honour.

The strategy of opting out as far as possible from contact with an 'oppressive', illegitimate government, continued for some closed communities (such as the Salihawa and Digawa) in Northern Nigeria through the colonial period and up to the present day. It may well be that they are heirs of the same tradition that gave rise to Abd al-Salam and his jamaa. Like his, their tradition is closer to that of the preacher than to that of the jurist or learned sufi; and was there a millenarian hope to lend a similar urgency and certainty to his convictions? But historians have tended to treat Abd al-Salam as simply ambitious and worldly – and somewhat inept, a figure of contempt even? Yet we know he had with him – until he was accused of ridda – a sufi scholar and saint noted for his miracles. I sometimes wonder, therefore, had Shaikh Uthman's jihad failed (as it very nearly did), how would we historians have discussed *his* arguments, had they survived his defeat? Does success legitimate revolt better than any text, and failure condemn it?

In answer to such a question, Michael Crowder was too worldly-wise a teacher simply to say 'no' and dismiss the persuasive power of success; but he was also too passionate a historian not to seek out the texts that showed how even failure might have legitimacy on its side. Furthermore, as an editor he consistently and strongly encouraged others *not* to allow, as the Hausa proverb has it, the elephant's footprint always to blot out the camel's (Sawun giwa ya taka ta rakumi).

Acknowledgements

This essay was first composed for the Table Ronde organized by the Institut de Recherche et d'Histoire des Textes at the Maison des Sciences de l'Homme (Paris), on 12 May 1986. I am grateful to M. Jean-Louis Triaud for initially encouraging me to present this analysis there.

Bibliographic note

The 'case' of Abd al-Salam and Bello's book *Sard al-Kalām* have been well-known for eighty years to historians of Nigeria writing in English. Copies of the Arabic manuscript text of *Sard al-Kalām* are widely available in Nigeria (the copy I have used here is from the Library of Bayero University, Kano) while a Hausa translation was published in volume 1 of R. M. East (ed) *Labarun Hausawa da Makwabtansu* (Zaria, 1932).

In the 1980s, the most interesting, detailed discussions have been contained in the Ph.D theses of M. T. M. Minna ('Sultan Bello and his Intellectual Contribution to the Sokoto Caliphate', London 1982) and O. Bello ('The Political Thought of Mohammad Bello [1781–1837] as revealed in his Arabic Writings, especially *al-Ghaith al-Wabl 'Sīrat al-Imām al-ᶜadl'*, London, 1983). A seminar at the Centre for Islamic Studies, University of Sokoto, on the life and ideas of Amir al-Muminin Muhammad Bello was held in April 1985; one of the papers presented there, by I. A. Lawal, discussed *Sard al-Kalam* and the Abd al-Salām case. There are poems, both in Arabic and Hausa, written by the jihad leadership, that relate to dissidents like Abd al-Salam; no detailed study of these has, I think, yet been done, nor has a detailed biography of Abd al-Salam been attempted.

Outside Nigeria, in 1986, the arabic text of *Sard al-Kalām* (based on a single manuscript) was published with a translation into German and an introduction, under the title *Das Sokoto-Kalifat und seine Ethnischen Grundlagen*, by Rainer Osswald (Beiruter Texte und Studien, Band 33; Orient-Institut der Deutschen Morgenlandischen Gesellschaft, Beirut, and F. Steiner Verlag, Wiesbaden). The analysis does not appear to include any new field data, and the interpretation is conventional, being based on the secondary literature of the 1960s and 1970s; less conventionally, and unusually for a study stressing ethnicity, he assumes without discussion that the Arewa were simply 'Hausa'.

Chapter Four

Shakespeare's *The Tempest:* A Preview of Colonial Rule

ELDRED D. JONES

W hen Shakespeare wrote *The Tempest*, England was at the beginning of its colonial experience. It was in fact as yet only at the stage of experiment. Raleigh's Virginia Colony was still news – generally bad news. When Sir Thomas Gates and Sir George Somers, having survived the wreck in the Bermuda Islands which it is now generally agreed inspired *The Tempest*, arrived to strengthen John Smith's Virginia Company in 1610, they found a settlement in disarray. Bad leadership, idleness and hostile Indians had combined to imperil the success of the enterprise. Leaving aside the Bermuda section of Strachey's account, here is part of his description of the state of the actual Virginia Colony:

> Onely let me truely acknowledge, they are not an hundred or two
> of deboist hands, dropt forth by yeare after yeare, with penury,
> and leisure, ill provided for before they come, and worse to be
> governed when they are here, men of such distempered bodies, and
> infected mindes, whom no examples daily before their eyes, either
> of goodnesse or punnishment, can deterre from their habituall
> impieties, or terrifie from a shameful death, that must be the
> Carpenters, and workmen in this so glorious a building.[1]

This extract presents the desired end – the 'glorious building', and the means, 'distempered bodies and infected mindes'. It gives, in short, another immediate example of the problem of government, in a new setting – that of an overseas settlement. The picture given is that of the colonists failing to govern themselves and each other well enough to achieve their aim. Then there were hostile forces – the original inhabitants

---

This chapter © Eldred Jones 1992

of Virginia who naturally did not take too kindly to this invasion of their homeland. Their effort to protect themselves and ward off their enemies was seen by the invaders as savagery, a lack of civility, even ingratitude. Strachey reports one such act when the Virginians seized and killed one of the colonists:

> . . . certaine Indians seised the poore fellow, and led him up into the Woods, and sacrificed him. It did not a little trouble the Lieutenant Governour, who since his first landing in the Countrey (how justly soever provoked) would not by any meanes be wrought to a violent proceeding against them, for all the practises of villainy, with which they daily indangered our men, thinking it possible, by a more tractable course, to winne them to a better condition: but now being startled by this, he well perceived, how little a faire and noble intreatie workes upon a barbarous disposition, and therefore in some measure purposed to be revenged.[2]

That account was confidently written by one who assumed the rightness of his action in taking over the territory of a 'savage', and who, despairing of ever converting – the savage to his assumed superior mode of behaviour his 'civility' – resorts to 'revenge'. The account represents the classic colonial situation, a situation which Shakespeare explores in the Prospero-Caliban relationship. This of course has been said before. Professor O. Mannoni's serious study of the psychology of colonization was translated into English in 1956 with a foreward by Philip Mason, under the title *Prospero and Caliban*.[3] Mason may or may not have influenced the choice of the English title, but it is significant that his own later exploration of the colonial syndrome was called *Prospero's Magic*.[4]

The Tempest has thus been recognized as Shakespeare's exploration of the colonial theme, and it is quite profitable to look at the play from that point of view. So much do we incline to allegorical interpretations – *The Tempest* as an allegory of the church, or the fall of man, for example – that we need as a corrective to look at its practical inspiration. It was inspired by, not just the wreck in the Bermudas, but I believe by the whole colonial experiment, both its potential and its pitfalls. Strachey's account extended beyond the wreck on the Bermuda Islands after all, and in Caliban, Shakespeare introduced the human element on the other side, something which the Bermudas – uninhabited (at least according to the account) – did not provide.

It is useful to look at the play as another exploration in a topical setting of an old problem, the problem of human government. Shakespeare had examined this problem over and over again, not only in the histories but in the tragedies and comedies as well. Professor R. A. Foakes' approach to the play (in *Shakespeare, The Dark Comedies To The Last Plays*) is quite illuminating. He sees the play as a step towards *Henry VIII* both being – by contrast to *Cymbeline* and *The Winter's Tale* – 'set in effect in modern times, and in the Christian context of the Duchy of Milan, or the kingdom of England; and both are designed to display human activities within the framework of government or rule'.[5] All I would like to add to this observation is that the arena is not the Duchy of Milan itself, but an outpost – a colony – with Prospero as the classic colonizer.

The labours of many scholars, particularly of Leslie Hotson and C. N. Gayley, have shown how closely Shakespeare was linked with men whose money was tied up in the Virginia Colony. He would thus quite probably have had access to unpublished documents, but even more, for a mind like Shakespeare's, to the talk of men who had actually been and seen, and others for whom the problems of colonization must have been dinner-table conversation. Leslie Hotson in *I William Shakespeare*[6], in which he follows up the people mentioned in Shakespeare's will into some fascinating by-ways of Elizabethan and Jacobean history, suggests an entirely plausible occasion in 1610 when Sir Dudley Digges, on a visit to Thomas Russell, the man whom Shakespeare named as overseer of his will, could have not only told Shakespeare about the Bermuda wreck and its sequel, but even have shown him Strachey's letter. Strachey's letter was published after *The Tempest* was written, yet the play's debt to it is clear. How did Shakespeare get his chance to study Strachey's letter before its publication? Here is Leslie Hotson's piecing out of the evidence for an answer:

Shakespeare's connection with Russell and the Diggeses affords an excellent occasion. Suppose him in 1610, according to the generally accepted belief, withdrawn from most of the activities of his London life to his home circle in Stratford, and consequently more frequently a visitor in the Russell-Digges household at Alderminster.

I find that two months after the arrival of Gates with the letter, and a fortnight after the *True Declaration* had been entered at Stationers Hall, Sir Dudley Digges came to Alderminster to make a settlement of money affairs with his stepfather. Articles were drawn up and executed in the presence of John Hanford, esquire, Russell's friend and mediator, on November 22. The agreement concluded, Russell drinks with his learned and eloquent stepson. And since they have had some 'jars' and do not always see eye to eye in the matter of family business, what is more likely than that Russell brings out his trump card to distract and charm Sir Dudley – his friend and all admired poet Shakespeare? Sir Dudley is full of the story of exploration and colonization. His friend Gates, 'best able to inform,' has told him more circumstantial and fascinating details of the adventure than have appeared in any accounts, and Sir Dudley has with him a copy of Strachey's letter. Russell will be deeply interested; his brother, Sir Maurice Berkeley, is a colleague of his stepson's on the Virginia Council. And Shakespeare – with his brave notions and gentle expressions, who could make a better audience? He had been struck by certain features of the strange and romantic story when it first came out; and he finds this intimate account stirring him still more. Digges is glad to trust his discretion with the copy of Strachey's letter. It is not long before the poet's quick imagination has shaped and transferred something of what he has heard and read.

> Ere I could make a prologue to my brains
> They had begun the play.

Why may we not take the afternoon of a poet with Sir Dudley Digges as the stimulus for some of *The Tempest's* mighty magic? It would be strange if the child of England's greatest astronomer, wholly possessed with the vision of adventure and discovery far away, should not strike delicate sparks from the poet's brain – a brain apprehensive, quick, forgetive, full of nimble, fiery, and delectable shapes.[7]

Even the short extract from Strachey's letter given earlier, suggests the incompatibility of the position of colonist and colonized. Theirs was a collision course. Shakespeare, within the limits he allowed himself (or social convenience allowed him), explores this problem in *The Tempest*, not just in the relationship between Prospero and Caliban (or even Prospero and Ariel, for the sprite too is a native put to forced labour) but also in the attempted *coup* of Antonio and Sebastian and in a comic key, of Stephano and Trinculo. Mutiny was a common occurrence in the early colonies. Indeed there is one mentioned in the Strachey account which, like that of Stephano, Trinculo and Caliban, misfired:

> They had now purposed to have made a surprise of the Store-house, and to have forced from thence, what was therein either of Meale, Cloath, Cables, Armes, Sailes, Oares or what else it pleased God that we had recovered from the wracke . . . always something of imperfection, and that as well by the property of the action, which holdeth of disobedience and rebellion (both full of feare) . . . there were some of association, who not strong enough fortified in their owne conceits, brake from the plot itselfe, and . . . discovered the whole order . . .[8]

This passage is not cited in an attempt to pin down a particular source for the Stephano/Trinculo/Caliban plot. Events like this must have been fairly commonplace in colonial experiments and therefore common talk in the houses of those who had the financing and running of colonies. Such incidents provided straws in the wind for a generalized look at the psychology of colonization.

Shakespeare generalized the experience, and complicated the issue by introducing a governor who ruled with supernatural powers. (Many a colonial governor must have wished for Prospero's magic books and his magician's wand with which to compel the obedience of reluctant subjects.) The new world also becomes transferred to the old – Prospero's island is in the Mediterranean somewhere between Africa and Italy. (It is worth noting that for the third time, Shakespeare goes to Africa for a husband or lover for an Italian woman – Aaron (*Titus Andronicus*), Othello, and now the King of Tunis. (This is not counting the failed attempt of the Prince of Morocco to win Portia in *The Merchant of Venice*.)

At the centre of the drama are Prospero and Caliban. The colonizer and the colonized, with their irreconcilable points of view. Caliban's claim is clear:

> This island's mine, by Sycorax my mother
> Which thou tak'st from me . . .[9]

Prospero's position is equally firm:

> Thou most lying slave,
> Whom stripes may move, not kindness! I have used thee,
> Filth as thou art, with human care, and lodged thee
> In mine own cell, till thou didst seek to violate
> The honour of my child.[10]

Prospero's position is condescending: 'I have used thee/Filth as thou art, with human care.' A similar situation would be recalled in the Strachey account cited earlier, in which the governor was portrayed as exercising great self-restraint 'for all the practices of villainy, with which they daily indangered our men, thinking it possible, by a more tractable course, to winne them to a better condition . . .' He, like Prospero, despaired. Both of course looked down from a height on their new found neighbours; both despised them. For Prospero, Caliban is 'filth'.

It is rash to express certainty as to whether Shakespeare as a private person sympathized with the position of Caliban or how he felt about Jews, or Negroes for that matter. But it is possible to see in his treatments – of Caliban, of Shylock and of Othello – the minority point of view.

At least, the minority case is put (as it is not seriously put in that other famous treatment of a Jew in Marlow's *The Jew of Malta*). Nor in *The Tempest* (to stick to one play at a time) is Prospero by any means a blameless character. Foakes observes of him:

> The standards Prospero applies are those of Milan, of his own civilization, and Caliban's version of what has happened raises some questions about the validity of those standards on the isle.[11]

How curiously this echoes Professor Mannoni's analysis of the colonizer's personality – and he too sees Prospero's behaviour as a reflection of this:

> The colonial's personality is wholly unaffected by that of the native of the colony to which he goes: it does not adapt itself, but develops solely in accordance with its own inner structure. It is inevitable, therefore, that misunderstandings should arise, for there can be no harmony between monads. What the colonial in common with Prospero lacks, is awareness of the world of others, a world in which others have to be respected.[12]

To Prospero, any suggestion or respect for what he calls 'filth' is preposterous, just as it was inconceivable to the Lieutenant Governor of Virginia, when he complained about the villainy of the Indians, that he was a trespasser in Virginia (to use a polite term) or that his invasion was the primary act of villainy. Whatever Shakespeare's personal point of view may have been, his presentation of the situation suggests that it was clear to him that there could not be any mutuality based on this kind of relationship. The only basis of co-existence in those circumstances was force. That is how Prospero and Caliban exist.

> If thou neglect'st, or dost unwillingly
> What I command, I'll rack thee with old cramps,
> Fill all thy bones with aches, make thee roar
> That beasts shall tremble at thy din.[13]

Shakespeare presents Caliban as physically repulsive. In the list of *dramatis personae*, he is described as 'A savage and deformed Slave', Prospero calls him 'filth', Stephano, 'monster'; so no doubt he was made up to look sufficiently repulsive for the audience to have reacted like Prospero to his foiled intent to 'people the isle with Calibans', with Miranda, Prospero's fair daughter, as his mate. Given Prospero's obsession with chastity, the very idea would have nearly unbalanced his judgement. There was no way in which a human relationship (this includes peopling islands) would have existed between Prospero, Miranda and Caliban. This attitude, I believe, would have been accepted by the generality of the seventeenth-century English audience who would probably have seen less to criticize in Prospero's conduct than Professor Mannoni or Professor Foakes in this century. But isn't it curious how Shakespeare responds to changing ideas?

I once saw a Swedish production of *The Tempest* – I mention this merely as an interesting curiosity – on a floating theatre moored to a pier in Stockholm. The production, I emphasize, was in Swedish which I do not understand, but it was vivid enough. Instead of a shipwreck, there had been a misadventure in outer space, and Alonso and his fellow astronauts had found themselves on this planet on which obviously Prospero and Miranda must have made an earlier forced landing in their cockle-boat of a spacecraft. It takes a bit of imagination to picture a spacecraft which would correspond to Prospero's

> A rotten carcass of a butt not rigged,
> Nor tackle, sail, nor mast. The very rats
> Instinctively have quit it . . .[14]

How all this was accommodated in the text I do not know but the Swedish audience seemed to be enjoying it all. One remarkable feature however which traversed the language barrier was how sympathetically Caliban was played. There was even a touching little scene at the end when he and Prospero were reconciled with a handshake. What I have described is, of course, quite a liberty with Shakespeare's play but I think it indicates that Shakespeare did suggest Caliban's point of view and that something could be made of this even in a more legitimate production.

Prospero's attitude to Ariel is only different from that to Caliban because Ariel is a less rebellious subject – quicker to come to heel. But even he is subject to Prospero's threats. Prospero had once rescued him from a cloven pine; now he threatens to re-immure him, this time, in harder wood;

> If thou murmur'st, I will rend an oak,
> And peg thee in his knotty entrails till
> Thou hast howled away twelve winters.[15]

These are the practical politics of colonialism; there can be no other, given the basis of the institution, the assumed superiority of one race or class over another.

But what about the men of equal 'civilitie', who come from the same civilization. They too have to govern themselves and each other. There was enough in the accounts of actual colonies and colonial experiments to show how difficult all this was: the idleness, the mutinies, the misgovernment. *The Tempest* reflects all this too: in the treachery of Antonio, the drunkenness and misplaced values of Stephano and Trinculo. The island like the colonies offered opportunities; but to be realized, these opportunities depended on human responses and these varied then; they vary now. Gonzalo's Commonwealth was put forward as one solution, the solution that poets had dreamt of and written about, the Golden Age.

> Gonzalo. I'th' commonwealth I would by contraries
> Execute all things. For no kind of traffic
> Would I admit, no name of magistrate.
> Letters should not be known. Riches, poverty,
> And use of service, none. Contract, succession,
> Bourn, bound of land, tilth, vineyard, none.
> No use of metal, corn, or wine, or oil.
> No occupation: all men idle, all,
> And women too, but innocent and pure.
> No sovereignty –
>
> All things in common nature should produce
> Without sweat or endeavour, treason, felony,
> Sword, pike, knife, gun, or need of any engine
> Would I not have; but nature should bring forth
> Of it own kind all foison, all abundance,
> To feed my innocent people.[16]

Experience had demonstrated that this could not be realized, and Gonzalo's rather confused account of an earthly paradise minutes before Antonio proposed his murderous plan of unsurpation, carries its own criticism. That solution was only for the books. In a practical situation, far away from the cushioning institutions of established government and accepted rules of social intercourse, man is thrown on his inner resources and whatever else he can muster – belief in God or Providence. Shakespeare gives Prospero the equipment of white magic but even he had no more control over the minds of men that the Duke in *Measure for Measure*. Things are only patched up at the end of *The Tempest*.

Notes

1. William Strachey, *The True Repertory of the Wrack and Redemption of Sir Thomas Gates*, (1610), first published in *Purchas His Pilgrims*. 1625. vol. xix, p. 48.

2. Strachey, vol. xix, pp. 62–3.

3. O. Mannoni, (*La Psychologie de la Colonisation*), tr. Philip Mason, *Prospero and Caliban: The Psychology of Colonisation*, (London, 1956).

4. Philip Mason, *Prospero's Magic* (London, 1962).

5. R. A. Foakes, *The Dark Comedies To The Last Plays* (London, 1971) p. 174.

6. Leslie Hotson, *I William Shakespeare, Do Appoint Thomas Russell, Esquire* (London, 1937: New York, 1938).

7. Ibid., p. 225.

8. Strachey, vol. xix, pp. 32–3

9. William Shakespeare, *The Tempest* (New Penguin Shakespeare, ed. Anne Righter, 1968) I, ii, 330–2.

10. *Tempest*, I, ii, 344–8.

11. Foakes, p. 148.

12. Mannoni, tr. Mason.

13. *The Tempest*, I, ii, 368–71.

14. *The Tempest*, I, ii, 146–8.

15. *The Tempest*, I, ii, 294–6.

16. *The Tempest*, II, i, 150–9; 161–6.

Chapter Five

The French Revolution and Race Relations in Senegal, 1780–1810

AMANDA SACKUR

In his book, *Senegal: a study in French assimilation policy,* Crowder traces the origins of assimilation to the egalitarian idealism of the French revolution.[1] He is not alone; it has become common currency in discussions on French policy.[2] Yet there is a tendency to accept such an association uncritically and little attention has, in fact, been paid to this early period. Clearly, it is impossible to ignore the French Revolution as an expression of radical ideas and as a turning point in French relations both within and outside Europe. However, whilst Enlightenment ideas and revolutionary enthusiasm did provide a climate which allowed the expression of a degree of egalitarianism as regards race, it is far from certain that this period saw the institution of a *policy* of assimilation for blacks. Indeed, it is questionable whether the Revolution even marked a break with old attitudes or established a new basis for colonial rule.

The importance of this point lies not only in understanding French colonial policy but also in contributing to knowledge of the local dynamics in Senegal. It forces a re-examination of the assumptions about race relations and therefore about the impact of the early French presence on Africans who lived in the settlements. Seen from the perspective of the two largest French trading posts in Africa, the Revolution appears less important than has hitherto been believed. Equally, by examining a few aspects of race relations in the period 1780–1810 we can see essential continuities more clearly. This view challenges notions of the easy nature of race relations in pre-colonial Senegal and is supported by closer study of the underlying nature of changes in France.

As Crowder points out, assimilation policy 'implied a fundamental acceptance of their potential human equality, but a total dismissal of

African culture as of any value.'[3] Both elements were long present in French thought about Africa. As early as 1685, the *code noir,* or regulations on the treatment of slaves in the Antilles, insisted on the conversion of slaves to Catholic Christianity and excluded the profession of any other faith from French territory.[4] Africans were seen as without religion and in extreme cases, without laws, society or civilization.[5] Although a degree of cultural relativism was expressed by the *philosophes,* this was a minor element in Enlightenment thought and was often a device to express criticism of elements of French society, not a serious attempt to promote respect for other cultures. By the 1780s, confidence in the superiority of French civilization and a certainty of its applicability world wide were dominant elements in attitudes to other cultures.

At the same time, the *philosophes* were concerned to explain how cultural differences (seen in terms of African 'backwardness') should have developed. Physiological differences suggested one reason and the bases for systematic scientific racism were expounded during the eighteenth century but most writers rejected this explanation, tending to favour environmental factors. Thus whilst despising blacks, they acknowledged black potential for 'improvement'.[6] Essentially, this ambivalence could be seen in Enlightenment attitudes to slavery and the slave trade. Most *philosophes* condemned its inhumanity and the degradation of fellow human beings but were uninterested in campaigning against it and were often prepared to tolerate its perpetuation in order to 'civilize' blacks. Moreover, in an extremely hierarchical society, most people were concerned to maintain what they saw as the proper degree of subordination. Shared humanity did not necessarily entail equality.

Race relations in France were based less on the philosophical positions of Enlightenment thinkers than on the constraints of an hierarchical society and the pressures placed on the poorer members of that society. There were, in fact, very few blacks resident in France, mostly concentrated in the Atlantic ports and large towns.[7] Throughout the eighteenth century, royal policy was to limit their numbers, rather than to integrate them into the general population. This policy reached its apogee in 1777 when draconian measures were promulgated. A total ban on the entry of blacks was introduced and all blacks already in the country were to be registered. Plans were made for the 'repatriation' of many to the West Indies.[8] Although fear of insubordination and unspecified *'désordres'* played a part in this decision, the main motivation appears to have been a perceived threat to the purity of French blood through miscegenation. The issue of marriage and sexual relations with blacks aroused strong feelings in France and in the colonies. Although undoubtedly rare, inter-racial marriages did occur. However, they appear to have faced widescale opposition. Despite the refusal of the Church to ban them, even priests appear to have been unhappy to officiate, especially when the bride was white.[9] There appears to have been less prejudice against sexual relations between white men and black women, perhaps because few were, in fact, marriages. In this they conformed to the variety of more or less exploitative relationships between richer men and poorer or more vulnerable women. Black and *métis* women were often seen as sexually desirable, clothed in the exotic aura of sexuality associated with the orient.[10]

Sexual relations were one of the most important elements of interaction between whites and Africans on the Senegalese coast. Formally banned, they flourished, most visibly in long-term relationships, often celebrated as marriages, with local, Wolof, rites.[11] It is not known how many Europeans married local women, nor how many entered into relationships which were less binding. Some men appear to have been polygamous although there is no definite proof. Certainly, polygamy fascinated European visitors to Africa, opening up intriguing possibilities which some claimed were more honest than Christian practice.[12]

Relationships with African women offered many advantages to the men out in Africa: a healthier lifestyle, better nutrition, access to locally-tested remedies for illness, more comfortable housing and general domesticity. Even those who did not live with their lovers gained an immense psychological advantage. Administrators commented that having someone to love made the uncomfortable and isolated existence in the trading posts bearable.[13] For senior officers and employees, alliances with local women also provided help in illicit trade. However, this aspect which has received much attention in historical accounts, should not be exaggerated. It is unlikely that the prospect of trade proved the initial or the primary motive for white men. On the other hand, there are examples of great strength of feeling in individual cases.[14]

Yet Cohen is wrong to claim that '[t]he liberal attitude towards blacks and coloreds that existed until the mid-nineteenth century was revealed in the willingness of whites in Senegal to intermarry.'[15] There was opposition to formal marriage and few white men contracted marriages which were legally binding in France.[16] *Mariages à la mode du pays* gave Europeans the advantage of domesticity without impinging on their lives in France; indeed, some of them left wives behind when they went out to Africa. One governor continued to write passionate love-letters to his aristocratic fiancée whilst apparently living with a prominent Goréen woman.[17]

The relationships thus established did not undermine any sense of hierarchy. As in the West Indies, whilst Catholic marriage implied equality, other unions maintained the hierarchy of race and class. In France, too, 'illegitimate' relationships dishonoured the woman involved but did not affect the status or respect of the man.[18] In some cases, particularly when the women were slaves, relationships were clearly exploitative. One account criticizes Frenchmen for selling their mistresses into the Atlantic slave trade when bored with them.[19] Some men may have seen slave women as freely available and subject to their whims, much as whites did in the West Indies. In 1725 a soldier was punished for raping and severely wounding a slave who refused his advances.[20] Sexual availability was an indication of subordination and sexuality itself an instrument of power rather than an expression of equality.[21] Other cases of disorder may have been due to similar causes; refusal appears to have triggered off anger amongst poor whites who resented the wealth of some local inhabitants.[22]

Although Cohen does refer to indications to the contrary, his picture is generally one which he describes as an 'easy relationship between the races in Saint-Louis and Gorée'.[23] Yet this is largely an exaggeration. It was perhaps relatively rare for men to condemn their colleagues for sexual relations with blacks but they did criticize other contact.[24] In the 1770s senior employees and officers petitioned the Ministry in protest at the governor's attentions to Africans.[25] A strong sense of racial differences pervades the French documentation and it would appear that all residents were aware of the hierarchical distinctions. In censuses and descriptions, whites are counted separately from blacks and some writers used the gradations of colour current in the West Indies.[26] Whites insisted on maintaining distinctions which established the subordinate role of blacks, whether Africans from the mainland or local inhabitants.[27] Discrimination in France also applied to Senegal; even the 'mayor' of Saint-Louis was refused admittance to France after the 1777 ordinance.[28]

The tone of French accounts and the attitudes revealed in such incidents as were recorded suggests that philosophers' treatises and theoretical models were less influential in determining race relations in Senegal than concepts of subordination and pervasive colour prejudice. A common attitude was that of the man who wrote, 'Il est essentiel de maintenir le respect et la subordination que ces gens-la [les noirs] doivent avoir pour un Europeen.'[29] This is not to say that an elaborate segregation was practised, nor that racism had developed a systematic rationale as it did in the nineteenth century. Europeans collaborated with local residents in trading ventures, socialized with them on some occasions and employed *métis* men in a limited range of occupations. Yet a persistent belief that blacks were inferior or ignorant lay behind the recognition by whites that they could not do without the collaboration of local inhabitants.

Two incidents in particular illustrate this feature of daily relations. They show that not only could prejudice surface in situations of conflict, but that it was also an element of normal social intercourse. Even more significant is the reaction of local people to expressions of prejudice. Their swift response shows that these were not incidents which proved exceptions to the rule of ordinary behaviour, although it may be that they were unusual in providing clear examples which could be refuted. Moreover, local residents, or at least those of influence, were not prepared to accept white prejudice.

The first example comes from a complicated case of commercial interests. In 1783 a French official named Gondreville died in Saint-Louis.[30] As was usual in these circumstances, an inventory was taken and among his goods was listed a small boat used for trading up the Senegal river. Soon after his death, this boat was claimed by a local man, Jean Blondin, who argued that Gondreville's only connection with the boat was that he had lent Blondin the three slaves with which Blondin had purchased it.[31] Not long afterwards another senior French official, Clergeau, also claimed ownership of it, on the basis that Gondreville had bought the boat in association with Clergeau, using Jean Blondin as a cover, and that Clergeau had later bought Gondreville's share.[32] The dispute was complicated by the fact that many of the whites involved in the transactions had since died or left Saint-Louis and by the formal ban on private trade imposed on all European employees.[33] There is no record of the final decision reached in this case but summaries prepared for the Minister suggest that both men lost their cases. Clergeau's case was believed to rest on a forged receipt, added to Gondreville's papers after the inventory was drawn up, whilst Blondin's appears to have been lost through lack of documentary evidence and the effect of local gossip.[34]

The most interesting document in the file, however, is a copy of a document prepared by the two claimants. It appears to be a written statement of Clergeau's arguments with Blondin's commentary in the 'margin'. Clergeau's section reveals contempt for Blondin and an attempt to use Blondin's colour against him; throughout the document he refers to 'Blondin' or 'le negre' without any title in contrast to Blondin's use of 'le Sieur'. In the course of the document, Clergeau uses 'le negre' six times, starting on the first page, implicitly appealing to the Minister's own prejudice. Later, he accuses Blondin of overstepping the limits of acceptable behaviour to whites:

> Le Negre Blondin Se permet vis-à-vis D'un Blanc une Liberté dont il Devoit etre Severement Puni, qu'il apprenne que Luy Seul Peut etre Capable De Soustraire Des Pieces, qu'il Deviene Plus Circonspect et Plus Respectueux.[35]

Quite clearly, Clergeau was appealing to strong prejudice which did not allow blacks the same rights as whites. It is not clear, however, to what extent he shared this view. Given that his case was very weak, he may have been using this as a rhetorical point, hoping to limit examination of the real issues. Nonetheless, he could not have used such a device unless unequal treatment was generally accepted.

Jean Blondin's commentary also shows that he recognized his relative weakness in disputing the word of a white. Although he defended himself vigorously, his defence reveals uncertainty that he will be treated fairly. The first element in his defence was to insist that all were equal before the law:

. . . aux yeux de la justice touts les hommes sont Egaux, Cet adage Reçu, Croit-il etre écouté parcequ'il Porte Sur Sa figure quelques Nuances de Blanc de plus que moy.[36]

In fact, Blondin does not appear convinced that this is true in practice. He repeats this assertion seven times in the course of approximately four sides of writing. However, he also goes further, insisting that he is worthy of belief, despite his skin colour:

Le Pur hazard L'à fait Naitre En Europe, il Est Blanc, je suis Né En affrique je suis Noir, aussi Croyable que Luy . . .[37]

In response to Clergeau's attack quoted above, he replies that "il est Permis à un Nègre de Se Déffendre En disant La vérité".[38] However, he also makes clear that he is not attempting to upset the established order of subordination, making four references to the respect he owes to Clergeau. The last is the most explicit and generalized statement of this ranking by colour:

. . . Sans M'Engager à m'Ecarter En Rien Du Respect que La Couleur Noire qu'il à Plut à dieu de me donner, doit à La Couleur Blanche qu'il a Plut à ce meme dieu dont nous tenons tout L'existence de donner En Partage à Mr. Clergeau.[39]

Without further information, it is impossible to tell how much Jean Blondin accepted such ideas as part of the 'natural order' or how much he was hiding his personal attitudes in order to make a good impression on someone he believed to subscribe to concepts of black inferiority. However, there may be a clue in the tone of Jean Blondin's arguments. On occasions he countered Clergeau's references to his colour by making them his own, referring to himself as 'Ce Nègre'. Apparently stung by Clergeau's attempt to use colour prejudice as an argument, he also turned the tables on the Frenchman, calling him 'Le Blanc Mr Clergeau' in response to 'le nègre Blondin'.[40] It does not sound as if he either believed in his own inferiority or was prepared to accept the racism of whites.

Clergeau did not succeed in his attempt to claim the boat but Blondin also failed to make good his claim. From the documents which survive, Blondin had a good case; it may be that prejudice played a part in his loss. Yet it would appear that two other factors were more important: the opinion of local residents that Blondin did not have the means to purchase a boat in 1782 and the lack of a crucial receipt.[41] This was an important element in commercial transactions of the time. Whilst Saugnier describes trade without written agreements in the 1780s, he also urged would-be traders to insist on documentation signed by witnesses.[42] Increasingly, judgements in disputes came to depend on the production of relevant documents and those who had not felt the need for written contracts lost court cases judged by Europeans.[43] This provided a major incentive to conform to European practices, at least where Europeans were involved in the transactions.

There were additional pressures to behave in ways which were comprehensible to whites. Formal insistence that all religions other than Catholicism were banned on French territory and the provision of religious services to the entire population encouraged the adoption of Catholicism. Baptism in particular was widely practised.[44] Yet Islam continued to flourish and local cults retained the respect of local populations.[45]

More important perhaps was the impact of French attitudes on local strategies. Intolerance of different cultures and an inability on the part of Europeans to adapt to African society may have played an important part in influencing creole behaviour.[46] In the first place, it became important to understand European business practices: learning French, using literacy and claiming a Christian identity were increasingly necessary in trade. Secondly, to avoid condemnation and to ease relations with potential business partners, it may have appeared sensible to minimize local cultural elements and present a 'European' front. Adopting elements of European material culture eased commercial transactions. Carnes' description of his brief visit to Gorée in the early nineteenth century shows how social intercourse provided a framework for trade. On arrival at Gorée, the American merchants left their ship to spend the day with an acquaintance of the shipper's. Carnes was agreeably surprised at the comfort and familiarity of the scene although he noted indications that the household he visited did not always adopt this style of life.[47] Undoubtedly, this type of reception persuaded visitors to do business with their hosts and provided a congenial atmosphere in which to conduct such business. In a more general sense, the ability to demonstrate a familiarity with European culture may also have helped locals to develop good relations with officials and resident traders, thus increasing their contacts and the numbers of recommendations to visiting captains.

However, daily contact with whites did not protect inhabitants from expressions of racism. The second incident which throws light on race relations in Senegal shows this very clearly. It occurred in 1808 when Gorée was under British occupation, having been captured in 1800. Although it did not concern a Frenchman, there is no reason to believe that there were substantial differences in attitude between the French and the British at this time. Many French authors expressed similar opinions.

The description of this incident comes from the journal kept by a Scotsman who lived on Gorée from 1807 to 1808. He has been identified as John Hill by Patricia Wilson.[48] In his journal he details a variety of social and professional engagements with both British and local inhabitants. However, even in these circumstances friction due to colour prejudice was not absent. Hill's entry for 17 April 1808 describes one such occasion: 'An unlucky observation escaped my lips this afternoon relative to the Ladies of Goree.'[49] Hill's account, which is the only description of this incident, goes on to give details. Discussing a brick with a friend, a British officer named Grant,

> . . . the colour being that of a dirty dull yellow, I observed without any intention of giving offence, 'that the colour approached pretty near to some of the young ladies in the Island.'[50]

Despite Hill's claim that he had not intended to offend, others who overheard this conversation interpreted the remark as an affront.

> The words had scarce dropt from my lips when a volley of *abuse,* was poured on me by his [Grant's] Girl . . . she threatened to acquaint all the girls of my language & dissuade them from holding company with me, in order to vex me if possible she took care to mention one or two that she knew I had a regard to . . .[51]

Nor was this the only response from those he had insulted. The entry for the following day continues the story:

> About 11 AM Lieut^t. Grant sent a message to me requesting I would come to his house. I obeyed out of respect to him when I entered, the room was crowded with female wanton's amongst whom was the girl supposed to be my favourite. After a few compliments I seated myself beside grant, & before I was aware, Miss Betsey told me here were plenty of bricks, I might begin to build a house if I pleased, then brought in her hand a piece of

the same brick alluded to yesterday, and plainly told me that she thought the brick was more like me than the girls, then held it so close to my face as actually to touch it, thus did she apparently triumph over me, but it was in the presence of her Gallant and in his room, otherwise she might have repented her insolence: All, however which I thought proper to do was to make her no reply, & took my hat and walk out of the room.[52]

The reaction to Hill's remark suggests that it made a strong impression on local women. Miss Betsey rebuked Hill at the time but obviously did not feel that this was sufficient. It is significant that her revenge involved the participation of other women; collective action was required to respond to an insult based on colour. Hill did not understand the hurt he had caused, he saw his remark as 'unfortunate' and believed that it was trifling since he had not intended to give offence. However, his reaction to Miss Betsey's revenge reveals the underlying attitudes which gave his joke such sting. After describing the charade to which he had been subjected, Hill wrote:

What a pity it is that Europeans in general, should so far forget their kindred & country women, as to pay so much attention & respect to french, Spanish, Dutch, Portuguise, English & even negro bastards, and many of adultrious bastards. . . . Tho' the most of them in their persons are tolerable fair women, yet they have a number of fashions exceeding unpleasant to Europeans & which put them in some respects upon a level with their slaves.[53]

In addition to this outburst, it is interesting to note Hill's initial reaction. Hill characterizes the women's retaliatory action not as self-defence but as 'insolence'. He does not spell it out but the assumption is that they should not have answered back to a white. Similarly, his decision to walk out without response was dictated by Grant's presence and the fact that the incident took place in Grant's rooms rather than any consideration for their sex. It is unlikely that he would have reacted in the same way to white women.

However, Hill does not appear to have been unusual in his attitudes. Intolerant of all local religious practices, Catholic, Muslim and 'animist', he was quite prepared to praise other aspects of African culture, even admitting that in terms of cleanliness Africans put the mass of his compatriots to shame.[54] It is unlikely therefore that Hill's remark expressed an unusual degree of prejudice. Indeed, the vehemence of Miss Betsey's response may have been due to frustration at a general level of racism which was difficult to combat because it was so widely accepted that it was rarely necessary for Europeans to express it.

Race relations in Senegal in the eighteenth century were not entirely easy. Whilst many men were more than ready to take local women, black or *métis,* as mistresses, this did not mean that they were prepared to accept inhabitants of the trading posts as their equals. Particularly in the second half of the century, Europeans were less prepared to adapt to local conditions. In part, this might be ascribed to the growing cultural gap between Europe and Africa, a process which accelerated in the nineteenth century. In the same way that regional culture and that of the poor in France was despised by aristocrats and wealthier members of the bourgeoisie *because* it was the culture of subordinates, Europeans in Senegal made little attempt to hide their attitudes to Wolof culture.[55]

Growing intolerance of differences in culture on the part of Europeans had, in turn, an impact on the local population. As the two incidents above demonstrate there were strong incentives for the elite to conform to European cultural norms. In addition to the contempt for African culture displayed by Europeans, the adoption of elements of French culture brought commercial rewards. Trade was facilitated and relations generally eased. Those who built houses in brick could make large sums from letting rooms to Europeans. Literacy was increasingly necessary for commercial and legal transactions.

Yet European racism and the avoidance of contact except on terms which maintained European superiority in the hierarchy may also have helped to limit the extent to which French culture was adopted. Lack of sustained contact minimized the necessity to alter existing structures, whether social, political or cultural. Even more importantly, Africans lacked the incentive to change. It was apparent that Europeans would not accept blacks as equals even if they adopted European culture. The outcome, I would argue, was a situational use of cultures by those who could afford to try to mitigate the effects of white prejudice.[56] However, assimilation was out of the question, for local inhabitants were made aware that colour distinguished them from Europeans.

The egalitarianism of the French Revolution offered the hope of new ideas which may have affected white attitudes but it quickly became apparent that prejudice on the basis of colour alone would not disappear. This fundamental colour prejudice and discrimination does not appear to have been altered by the Revolution or the egalitarian measures taken in 1794. Indeed, Napoleon insisted on increasing social distance between the colours, in line with his policies of re-instating slavery and expelling blacks from France.[57] In the instructions to Blanchot issued in 1802, a local militia is allowed, 'sans les incorporer dans la nouvelle garnison afin de maintenir toujours la distance de couleurs.'[58] Nor did those who had served in Senegal disagree. A former official who wrote an exposition on his views of the colony in 1814 dismissed the possibility of local participation in administration and advocated 'la ligne de démarcation' between them and Europeans to avoid 'une dangereuse familiarité'. Believing assimilation to be counter to the 'caractère natal' of the *métis,* he proposed to 'les isoler dans leurs moeurs et leurs usages'. Blacks, according to Picard, were easier to manage than the 'demie civilisation' of the *métis;* they were lazy, profoundly ignorant and committed thieves. France should therefore impose a firm rule, treating the inhabitants with justice and humanity but excluding them from influence and maintaining a strict distance.[59] The Revolution appears to have made no lasting impact on attitudes towards assimilation. In the early nineteenth century both the French in Senegal and the British in their colonies developed a strong concern for maintaining social distance.

Yet given eighteenth century attitudes to blacks, the Revolution did attempt to make radical changes in their status. This period saw the expression of egalitarian ideas which were not necessarily new but which had not been fully developed before. In 1788 the Société des Amis des Noirs, an abolitionist campaigning group, was founded. The following year, Brissot argued that the deputies owed 'as much to [their] fellow citizens of the colonies as to those of Europe, as much to black Frenchmen as to white.'[60] Of approximately 2000 *cahiers de doléances,* 49 called for the end of the slave trade or slavery itself, often in egalitarian terms, calling slaves 'our fellow human beings' or 'unfortunate brothers'. One called for liberty for slaves, 'to which they have as much right as we, since they are our equals.'[61] In fact, the Declaration des droits de l'homme et du citoyen, published on 26 August 1789 appeared to recognize this point in article 1: 'Les hommes naissent et demeurent libres et égaux en droits. . .'

The declaration of 16 Pluviôse an II (4 February 1794) which abolished slavery in the French possessions and decreed that all inhabitants of French colonies, regardless of colour, were French citizens entitled to all the civic rights attached to this status, has been described as 'one of the most radical acts of the entire revolution.'[62] The declaration was accompanied by festivities and propaganda to celebrate the event. On 30 Pluviôse a celebration was organized at the Temple de la Raison, prints bearing captions such as 'Moi, libre aussi' were sold, songs about the liberation of slaves were widespread and pantomimes glorifying the benevolence of the French were produced.[63]

Since the issue of equality had been raised in 1789, it is significant that this measure was so long delayed. The reasons for the delay (and also for eventual passage) reveal much about eighteenth century attitudes to 'race' and explain why the radical measures of 1794 were to have such a short-lived impact on French policy.

In the first place, the egalitarian ideas expressed in the declaration of 16 Pluviôse were more the logical extension of theoretical viewpoints than widely held attitudes. Discrimination against blacks and 'hommes de couleur' was an important element of race relations in France, whatever the theories of philosophers. Government policy to restrict, if not eliminate, the presence of blacks in France, a policy which was renewed by Napoleon, enshrined a concept of blacks which was far from egalitarian and opposed the categories of 'black' and 'French'. Hostility to blacks was not confined to the government. In an atmosphere of competition for work and charity, the poor often turned on blacks as threatening their livelihood.[64] Even in Year II, there were limits to the general enthusiasm. Police spies reported discontent among some groups that blacks were to be considered equals and a play about inter-racial marriage was forced off the stage.[65] Advocates of equal rights such as Grégoire, Raynal, Condorcet, Mirabeau, Brissot and La Rochefoucauld were not, therefore, representative of a new trend in public attitudes. Because there was no consensus for radical measures on questions of race and citizenship, it was not difficult for Napoleon to reverse this measure in 1802. Thus, far from marking a new departure or embodying Enlightenment ideas of equality and universalism which had gained widescale acceptance, the 1794 declaration can be seen as a brief aberration with limited influence on attitudes or policy.

Even more important in delaying the implementation of egalitarian policies towards blacks was the existence of powerful interests in favour of the maintenance of slavery and the slave trade. White colonists and plantation owners on the one hand and representatives of the ports on the other organized themselves into two effective pressure groups to lobby against changes. The deputies to the various assemblies, overworked and largely ignorant of colonial affairs, were persuaded that French prosperity depended on the maintenance of the status quo. Thus although a few measures were taken to improve the position of free 'hommes de couleur', the issues of slavery and the slave trade were largely avoided by putting off debates or by the use of ambiguous wording which allowed local decisions in the West Indies to circumvent the spirit of the declaration.[66] When the Convention eventually addressed colonial questions, the situation had changed dramatically. Rebellions of planters in the colonies and the British threat in the Caribbean meant that 'une motivation essentiellement politique', to quote Jean Tarrade, favoured the abolition of slavery.[67] Sonthonax had already declared an end to slavery in Saint Domingue to rally blacks to the Republic in 1793; the declaration of 16 Pluviôse an II merely extended this strategy to fight the counter-revolutions and British expeditions throughout the region.[68] Once the move had been made, the general mood of egalitarian fervour of the time seized on the declaration and incorporated it into propaganda. As Cohen points out, this propaganda was 'part of the enthusiasms of the moment, but did not signal a transformation in general assessment of the black man.[sic]'[69]

The political rather than ideological nature of this policy can be seen in the way in which it was applied. In Saint-Domingue, where Sonthonax had first declared the emancipation of the slaves, the British were indeed expelled but the Republic failed to consolidate its control and the colony was, in effect, lost. Guadeloupe was also retaken from the British with the use of blacks in the armies. However, Victor Hugues, the energetic commissioner, interpreted the declaration in his own way, gradually re-imposing a system of compulsory plantation labour once the British threat was over. Within a year many features of the old system had been re-instated, including the death penalty for blacks who left their plantations without permission.[70] Other islands in the Caribbean remained in British hands until 1802. Outside the Caribbean, the declaration had even less effect; in the Mascareignes the commissioners who brought the text to the colonies were sent back and slavery continued without interruption. In Senegal there was no counter-revolution by slave owners and no attempt to abolish slavery. The slave trade to the West Indies was halted, but this was probably as much the result of shipping problems during the war as it was due to adherence to the declaration. Slaves continued to be imported into the trading settlements in large numbers.[71]

Yet in France, the Revolution did accelerate a trend towards imposing a single, uniform culture on French territory. Despite token comments accepting the validity of other ways of organizing society, French *philosophes,* in common with other Enlightenment writers in Europe, saw history as the progress of reason, perfecting French civilization. Once this had occurred, Reason again dictated that, given the essential equality of men (women were not even considered) all societies would benefit from its spread, whatever their colour or culture.[72] For many, the reforms and massive changes of the revolution heralded this state and thus the revolution gave great impetus to earlier trends, lending an almost missionary zeal to the war effort. Over the period 1792–1814 'the concept of civilization acquired for the first time a quasi-scientific status, which was increasingly to be employed as the cultural legitimation of European imperialism.'[73] However, it was under Napoleon that this impulse was translated into action. Cultural assimilation was directed at both the French regions and territory gained in the war. The moral obligation to spread the benefits of 'civilization' was seen as particularly applicable to Europe itself, only later developing into a missionary drive throughout the world. It was under Napoleon, too, that limitations were imposed on the possibility of assimilation. Cultures which differed radically from a Parisian, bourgeois ideal were seen as unsuitable for assimilation, at least in the near future.[74]

Outside the Caribbean colonies, there appears to have been little attempt to introduce a new political system or to extend French culture to the colonies. Even in Guadeloupe, the only Caribbean island under firm French control in the period, power rested firmly with the commissioners sent out from the metropolis, or to be more accurate, with one of the three commissioners: Victor Hugues. In Senegal, very little changed in the revolutionary years. Neither the ministry in France nor the commandants in Saint-Louis felt it necessary to institute democratic assemblies although it is possible that for a brief period an elective council of local inhabitants was convened to advise the administration. The records are far from clear and it is impossible to tell when, if ever, this council existed, what its functions were or what real power it held. There is nothing to suggest that the council influenced the administration; it probably operated only when no French interests were concerned. Indeed, the fact that a distinction can be drawn between French and local interests reveals how little political assimilation was valued.

The evidence of the impact of the Revolution on the Senegalese of Saint-Louis and Gorée is not altogether clear. The years of greatest turbulence in France appear to have had no immediate impact on local attitudes. French records mention only one major disturbance, in 1799, but it was caused by West Indian soldiers, not local residents. On the other hand, 1802 saw the most spectacular revolt against the administration of the whole period of French trading contact with the Senegalese coast: in July, armed men seized the Governor, his wife and his closest aide from their beds and forcibly deported them to Gorée, then in British hands. This was not a revolt against French, or indeed foreign, rule but a protest against the high-handed and dubious practices of the Governor; once he was deported, Saint-Louis settled down very quickly. Some of the participants were in fact French.[75] Nonetheless, the action may have been influenced by the events in France over the previous thirteen years. In an extremely polemical pamphlet, Laserre, the deported Governor, claimed that revolutionary ideas were to blame for the uprising. According to his version, the local participants claimed that the Revolution had ended the prerogatives of colour which had existed before and shouted slogans including 'Vive la convention! Vive Robespierre!'.[76] Unfortunately, it is far from certain that Laserre's account is accurate and there is no supporting evidence for this aspect. However, if he was not merely appealing to the anti-revolutionary prejudices of the times, his description provides interesting glimpses of local reactions to the Revolution. In the first place, the timing, linked to references to the Convention, would suggest that it was a response to the reversals of revolutionary gains. Support for the Convention, long dissolved, and for Robespierre, who had not been a major advocate of the changes in 1794, also raises questions of how closely the Senegalese had been following events in France. It would appear that they did not feel that the details were an important concern. Since the period saw very little change either in French attitudes or in colonial policy, this was probably a fair assessment. Secondly, if Laserre is to be believed, the aspect of the Revolution which most concerned Saint-Louisien leaders was not the question of democratic rights or local participation in administration but that of fundamental racism. This supports the conclusion from analysis of the two incidents above. Local inhabitants were both aware of French racism and constrained by it.

The half-hearted implementation of revolutionary decrees in Senegal and the lack of change in French policies both suggest that the impact of the Revolution on colonial theory has been exaggerated. Similarly, the continuation of racial prejudice amongst Europeans out in Africa appears unaltered in the early nineteenth century. If anything, it increased. It is clear that the ideas expressed by a few philosophers and revolutionaries in France had little effect on race relations in eighteenth-century Senegal. The radical measures of 1793–4 were, in fact, a temporary rejection of ideas of subordination and racial difference which were still widely held in the late eighteenth century. With the rejection of radicalism and a return to authoritarian rule the changes were easily reversed. Indeed, in 1817 when France began to see Senegal as a colony rather than a simple trading post, a new emphasis on racial difference and the need for maintaining distinctions was also part of that development.[77] Moreover, the administrative imposition of cultural uniformity, although implicit in revolutionary ideology, was actually implemented more effectively by the *ancien régime* and the Empire. Thus to understand the origins of French assimilation policy, it is necessary to give new attention to the nineteenth century. Ideas expressed at the height of egalitarian enthusiasm may indeed have inspired later theorists but the creation of new policy stemmed from nineteenth century developments. If the Revolution affected later colonial policy, that influence was moral rather than practical.

Notes

1. M. Crowder, *Senegal: a study in French assimilation policy*, (Institute of Race Relations; London, 1962), pp. 1–2.

2. H. O. Idowu, 'Assimilation in Nineteenth Century Senegal', *Bulletin de l'I.F.A.N.* série B, vol. XXX, No. 4 1968 p. 1422; E. Isichei, *History of West Africa since 1800*, (London, 1977), p. 202; R. F. Betts, *Tricouleur: the French Overseas Empire*, (London, 1978). p. 38.

3. Crowder, *Senegal* p. 2; see also Idowu, 'Assimilation' pp. 1437–8.

4. This applied to all residents, whatever their colour. For the terms of the code noir see P. Baude, *L'affranchissement des esclaves aux Antilles Françaises principalement à la Martinique, du début de la Colonisation à 1848*, (Fort de France, Imprimerie du Gouvernement, 1948), pp. 105–15; for similar regulations in Senegal see, for example, Archives Nationales de France (A.N.F.) Colonies C⁶6 Reglemens de la Compagnie Royalle du Sénégal et Costes

d'Affrique, 14.3.1721, article 3; A.N.F. Colonies C⁶16, liasse 1775, Ordonnance concernant la police Générale de L'isle de Gorée, 28.1.1775, articles 14–16.

5. This discussion is taken largely from W. Cohen, *The French Encounter with Africans: White Response to Blacks, 1530–1880*, (Bloomington, 1980), pp. 60–99, 130–54; N. Hampson, *The Enlightenment: An evaluation of its assumptions, attitudes and values*, (London, 1968, 2nd ed. 1982); D. C. Potts and D. G. Charlton, *French Thought since 1600*, (London, 1974), pp. 23–39; S. Woolf, 'French Civilization and Ethnicity in the Napoleonic Empire', *Past and Present* No. 124, August 1989 pp. 96–98; P. Mark, 'Fetishers, "Marybuckes" and the Christian norm: European images of Senegambians and their religions, 1550–1760' *African Studies Review*, Vol. XXIII, No. 2, 1980, pp. 91–9.

6. M. Duchet, *Anthropologie et histoire au siècle des lumières*, (Paris, P.U.F. 1971), pp. 203–4; Cohen, *The French Encounter with Africans*, pp. 73–9, 89–95.

7. S. T. McCloy, *The Negro in France*, (Lexington Kentucky, 1961), p. 5; Cohen, *The French Encounter with Africans*, pp. 111–2.

8. A. N. F. Colonies F¹B3, dossiers I – VI; Bibliothèque Nationale, Paris, Mss Joly de Fleury 1027, ff. 239–42; H. W. Debrunner, *Presence and Prestige: Africans in Europe. A history of Africans in Europe before 1918*, (Basel: Basler Afrika Bibliographien, 1979), pp. 138–40.

9. A. N. F. Colonies E 358, dossier Rottier Belair, Antoine; Mss Joly de Fleury 1027 ff. 234–46; 2424 ff. 258–60, 359; A. Gautier, *Les soeurs de Solitude: la condition féminine dans l'esclavage aux Antilles du XVIIᵉ au XIXᵉ siècle* (Paris, Editions Caribéenes, 1985), pp. 151–152; for an interesting parallel, see V. Martinez-Allier, *Marriage, Class and Colour in Nineteenth Century Cuba: A Study of Racial Attitudes and Sexual Values in a Slave Society*, (Cambridge, 1974), pp. 42–56.

10. F. Henriques *Prostitution and Society: a survey*, 3 vols. (London, 1962–8,) vol. II p. 132; R. Kabbani, *Europe's Myths of Orient: Devise and Rule*, (London, 1986), pp. 6–7, 14–36; Gautier, *Les soeurs de Solitude*, pp. 151, 154, 160–1; D. H. Lamiral, *L'Affrique et le peuple Affriquain considérés sous tous leurs rapports avec notre commerce et nos colonies*, (Paris, 1789), p. 44.

11. P. Cultru, ed. *Premier voyage du Sieur de la Courbe fait à la coste d'Afrique en 1685*, (Paris, 1913 pp. 36–9); A. Delcourt, *La France et les établissements français au Sénégal entre 1713 et 1763*, (I.F.A.N. Dakar, 1952), p. 124; G. E. Brooks Jnr., 'The Signares of Saint-Louis and Gorée: Women Entrepreneurs in Eighteenth-Century Senegal' in N. J. Hafkin and E. G. Bay, eds. *Women in Africa: Studies in Social and Economic Change*, (Stanford, California, 1976) pp. 34–8; J. Corry, *Observations on the Windward Coast of Africa*, (London, 1807; reprinted Frank Cass, 1968), pp. 11–12.

12. N. I. de Moraes, 'Contribution à l'histire de la Petite Côte', 4 vols. unpublished thèse de doctorat, Université de Paris I, 1976, vol. II pp. 268–70; W. Smith, *A New Voyage to Guinea describing the customs, manners, soil, climate, habits, buildings, education, manual arts, agriculture, trade, employments, languages, ranks of distinction, habitations, diversions, marriages and whatever else is memorable among the inhabitants, likewise an account of their animals, minerals etc.*, (London: Nourse, 1744), pp. 244–7.

13. Service Historique de l'Armée de Terre: Génie. article 14, dossier Afrique: 'Mémoire sur un Etablissement dans la Rivière de Gambie, may 1779 abord l'Epervier', f⁰ 1r⁰; Archives Nationales du Sénégal, 5D1 no. 6 Mémoire sur l'Ile de Gorée par le Chᵉʳ de Mesnager, 14.5.1768 p. 4.

14. P. Cariou, 'La rivale inconnue de Madame de Sabran dans l'Ile de Gorée', *Notes Africaines*, No. 45, Jan. 1950, pp. 13–15; A.N.F. Colonies C⁶15 hasse 1766 Extrait de la Correspondence de Demesnager, 31.10.1766, f° 3r°.

15. Cohen, *The French Encounter with Africans*, p. 124.

16. Archives de la Compagnie des Indes, Lorient, 1723, cited in A. Lacroix 'Les Français au Sénégal au temps de la Compagnie des Indes, 1719–1758', unpublished

dissertation, Bastia, p. 61. No precise reference given; A.N.F. Colonies C⁶15, liasse 1766, Demesnager au Ministre 15.5.1766 p. 9.

17. E. Magnieu & H. Prat, eds. *Correspondence inédite de la comtesse de Sabran et du Pan chevalier de Boufflers 1778–1788,* (Paris, 1875); Cariou, 'La rivale inconnue de Madame de Sabran', pp. 13–15.

18. See Martinez-Allier, *Marriage, Class and Colour* pp. 109–12; Gautier, *Les soeurs de Solitude,* pp. 158–60, 162–81; E.-M. Benabou, *La prostitution et la police des moeurs au XVIIIᵉ siècle,* ed. P. Goubert, (Paris: Librairie Académique Perrin, 1987).

19. J. G. Pelletan, *Mémoire sur la colonie française du Sénégal avec quelques considérations historiques et politiques sur la traite des Nègres,* (Paris: Panckoucke l'an IX [1801]), p. 99.

20. A. N. F. Colonies C⁶9 Lettre-journal, St. Robert à la Compagnie, 18.6.1725 ff. 30rᵒ-vᵒ; see also A. N. F. – Section d'Outre-Mer, Dépôt des Fortifications des Colonies Gorée II, carton 76, no. 24 Brizon de Palmaroux à de Fulvy 20.7.1741 ff.2rᵒ-vᵒ.

21. M. Foucault, *L'histoire de la sexualité,* 3 vols. Vol. I *An Introduction* trans. R. Hurley, (Harmondsworth: Penguin 1979), pp. 81–105; Gautier, *Les soeurs de Solitude,* pp. 151, 158–64.

22. A. N. F. Colonies C⁶33 Blanchot au Capitaine Sacray, 28 Nivose an XI; A. Lacroix, 'Michel Adanson au Sénégal (1749–1753)', *Bulletin du Comité d'Etudes Historiques et Scientifiques de l'Afrique Occidentale Française,* vol. XXI no. 1, Jan.–March 1938, pp. 88–89; C. Becker & V. Martin, eds. 'Mémoires d'Adanson sur le Sénégal et l'île de Gorée,' *Bulletin de l'Institut Fondamental de l'Afrique Noir,* série B, vol. 42, no. 4 Oct. 1980 pp. 736–7.

23. Cohen, *The French Encounter with Africans,* p. 126.

24. A. N. F. Colonies C⁶11, Rapport de Saint Adon à la Compagnie et Conseil Supérieur du Sénégal, 2.12.1736; A. Lacroix, 'Michel Adanson au Sénégal' pp. 58, 107.

25. A. N. F. Colonies E 2, dossier Ailleboust de St. Vilmé, J.-B., Ailleboust et al au Ministre, sans date, ca. 1773 ff.1vᵒ-3vᵒ.

26. For example, A. N. F. Colonies C⁶14, liasse 1758, Tableau des habitans éxistans sur l'Isle du Sénégal, 1ᵉʳ Juillet 1758; Archives Nationales du Sénégal 3G2/123, Denombrement Général des Habitants de lIsle de Gorée, 11.7.1767; A. Pruneau de Pommegorge, *Description de la Nigritie,* (Paris, Maradan, 1789), p. 2.

27. M. Adanson, *Histoire naturelle du Sénégal: les coquillages, avec un Voyage au Sénégal,* (Paris, 1757), pp. 28–9.

28. Archives Nationales du Sénégal 1B1, pièce no. 212, La Luzerne à Blanchot, 23.4.1789.

29. A. N. F. Colonies E 2, dossier Ailleboust de St. Vilmé, J.-B., Genlis, Observations . . . sans date (ca. 1773) p. 2. In this and all quotations, the original spelling and punctuation have been retained.

30. A. N. F., Colonies E 208, dossier Gondreville, Jean-François Chabardin dit, (A.N.F. Colonies E 208) Extrait des Registres de la Paroisse St Louis du Sénégal certificat d'inhumation, 12.3.1783.

31. A. N. F., Colonies E 208, Copie de la lettre de M. Daire a M. Dumontet . . . de Podor Le 2 avril 1783; Daire à Dumontet 1.5.1783; Copie du billet . . . signed Blondin fils 18.6.1782; Mémoire de Blondin au Marechal de Castries, 6.7.1783.

32. A. N. F., Colonies E 208, Dumontet au Ministre, 21.7.[1783]; untitled copy of submissions by Clergeau and Blondin, signed Jean Blondin, 12.7.1783.

33. A. N. F., Colonies E 208, submissions by Clergeau and Blondin, fᵒ1; for the ban on trade, see S. Zilombo, 'The Economy and Society of Saint-Louis du Sénégal with Special Reference to the Emergence of Eurafrican influence, 1659–1809' unpublished Ph.D. thesis, University of Birmingham 1985 pp. 204–14, 238–9; L.-P. Raybaud, 'L'administration du Sénégal de 1781 à 1784: l'affaire Dumontet' *Annales Africaines,* (Dakar, 1968), pp. 146–64.

34. A. N. F., Colonies E 208, Minute, 'Batteau de la Succession du Sʳ Gondreville', n.d.

35. A. N. F., Colonies E 208, submissions by Clergeau and Blondin, fᵒ3rᵒ.

36. A. N. F., Colonies E 208, submissions by Clergeau and Blondin, fᵒ1rᵒ.

37. A. N. F., Colonies E 208, submissions by Clergeau and Blondin, fᵒ4rᵒ.

38. A. N. F., Colonies E 208, submissions by Clergeau and Blondin, fᵒ3rᵒ.

39. A. N. F., Colonies E 208, submissions by Clergeau and Blondin, fᵒ4vᵒ.

40. A. N. F., Colonies E 208, submissions by Clergeau and Blondin, fᵒ1vᵒ.

41. A. N. F., Colonies E 208, Minute, 'Batteau de la Succession du Sʳ Gondreville', n.d.

42. Saugnier, *Relation de plusieurs voyages à la cote d'Afrique à Maroc, au Sénégal, à Gorée, à Galam &c. avec des détails intéressans pour ceux qui se destinent à la traite des nègres, de l'or, de l'ivoire &c. tirées des journaux de M. Saugnier qui a été longtemps esclave des Maures et de l'empereur du Maroc,* (Paris, Greffier jeune 1791), pp. 271–2.

43. See, for example, Archives Nationales du Sénégal, Archives du Greffe, Saint-Louis, 1786–1789 no. 19, 14.3.1789, and no. 25, 9.3.1789.

44. Archives Nationales de France – Section d'Outre-Mer, Registres parroissaux de Saint-Louis et Gorée; Verdun de la Crenne, Chevalier de Borda & Pingré, *Voyage fait par ordre du Roi en 1771 et 1772 en diverses parties de l'Europe, de l'Afrique, et de l'Amerique, pour verifier l'utilité de plusieurs méthodes et instrumens servant à determiner la Latitude et la Longitude,* 2 vols. (Paris, 1778, Imprimerie Royale vol. I),p. 151.

45. Prélong, 'Mémoire sur les Iles de Gorée et du Sénégal', *Annales de Chimie* tome XVIII, Sept. 1793 pp. 297–8; J.-B. Durand, *Voyage au Sénégal en 1785 et 1786* 2 vols. Paris, Agasse, l'an X [1802] vol. II pp. 25–6; Abbé D. Boilat, 'Mission à Joal' 1846, ms in collection of Société de Géographie de Paris, S. G. carton BO –BON, no. 109, pp. 21–2.

46. Following some eighteenth-century usage, 'creole' here refers to locally born, or long-term residents (almost all African) rather than temporary visitors from the mainland or new arrivals.

47. J. A. Carnes, *Journal of a Voyage from Boston to the West Coast of Africa,* (Boston, Massachusetts, 1852), pp. 40–8.

48. P. Wilson, 'Christian Linguists in Senegambia' unpublished dissertation for M.Th., Aberdeen University 1978 pp. 1–23.

49. Hampshire Record Office, Mildmay Papers 15 M 50 / 1574 Pocket book, (H. R. O. Pocket book) p. 57.

50. H. R. O. Pocket book, p. 57.

51. H. R. O. Pocket book, p. 57.

52. H. R. O. Pocket book, pp. 58–9.

53. H. R. O. Pocket book, pp. 59–60.

54. H. R. O. Pocket book. For religion see pp. 53–6; for hygiene see pp. 25–7.

55. Pelletan, *Mémoire* p. 55; Verdun et al, *Voyage fait par ordre du roi,* p. 144.

56. See my forthcoming thesis, 'The Development of Creole Society in Saint-Louis and Gorée, 1719–1817', London University.

57. Debrunner, *Presence and Prestige,* pp. 152–3; Cohen, *The French Encounter with Africans,* pp. 118–20.

58. C. Schefer, *Instructions Générales données de 1763 à 1870 aux gouverneurs et ordonnateurs des établissements français en Afrique occidentale,* 2 vols, (Paris, Champion 1921), vol. 1 p. 189.

59. A. N. F. Colonies C⁶28, 'Des Possessions françaises en Afrique par Mʳ Picard', 1814 pp. 57–62.

60. J.-P. Brissot, *Lettre à MM. les députés des trois ordres,* Paris 1789 p. 30. Cited in D. Geggus, 'Racial Equality, Slavery, and Colonial Secession during the Constituent Assembly' *American Historical Review,* vol. 94, no. 5 Dec. 1989, p. 1293.

61. Cohen, *The French Encounter with Africans,* p. 141.

62. Geggus, 'Racial Equality, Slavery, and Colonial Secession', p. 1290.

63. Debrunner, *Presence and Prestige*, p. 150.

64. Cohen, *The French Encounter with Africans*, p. 113; for rivalry amongst the poor in France, see O. Hufton 'Towards an understanding of the poor of eighteenth century France' in J. F. Bosher, ed. *French Government and Society: Essays in memory of Alfred Cobban*, (London, 1973), pp. 152–3, 162–3.

65. Debrunner, *Presence and Prestige*, p. 150.

66. Geggus, 'Racial Equality, Slavery and Colonial Secession', pp. 1290–1308; J. Tarrade, 'Les colonies et les principes de 1789: les Assemblées révolutionnaires face au problème de l'esclavage' in J. Tarrade, ed. *La Révolution Française et les colonies*, (Paris: Harmattan, 1989), pp. 16–26.

67. Tarrade, 'Les colonies et les principes de 1789' p. 33.

68. Ibid. pp. 10–11, 28–33.

69. Cohen, *The French Encounter with Africans*, p. 142.

70. L. C. Abenon, 'L'ordre révolutionnaire en Guadeloupe: travail et libérté, 1794–1802' in M. Martin and A. Yacou, eds., *De la Révolution française aux révolutions créoles et nègres*, (Paris: Editions Caribéenes, 1989), pp. 97–104.

71. Durand, *Voyage au Sénégal*, vol. II pp. 26–27; P. D. Curtin, *Economic Change in Precolonial Africa: Senegambia in the Era of the Slave Trade*, 2 vols., (Madison: University of Wisconsin Press, 1975.), vol. I pp. 162–3.

72. Idowu, 'Assimilation' p. 1437.

73. S. Woolf, 'French Civilization and Ethnicity,' p. 96.

74. Ibid. pp. 110–18.

75. for a description of these events see L. Jore, *Les établissements français sur la côte occidentale d'Afrique de 1758 à 1809*, (Paris, Société Française d'Histoire d'Outre-Mer, 1965), pp. 140–93.

76. Col. L. H. P. Laserre, *Mémoire pour le colonel Laserre, ex-commandant au Sénégal, déporté par suite de l'insurrection qui a éclaté dans la colonie pendant la nuit du 4 au 5 thermidor an X, contenant le compte rendu de sa gestion, le récit des événemens de l'insurrection et la réfutation des calomnies que les insurgés ont dirigés contre lui*, (Paris: Fain, an XIII [1805]) p. 31, see also p. 33.

77. A. N. F. Colonies C⁶28, Des Possessions françaises en Afrique par Mr Picard, 1814 pp. 57–62; C. Schefer, *Instructions*, vol. I p. 189; for a comparison with British attitudes see K. Ballhatchet, *Race, Sex and Class under the Raj: Imperial Attitudes and Policies and their Critics, 1793–1905*, (London, 1980), pp. 2–5, 96–7.

62. Geggus, 'Racial Equality, Slavery and Colonial Secession', p. 1300.

63. Debbasch, *Couleur et liberté*, p. 151.

64. Cohen, *The French Encounter with Africans*, p. 117. On slavery amongst the poor in Europe, see O. Hufton, *Towards an understanding of the poor of eighteenth-century France*, in J. F. Bosher, ed. *French Government and Society: Essays in memory of Alfred Cobban* (London, 1973), pp. 145–65. 162–0.

65. Hardman, *France and Russia*, p. 154.

66. Geggus, 'Racial Equality, Slavery and Colonial Secession', pp. 1290–1308. J. Tarrade, 'Les colonies et les principes de 1789: les Assemblées révolutionnaires face au problème de l'esclavage', in J. Tarrade ed. *La révolution française et les colonies* (Paris, Harmattan, 1989), pp. 16–20.

67. Tarrade, 'Les colonies et les principes de 1789', p. 17.

68. Ibid, pp. 16–17. 20–9.

69. Cohen, *The French Encounter with Africans*, p. 141.

70. A. G. Abénon, 'L'ordre esclavagiste en Guadeloupe (travail et liberté), 1794–1802' in M. Martin and A. Yacou eds, *Esclavage et libération dans les sociétés antillaises et latines* (Éditions Caribéennes, 1988), pp. 97–104.

71. Durand, *Voyage au Sénégal*, vol. II, pp. 20–27. R. L. Curtin, *Economic Change in Pre-colonial Africa: Senegambia in the Era of the Slave Trade*, 2 vols, (Madison, University of Wisconsin Press, 1975), vol. I, p. 143.

72. Durand, *Assemblée*, p. 237.

73. S. Wood, *French Revolution and Education*, p. 28.

74. Ibid, pp. 110–14.

75. For a description of these events, see C. Jory, 'Les colons restent fidèles à la métropole d'Afrique: 2e–1789 à 1809', (Paris, Société Française d'Histoire d'Outre-Mer, 1986), pp. 180–93.

76. Col. L. H. P. Laserre, *Mémoire pour ... règlement intérieur, économie à ... le dépose sur celle P. ... Institution qui rente dans la réalité pensée à ... tant de ... l'Institution en ... comptant le temps à ... semblait le texte des survenues de l'Institution à la ...*, in XIII, (France 1835), p. 43; see also p. 42.

77. A. N. F. Colonies C98 Les Possessions françaises en Afrique par MP 1890s. 2844 pp. 31–02. G. Sabel, *Mémoires*, vol. I, p. 186. For a comparison with British attitudes see K. Ballhatchet, *Race, Sex and Class under the Raj: Imperial Attitudes and Policies and their Critics, 1793–1905*, (London, 1980), pp. 5–8 96–7.

Chapter Six

Early Resistance to Colonialism: Montague James and the Maroons in Jamaica, Nova Scotia and Sierra Leone

MAVIS C. CAMPBELL

I f the 'key to human dignity lies in action,' then the Maroons of the New World possessed this trait fully, for their lives bespoke resistance – and resistance is action. Everywhere in the region where slavery existed, the Africans were sure to resist in myriad ways, including making good their escape. The most successful of those who escaped ended up establishing their own communities along African socio/political/military lines in far-away places inhospitable to the pursuers. These communities have come to be known as Maroon societies in the English-speaking world, and the inhabitants as Maroons.[1]

In Jamaica, after numerous concerted but unsuccessful efforts were made by the British to dislodge the Maroons from their mountainous domains, formal peace treaties were finally made with them in 1738–9. These treaties granted them lands and gave recognition to their quasi-autonomous existence.[2] This was indeed a remarkable achievement of resistance. Here we have a group of free blacks during this early period of the colonial process who stoutly refused to have their lives fashioned by the dictates of their masters. And the Jamaican model was not the first of its kind in the hemisphere. The Spanish colonial masters also had perforce to make peace treaties with some of their Africans who fought valiantly for their freedom, as early as the 1540s, 1570s and the early 1600s in Hispaniola, Panama and Mexico respectively.[3] Of all these early free black communities, however, only in Jamaica and Surinam have they continued as semi-autonomous groups up to the present. In the Spanish territories they eventually became merged with the wider society.

The early presence of these free African communities co-existing within slave societies had within them inherent dangers for the colonial

This chapter © Mavis Campbell 1992

authorities. In Jamaica, however, their fear that the quasi-independent Maroons might have joined forces with the plantation slaves against them was to prove unfounded. This was largely because the Maroons stuck faithfully to the clauses in the treaties obliging them to search for and return runaways. But this did not prevent the colonial government from reneging on the Maroons by flagrantly whittling away most of their traditional practices as well as their rights under the treaty arrangements. Tension thus ineluctably grew between the Maroons and the colonial government which finally culminated into open hostilities in 1795. This was with the largest group, the Trelawny Town Maroons, and the resistance movement was led by their redoubtable leader, Captain or Colonel (as the records variously designated him) Montague James.

Montague James is not the best known of Maroon leaders in the region. Cudjoe, who figured during the early decades of the eighteenth century and negotiated the 1738 peace treaty in Jamaica, and Nanny (now a national hero of this country), are certainly more popularly known. Yet it is on Montague James that we have the greatest body of documentation. We have accounts of him in Jamaica, Nova Scotia and Sierra Leone, and are thus in a position to give a fairly well-rounded characterization of him. This could hardly be done with the shadowy sketches we have of Cudjoe or Nanny, for instance. Despite his name (most Maroons in Jamaica anglicized their names after the treaties), there is suggestive evidence that he was an Ashanti[4] or at least an Akan from what is now Ghana. Exactly when Montague became leader of the Trelawny Town Maroons is not clear, but it was either during the late 1770s or early 1780s.[5] The official title for this position was 'Captain,' but it appears that his military title was that of 'Colonel.' Montague was so favoured by the colonial powers that by the late 1770s he held a special position within his community. At this period the principal white superintendent, required under the 1738 treaty to reside among them, was John James. James' influence among the Maroons and with the colonial administration was so immense that he was made 'major-commandant' not only of the Trelawny Town Maroons, but of all the Maroon groups within the island. This greatly increased his duties and for this reason he effected the appointment of Montague James as 'assistant superintendent of Trelawny Town,' under a special commission and with a salary intended to have been £200 per annum.[6] Montague James was thus, as far as the records can tell, the only Maroon leader to have held such a commission which would normally have gone to a white colonist. From all accounts, Montague served the colonial government with dedication and loyalty both as captain and as assistant superintendent of the Trelawny Town Maroons.

Montague's life as a leader had, in large measure, most of the attendant paradoxes and contradictions that Third World leaders encounter within a colonial context. He, like many others to come, became co-opted into the colonial system, very often unavoidably serving its interest in a manner antithetical to the interests of his own people. In Montague's case, this must have been most pronounced where his official duty required him to wrest freedom from those who wanted to escape from the brutality of slavery. As captain of the Maroons in his town, he was obliged, under the treaty, to search for, and return runaways to their masters. From the evidence, Montague served faithfully in this capacity. Indeed, so well did he perform this function that his health became impaired from being so frequently out in search parties especially at nights. For the recovery of his health we find him away from the island (destination unknown, and at whose cost, not clear), for eighteen months.[7] Whoever was responsible for Montague's 'sick leave,' it seems remarkable for the period and must serve as an indication of his usefulness to the colonial powers. In extenuation, perhaps, it should be mentioned that the captaincy of Maroons in the different communities did not carry official salaries. Their chief source of income, therefore, came from serving in search parties and from returning runaways for which they were paid on a *per capita* basis. As for Montague's new appointment as assistant to James, which nominally carried the salary of £200 per annum, like every other salaried person on the island at that time, he too, was not paid on a regular basis. Repeatedly, by himself or more often, in combination with John James, he made representations to the Assembly to be reimbursed. On a few occasions we find him receiving £100, at other times £200, for varied periods.[8]

As assistant to James, some of Montague's new duties would also have involved him in veritable espionage on his own people. By the 1780s, while many Maroon rights were being abrogated by the colonial state, concomitantly the powers of the white superintendents in Maroon towns increased. Among their many new duties, superintendents were to ensure that the earnings of Maroons complied with the limitations fixed by law, to discipline the Maroons to see that they did not reside outside their towns beyond a certain time stipulated by law, and to enforce a host of other such regulations intruding on the personal lives of the Maroons.[9] As assistant to James, Montague would, of necessity, have participated in enforcing these rules. And even if they went against his own personal views, the evidence suggests that he performed his duties with the usual loyalty and diligence. The numerous petitions that John James wrote on his behalf importuning the government to pay him for his services attested to this. That of 24 November 1790 pointed out that upon Montague's appointment in 1788,[10] a salary of £200 was granted him by the Assembly, and although he had since continued to exert himself with every 'diligent attention,' yet after applying for his salary it was refused by the receiver general.[11] In this instance Montague was fortunate when three months later a report of the Assembly agreed that he 'ought to be paid' £200 for his services in 1790.[12]

Montague, like so many leaders within a colonial complex, would seem to have become alienated from his people – at least for a time. In 1792 for instance, he and three of his officers petitioned the governor for additional lands over and above the 1500 acres allotted to them under the treaty. In justifying their request, they argued that a large part of their land was unfit for cultivation, the arable section was over-cultivated and was thus suffering from soil exhaustion, while at the same time their population had increased and was increasing.[13] The evidence we have of some tension between the Maroon officers and the rank and file came from the Assembly's response. The committee reviewing the petition visited Trelawny Town and claimed that they found none of the Maroons, apart from the four officers who signed the document, acquainted with its contents, and that no meetings were held to articulate these grievances. If this is correct, then it would indeed have been a breach of the Maroon system of government, which was based on consultations all down the chain of command from the leadership to the bottom. But the committee also reported that they did find a general wish in Trelawny Town for more lands.[14]

This petition was to become a decisive turning-point in Maroon/government relations. The request for more lands was brusquely rejected; four days later the popular Major James was removed from his post as superintendent, on the pretext that he violated the law by not residing in Trelawny Town. (Apparently James was also removed from the post of major-commandant of all the Maroons.) In the process, Montague, too, was removed from his position. The Assembly decided that the warrants granted to him were 'highly improper and illegal, and that instead of encouraging by reward, the House will discountenance all such proceedings.'[15] This was a reply to what was to be the last of the numerous petitions from John and Montague James, asking to be paid for their services. Indeed, if John James went, so would Montague because Montague owed his position to James alone. The whole episode represented a new hostile attitude to Maroon affairs, for reasons too complicated to be delved into here. But the final outcome, three years later, culminated in the Trelawny Town/Government war which ended in the deportation of the group to Nova Scotia and finally to Sierra Leone.

Who was Montague James? From the above brief sketch we see him as a 'good' colonialist – a coopted one – rendering faithful service to his overlords, and much under the spell of the powerful John James. There is no doubt that by the 1790s the reputation of the Maroon Chief had declined under James' ascendancy. R. C. Dallas characterized Montague at this time as hardly more than a pathetic figure, wearing 'a gaudy, laced, red coat, and a gold-laced hat with a plume of feathers. None but their captains and officers sat in his presence, except upon the ground. He was the first helped at meals; no woman ate with him, and he was waited on by the young men. He presided in the councils, and exercised an authoritative tone of voice to enforce order, which, however, he seldom effected; for he was, in fact, considered in no better light than as an old woman, but to whom the shadow of respect was to be paid, as he bore the title of Chief.'[16] The records consulted do not bear out Dallas' profile of Montague. However, Montague's behaviour at the beginning of the war does not conform to the usual behaviour pattern of Maroons. Put succinctly, the war began when a few Maroons were chastized for some petty theft by some slaves. This was the greatest humiliation to the Maroons who held the slaves in contempt, as the slaves in turn hated them for helping to prevent them escape from slavery. But, above all, it was one of the violations of the treaty. An act of petty theft would normally and traditionally have been tried by the Maroons themselves. The Trelawny Maroons postured and used strong language as they would in such situations, and, with different administrators who understood Maroon ways, the matter might well have been settled peacefully. But the governor, the Earl of Balcarres, a neophyte to Maroon affairs, flexed his muscles and sent out a huge force against the Maroons, at the same time asking them to surrender.[17] It is surprising that although the Maroons committed no act against the state, Montague and some of his people surrendered to Balcarres. This was not in keeping with the old Maroon fighting spirit. But ironically, it was Balcarres' brutal treatment of them that brought back that spirit. 'All [who surrendered], not excluding the white-haired veteran Montague, had been put in irons and hurried off to prison – perhaps to death,' Gardner wrote.[18] Dallas, however, said, 'They were all, old Montague excepted, bound with their hands behind, and . . . sent into confinement at Montego Bay. . .'[19] Excepted, probably, from being bound, but certainly not from being imprisoned, for Montague *was* also imprisoned.

Montague's imprisonment transformed him into a real Maroon leader again and no longer James' minion as he had been for so long. Apparently, his strategy was to appear subdued and contrite in confinement; and it paid off when he and some prominent members of his group were sent back to Trelawny Town to appeal to the others to surrender. They did not return but became some of the outstanding stalwarts of the war. Montague became their undoubted leader and was even more determined than some of the younger ones to pursue the war relentlessly. Never would he forget the treatment he and his people received from Balcarres; he was known to have declared that he would rather rot in the woods than surrender.[20] It appears that Montague soon became the brain behind the revolt, leaving the more active combat to the younger men and women. Given Balcarres' great force, the strategy was to have small, well-trained sorties under tough and disciplined leaders, attacking plantations all over the island, and avoiding open combat. The tactic of attacking far and wide also made it difficult for the unwieldy force to pursue the Maroons with any degree of swiftness. The overall policy was most effective and many planters were actually forced to evacuate their estates.[21] Without a doubt, the war was going in favour of the Maroons and the colony close to a state of desperation until Balcarres brutally introduced bloodhounds from Cuba. The Maroons feared these savage dogs, as Balcarres well knew.

At any rate, old Montague was not prepared to give up without a fight. He thus tried to employ a delaying tactic. Three days after the arrival of the dogs (20 December 1795), we find him signing a truce with George Walpole, the officer commanding the government forces. This was a very basic document obviously drawn up in a hurry. Under it, the Maroons, 'on their knees', would beg His Majesty pardon; they would be prepared to return to their old town (now confiscated by government), and would return all runaways. In addition, they entered into a secret pact with Walpole, obliging the general to agree 'on his oath . . . that they should not be sent off the island.'[22] Eight days later, the treaty or truce was formally signed by Walpole, Montague, Balcarres, and duly ratified. But in ratifying the truce, Balcarres gave the Maroons three days (until 1 January) 'to come in body' to surrender at Spanish Town. The Maroons, their women and children, their arms and other supplies were scattered all over the steep mountains, and it would have been impossible for them to have 'come in' in three days. Thus they were set up for failure and when the Maroons did not – and could not – all 'surrender' by 1 January, Balcarres could use this as a pretext to deport them on grounds of bad faith. Gardner appropriately observed: 'If this was the record of a great continental war, instead of a conflict with three hundred black woodsmen, the question would long be earnestly discussed whether Balcarres did not really design, when he signed the treaty, to occasion the embarrassment which followed. The Maroons were accused soon after of breach of faith, and on this plea were sent from the island.'[23] The evidence in favour of Gardner's proposition is overwhelming. Balcarres had openly boasted that he viewed the treaty 'signed by Major General Walpole on the one part, Colonel Montague James, the Chief of the Maroons on the other part, and ratified by me, absolutely as nothing.'[24]

But what was in Montague's mind when he signed the truce? There is every reason to believe that Montague saw it as a ruse to play for time to reposition themselves in the mountains – reminiscent of the tactics of some of the Maroon leaders as early as the seventeenth century. The notion of asking His Majesty pardon on their knees should be seen as a metaphor. It was a time-honoured tactic of the Maroons, when cornered, to appear penitent – as Montague and his followers did to good effect when they were released from imprisonment to persuade their people to submit. Montague, who was determined to rot in the woods rather than surrender, had no intention of going on his knees to ask anyone for pardon. But the odds were heavily weighted against him, especially when he discovered that some of his most trusted officers had surrendered to Walpole. And, what was perhaps most disheartening to Montague, Walpole was using some of them most effectively as couriers to persuade others to 'come in.' Nevertheless, even on 25 December, after the truce was signed, Walpole was complaining about the defiance of the Maroon leader. He saw 'old Montague . . . as far as I can guess, the obstacle to peace, as much as he dares: Some of the Maroons were heard to tell him, that they would have peace, whether he would or not,'[25] and here was the rub. The force of circumstances was now too much for the intrepid Montague: news of the brutal potential of the bloodhounds was well circulated within the Maroon ranks, and Walpole used the threat of the dogs with skill – threatening all the while to unleash them if the Maroons did not lay down their arms. But perhaps most discouraging of all to Montague must have been the near 'mutiny' of some of his people. On or around 5 January, he, with a group of his most loyal followers, presented himself to Walpole.[26]

Montague's imprisonment by Balcarres foreshadows what would befall many colonial leaders in modern times, who came to see this kind of incarceration as a veritable 'university' for the training of political leadership. Like many who were first coopted into the colonial complex, Montague too, finally left his mark on history through active resistance. By so doing he reclaimed his dignity and lost his 'inessentiality' in Fanon's terms.[27] Equally, his action represented another critical side to resistance–value. Resistance to the colonial power is an affirmation of *value* of the colonized. It is as much a conscious and positive affirmation of self-worth as it is a rejection of the negative stereotypes of the colonized held by the colonial authorities. Balcarres, with his brutal arrogance, certainly helped to bring back the traditional self-confidence of Montague and his people who were proud of their history of successful resistance. That they were tricked into deportation, does not change the argument, because, as we shall see, they never returned to the kind of dependency they developed under John James, but continued to resist colonial intrusion in Nova Scotia and Sierra Leone.

Balcarres and the Jamaican authorities in collusion with the Colonial Office in London violated the treaty and deported the Maroons of Trelawny Town, nearly 600 of them, in 1796. So obsessed were they with the idea of deportation that they did not even care where the Maroons were to be sent. That their first destination was Nova Scotia was merely due to the fortuitous circumstance of the availability of a vessel at the Kingston Harbour about to sail for this territory.[28] Whatever the trumped-up charge for deporting Montague and his people, in reality, the thinking behind this drastic step was based, at this time, on the twin preoccupations of security and economics. Deportations of this kind should be seen in the context of the British colonial policy of that time of moving subject peoples back and forth to satisfy some perceived need or anxiety of the 'Mother country.' In the Caribbean, for instance, any element deemed disruptive of the plantation economy, would be impatiently considered dispensable; and transportation or deportation was generally thought the most effective solution. The Maroons, for instance, were to take the same course as that of the Afro-Americans who fought with Britain during the American War of Independence and were shuttled off, first to Nova Scotia in 1783, and finally to Sierra Leone in 1792 – just some five years after the 'Black Poor' of Britain were repatriated there too.

Up until the end of the eighteenth century it did not matter much to Britain where 'troublesome' elements were sent. Not long after the deportation of the Maroons to Nova Scotia, the Garifunas or Black Caribs, another group that resisted colonial authority, were deported from Saint Vincent. This step had been contemplated for them ever since 1772. They were to be sent – anywhere – but preferably to some unfrequented parts of the 'the coast of Africa' or to some adjacent desert island.[29] This was only to happen in 1797, and then they were sent not to Africa, but to Roatan, an island off the coast of Honduras.[30] It also did not matter to the British which occupations they were to follow, merely that they should fend for themselves. Some aid would be given to them for a limited time, after which they were expected to provide for their own subsistence. The wave of deportations from the Caribbean in the latter part of the eighteenth century rested on two British preoccupations: heightened fears for security generated by the Napoleonic wars in the region, and the colonial planters' perceptions of land scarcity.[31]

By the beginning of the nineteenth century, however, with the development of new ideas about trade with Africa, it began to matter very much what occupation the deported would pursue. Agriculture for the purposes of 'legitimate' trade was to be the order of the day. Africa was to be the producer of primary goods for the burgeoning industries of Britain; and Africa in turn, was to be a principal receptacle for Britain's manufactured goods. The new mercantilism was based no longer on the slave trade but on legitimate trade in goods like palm oil, which with its manifold used became a criticial commodity. These deported subject peoples, then, were no longer to be left to a marginalized economic existence, but targeted to play a key role in the emerging world economic system.

In the event, Montague and the Trelawny Town Maroons were to be subject to two different 'philosophies' in their deportation. In Nova Scotia the most that was expected of them was subsistence living, after the usual initial assistance from the colonial authorities. Thereafter, they were expected to cultivate the lands allotted to them and not be a charge on society. The problem with this policy was that the Maroons had no mind to settle in Nova Scotia. For how could anyone expect Maroons from their delectable mountains in Jamaica to live in such a cold climate? The question was unanswerable.

Montague again led the resistance movement in Nova Scotia. In this case it was against climate and it was conducted not on the battlefield but in the diplomatic/political arena. But even before they left the shores of Jamaica, while still on board the *Asia,* they sent two of their most diplomatic petitions to the Earl of Balcarres and the Duke of Portland. That to Balcarres, the more subtle of the two, said, in part, that

'Your Petitioners Sensible of Your Honors Great Goodness and Mercy in ratifying the acceptance of certain Proposals made by Colonel Montague James, yet conscious how much they have offended are afraid that their abode in this Island might be attended with fatal Consequences to themselves and to Families.

That if they were settled on lands in any other parts of his Majesty's Dominions they might again obtain an opportunity of proving the Sincerity of their Repentance and how anxious they are to prove themselves faithful subjects. . .'[32]

The tact and finesse of the first paragraph of this petition should not go unnoticed. It is an adroit balancing act between morality and necessity. Montague and his people are here subtly reminding Balcarres of the sanctity of 'certain proposals' made in the treaty between the Maroon leader and General Walpole which was ratified by the goodness and mercy of the Governor himself. But now necessity saw the contract broken because the Maroons 'offended' the colonial authorities and their lives would have been endangered had they remained on the island. Montague knew that the Maroons had done nothing to offend the colonial state but quite obviously the situation demanded much diplomatic nicety. If the government could be made to see the moral issue of the breach of contract perpetrated against them through deportation, and if they, for their part, did nothing to aggravate the situation, and were allowed 'the opportunity of proving the Sincerity of their Repentance,' then perhaps they might even be allowed to return to their beloved Jamaica? Less than a year after their arrival in Nova Scotia, they began sending petitions and memoranda. Some were sent to individuals like General Walpole, now residing in Britain, after leaving Jamaica in disgust because of the bad faith shown by the government in deporting the Maroons. Others were sent to the Colonial Office in London, to the House of Commons, and even to the King, all asking to be removed to a warmer climate.[33] Initially the Colonial Office under the Duke of Portland was furious, and the Maroons were told that they were expected to remain in Nova Scotia. This stiffened their resistance. They thus developed the strategy of doing no work at all, and their lands, for the most part, remained uncultivated. This was too much for the tight-fisted Portland, who saw in this the possibility that his government might have to foot their maintenance bills. To make matters worse, Jamaica was simultaneously threatening not to subscribe another penny more than the £25,000 the Assembly had voted for Maroon subsistence in Nova Scotia. The money was to last for a year, after which time they were to maintain themselves. The Maroons were even more determined not to remain and they continued to send petitions to Britain and to live in 'idleness' as the Nova Scotians saw it. Clearly an impasse was reached. Finally, the authorities gave in to the determined resistance of Montague and his Maroons. Undoubtedly, the new thinking on Africa helped the Maroons' case. Portland approached the Sierra Leone Company about settling them in Freetown, and after some demur, the company finally agreed.[34]

Indeed, the transportation of the Maroons from Nova Scotia to Freetown was most auspicious for the biographer of Montague James. It enabled me to take a closer look at him. Earlier, I asked who Montague was and at that point I saw him as a coopted colonial subject doing the bidding of his rulers. Later I saw him as the more typical Maroon leader, resisting the bad faith of the colonial administration with determination, but tricked into deportation; and eventually there came to light another side of this fascinating man, reflecting a high degree of diplomatic adroitness. Still, we were not able to get close to him. Whether before or after the treaties of 1738–9, Maroon leaders are not easy to get close to. Before the treaties, under conditions of guerrilla warfare, they had perforce to live in secrecy. After the treaties, they lived in a kind of 'reservation,' and since they did not write memoirs or history, they still were not accessible to the non-Maroon. Thus it was fortunate that the Sierra Leone Company chose George Ross, one of their employees, to supervise the transportation of the Maroons from Nova Scotia to Sierra Leone. This by itself might not have been very significant. But the directors of the company gave Ross strict instructions to acquire intimate knowledge of the Maroons, 'their capacities, dispositions, manners and customs. . .' and to accomplish this, Ross was first sent to reside with them in Nova Scotia for nearly a year before embarking for Sierra Leone.[35] In this capacity, Ross became an observer-participant and there is no doubt that he developed a deep understanding of Maroon life-style, customs and manners.

But Ross also kept a diary *en route* from Nova Scotia to Sierra Leone which he continued when he became superintendent of the Maroons up until 1801. It is from his entries that we became aware of his knowledge of the Maroons. In this respect Ross could be seen as an important – perhaps the first – ethnographer of the Maroons. And we are grateful to him for the closer view we have of old Montague James. We see Montague as the veteran soldier, the negotiator, diplomat, humanitarian and even slightly inebriated with Ross on a few occasions.[36]

Montague featured throughout Ross' journal from the very first entry. It should be noted that he is more often referred to as 'The General,' at other times, as 'old Montague,' or just plain 'Montague.' From the first day on board the *Asia* transporting them, Montague's skill was required to resist – in this case, dishonesty. It was soon discovered that the Maroons were short-changed of their allowances, and Montague, with the aid of Ross and others, protested vigorously and finally succeeded in stopping the peculation. Perhaps the most galling to the Maroons was the knowledge that their rum was being tampered with: they were receiving 'grog' (a mixture of rum and water) instead of their customary full-spirited Jamaican rum.

Every account of Montague in this diary showed him a most wise, judicious, humane and even-tempered leader. Ross had perforce to rely on him constantly for guidance across the Atlantic as well as in Sierra Leone when he became their superintendent. Montague seems to have possessed that rare inner security that enabled him to govern and exercise influence through dignity and strength of character rather than by the *force majeure*. Throughout the diary we see him, as chief of the Maroons, governing by consultation and discussion, and no longer alienated from his people as we saw happen for a time in Jamaica when he was part of the colonial apparatus. And yet he was to serve the colonial powers again immediately upon his arrival in Sierra Leone. The Afro-American settlers were in a state of rebellion against the payment of quit rents on land and the Sierra Leone Company had just reached the point where they thought the rebels had gained the upper hand. The arrival of the Maroons could not have been more timely. Montague was immediately introduced to the Governor of Sierra Leone and his speech to this official is instructive. He told him that the Maroons had come to Sierra Leone not for regrets, but for 'good.' 'They liked King George [III] and white people very well and if the settlers did not like King George, and the colony's government, the Maroons would be ready for them.' (Entry of 1 October 1, 1800.) And so they were. As is known to history, the Maroons soon helped to crush the rebellion decisively and Ross' journal is full of praise for them. A part of his entry of 1 October, 1800, said that 'all joined in praising the Maroons for a set of the finest Fellows and the Best Bushmen ever was.'

But the other qualities of Montague's character soon surfaced. A few weeks later, when all was quiet in the colony, he solicited Ross' aid in requesting the governor to intercede on behalf of the rebels. As punishment, some were banished to the Bullom Shore, considered isolated and barren. Montague wanted them to live among the Maroons instead. He, no doubt remembering their experience in Jamaica, told Ross that the Maroons did not wish that any people should be driven away from their original place of residence. What was more, they did not like the idea that the Maroons would inherit the evacuated lands of the banished rebels. Ross, who was against Montague's recommendation, told the Maroon leader that although he admired his motives as 'humane and generous', nevertheless the Maroons, newly arrived, could not have known the extent to which the rebels had forfeited their right to the lands they occupied. Montague did not accept Ross' reply but did not say so. Instead, he proceeded diplomatically to praise Ross, whose guidance he would always seek and he, Montague, would never think of going behind Ross's back to apply directly to the governor without Ross' consent, and so on. Ross who understood Maroon diplomatic periphrasis fully (thanks to those months he spent with them in Nova Scotia and en route to Sierra Leone), confided to his diary: 'I perceived him very intent and indeed urgent on the business. I told him I saw no harm that could come of his applying to the Governor. . . ' and duly sent a letter to the official with Montague's wishes. (Entry of 11 October, 1800.)

Although the outcome of Montague's compassion for the settlers is not clear, nevertheless, the whole episode serves to give a more nuanced view of the Maroon chief. The diplomatic and subtle way in which he introduced the subject to Ross added to what we already know of his skill in this direction. Now we have a better view of his humanity and his even-tempered approach to a problematic situation. In willingly going to battle against the settlers, as a military man, Montague was responding almost viscerally to a fighting situation. In fact, it is not unfair to say that the Maroons were excited with the opportunity to do battle again. There was no dissenting voice among them when solicited to fight. The council minutes of 2 October, 1800, said 'to this with one heart and one voice they expressed a cheerful consent and offered whatever succours [?] of men the government might chuse to call out.'[37] The fighting men and women were out of practice, having been inactive in Nova Scotia for over two years and their cramped position *en route* to Sierra Leone was not their preferred life-style. One official of the Sierra Leone Company was known to jest that 'the chiefs made an unanimous and hearty offer to take the field glad . . . to stretch their legs a little.'[38] In their engagement with the settlers, we find, for instance, different groups going out to survey the mountains in search of the rebels rather reminiscent of their party duties in Jamaica. One particular sortie consisted of the governor himself, Ross, a party of some sixty Maroons, out at 8.00 in the morning with 'the old General at our head in top spirits.' (Entry of 6 October, 1800.) Yet, when the battle was successfully resolved, Montague could plead the cause of the rebels he helped to defeat.

It need hardly be said that the assistance of the Maroons in defeating the settlers was to create hatred and fear for the Maroons. But it is not too far-fetched to say that Montague, ironically, could be seen as having initiated the process of improved relations between these two groups. Tension did last for a long time but by mid-nineteenth century the Maroons and the settlers were to grow together through marriage, business and religious affiliations and to become the cornerstone of the Creole society of Sierra Leone.

The Maroon sojourn in Sierra Leone, as noted earlier, came under Britain's new mercantile philosophy which saw Africa's economic importance in agricultural commodities rather than in the slave trade. The Afro-Americans were thus expected to become farmers in Sierra Leone. Upon the occasion of their departure from Nova Scotia, imperious commands were sent repeatedly from the Colonial Office to the Nova Scotia governor ordering the Maroons to arrive in Sierra Leone with 'implements of agriculture.'[39] Thus equipped, they should be seen as scheduled to be industriously engaged in the husbandry of Africa. The Maroons, a military people, again resisted colonial dictates. Instead, they went into small-scale commerce, becoming trading intermediaries between Europe and the hinterland of West Africa. They also went into the civil service and the professions, where many rose to positions of leadership.

As for Montague, although we do not know his exact age, we know that when he arrived in Sierra Leone he was considered 'very old' and ailing, as he was considered 'white-haired' and old from the 1790s. Not even the aggressive economic philosophy of the age would thus have expected him to be engaged in farming. His private life remains, if I may borrow from Churchill, a mystery wrapped in a puzzle within an enigma. In characterizing Montague's hierarchical tendencies in Jamaica, Dallas had noted that 'no woman ate with him.' If this is correct, then it may have been merely a transferred African cultural mode where men and women would eat separately from one another. Ross' journal, on the other hand, made no mention of a wife or family for Montague. In looking at the possessions under his name from Nova Scotia to Sierra Leone (12 different cases depicting much affluence),[40] one can see both female and male garments among the clothing items. We find 31 pairs of trousers, 25 shirts, 19 vests, among the obvious male items. For the obvious female items we find, 19 gowns or 'gounds,' 1 box of trinkets, 15 petticoats, 11 pairs of stockings, 11 shifts (a kind of woman's slip or loose dress). Clothing items such as coats, hats, shoes, handkerchiefs are listed with no gender identification. Every female item listed could have belonged either to a young girl or to an adult women. We have another clue suggesting that Montague had a small family. After Ross' resignation as superintendent of the Maroons in Sierra Leone (May 1801), his successor requested a kind of census of the Maroons. Here we find in Montague's household, himself (one male) and two 'females':[41] a wife and a daughter, or possibly two daughters? We simply are not certain, although a few hints below may argue for the latter.

There is no doubt that Montague was greatly esteemed in Sierra Leone. He may have been among the first – possibly the first – Sierra Leonean to have receive an old age pension. In March of 1801 the Council resolved that, 'In consideration of the meritorious conduct, increasing bodily infirmities, and destitute conditions of Colonel Montague James of the Maroons, Resolved that in addition to the ration of provisions which he now receives in common with the rest of the Maroons, a pension of one Dollar per week be paid him by the Accountant to commence from the 21st day of March 1801; and that the Superintendent be requested to communicate this resolution to Colonel Montague.'[42] Here again, there is no mention of a spouse and the next resolution from the Governor and Council could be seen as providing more circumstantial evidence showing that Montague did not have a wife while in Sierra Leone. A few months later, this same body moved that because of the good conduct of Colonel Montague James of the Maroons, they were 'desirous as far as lies in their power to relieve the infirmities of his old age, and declining state of health.' To effect this, they resolved that the superintendent of the Maroons (now Lieutenant Henry Odlum) be requested to take Montague into his house to board on an allowance of £50 per annum.[43] Yet another resolution of the same month again authorized Odlum to provide Montague 'with a few necessary articles of household furniture.'[44] Montague's health must have improved somewhat for he was to be appointed to the highest office in a colonial polity. In 1809 Governor Thompson appointed him a one-man 'provisional government . . . to execute the office of Governor and Council,'[45] during a short absence of the governor from the colony. This must be the ultimate statement of the respect he enjoyed in Sierra Leone, possibly the first black to have held such a position even if for a short time, in any part of the British Empire. That he could, a year later, become responsible for at least one 'liberated African'[46] as an apprentice, may also suggest improved health. Unfortunately, though, we can trace no more documentation on Montague from this period. I had hoped A. B. C. Sibthorpe in his gossipy work on Sierra Leone would have supplied some more information on him. But all that Sibthorpe gives us is a list of 'Names of Note' during W. Dawe's governorship,[47] which include many Maroons, including Generals Montague and Shaw. We know nothing of Montague's death. We may infer that this happened between 1811 and 1812. This is implied by the absence of Montague's signature or mark on a very important Maroon petition to the Sierra Leone government in 1812, protesting a militia act they considered too rigid in its application.[48]

Montague's life must be one of the most interesting and varied of Maroon leaders, spanning not only their homeland – the Caribbean, Central and South America – but also British North America and West Africa. It is when we see the Maroons in a wider setting that we are even more aware of the disservice done to them when they are treated uncritically, as merely romantic, exotic and one-dimensional figures. Montague's life, whether in Jamaica, Canada, or Sierra Leone was one of complexities, paradoxes and contradictions, where he was constantly faced with difficult choices. His life throws into relief some fascinating aspects of British imperial history, and shows how complex race relations can be. In Jamaica we see him holding a commissioned position held normally by white colonists. In Canada his military rank of colonel was formally confirmed by the Lieutenant Governor, Sir John Wentworth, who practically doted on the Maroons generally, and devoutly wished to have them settled in his colony. His disappointment was intense when Montague and his people resisted his overtures. In Sierra Leone we saw Montague being treated with immense concern and consideration, culminating, finally in his extraordinary appointment to the highest office within a colony.

Yet one should not be naive about all this. Such treatment was neither representative nor should it be regarded as a part of British colonial 'policy' with any semblance of a linear progression. It is not over-cynical to see it as an exceptional situation; such 'lapses' only occurred when British interests were decidely not jeopardized. However, an important dimension of British imperial history would be absent if it did not take into consideration the life of Colonel Montague James.

Notes

1. Although the term Maroon is the generic one usually applied, other usages, such as 'Quilombos' and 'Mocambos' are used by the Portuguese, or 'Palenques' or 'Cumbes' in some Spanish speaking countries. The etymology of 'Maroon' is uncertain, but it is generally believed that it derives from the Spanish word, *cimarron* depicting one living a wild existence. See also note 2 below.

2. For an up to date history of the Maroons in Jamaica, see Mavis C. Campbell, *The Maroons of Jamaica, 1655–1796. . .* (Massachusetts, 1988).

3. Ibid., chap. 1.

4. Among the hints, we find Montague, slightly inebriated, and singing an old 'Koromantyn song with great earnestness'. See George Ross' diary which this author has edited as *Back to Africa: George Ross and the Maroons from Nova Scotia to Sierra Leone.* Entry of 23 October 1800 (forthcoming).

5. The documents are rather confusing about these appointments. In a petition of 10 March 1792, it is mentioned that Montague was appointed Captain of the Maroons in 1767, but this is most likely an error and is probably the date when John James, the white superintendent was appointed. See *Journal of the Assembly of Jamaica (JAJ)* Vol. IX, 10 March 1792.

6. Ibid., Petition of John Montague James, same date; and Vol. VII, Petition of John James, 5 December, 1781. In order not to confuse the two James, Montague will always be addressed by his first name.

7. *JAJ,* Vol. 8, Petition of John and Montague James, 20 December, 1788.

8. Ibid., Vol. 9, 10 March, 1792; Vol. 7, 26 February 1783; on this occasion he was paid £100, 'as assistant superintendent of Trelawny Town'; also Vol. 8, 20 December, 1788, among others.

9. See Campbell, *The Maroons,* chapter 6.

10. This is an obvious error. A part of the petition said, the House in 1788 ordered £200 to be paid to Montague, but further, the same petition also said ever since 1788 when he acted as Captain of Trelawny Town, he received no pay. But Montague did indeed receive £200, December 1788; see *JAJ* Vol. 8, 4 and 19 December 1788.

11. *JAJ,* Vol. 9, 10 March, 1792; Vol. 8, 24 November, 1790.

12. Ibid., Vol. 8, 24 February, 1791.

13. Ibid., Vol. 9, Petition from Maroons of Trelawny Town, 7 March 1792.

14. Ibid. Mr. Vaughn's Report on Maroons of Trelawny Town, 6 December, 1792.

15. Ibid., 19 and 20 December, 1792.

16. R. C. Dallas, *The History of the Maroons. . .* (London: T. N. Longman and O. Rees, 1803), Vol. 1, p. 136.

17. Ibid., pp. 78–260; Campbell, *The Maroons,* chapter 7.

18. W. J. Gardner, *A History of Jamaica. . .* (first published 1872; reprinted London: Frank Cass, 1971), p. 228.

19. Dallas, *History* I, p. 181.

20. Campbell, *The Maroons,* pp. 230–321.

21. Ibid., p. 224.

22. *JAJ,* Vol. 9, 20 and 23 December, 1795.

23. Gardner, *History of Jamaica,* p. 233.

24. CO 137/96 Balcarres to Portland, 30 January, 1796.

25. *JAJ,* Vol. 9, Walpole to Balcarres, 28 December, 1795.

26. Ibid. Vol. 9, Walpole to Balcarres, 5 and 8 January, 1796.

27. Frantz Fanon, *The Wretched of the Earth,* (New York, 1963), p. 36.

28. CO 137/96, Balcarres to Portland, April–May 1796; CO 217/67, Balcarres to Wentworth, 3 June 1796.

29. CO 267/10, Paul Le Mesurier [?] to John King, 16 August, 1796. It should be noted that the Maroons were also mentioned in this letter to be settled at the same area. For more on the Garifunas, see Nancie L. Gonzales, *Sojourners of the Caribbean: Ethnogenesis and Ethnohistory of the Garifuna* (Urbana and Chicago: University of Illinois Press, 1988), pp. 19–20.

30. Ibid.

31. Ibid. See also Michael Duffy, *Soldiers, Sugar and Seapower: The 'British' Expeditions to the West Indies and the War Against Revolutionary France* (Oxford, 1987), chapter 1 and pp. 257–63, particularly, for some of the deportations in the region.

32. CO 137/96, Maroon Petition to Balcarres, 27 April 1796.

33. These petitions, along with other primary materials on the Maroons in Nova Scotia, have now been published by this author under the title *Nova Scotia and the Fighting Maroons: A Documentary History* (Williamsburg, 1990), *passim.*

34. CO 217/67, Portland to Wentworth, 15 July 1796, was the first among a long series of communications on this matter. See also, CO 217/70, John Gray to Wentworth, 24 June, 1799. Ibid., Documents 61, 65, 66, 67, 68, 69, 70, 71, 72 etc. for a long series of communications on this matter.

35. CO 217/70, Portland to Wentworth, 8 October, 1799.

36. See note 3 above; also, entry of 22 October, 1800.

37. CO 270/5, Council Minutes, 2 October, 1800.

38. Quoted by Ellen Gibson Wilson, *The Loyal Blacks. . .* , (New York, 1976), p. 393.

39. Among others, see, CO 217/73, Portland to Wentworth, January (n.d.), 1800. W. O. 1/352, Portland to Chairman of Sierra Leone Company, 5 March, 1799.

40. The document said 13 cases but this is clearly a miscount. See An Account of Maroon Property Embarked with them from Nova Scotia to Sierra Leone, CO 217/74, Wentworth to Portland, 6 August 1800, in Campbell, *Nova Scotia and the Fighting Maroons,* Document 118.

41. Council Minutes of Sierra Leone, 2 April, 1802.

42. Ibid., 26 March, 1801.

43. Ibid., 2 June, 1801.

44. Ibid., 12 June, 1801.

45. James W. St. G. Walker, *The Black Loyalists: The Search For a Promised Land in Nova Scotia and Sierra Leone 1783–1870* (New York: Africana Publishing Co., 1976), p. 272; Fyfe, *A History of Sierra Leone,* (London, 1962), p. 108.

46. CO 267/27, Thompson to Castlereagh, 1 January, 1810.

47. A. B. C. Sibthorpe, *The History of Sierra Leone* (New York, 1970) p. 15.

48. CO 267/34, Maroon Petition to Governor and Council, 1812 (n.d.).

Chapter Seven

The Place of Sierra Leone in African Diaspora Studies

AKINTOLA J. G. WYSE

S tudies on the African diaspora, where they particularize the provenances of slaves imported to the New World, areas of slaving activity, and ethnic, cultural inputs to New World societies, have tended to concentrate on the Yoruba, Hausa, Akan, the Fon of Dahomey, Angola and Congo.[1] Sierra Leone is consigned to a footnote status, to the extent that, even when his own evidence argues the contrary, a writer claimed that 'the rivers of Sierra Leone, which continued to the east of the Guinea rivers, did not contribute any appreciable contingent to the slave trade.'[2]

Yet, given its background, not only as a receptacle for returned emancipated and rescued Africans, but also as part of the catchment area from which slaves were acquired at various times during the Atlantic slave trade, Sierra Leone is central to the African Diaspora.[3] As a home for returned Africans it epitomizes what I call the reverse drive quotient of the Atlantic crossings of the slave trading era. Also, the people on whom I will be focussing here, the Krio (Saro, as they were known in other parts of Africa), represent the cultural transfer of Western values and civilization to Africa which they themselves disseminated throughout the continent. Not only that, through their peregrinations they created their own diaspora, taking a coastal and inward sweep, a diaspora within a diaspora.[4] And they carried with them problems such as relations with autochthonous populations, and cultural transfers, which have been identified as common parameters in the global experience of returnee groups.[5]

While recognition is given here to the pioneer work of Herskovits in this area, it is also pleasing to note that more recent research efforts

---

have tried to identify and articulate the place of Sierra Leone in, and its contributions to, diaspora studies.[6] In several conferences on the diaspora, especially those organized by UNESCO, the significance of Sierra Leone in this area was highlighted. References were made to common links with societies in the Caribbean and parts of continental America, the similarities in food, dress, customs and rites; and there were calls (which still remain largely unanswered) for comparative investigations both into these societies and into the various ethnicities which formed the Krio of Sierra Leone.[7]

Scholars like Johnson Asiegbu, who have studied the Krio before, are now taking a second and even third look.[8] A course on the Atlantic slave trade and the diaspora was recently included in the syllabus of the Department of History at Fourah Bay College, and it is proving to be highly popular. A recent study by MacSam Dixon-Fyle on the Saro presence in Port Harcourt indicates a movement away from the known areas of Krio outreach in the Yoruba-speaking areas to the lesser studied areas of the eastern parts of Nigeria, the Cameroons, Fernando Po (as indicated by the articles of Browne and Lynn) and even Southern Africa.[9] And evidence coming to light suggests that Sierra Leonean groups other than the Krio have also had a presence in, for example, Calabar and Port Harcourt. Even more illuminating, a dimension of the diaspora hitherto unarticulated, is the contribution of Sierra Leone to the evolution of the Gullahs – a group of black people with a distinctive culture and speech form living in South Carolina and its sea islands, and coastal Georgia. Dramatized in the media as the Sierra Leone/Gullah connection, investigations carried out recently by this writer and others yielded interesting insights into the American connection with Sierra Leone on the one hand, and the constituents of the ancestry of the Krio on the other.[10] It has some implication for Sierra Leone historiography which tends to see the ancestors of the Krio as strangers from across the sea with no connection with people in the interior of Sierra Leone.

A detailed account of the Krio, as a dimension of the African diaspora, has been published in J. E. Harris' edited volume, *Global Dimensions of the African Diaspora* and we can only summarize it here.[11] The Krio are descendants of emancipated returnees from Britain, the Black Poor, whose release from servility was derived from the famous Lord Mansfield judgement of 1772 and the efforts of humanitarians who actually founded Sierra Leone in 1787 for their resettlement; also the New World Africans – the Nova Scotians (1792) and the Maroons (1800) – and thousands of liberated/recaptive Africans from various ethnic backgrounds in Western Africa who were rescued by the Royal Navy patrol from slave ships and resettled in Sierra Leone between 1808 and 1864. Other groups, private individuals, like Paul Cuffee, the black entrepreneur, selected Sierra Leone as a base for carrying out the programme of the back-to-Africa movement. He personally funded and mounted expeditions of immigrants to Sierra Leone, between 1811 and 1817. Certain leaders in the American establishment, for instance, Thomas Jefferson, did toy with the idea of taking over Sierra Leone from the British if they gave it up, as seemed to be a possibility at one time. As a matter of fact, the Liberian colony that was eventually established in 1822 was modelled on the ideals represented by the Sierra Leone experiment.[12]

The concept behind the founding of Sierra Leone as a haven for returned Africans displaced by the slave trade, and as a socio-cultural experiment which aimed at making the peninsula a nursery from where western values, western civilization, including Christianity, were to spread throughout 'darkest Africa', has been much discussed in various works.[13] Some have applauded the achievements of the descendants of these early converts and have praised their conquest of the human spirit.[14] Others have not been so charitable about the benefits they brought to the African societies with which they came into contact.[15] Still, once the various groups had been resettled in Sierra Leone and had been provided with the infrastructures of a western society – church, school and college, administrative structures – by British philanthropy and government agencies, and also by their own efforts, the early settlers, returnees from the New World and the recaptives, were able to evolve a society, Kriodom, that retained both much of its African past and demonstrably subscribed to the prescriptions of Western civilization. Indeed, they became cultural vectors, agents of Western civilization; and they took this wherever they went, becoming role models for the host societies.[16]

The 'Krio diaspora' is said to have begun in 1839 (though it might have started even earlier) when some recaptives, mostly Yorubas, petitioned the British government to permit them to go the lands of their ancestors, in this case Badagry, to share with their less fortunate brethren the benefits of Western civilization they had acquired in Sierra Leone.[17] Though they were refused this permission, they took the initiative of going to Badagry to spread the gospel, promote trade and generally to bring Africa into the mainstream of a world civilization. By this they anticipated the programme for the development of Afro-European relations so brilliantly articulated by the philanthropist Thomas Fowell Buxton in his *The African Slave Trade and its Remedy* (1840) and epitomized in the Niger Expedition of 1841.[18] The outreach of Sierra Leoneans dating from this period was self-propelled. In subsequent years many Sierra Leoneans were to be found in many places outside their homeland: in Yorubaland, the Gambia, the Upper Guinea, Lokoja and parts of what became Northern Nigeria, the Cameroons (Victoria), the hinterland of Sierra Leone (declared a British Protectorate in 1896), the

Congo, French West Africa, and even in South Africa. While this exodus alarmed the Revd. N. H. Boston, Colonial Chaplain in the Gambia, who complained in 1912 about 'the depopulation of Creole villages whence thousands of Sierra Leoneans [were] emigrating not only to the Protectorate and northern rivers, but into all the countries along the coast and to the Congo in the South',[19] many articulate Krio advocated the expansion of British spheres of influence and actively supported Britain's *mission civilisatrice*. Thus Dr. H. C. Bankole-Bright, a leading activist of the inter-war years, was to boast to the governor of Sierra Leone in 1926: 'If you have Nigeria today, you have to thank our fathers from Sierra Leone who were the early pioneers, and we their children are proud to think that it was under their influence that the treaties were signed by virtue of which England owns Nigeria today . . .'[20] And Christopher Fyfe has noted that 'the dynamic, expansive element in British West Africa [during the nineteenth centure] . . . was not inspired from London. It was provided by the Sierra Leone Creoles.' Some Sierra Leoneans also joined the expanding settlement for emancipated slaves established at Freretown, near Mombasa, by the British in 1864. Their descendants are still well known in that part of East Africa.[21]

The population of the Krio was never large, and because of the unavailability of statistical information it would not profit us at this stage of our knowledge to dwell on the numbers game. But accounts of areas of Krio presence studied suggest that a good number of immigrants left the peninsula. In Lagos, where the Saro were given a piece of land, Olowogbowo, to settle, it is reckoned that by 1865 they made up 20 per cent of the population of the city.[22] In the Protectorate of Sierra Leone, the Chalmers Report on the Hut Tax War of 1898, memorial tablets in churches, and sundry official documents point to the fact that hundreds of Krio immigrants were to be found in the Protectorate.[23]

Of the areas studied, the most written about is Yorubaland. And Kopytoff, Ajayi, Webster, Baker and Ayandele, to name just a few, have told us about the impact the Saro had on the host people. They were responsible for introducing Christianity in that area, they promoted education, establishing the first secondary schools, they pursued trade, and founded the first Chamber of Commerce, and they were pioneer political activists. Their ideals and activities set the tone of society.[24]

These roles were replicated in other areas of sojourn, as for example, chronicled by K. A. B. Jones-Quartey in the case of Accra.[25] Indeed, Krio immigrants produced families that became common to Freetown, Lagos, Accra, Calabar and Banjul. The Krio impact symbolized by such names as Easmon, Hayford, Renner, Dove, Dove-Edwin, Macauley and Forster, reinforced by a common educational and cultural background injected a cosmopolitanism into West African society. As J. F. A. Ajayi puts it: 'This dispersal of people from Sierra Leone to different parts of West Africa, the Gambia, Gold Coast, Lagos, the Niger, Calabar, Fernando Po, Victoria gave rise to a class of educated Africans with relations all over West Africa; thus giving a certain reality to West Africa as the political basis of their nationalism.'[26]

Accounts for other areas are not so full. A recent honours history dissertation by Yaya Jalloh makes an intriguing point that the Gambia almost became a colony of Sierra Leone, and it adds to the snippets of information about Krio immigrants contained in A. MacMillan's *Red Book of West Africa* (1968 edition).[27] The Sierra Leone presence in Victoria (Cameroon), the Congo and South Africa has yet to be investigated. Contemporary newspapers did talk about many Sierra Leoneans who went to work in the Congo and returned as 'Congo Massas', rich catches for indigent Krio girls. And Cookey also relates that the protests made by Sierra Leonean workers in Leopold's Congo led to investigations into the atrocities of the Leopoldian system.[28] We also know that Sierra Leonean workers were in German South West Africa (Namibia) and that a group of them founded the West African Club (open to all West Africans) in the Cape of Good Hope, South Africa, in 1901. Beyond this little is known about the Sierra Leone diaspora in these regions. Revd. H. M. Grace's suggestion to the Colonial Office in 1939 to investigate the Krio communities along the entire West Coast might have given us some idea of the spread of their people if the advice had been followed.[29]

Recently, interest in the Sierra Leone or Krio presence in other areas has been aroused. Findings of this author debunk the claims of some scholars that 'the Creole community tended to be more interested in the land they originally came from, especially in the case of Yorubaland, rather than its Temne, Mende or Limba neighbours.' Evidence exists that points to a strong Krio presence in the Protectorate, in the 'colonies' established, especially in railway towns, of lone Krio pastors, like P. P. Hazely and Henry O. Johnson, who sojourned for years among the Limba and Mende and the many familial relationships established between the 'settlers' and the host people.[30]

MacSam Dixon-Fyle's article on the 'Saro at Port Harcourt 1913–1949' ushers in a new dimension to studies on the Krio diaspora. Much more attention is now being shown outside the traditional areas of study, and focus is being centred on the Saro presence in the eastern parts of Nigeria, for example, Port Harcourt, Calabar, and Owerri. Apart from identifying pioneers who made notable contributions to the development of Port Harcourt, Dixon-Fyle has opened up a new perspective for investigation, and that is that not all the Sierra Leoneans in the diaspora in West Africa were Krio.[31] Although Dixon-Fyle's time-frame refers to a more recent period, it nevertheless agrees with my own observations on the Sierra Leone presence in Calabar. There I found out that non-Krios had been among those Sierra Leoneans who went to stay in Calabar in the nineteenth century. There is a place in Akpakpa, Calabar, called Mende Compound, where Mende immigrants used to settle. They produced foofoo – a derivative of cassava, used by the Krio to prepare a popular dish in their cuisine. Temne rice planters also were to be found among the Sierra Leoneans.[32] Today, there are still descendants of these settlers among the Sierra Leonean community, who continue to recognize their ancestral homes, and promote 'national solidarity', through a Sierra Leone Descendants' Union (formerly, Friendly Society). The number is small, but a few children of Efik fathers or mothers still carry such ethnic Mende names like Kenye. A visit to the cemetery at Port Harcourt revealed at least one Mende name on a tombstone – Vangahun: Pa J.N. (Vangahun) Coker or Saro Coker. What this suggests is that, at least, with reference to Calabar and Port Harcourt, it would no longer be accurate to talk about a Krio diaspora but more properly a Sierra Leone diaspora. And information about the leading Sierra Leonean citizens in Calabar, the lawyers, artisans, maritime engineers and commercial men, point to an impact no less significant than that which has been proved in the case of Yorubaland. Local people still speak fondly about the Benjamins (one of whose sons, S. E. Benjamin, is President of the Sierra Leone Descendants Union in Calabar), the Thorpes, the Joneses, the Reffels, and the Potts-Georges. The eccentric are also remembered. For example, Pa Sam Cole, a carpenter who lived in Creek Town, and populated a whole village with his wives and children. His daughter, Mama White, now an old woman, was still alive when this author was in Nigeria in 1985. Pa Haven, a midget, who worked as a clerk of Lawyer Gibson, was remembered for his habit of standing on a chair when he wanted to chastize his wife. Streets have been named after the famous, such as Gibson Street and Beccles Davies Street. Sierra Leonean lawyers also played important roles in the judicial system. Some, like A. E. Gibson, became judges.[33] Indeed, Adewoye attests that in the first quarter of this century over 60 per cent of the lawyers in Calabar were Sierra Leoneans.[34]

The Sierra Leone immigrants in Calabar were the pioneers in such technical professions as marine engineering (H. M. Harris), black-smithery (Pa Conger-Fynch), and engineering (C. W. Potts-George). The Reverends H. L. Forde, Melville Cole, Potts-Johnson, Doherty, Renner and Showers represented the clergy, and Isaac Rutherford Benjamin carried the flag for the educationalists. The press was run by a Krio, Pa Theo John. These elite were the custodians of the social register of Calabar and they sustained the civil service, for example, as legal clerks, surveyors, post masters (Barclay Macauley was Calabar's first Post Master), and marine clerks.

On the other side of the Atlantic Ocean, the work of Lorenzo Turner on African survivals in the culture of the Gullahs of South Carolina has been built upon by recent investigations on the Gullah carried out by this author and other Sierra Leonean scholars.[35] My investigation points out that many slaves in South Carolina, may have originally come from Sierra Leone. Adverts on runaway slaves include references to Temne, Limba, Kissi and Mende slaves.[36] This evidence is substantiated by documents on the slave trade which specifically mention Sierra Leone as a provenance of some of the slaves imported into South Carolina.[37] Even more intriguing, many slaves who escaped to the British lines during the American Revolution came from South Carolina, and those who signed to come to Sierra Leone from Nova Scotia in 1792 included some of these slaves. One was able to identify in the list of returnees, the Nova Scotians, a number of slaves who originally came from Sierra Leone. One of these was John Kizzell, planter, merchant, diplomatic agent of Governor Columbine and preacher, who had been captured during the American Revolution and sold to a plantation owner in South Carolina.[38] He escaped and joined the British lines. He returned to his homeland with the Nova Scotians in 1792, moved into the interior and established a church among the Sherbro. He was a collaborator of Paul Cuffee and he helped him found the Friendly Society, a mutual aid society in 1811 'to break the white stranglehold' on the Sierra Leone economy. He also acted as the contact person for the first mission of Mills and Burgess sent by the American Colonization Society in 1818 to search for a colony to resettle emancipated slaves from the United States of America – the future Liberia. As a matter of fact, John Kizzell is one documented case where a Nova Scotian immigrant freely moved between Freetown to promote his business and his other base at Camplar, Sherbroland, which became his final home. Another Nova Scotian immigrant identified from the list is David George, the Baptist leader, who escaped from Savanah to Charleston, and brought fifty-nine of his congregation to Sierra Leone.[39]

Much has still to be discovered about Kizzell, but the fact that some of the Nova Scotians had originally come from Sierra Leone points to an interesting perspective of Sierra Leone historiography which must now recognize that the Nova Scotians were not the complete strangers that they were reckoned to be, without any connection with Sierra Leone, but that they were returnees to their ancestral home. This is the reverse drive of the African diaspora – the return of people and/or their descendants who had been snatched from their natal homes and sold across the Atlantic.

The return was more than a physical rehabilitation. The returnees came back with both an acquired culture and the survivals of their African past. As participants and observers in the climate of the American Revolution, the Nova Scotians came to Sierra Leone in an independent and challenging spirit, with revolutionary ideas and with churches of their own. Their Jacobin tendencies of course put them on a collision course with their British patrons as shown in the Nova Scotian Rebellion in 1799–1800, and on other occasions.[40] They also came with skills acquired in the New World; – there were, for example, carpenters and sawyers, masons and coopers. And the farmers still retained the skills related to rice technology which their ancestors had taken with them to the New World.[41] So it was not surprising that when the Nova Scotians came, they planted rice on the slopes of Wansey Hill, renamed Tower Hill in 1805. Isaac Anderson, a revolutionary leader of the Nova Scotians, for example, sent casks of rice to John Clarkson, the man who brought the Nova Scotians to Sierra Leone. And when the British suppressed their Nova Scotian rebels after their second rebellion in 1802, they killed the 'finest African farmers in the Sierra Leone Settlement.'[42]

The significance of the Nova Scotians in the study of the diaspora is that they provided the western background of the ancestors of the Krio, and were the group to whose social prescriptions all subsequent immigrant groups, which eventually made up Krio society, had to acknowledge and conform.[43] They also initiated the outreach of their descendants into the surrounding areas as they went into the interior as teachers, traders and as refugees.[44] But much more important, they presented an identifiable link between Sierra Leone and the Gullahs of South Carolina. Interest in this Gullah connection has mounted increasingly, and much is being made of it in the media and official circles in Sierra Leone. Further, with the publications of scholars like Littlefield, a new investigative approach has been supplied on the Sierra Leone contribution in the New World, both materially and culturally. Studies by Beltran and King, for instance, tell us about large contingents of Sierra Leone slaves in various Latin American societies.[45] If the trend continues, we expect to see a body of literature that would particularize and identify the Sierra Leonean provenance of slave societies in the New World as has been done, for example in the case of Nigeria and Ghana. While older works by George Walker and Helen Gibson Wilson on the Nova Scotians have sufficiently documented this New World returnee group in the history of Sierra Leone, Mavis Campbell's recent effort on the Maroons should complement studies on the diaspora from the other side of the Atlantic on two major constituents of the society which evolved in the Sierra Leone peninsula.[46]

Although Michael Crowder himself did not study Sierra Leone from the perspective of the diaspora, he was keenly interested in the Krio. He published an article on the formation and structure of their society in 1958 and made references to their presence in various parts of Africa in several of his books.[47] And before he died he was working on the American connection with Sierra Leone seen through the career of the Revd. Edward Jones, the Amherst graduate who was the first black Principal of Fourah Bay College, 1841–60.[48] He also played host to me when I delivered, at his invitation, a lecture on 'The Sierra Leone-Gullah Connection: Documented or Conjectured?' at Amherst in December 1987 and he sent me a copy of an article in the *National Geographic Magazine* of December 1987 ('nowhere to lay down weary head') which was of some relevance to my Gullah investigation. We had useful discussions on how the unarticulated American dimension of the Sierra Leone diaspora could be highlighted. And had he lived, his ideas would have surely taken a more positive shape. But wherever he now reposes in a well-earned rest, the spirit of Michael Crowder will be assured that Sierra Leonean historians are taking up the challenges.

I am sure that he would not disagree with my conclusion that Sierra Leone is central in diaspora studies. It holds this important place, not only because the Krio, apart from having their own diaspora, epitomize a dimension of the global diaspora, but also because Sierra Leone reflects the many ramifications of Afro-European relations deriving from the Atlantic slave trade. As a repository of returned Africans, the reverse drive of the Atlantic crossings, it provides a good background for studies of cultural interpretation on the one hand, and on ethnicity, on the other, such as those of Koelle in his *Polyglotta Africana*, and subsequent scholars like Herskovits, Little, Curtin and Vansina.[49] The revolt of Sengbe Pieh in 1839 and his seizure of the *Amistad* slave ship taking him and his fellow Sierra Leoneans to slavery in the New World, the protests of Sierra Leone immigrants in the Congo against the horrid rule of Leopold I of Belgium, and documented protest activities elsewhere in West Africa, contained in general works on the political history of West Africa, are dimensions of Sierra Leone's contribution to the black man's fight against slavery and white overrule.[50]

Finally, although it has been suggested that Sierra Leone did not make a major contribution to Pan-Africanism, we should remember the activities and opinions of men like Edward Blyden, the West Indian pan-Negro patriot and guru of African cultural nationalism, who adopted Sierra Leone as his home, of Orishatukeh Faduma, the American-trained educationalist, and of many others who identified with Marcus Garvey's movement for the global emancipation of the black man. Their achievements are sufficiently known not to delay us here, but mention is made of them to remind us that, if we are to take an overall view of the African diaspora, Sierra Leone did not play a negligible role in it.[51]

Notes

1. This perception is evident in general works on the diaspora. For example, while most references would be made to specific Gold Coast/Coromantine, Senegambia, Igbo, Yoruba or Fon, Congo or Angola inputs, few would cite specific Sierra Leonean

provenances. Except for these few, Sierra Leonean inputs are hidden in generic or geographical terms which refer to slaves from the Guinea Coast, the Windward Coast or simply Africa, etc. But see a selection of works: Graham W. Irwin, *Africans abroad: a documentary history of the Black Diaspora in Asia, Latin America and the Caribbean during the age of slavery*, (New York, 1977); Herbert S. Klein, *African Slavery in Latin America and the Caribbean*, (London, 1986); for some references to Sierra Leone slaves: M. J. Herskovits, 'On the provenience of New World Negroes', *Social Forces*, XII, December 1933, pp. 247–62; 'The Significance of West Africa for Negro Research', *Journal of Negro History* (hereafter *JNH*), January 1936, pp. 15–29; Donald D. Wax, 'Preferences for Slaves in Colonial America', *JNH*, LVIII, October 1973, pp. 371–401; Allan Kulikoff, 'The Origins of Afro-American Society in Tide Water Maryland and Virginia, 1700–90', *William and Mary Quarterly*, 3rd Series, XXXV, April 1978, pp. 226–59; cf. W. R. Higgins, 'The South Carolina Negro Duty Law', M.A. thesis, University of South Carolina, 1967; Joseph E. Holloway, 'The origins of the Afro-American Culture (Mimeo) 42 pp; John Bennett Papers (Notes and Scrapbooks deposited in the South Carolina Historical Society Archives, Charleston, S.C.) for references to the 'indolent Timani' and the 'big headed Veys'; D.C. Littlefield, *Rice and Slaves: ethnicity and the slave trade in Colonial South Carolina* (London, 1981) gives some statistics of Sierra Leonean slaves, but conveys an impression of marginality about Sierra Leonean inputs, p. 113. However, documentary evidence of Sierra Leone imports can be obtained from Elizabeth Donnan, *Documents illustrative of the history of the Slave Trade to America* (Washington, 1935) Vol. IV; Philip M. Hamer and George C. Rogers Jr. (eds), *The Papers of Henry Laurens* (Columbia, 1970), II and III and other editions, Vols. IV–IX (1974–1981). Philip D. Morgan, 'The development of slave culture in 18th century plantation America', Ph.D. thesis, University of London 1977, discusses the cultural sustenance of African slaves without specifying tribal provenances. But see M. G. Smith, 'The African heritage in the Caribbean', in Vera Robin (ed), *Caribbean Studies: A Symposium* (Seattle: 1957), p. 35; Roger Bastide, *African Civilization in the New World* (London: 1971); Charles Joyner, *Down by the Riverside: A South Carolina Slave Community* (Chicago: Urbana, 1984), Chapter 7; Davey Pavy, 'The provenience of Columbia Negroes' *JNH*, LII, 1 January 1967, pp. 36–58.

2. G. Aguirre Beltran, 'Tribal origins of slaves in Mexico', *JNH* XXI, 3, July 1946, pp. 269–352; cf. W. Robert Higgins, 'The geographical origins of Negro Slaves in Colonial South Carolina', *The South Atlantic Quarterly*, LXX, 1971, Winter, No. 1, pp. 34–47; Elizabeth Donnan, 'The Slave Trade into South Carolina before the Revolution', *American Historical Review*, July, 1928, XXXIII, 53, pp. 804–28; M. J. Herskovitz, 'The present status and needs of Afro-American research', *JNH*, XXXVI, 2, April 1951, pp. 123–47.

3. E. Donnan, *Documents illustrative* IV; Capt. William Snelgrave, *A new account of some parts of Guinea and the slave trade* (1734), (London: Frank Cass, 1971 edition); John Mathews, *A voyage to the River Sierra Leone*, (London, 1788 (2nd ed. 1971)); Walter Rodney, *A History of the Upper Guinea Coast, 1545–1800* (Oxford, 1970); 'Upper Guinea and the significance of the origins of Africans in the New World', *JNH*, LIV, 4, 1969, pp. 329–45; Adam Jones, *From Slaves to Palm Kernels: A History of the Galinhas Country, 1730–1890* (Wiesbaden, 1983), and Marian Johnson, 'Slaves from the Windward Coast', *Journal of African History* (hereafter *JAH*), 21, 1, 1980, pp. 17–34; Nicholas Owen, *Journal of a Slave Dealer: a review of some remarkable axcedents in the life of Nics. Owen on the coast of Africa and America from the year 1746 to the year 1757*, edited with an introduction by Eveline Martin, (London, 1930). F. W. Butt-Thompson's claim (*Sierra Leone in History and Tradition*, (London, 1926), p. 16 that Andrew Battell found a camp of 500 Temne slaves from Sierra Leone in the Congo in 1589 is yet to be corroborated.

4. C. Fyfe, *A History of Sierra Leone*, (London, 1962). 'Reform in West Africa: the abolition of the slave trade' in J. F. A. Ajayi and M. Crowder (eds), *History of West Africa*, (London, 1974) II, pp. 30–56; 'The dynamics of African Diaspora: the transatlantic slave trade', in M. Kilson and Robert I. Rotberg (eds), *The African Diaspora: interpretative essays* (Harvard University Press, 1976), pp. 57–74; P. E. H. Hair, 'Áfricanism: the Freetown Contribution', *Journal of Modern African Studies* (hereafter *JMAS*), V, 1967, pp. 521–39; J. W. St. George Walker, *The Black Loyalists: the Search for a promised land in Nova Scotia and Sierra Leone, 1785–1870* (London, 1976); T. F. V. Buxton, 'The Creole in West Africa', *Journal of the African Society* (hereafter *JAS*), XII, 1912–1913, pp. 385–94; K. L. Little, 'The Significance of the West African Creole for Africans and Afro-American Studies', *African Affairs*, 49, 197, 1950, pp. 308–19; *Sierra Leone Guardian and Foreign Mails (SLGFM)*, 21 March, 1919.

5. Joseph E. Harris (ed), *Global dimensions of the African Diaspora* (Washington, 1982).

6. Herskovits, references cited in note 1 above and *The Myth of the Negro Past* (1941) 4th printing, (Boston, 1967); A. J. G. Wyse, 'The Krios of Siera Leone from the perspective of the African diaspora' in Harris (ed) *Global dimensions*, pp. 309–37; Fyfe, 'Reform in West Africa.'

7. See, for example, papers presented at the Diaspora Conference at Howard University, Washington, 1979, published in Harris (ed), *Global Dimensions*; Final Report on the *UNESCO Conference on 'The African Cultural presence in the Caribbean and in North and South America, Bridgetown (Barbados)*, 21–25 January, 1980; Final Report on the *UNESCO Conference on 'The Cultural Contributions of Blacks of the Diaspora to Africa'*, Cotonou (Benin), 21–25 March, 1983.

8. J. U. J. Asiegbu, *Sierra Leone Creoles in British Nigeria Revisited, 1857–1920* (published by Lantern Books and Blackwells, 1984) is a companion book to his earlier effort, *Slavery and the Politics of Liberation, 1787–1861* (London, 1969), personal communication, 9 May, 1984.

9. MacSam Dixon-Fyle, 'The Saro in the political life of early Port Harcourt; 1913–1949', *JAH*, 30, 1989, pp. 125–38; Robert T. Browne, 'Fernando Po and the Anti-Sierra Leone Campaign, 1828–34', *International Journal of African Historical Studies*, VI, 1973, pp. 249–64; Martin Lynn, 'Commerce, Christianity and the Origins of the "Creoles" of Fernando Po', *JAH*, 25, 1984, pp. 253–78.

10. The findings of this writer have not yet been published, but his comments have been publicized in two public lectures at Amherst College, Mass., 3 December 1987, 'The Sierra Leone/Gullah connection: linkages – conjectured or documented?' and at the USIS Auditorium, Embassy of the USA, Freetown, 17 February 1988, 'The Sierra Leone/Gullah Connection: some historical and linguistic pointers.' See also media coverage: The *Miami Herald*, 21/1/88; *Greenboro News and Record*, 29/1/88, *Daily Times – News*, 21/1/88; *The New York Times*, 25/10/87.

11. Wyse, 'The Krios of Sierra Leone . . . African diaspora', and *Searchlight on the Krio of Sierra Leone*, (Inst. of African Studies Occasional Papers, No. 3, Fourah Bay College, 1980) 42 pp.

12. Fyfe, *A History of Sierra Leone*, op. cit.; Fyfe and Jones (eds), *Freetown: a symposium* (Freetown, 1968); Arthur Porter, *Creoledom* (London, 1963); J. Peterson, *Province of Freedom: A History of Sierra Leone, 1787–1870* (Evanston, Ill., 1969); L. Spitzer, *The Creoles of Sierra Leone: responses to colonialism, 1870–1945* (Wisconsin, 1974); A. J. G. Wyse, *The Krio of Sierra Leone: an interpretive history*, (London, 1989) offer a good background study here. For the American angle see Lamont D. Thomas, *Rise to be a people: a biography of Paul Cuffee* (University of Illinois Press, 1986); R. West, *Back to Africa: a history of Sierra Leone and Liberia* (New York, 1970); Mary Beth Norton, 'The fate of some black loyalists of the American Revolution', *JNH*, LVIII, Oct. 1973,

pp. 402–26; Archibald Alexander, D.D., *A History of Colonization on the Western Coast of Africa* (Philadelphia, 1846). For accounts of the Barbados men (1819) and the Ascension men (1828) see Capt. F. W. Butt-Thompson, *The first generation of Sierra Leoneans* (Sierra Leone, 1926), pp. 39–40.

13. Ibid., J. D. Hargreaves, *A Life of Sir Samuel Lewis* (London, 1958).

14. J. F. A. Ajayi, *Christian Missions in Nigeria 1841–91: the making of a new elite* (Evanston, Illinois, 1965) and 'The development of secondary Grammar School Education in Nigeria', *Journal of the Historical Society of Nigeria (JHSN)*, II, 4, December 1965, pp. 317–35; 'Origins of Nigerian Nationalism', *JHSN*, II, 4, 1961, pp. 196–210; Hair, 'Africanism', Elizabeth Isichei, *The Ibo people and the Europeans: the genesis of a relationship to 1906* (London, 1973), p. 91.

15. For instance, E. A. Ayandele, *The missionary impact on modern Nigeria, 1842–1914* (London, 1966), and *The educated elite in the Nigerian Society* (Ibadan, 1974); 'James Africanus Beale Horton, 1835–1883: prophet of modernisation in West Africa', *African Historical Studies*, IV, 3, 1971, pp. 691–707. But see Bolande Awe's summarization, 'The cultural contributions of the blacks of the diaspora to Africa, with special emphasis on Nigeria', paper presented at the *UNESCO Conference on The Cultural Contributions of the blacks of the Diaspora to Africa, Cotonou (Benin)*, 21–25 March 1983, 12 pp.

16. See cited works of Fyfe and Wyse, for example, in Note 12 above; J.H. Kopytoff, *A Preface to Modern Nigeria: The Sierra Leoneans in Yoruba, 1830–90* (Wisconsin, 1965); Pauline Baker, *Urbanization and Political Change: The Politics of Lagos, 1947–1967* (Berkeley, 1974); Patrick Cole, *Modern and Traditional Elites in the Politics of Lagos* (London, 1975).

17. Note 16 above; Carl Campbell, 'John Mohammed Bath and the free Madingoes in Trinidad: the question of their repatriation to Africa, 1831–8', *Journal of African Studies*, IV, Winter 1975/76, pp. 476–95; N.I.K. Eleady-Cole, 'Education in Sierra Leone, 1787–1914', M.A. thesis, London, 1967, p. 49; Asiegbu, *Slavery and the Politics of Liberation*.

18. C. Fyfe, 'Four Sierra Leone Recaptives', *JAH*, 2, 1, 1961, pp. 77–85; J. B. Webster, 'The Bible and the Plough,' *JHSN*, II, 4, Dec. 1965, pp. 418–34.

19. *SLWN*, 7, September 1912.

20. J. D. Hargreaves, *A life of Sir Samuel Lewis: Sierra Leone Legislative Council Debates*, 9 December 1926; C. Fyfe, *A History of Sierra Leone, op. cit.*, p. 462; A. J. G. Wyse, 'The Krio Factor in West African History', *The Calabar Historical Journal*, III, 1, September 1985, pp. 109–35.

21. Quote is from C. Fyfe, *Africanus Horton: West African Scientist and Patriot* (Oxford, 1972), p. 17. The Sierra Leone input in Freretown is mentioned in Joseph E. Harris, *West African Slave Trade and repatriation in Kenya*, pamphlet, Howard University, 1974. 31 pp.

22. Baker, *Urbanization*, p. 21; J. B. Webster *et al*, *The revolutionary years: West Africa since 1800* (London, 1980 edition), p. 137. R. R. Kuczynski's *Demographic Survey of the British Colonial Empire, West Africa* (London, 1948) Vol. 1, as I have argued in *The Krio of Sierra Leone*, Ch. II is not reliable as a census guide.

23. A. J. G. Wyse, 'An investigation into negative reports on Krio impact in the interior of Sierra Leone' (Mimeo); cf. Elizabeth Isiahei, *History of West Africa since 1800* (Hong Kong, 1977), p. 135.

24. See cited works in notes 12, 14, 16, 18, 20, 21 and 22 above; A. G. Hopkins, 'The Lagos Chamber of Commerce, 1886–1903', *JHSN*, III, 2, December 1965, pp. 365–76.

25. K. A. B. Jones-Quartey, 'Sierra Leone's role in the development of Ghana, 1820–1930', *Sierra Leone Studies (SLS)*, 10, 1958, pp. 73–83.

26. Quoted in Ajayi, 'Origins of Nigerian Nationalism', pp. 196–210; J. D. Hargreaves, 'The Creoles and the expansion of Sierra Leone: a sub imperialism manqué', in *Études Africaines offertes a Henri Brunschwig* (Paris, Eness, 1982), pp. 225–33 discusses Krio outreach to Francophone West Africa.

27. Yaya Jalloh, 'The Gambia-Sierra Leone relations, 1787–1987' B.A. Hons. Hist. Diss. (1988).

28. *SLWN*, 25 May, 1901; 31 December 1910; S. J. ·S. Cookey, 'West African Immigrants in the Congo', *JHSN*, III, 2, 1965, pp. 261–70.

29. CO267/674/32010 Jardinè to MacDonald, 11 December 1939. Min. by Revd. H. M. Grace.

30. See note 23; P. E. H. Hair, 'Freetown and the Study of West African Languages, 1800–79', *Bulletin d'Ifan* 21, 3/4 July–October 1959, pp. 579–86.

31. See note 9 above.

32. Research notes collected by this author while in Calabar, Nigeria.

33. Interviews with Sierra Leonean descendants conducted by the author in Calabar, 1985.

34. O. Adewoye, 'Sierra Leonean immigrants in the field of law in Southern Nigeria, 1862–1934', *SLS* (NS), 26, January 1970, pp. 11–26.

35. The others are Dr Joko Sengova, a linguist, and Dr Cyrus Macfoy, a botanist. The latter made a comparative investigation of herbs, plants and other pharmacopoeia in South Carolina which may be similar to certain flora in Sierra Leone. See Lorenzo Turner, *Africanisms in the Gullah dialect* (1949), Reprinted, New York, 1969.

36. Eighteenth-century newspapers in South Carolina used to advertise runaway slaves, paying attention to their physical features and making references to their ethnicity. Those consulted and which specifically identified Temne, Limba and Kissi slaves, for instance, were the *South Carolina Gazette and Country Journal, South Carolina Gazette*, and *South Carolina Weekly Gazette* (1730s–1780s in microfilm, South Carolineana Library, Columbia, SC); G. Heuman (ed), *Out of the House of bondage: Runaways, resistance and marronage in Africa and the New World* (London, 1986).

37. Donnan, *Documents*, IV; *Henry Laurens Papers*, III–VIII.

38. A set of documents entitled 'List of blacks in Birth Town who gave in their names for Sierra Leone in 1791' (CO217/63, Public Record Office, London), by courtesy of C. Fyfe, has a list of 518 and 26 (who got to Halifax by stealth) slaves from Birth Town who gave up their names for Sierra Leone in 1791. The actual number on the list is 155. Of these, 49 were African-born, and Isaac Anderson, John Gordon, John Kizzell, Frank Peters, and Mingo Leslie, for instance, were among those who actually arrived in Sierra Leone in 1792. Another set of documents containing names of slaves, over 3,000 who were admitted into the British areas of control after the cessation of hostilities following the American War of Independence in 1783 is in microfilm in the Central Library of the University of South Carolina (M-154-29 British Headquarters Papers, Sir Guy Carleton Papers # 10386 (3) - # 10437 (275) Book of Negroes registered . . . 1783) See also Alexander, *A History of Colonization*, p. 71 who refers to the Nova Scotians as 'fugitive slaves of the Southern States who . . . transferred in mass to the western Coast of Africa'; Benjamin Brawley, *A Social history of the American Negro*, (New York, 1921), pp. 173–4.

39. L. D. Thomas, *Paul Cuffee*, pp. 53–5; Benjamin Brawley, *The Negro in the American Revolution*, (Chapel Hill, 1961), pp. 163–167; Ellen Gibson Wilson, *The Loyal Blacks*, New York, 1976, pp. 368–370.

40. On the Nova Scotian impact, see St. George Walker, *The Black Loyalists*; Ellen Gibson Wilson, *The Loyal Blacks*; A. F. Walls, 'The Nova Scotian Settlers and their Religion', *Sierra Leone Bulletin of Religion*, I, 2, December 1959, pp. 19–31.

41. CO217/63 List of blacks in Birth Town.

42. Ellen Gibson Wilson, *The Loyal Blacks*, p. 400.

43. Wyse, *The Krio of Sierra Leone*.

44. C. Fyfe, 'European and Creole influence in the hinterland of Sierra Leone before 1896', *SLS* (NS), 6, June 1955, pp. 77–85; A. Ijagbemi, 'The Freetown Colony and the

Development of 'Legitimate Commerce' in Adjoining Territories', *JHSN*, 5, 2, June 1970, pp. 247–65.

45. C. Littlefield, *Rice and Slaves*; Beltran, 'Tribal Origins of Slaves in Mexico'; J. F. King, 'Descriptive data on Negro Slaves in Spanish importation records and Bills of Sale', *JNH*, XXVIII, 2 April, 1943, pp. 204–230.

46. Mavis Campbell, *The Maroons of Jamaica: a history of resistance, collaboration and betrayal* (Third World, 1989).

47. M. Crowder, 'An African Aristocracy', *Geographical Magazine* XXXI, 4, August 1958, pp. 183–90.

48. M. Crowder, 'From Amherst to Fourah Bay: Principal Edward Jones', paper presented at the *International Symposium on Sierra Leone*, 19–21 May 1987, 25 pp. This author has (in mimeo) a short piece on 'Edward Jones: Amherst's first black graduate in Sierra Leone, 1831–64' 13 pp. I understand that Dr Davidson Nicol is working on Jones, and he has a short article on 'An Afro-American Educator and Traveller in the 19th century: the Revd. Edward Jones' (Mimeo). 19 pp.

49. S. W. Koelle, *Polyglotta Africana*, (London, 1854). Reprinted with an introduction by P. E. H. Hair (Freetown, 1963); P. Curtin and Jan Vansina, 'Sources of the Nineteenth Century Atlantic Slave Trade', *JAH*, V, 2, 1964, pp. 165–208, J. R. Griffith 'On the races inhabiting Sierra Leone'. (Paper in Sierra Leone Collection, Fourah Bay College Library, Mt. Aureol, C. 1886.)

50. On Sengbe Pieh and the Amistad revolt, see W. E. B. DuBois, *The Suppression of the African Slave Trade to America, 1638–1870* (Mass. 1896). Reprinted, New York, 1969; Lewis Tappan, *Life of Arthur Tappan*, (New York, 1871). Arthur Abraham, 'Sengbe Pieh: a neglected Hero?' *Journal of the Historical Society of Sierra Leone* II, 2, July 1978, pp. 22–30. Krio political activities in West Africa are discussed in most standard works, but see Ian Duffield, 'John Eldred Taylor and West African Opposition to indirect rule in Nigeria', *African Affairs*, 70, 280, July 1971, pp. 252–68; E. A. Ayandele, *African Historical Studies*, (London, 1979).

51. G. Cleo Hanciles, 'Sierra Leone's contribution to the growth and development of conscious Africanism', M.A. thesis, Sierra Leone, 1979, I. Geiss, *The Pan African Movement*, (London 1968); R. W. July, *The Origins of modern African thought*, (London, 1968).

Chapter Eight

The Lebanese in Colonial West Africa

TOYIN FALOLA

In *West Africa Under Colonial Rule*,[1] Michael Crowder provides a five-page synthesis on the Lebanese in West Africa. His main concern was to show that the Lebanese, beginning from the 1920s, controlled the West African retail trade by displacing African and European traders. He explains why the Lebanese were able to achieve this, and his overall assessment of their contribution is very positive:

> . . . their role in opening up West Africa to increased international trade cannot be exaggerated. Where European firms were too timid, or African businessmen lacked the resources, they pioneered new markets.[2]

As much as possible, I intend to follow Crowder's outline. I will expand on his synthesis and fill some of the gaps by developing new themes – on race relations, conflicts, and socio-cultural issues. The historical context is also retained, that is, immigrants in colonial Africa.

Migration and mobility

From the second half of the nineteenth century to the present the Lebanon (known as the Province of Syria in the nineteenth century), has witnessed massive migrations of its citizens to Africa, Persia, India, China, Japan, Australia, USA, the British Isles, and South and Central America.[3] These migrations stemmed from a combination of factors, the primary one being the quest to escape from poverty.[4] Hanna has shown that most of the Lebanese migrants were so poor that they had to raise loans to be able to travel and had to repay and remit money to Lebanon to sustain members of the families they had left behind.[5] However, as education improved in Lebanon, the middle class joined in the migration, though most went to the USA.[6] Irrespective of their previous occupation in Lebanon, the majority of the migrants took to commerce and compared to their previous condition, many, prospered greatly in their new homes.

For the earliest immigrants, the choice of West Africa was accidental or unintended. Their preferred destinations were either Brazil or the United States, through Marseilles. Many found their way to Dakar and later to other places because they lacked adequate funds or documents to travel to the US or Brazil. Some failed the health tests or were simply ignorant of their destinations.[7]

The Lebanese presence was noticed in West Africa in the 1880s.[8] Once there, most decided to settle as they could not return home or because they had found a solution to poverty, and because they could remit money to repay their debts in Lebanon.[9] The initial settlers established the communities that attracted other Lebanese and the Lebanese communities grew rapidly. The number of immigrants is difficult to calculate because most available data cover those who travelled by ship or by air (from the 1950s) and not by land; the records on immigration were better kept after the 1920s but those on deaths and births are inadequate, and the Lebanese were not too eager to disclose the numbers of their families and relations.

However, we have sufficient data to indicate the growth of migration, and understand the pattern. From the few figures available from the late nineteenth century, it is clear that the number rose substantially during the colonial period, and the Lebanese were in virtually all the West African countries by the First World War. In French West Africa, from 28 in 1897 the figure rose to 276 in 1900, 1,110 in 1909 and over 3,000 in 1929. In Guinea, the number rose from 2 in 1892 to 163 in 1900, 697 in 1909, 909 in 1930, and 1367 in 1936.[10] In 1897, 10 were reported for Senegal but by 1960 the figure had risen to 10,000.[11] In Nigeria, from a figure of 90 in 1911 it grew to 1,250 in 1959.[12] A pro-Lebanese source put the total figure for 1960 at 13,900 for the English-speaking countries and 17,200 for the French-speaking.[13] In 1962, the Lebanese Foreign Ministry issued its own official census as follows: Senegal (10,170), Nigeria (6,150), Guinea (3,008), Sierra Leone (2,900), Liberia (2,697), Ghana (2,200), Ivory Coast (1,854), Portuguese Guinea (1,050), Gambia (650) and the Republic of Benin (95).[14]

The remarkable migration of the Lebanese is owed to many sources. First, the success of the pioneers encouraged others to follow. The pioneers were quick to advertise their success, through letters which exaggerated their achievements and stories which romanticized their life-styles in their new homes.[15] Second, the economy of West Africa grew during the colonial period, at a time when Lebanon was experiencing great difficulties, especially in the 1930s and 1940s. In the words of Fuad Khuri, the slogan became 'those who fail their future in Lebanon search for it in Africa'.[16] Third, in the 1920s and 1930s, USA, the country most favoured by the migrants, reduced the immigration prospects of the Lebanese who were then forced to explore other places.[17] Finally, migrants in West Africa sponsored others from Lebanon. Relations and friends were provided with information and money to travel. To the Lebanese, kinship was an important factor in emigration and the organization of business. Kinship provided labour (for use by the entrepreneur), capital and credit (the sponsor was expected to assist with money and trade goods when a new shop was to be established), and marriage partners, since many Lebanese, especially the Muslims, married from within their lineages.[18]

Because kinship played such a large role in the migrations, Lebanese from the same region and religion settled in the same areas in West Africa. For example, settlers in Dakar were from Tyre (South Lebanon), those in Accra were from Tripoli (North Lebanon), those in Kano from Juwaiyya (South Lebanon) and those in Calabar and Lagos were mainly from Mizyara in North Lebanon.

The patterns of migrations were more complex after the initial ones of the nineteenth century.[19] Throughout the colonial period, three patterns of migration were constant and simultaneous: migrations from other continents, notably from Asia; migrations from within West Africa; and internal migrations within a country.

In the first inter-continental pattern, the majority of the Lebanese came from Asia, and a few others from Egypt, Argentina and Venezuela. There were outward flows as well, again mainly to Lebanon, though many (as high as 20 per cent in Sierra Leone) went to Europe and North America. The preference was for Britain and France, mainly because of associations with the citizens, and knowledge, of these countries. The reasons for outward flow included the need for retirement, investments elsewhere and diminishing opportunities in West Africa.

The Lebanese changed locations within West Africa, giving rise to a second pattern of migration which was intra-regional. This pattern of migrations suggests that the Lebanese were aware of opportunities in many countries, and had a network which made it possible to share information and arrange the migrations. Countries such as Burkina Faso, Mali and Sudan received the Lebanese probably from the French coastal territories of Senegal, Ivory Coast and the Republic of Benin. During the Second World War, when French West Africa had problems of supplies of imported goods, many Lebanese traders travelled to Liberia,

Sierra Leone, and Portuguese Guinea. Their economic interests included smuggling trade goods, and scarce CFA currency, later to be resold at high profits. In the 1950s the lucrative diamond industry in Ghana, Sierra Leone, Guinea, Liberia and Ivory Coast stimulated extensive intra-regional migrations to participate in this industry, either as smugglers or legitimate dealers.

The third pattern of migration was movement between towns and villages in the same country to exploit and extend commercial opportunities. Up until the First World War many Lebanese avoided the hinterland but when knowledge of the potential became known, and transport facilities improved, the Lebanese began to penetrate with vigour. Those who dealt in produce travelled extensively because of the need to collect goods, and transport them to depots. The railways provided the best opportunity: not only did the Lebanese use them to travel, but they turned the stations into markets, selling as hawkers or by setting up mobile shops. From the 1920s onward the use of lorries led to a deeper penetration of the hinterland. In the 1950s, the Lebanese began to withdraw from the villages to concentrate their activities in the cities. In the case of Sierra Leone, Laan has suggested that the withdrawal was caused by the preference for better facilities and housing, in the cities, the reduction in transport costs, and the increase in the use of private cars.[20] Some of these reasons are of wider application. For instance, it is true that the increase in the use of lorries made it possible to transport goods from many places to a central location, instead of duplicating stores in many villages. The use of private cars by the affluent Lebanese not only made living in the city more attractive but it was easier to travel to the villages and return to the city after business transactions. The improvement in housing, with the best houses located in the cities with better social services and communication facilities, also made the successful Lebanese prefer city life. The Lebanese were among the landlords of these new houses, rightly described by Crowder as 'large and hideous unarchitectured concrete-block houses, with crude concrete verandahs, painted in gaudy colours'.[21]

To minimize the conflicts generated by the Lebanese migrations and mobility, the colonial governments used immigration ordinances to check the influx and monitor the activities of the migrants. In the 1920s the colonial governments insisted on the registration of aliens – defined as foreigners with no connection with the colonial metropolises.[22] A migrant then required a passport and visa, evidence of physical fitness, and a deposit of a sum of money to meet the cost of repatriation. The enforcement of these regulations varied from one country to another, and with the ingenuity of the Lebanese at manipulating the immigration rules. Throughout the colonial period, immigration rules were revised to make the conditions of entry more difficult, especially under the pressure of nationalist movements after 1945.

In his contemporary study of the economy of British West Africa from 1949 to 1952, Peter Bauer concluded that the immigration regulations were inimical to Lebanese economic activities because new Lebanese were refused entry; those on the ground would find it difficult to expand because of lack of access to non-African staff; while the Lebanese importers could not expand the scope of their businesses.[23] In the 1950s the general policy was to prevent the entry of migrants who had little money to invest.

To overcome immigration problems and protect their investments, the Lebanese explored the options of naturalization. This became a political issue, and the colonial governments were very cautious in approving the applications. For instance in Nigeria, three applications were successful in 1945 and fifteen in 1959.[24] In Sierra Leone, the government refused to process applications after 1930. In the dying years of colonial rule, the policy was to enable Africans to progress 'without the eventual complications of pressure from powerful and strongly entrenched non-African interests'.[25] The nationalists were allowed to negotiate the conditions for the continued stay of the Lebanese, and some of the agreements became part of the independence constitutions. The Afro-Lebanese were treated as citizens while provisions were made in the various constitutions for naturalization.

Lebanese ventures

None of the Lebanese businesses in the early years was big. The early migrants had little or no capital, skill, or access to credit to bring them any early success. And they had neither the language nor the qualifications to find wage employment. Therefore the early migrants dealt in very small imported items – cheap and fake goods. Many of them sold coral beads, from which they got their popular name of 'coral men', believed to have been coined by the Creoles of Sierra Leone. The choice of such items was an excellent strategy. Consumers who appreciated imported items but had little purchasing power turned to the Lebanese for imitations and small quantities. The Lebanese did not create a new trade but simply exploited existing structures by concentrating on sectors and people not adequately catered for by the African and European traders. By paying little or no rents on shops, working hard as hawkers and peddlers, making low profits and living cheaply, the early Lebanese traders were able both to survive and to expand. Lack of data on the early immigrants makes it difficult to analyze the process of capital formation; but what is clear is that the Lebanese promoted and intensified dependence on the European firms for trade goods and on the Africans for customers.

By about 1920, many of the migrants had achieved some success. In Senegal, the ten Lebanese in 1897 were described as poor. However, by the beginning of this century not only did their numbers increase but they had also established a monopoly on retail trade in St. Louis.[26] In Guinea, they were successful in the rubber trade; two of them were mentioned in the trade in 1898, and the number grew to 150 in 1899 and 600 in 1904. Their French rivals lost to them because the Lebanese were willing to pay higher prices to producers. In Sierra Leone, where no Lebanese was reported to be a successful merchant in the 1890s, by the second decade of this century, they had become so prominent that they had shops in twenty-four towns and were heavily involved in general merchandise, rice and kola.[27]

In the decades that followed, the Lebanese expanded in many areas of commerce. In the 1920s they consolidated their hold on retail and middleman trade. Together with the European traders, the Lebanese dominated the exchange sector of the economy. Except in Ghana and south-western Nigeria where Africans were active in the cocoa trade, the Lebanese became the most prominent middlemen in West Africa. Success in trade promoted the diversification into other sectors such as mining and manufacture.

Most of the Lebanese were involved in general merchandise, that is, trade in imported manufactured items. The shops of the Lebanese were located in the business districts of many towns, from where they were able to reach hundreds of urban dwellers and establish contacts with the villages. The Lebanese also recruited agents, mainly Africans, who carried the goods to remote villages. In periods of slump, the Lebanese themselves moved out to the villages to hawk their products.

Pedlar has pointed out that a successful Lebanese retailer could at the same time be a wholesaler or semi-wholesaler.[28] A Lebanese trader did not make a neat distinction between wholesale and retail. A successful Lebanese shopkeeper not only sold in small quantities to his customers but could sell in bulk as well to the other Lebanese, African retailers, and his own agents. The big Lebanese shopkeepers bought goods in large quantities from the European traders while a few of them were able to import direct from Europe. The ambition of a Lebanese trader was to become an importer, and some succeeded, especially in the 1950s, when exchange control and import licenses were liberalized. Many did not succeed as importers because the European companies were better organized in this sector, and the Lebanese lacked the necessary capital and access to manufacturers in Europe. The Lebanese who engaged in the import trade added to their skill the knowledge of bookkeeping, advertising, making contacts with manufacturers and writing business letters.

The Lebanese were also very active in the agricultural export trade: they travelled out to the villages to collect produce; they established buying stations in strategic locations; they hired indigenes as agents; and they served as middlemen to the European firms. Only during and after the Second World War, did control measures by the government and the establishment of marketing boards, to regulate prices and allocate quotas to buyers, diminish the extent of Lebanese participation. The Lebanese were involved in almost all the major products. The history of some of these products has been written, and my concern here is only to use a few to illustrate the involvement of the Lebanese.

In the groundnut trade, the success of the Lebanese varied from one country to another, depending on the nature of the competition between them and the European companies. For instance in Senegal, groundnut exports rose from 15,000 tons in 1898 to 500,000 tons in 1930. The trade drew many new European companies and producers in the 1930s,[29] who came to rely on the Lebanese to make contact with primary producers who were scattered in many locations. Lebanese numbers increased: they filled the vacuum created by the French who left for military service during the war; and they were able to cope with the less exciting life in the villages and with low profits. Many Lebanese became independent operators, though competition with the European firms was very intense.[30]

In Nigeria, the active penetration of the Lebanese was after the First World War, when the European companies had to adjust to a slump and compete with one another. Hogendorn refers to the emergence of four prominent Lebanese: Ferris George, Saul Raccah, Joseph Elyas and Joseph George.[31] These men and others imitated the trading practices of the Hausa, worked hard, and obtained credit facilities from the European firms.[32] As their businesses expanded, the successful ones like Ferris George, were able to hire Hausa traders as middlemen and agents, to export to Europe,[33] and to challenge the supremacy of the European firms. In the 1930s they were accused of displacing small-scale Hausa traders and of unfair fierce competition with the European firms.[34] In spite of attempts by the European firms to use 'stable prices' and 'buying quotas', to resist the Lebanese challenge, the Lebanese continued to be successful. They reduced their overheads by maintaining few out-stations, by offering higher prices than European buyers, and by seeking cheaper shipping rates. A success story *par excellence* was the trading career of Saul Raccah, whose business expanded to rival that of the United African Company (UAC). By 1938–9 Raccah was able to handle a third of Nigeria's total groundnut exports.[35] But control measures during the Second World War enabled the European firms to regain their supremacy. The West African Produce Board (WAPB) was founded in 1942 to control exports. In 1943–4, the board granted a quota of 28.63 per cent to the Lebanese and 71.37 per cent to the European companies.[36] The various firms continued to sell on the basis of the quota allocated to them, and several Lebanese firms continued to be on the list. In the 1940s a licensed buying agent required a minimum capital of £10,000, a sum which was large and which suggests the financial worth of the Lebanese dealers. In the last years of colonial rule in Nigeria, Lebanese investments suffered a decline: the Nigerian Groundnut Marketing Board, the successor of the WAPB, showed preference to Nigerians by denying allocations to many Lebanese applicants.

Cocoa was another cash crop, with Ghana and Nigeria as the main producing countries. In south-western Nigeria, four Lebanese became successful cocoa merchants: J. Nabham, F. J. Nabham, N. Abizakhem and C. Zard. During the war years, when quotas were allocated by the WAPB, C. Zard was recognized as a merchant. In 1943–4 season, he was given 5.76 per cent of the total allocation.[37] In subsequent years, four Lebanese figured prominently as licensed buying agents: A. K. Zard, N. K. Zard, C. Zard and N. Abizakhem.[38]

The Lebanese were also involved in the rubber, palm kernels, and cotton trades, all to the extent made possible by government control and the profit to be made. Where the role of the Lebanese was heavily criticized, their operation was small. Where a government agency established a monopoly, the Lebanese had to divert their attention elsewhere. Cotton export is a good example; the trade was dominated by the British Cotton Growing Association and several European companies. Only a few Lebanese were allowed to participate.[39]

While the Lebanese generally avoided the trade in foodstuffs, which Africans dominated, there were some exceptions where good profits were to be made. In Sierra Leone, their involvement in rice – the main staple – and in kolanuts was very substantial.[40] At different periods, Lebanese established poultries, piggeries, dairy farms and banana plantations. They also traded in corn and palm oil. Several were interested in livestock, and they succeeded in distributing beef in such cities as Lagos and Kano.[41]

Many Lebanese also became involved in the transport business. So successful were they that they dominated lorry transport in northern Nigeria for most of the period and in the Sierra Leone Protectorate in the 1930s. In the 1950s they made huge investments in new lorries.[42] Several of them won contracts to carry mail for the government while others specialized in the spare-parts trade, travel agencies,[43] and vehicle repair and maintenance. In Sierra Leone, some Lebanese had launches to transport fish.[44]

Also in the service sector, many Lebanese worked as money lenders, charging high interest rates, or as seamstresses, barbers and medical doctors. In the 1950s a few of them went into banking.[45] They were generally successful in the entertainment industry, with heavy investment in horse-racing, night clubs, casinos, cinemas and hotels. Many cinema houses were associated with the Lebanese, either as proprietors, film agents, or operators. They invested in property: in Nigeria, successful men such as P. T. Solomon in Calabar, Zard in Ibadan and Joseph Nabham in Lagos, were notable property dealers and estate agents.[46] The post-1945 construction boom led to the influx of more Lebanese contractors, builders and artisans.

In the 1940s and 1950s Lebanese with substantial capital diversified into manufacturing. George Calil established a groundnut mill in Kano in 1942. Two others followed his footsteps, and by the 1950s they were together producing 15,000 tons of cake and 10,000 tons of oil.[47] In the 1950s the liberalization of rules on investments and tax exemptions encouraged many Lebanese to register private companies and to collaborate with indigenes and nationals of other countries to float a number of new companies.[48] This was the era of Lebanese involvement in the manufacture of building materials, for example, cement and floor tiles; also textiles, electrical goods, shoes, kapok, metal products, soap, candles, bottles, etc. Those who wanted to avoid the criticisms associated with the retail trade (discussed below) diversified into manufacture which required more capital. Some of these industries later grew to become big, with nominal capital above £50,000.[49]

Finally, the Lebanese engaged in mining. In 1954 a Lebanese invested a sum of £10,000 in mining in Jos.[50] In Sierra Leone, they were conspicous in gold and diamond mining. Between 1934 and 1944, the Lebanese were the most successful of the small miners. In the 1950s, the decade of the diamond boom, the Lebanese made huge fortunes by buying diamonds, and many of them were able to use the profits to expand their shops and diversify into other sectors of the economy.[51]

Features of Lebanese entrepreneurship

The characterization of the Lebanese primarily as middlemen between the big European firms and the African producers or traders, while correct to some extent, is inadequate to explain their economic activities.[52] First, not every economic activity involves relations between Europeans and Africans, for example, the trade in such food items as rice. Second, there were Lebanese merchants directly involved in the import and export trades. The point to emphasize is that Lebanese activities were too diverse to fall entirely into the very simple category of middlemanship.

While it is true that many Lebanese dealt in imported items, their business cannot be described as 'foreign business' or a 'foreign sector of the economy' as some scholars have concluded. They were foreigners, but they operated as local merchants. Many of them sold foreign goods but the key sector where they operated was the internal distribution within West Africa. Their aim was to exploit opportunities in West Africa by drawing resources and goods from within and responding to local changes.[53] This explains the resilience of their businesses: the Lebanese were able to respond to the devastating impact of the two World Wars, the depression of the 1930s, and changes in the economy of Europe.

Van der Laan has pointed attention to another important feature: the continuity of Lebanese enterprise.[54] A Lebanese business used the same place and location for a very long time. The operations, too, were constant. There was a main reason for this continuity: the Lebanese could not just wind up the business and return home. The rewards of continuity were good: it was easier for the Lebanese entrepreneur to cope with problems and to hope for the best in difficult years; and it also enabled the Lebanese to have reliable customers and creditors.

Lebanese entrepreneurs sought access to capital from other Lebanese and from European traders and banks. The European firms were generous in supplying goods on credit to the Lebanese, mainly because by their selling in small quantities to the Africans they were only performing a function ancillary to that of the big European importers. There were, however, often tensions in the relationship between them, caused partly by the desire of the Lebanese to import and thereby undercut the European firms; to acquire credits from more than one company and thereby reduce dependence; to buy in cash and thus reduce the profit margin built into credit; and to push up the ceiling of credit accounts and have access to more goods, thereby increasing the risk of the European companies. Nevertheless, the European firms preferred the Lebanese to the African traders because they thought that they were more reliable. It is doubtful whether honesty, and not shrewdness, was the real issue. Van der Laan points out the main reason in the case of Sierra Leone:

> They knew what penalties awaited a shopkeeper who defaulted on his debts to a European supplier. The European community was small and the news would soon go round. He would be blacklisted and have problems in getting stocked up, unless he paid cash. British officials would hear, too, and he did not want a bad record with them as it might lead to his deportation. A Lebanese could not easily disappear leaving his debts unpaid; and fleeing the country would require a great deal of money and would probably mean travelling on a British ship. If he settled in another part of Sierra

Leone he was bound to be recognized sooner or later, because there were so few white men in the country.[55]

A Lebanese enterprise was a family business. The advantages were obvious: continuity of operation was guaranteed as the sons took over the business from their fathers; overheads were low because wages were not necessary to family members; and supervision was easy and thorough. There were disadvantages as well: expansion was limited to a size that could be supervised by the family and the opening of new branches was difficult.[56]

When the business was bigger than the family could manage, extra hands were hired. The hired labour was expected to work long hours for little pay. The working conditions created ill-feeling between the Lebanese and their African workers, and added to the widespread opposition to the Lebanese. Africans in the service of the Lebanese engaged in covert resistance of various kinds: stealing, indolence at work, leaking trade secrets to rivals, etc. Cases of overt resistance are also reported. In Calabar in 1948, the Syrian and Lebanese Workers' Union wrote a petition to the Commissioner of Labour in Lagos, to complain that they were cheated by the Lebanese in several ways: wages were low; working hours were long; and appointments were terminated without notice.[57] When the workers were given the opportunity to discuss their problems with the Commissioner, they demanded a minimum wage, the regulation of working hours, and the right to observe public holidays, enjoy annual leave and medical facilities. Acting on the instruction of the Commissioner, the Labour Officer in Calabar conducted an investigation into the labour conditions in Lebanese businesses. He discovered that the highest salary of £5 per month was received by only one person (the operator of Patsol Cinema) and the others received between 8s. and 60s. a month whereas other employers paid between 20s. and 85s. a month.[58] The Labour Officer also found out that many of the workers received wages not sufficient to live on. The Lebanese agreed to increase the wages to between £1 and £1.10s. a month, regulate the working hours to between 7 a.m. and 12 noon and 2 p.m. to 5.30 p.m., grant a one-week annual leave with pay, observe public holidays, and give a month's notice before terminating an appointment. Many of these remained as promises, and the workers continue to grumble.[59]

The Lebanese flexibly responded to the circumstances in which they operated. They were quick to respond to new laws, conforming to or bending them to suit their purposes. In relating to the European traders and firms they stressed economic issues and ignored moral and social considerations. In dealing with the Africans, they heeded conditions: political, for example, relations with chiefs who behaved as patrons; and moral, for example, respect for customs and local religions. The business methods of the Lebanese were borrowed extensively from both the African and European traders, and also came from their own experience. They understood the techniques of bargaining, haggling, peddling, selling in small quantities, etc. – all associated with indigenous practices. They equally imitated the European traders, especially the methods of advancing credit and keeping shop. The Lebanese imitated one another, especially the successful ones, in their methods of selling and buying. They were astute in assessing the demands of their African consumers. They knew that the farmers spent much on general merchandise, and they went further to encourage them to buy on credit and pay later in cash or crops. They satisfied urban consumers by stocking goods in high demand. A good rapport was established with the customers by discussion with them and tolerating regular window-shopping. The Lebanese undoubtedly often hoarded, inflated prices, used false weights, and avoided tax.

But colonial society provided the Lebanese with the opportunities to start a new life, embark upon business and expand. In spite of all their ordeals, the discrimination against them and the competition, the Lebanese retained a strong desire to succeed; they hardly contemplated failure, and they were always confident of success. The evidence of this was mostly in material acquisitions: building concrete houses, possessing cars, wearing good clothes, and having bank accounts. Heavy expenses were incurred on further investments, pilgrimages to Mecca by Muslims, sponsoring relations and friends to come to West Africa to join them and begin new businesses, marriages, health, retiring to Lebanon, and bequeathing a successful business to the next generation.

Social life and politics

The Lebanese lived close to their shops, when they did not in fact use the same building as shop and residence. The early Lebanese migrants rented these houses, but built their own as their conditions improved.

Social relationships were closely connected with economic activities. Outside of the family network which was the core of the business, the Lebanese put their trust in those related to them by ethnicity or religion. Relations with others were either utilitarian or inevitable. They needed the Europeans for goods and for status values, and the Africans for labour and markets. Many of the men, in fact, married Africans, especially those who were poor and unable to sponsor partners from Lebanon. Lebanese women hardly had contacts with Africans. Where their number was too small to support autonomous institutions, they worshipped with Africans and sent their children to the same schools. Most learned to speak the indigenous languages, which was necessary for business.

The Lebanese constituted an ethnic minority wherever they resided. They lived together in one quarter or neighbourhood, generally named after them, for example, Lebanon Street in Ibadan. They came together for social functions and sports. Most of them belonged to unions formed for the expression of their specific, general interests, which enabled them to make demands for more land and other privileges. Where the community was large they united to establish schools and places of worship.

The Lebanese did not fully integrate into the society and that is not peculiar to them, as many studies on the Asian diaspora have shown. Pierre L. van den Berghe has argued that a 'life condition' of minorities is vulnerability;[60] for example, they are victims of pogroms, genocide, expulsions, expropriation. The primary concern of minorities is to overcome vulnerability either through assimilation and loss of ethnic identity or by organizing themselves 'in the protective cocoon of an ethnic enclave, to keep a low profile, and to be left alone'.[61] The option of assimilation is not a realistic one because the host society prevents entry into the ruling class while the lack of access to land makes a downward mobility into the peasant class difficult. Migrants, concluded Berghe, 'are virtually forced into a mercantile niche: they become an urban petty bourgeoisie specialising in labor-intensive economic services. Survival and success in that niche, in turn, impose ethnic enclaving organisation'.[62]

However, the Lebanese were not homogeneous as a group. They did not all belong to the same class or religion, and were also divided by sub-ethnic peculiarities. Differences were reflected in intense commercial rivalries, personal animosities and clashes, and devastating rumours to discredit the successful ones. As much as possible, business tricks and secrets were kept in the family and assistance was denied to rivals and competitors. The Lebanese did not create an exclusive trading diaspora with a strict regulation of members; rather, every Lebanese did what he thought best to advance his interest.

The feuds and differences among the different groups in Lebanon were transferred to West Africa, to the extent that many resorted to the police and the courts for settlement. The Lebanese belonged to different religions. Those from the Tripoli region were Sunni Muslims; their number was few, and others saw them as arrogant and privileged. The bulk were Shi'ite Muslims from south Lebanon, a poor minority group. In West Africa, the Shi'ites discouraged public worship, proselytizing, and unnecessary relations with the others. Other sects included the Druses and the Ismailis.[63] Most of the Christians were either Catholics, Maronites from the El-Metu and Tleill groups, or the Greek Orthodox, mainly the Rahbe group. The Maronites avoided interaction with the Greek Orthodox. Where the Lebanese had the resources and facilities to establish churches and schools, each sect catered for the needs of its members. Where resources were lacking, they either kept to themselves or shared facilities with those they could tolerate: the Greek

Orthodox chose Protestant institutions; the Maronites chose the Catholic ones, avoided the Muslims and used available means to educate their children.

Finally, the Lebanese were divided by wealth. There was a marked distinction between the rich and the poor. In the 1950s these distinctions were shown, for example, in the sizes of shops, quality of dress, types of accommodation, and ownership of cars. There were many cases when the poor were isolated, and it was not uncommon for the rich to criticize the poor for lack of good judgement and to attribute their misfortune and poverty to gambling, laziness, and excessive drinking.

Although the primary interest of the Lebanese was in commerce they realized that politics was necessary to achieve this goal. They presented themselves as law-abiding and peaceful people. The Lebanese were successful in seeking the cooperation of the African rulers, especially in the early years when they had to negotiate with them for land and shops. They showed respect, and gave large gifts to the chiefs in return for support and protection. The Lebanese also cultivated the goodwill of the colonial officials, supported government activities, responded to calls for donations, and avoided conflicts. In return, the colonial administrators served as the godfathers, offering protection to the Lebanese against African prejudices, attacks on their shops, and in rejecting requests to expel them. In the decolonization years, the Lebanese identified would-be leaders and influential political parties and they found the means to support them. For instance in Nigeria, it was alleged that they made financial contributions to the Northern Peoples Congress, the party which controlled the north and the federal government during the First Republic (1960–6).[64]

Race relations and conflicts

Trade, the main interest of the Lebanese, was a major source of conflict and often assumed the dimensions of warfare, where every strategy was fair. The colour, business practices, and life-style of the Lebanese were objects of attack, in order to minimize the threat which they posed to their actual and potential rivals. The Lebanese, Europeans and Africans, the three actors in the competition, invented stereotypes for one another, so as to explain attitudes and justify actions. The Lebanese self-presentation, especially in relation to the Africans, was either as Europeans or the race next to them in achievement. The Lebanese saw themselves as victims of undeserved envy and hostility, in spite of being law-abiding, peaceful, and useful agents in the development of Africa.[65] They believed that they were superior to the Africans but inferior to the Europeans whom they could match with hard work.

The Lebanese disputed vigorously the negative comments made by their African and European critics. On the criticism that they did not keep business records, their reply was that this was not necessary since they could not read or write and that competitors must be denied access to secrets. They did not see the need for hired labour since their businesses were small in scale. They denied the allegation that they were competing with the Europeans who supplied them with goods. They rejected the charge that they lived in slums because they were too thrifty: every Lebanese trader was said to live a style compatible with his income.[66] To the criticism that they repatriated their profits, the Lebanese wondered whether the money belonged to the Africans in the first place, since they themselves created the opportunities to make the money. They did not believe that they displaced African traders since they, too, arrived as poor immigrants and had worked hard to build up their capital.[67]

Many Africans accepted the Lebanese view of themselves as being next to the Europeans. These Africans believed that the Lebanese were more knowlegeable and that much of their business practice was worthy of emulation. The Lebanese were characterized as hardworking and endowed with superior ability and to be able to establish an ascendancy over African traders. Some even appreciated that their role as middlemen and in competing with the European firms reduced prices. Not all Africans agreed with these characterizations. The Creoles of Sierra Leone believed that the Lebanese were culturally inferior. There were many Africans who did not associate positive values with the Lebanese commercial success, describing them as stingy, clannish, sly, arrogant and dishonest. One observer concluded that they were nothing but a 'damned nuisance – they undermine and wreck African prosperity – make all the money they can – and take it elsewhere'.[68]

The Europeans did not see the Lebanese as equals. Indeed, the French refused to promote any meaningful contacts with the Lebanese, while the British discouraged them from attending their clubs and taking part in their sports. Generally, the Lebanese were treated as inferiors; they were imitators who ruined business for good traders, they cultivated no decent taste and had no civilized style. The Europeans were segregated from them, with racial leasehold clauses to prevent the rich Lebanese from living close to them. To the Europeans, who believed that the purpose of colonialism was to civilize the Africans, the presence of the Lebanese was seen as an obstacle. In Senegal the President of the Chamber of Commerce in the 1930s thought that the role of the Lebanese should be curtailed because they had little to teach the Africans:

> In order to provide [the civilizing mission] one must oneself have
> a sufficient degree of civilization. Outside the Libano–Syrian elite

there are a number of Syrians in Senegal who have descended to a level not very far from the natives among whom they live.[69]

However, many contemporary Europeans believed that the Lebanese fulfilled a useful role as middlemen, thereby aiding the development of commerce, especially as they were able to penetrate to the villages.

The Europeans thought that the Lebanese were superior to the Africans. Compared to the Lebanese, Africans were seen as incompetent, lazy and inexperienced. A Frenchman based in Senegal captured the minds of many when he confidently asserted that:

> The Lebanese are different from the Africans, they're more like the Chinese; they work very hard. They are also much harder than we are on the Africans, which is how it should be – 'the rule of the stick.' We Europeans haven't understood how to handle them. We wear kid gloves and are too kind, and they do not work.[70]

The official position was close to this: the Lebanese were better than Africans and were good at making money.[71]

The Lebanese had to compete with the European traders who had better access to capital and goods. As early as 1898, a law was passed in Guinea to prevent the Lebanese from trading in the markets because of the rivalry with the French. In Senegal Lebanese shopkeepers clashed with the French shopkeepers in the depression years when profits fell. The French shopkeepers, in order to survive, demanded protection and attacked the Lebanese on account of their effective competition with them. Early in the 1930s anti–Lebanese campaigns became better organized by the Syndicat Coopératif Economique du Sénégal (SCES), an organization set up to protect the interest of French shopkeepers. The association used the monthly *France-Afrique Noire* to warn the public of the dangers posed by the Lebanese. It publicized the 'shoddy deals' of the Lebanese, called on the government to restrict their immigration and regulate their practices.[72] The Lebanese also had many clashes with the big firms in the groundnut trade; the firms accused them of accepting adulterated products and underselling them.

African traders also regarded the Lebanese as rivals. In 1914 the Creoles asked the government to expel them from Sierra Leone.[73] In Nigeria in the late 1920s and early 1930s, retailers appealed to the chiefs to prevent the Lebanese from attending the markets in the villages and some towns.[74] In 1928 hundreds of them were expelled from Liberia. Everywhere, their success and business practices generated envy and hostility, and nowhere with more effect than in Sierra Leone. There were riots in 1919 which began in Freetown on 18 July, spread to other

major cities, and continued until 7 August.[75] The riots resulted in the
death of a Lebanese and the looting of many shops. The police had to
intervene and all Lebanese were held in custody for eight weeks, so as
to protect their lives. The cause of the riots was the belief by the Sierra
Leoneans, especially the Creoles, that the Lebanese were responsible for
inflation and the shortage of rice – the staple food. The Colonial Office
in London rejected the proposal that the Lebanese should be deported
and ordered the Governor to protect them and compensate those who
lost money and goods. This support encouraged the Lebanese to further
consolidate their businesses while it increased Creole hostility.

In the 1920s there was a press war on the Lebanese. The press
represented the interest of the consumers who felt cheated, the African
merchants who believed that the Lebanese were taking a lion's share of
the business,[76] and the European firms, who thought that the business
practices of the Lebanese undermined trade. The usual criticisms were
levelled at the Lebanese: they were unscrupulous and dishonest in their
methods; they corrupted the chiefs and politicians with bribes; they
repatriated their profits since they had no interest in the development
of Africa; they kept no business records; they were a menace to the
pursuit of decent trade. These criticisms usually ended with suggestions
to curtail their activities, control their immigration or expel them
altogether.[77]

After 1945, when the agitation for independence intensified, the
opposition to the Lebanese mounted as part of the demand for the
control of the economy by Africans. African politicans expressed the fear
that the Lebanese could use their economic power to either gain political
power or influence the course of political events. In French-speaking West
Africa, small traders, including French shopkeepers in Senegal, embarked
upon many anti-Lebanese campaigns. The Lebanese were blamed for
economic problems ranging from unemployment and inflation to usury.
In Senegal the government was advised to employ violence to deal with
the Lebanese.[78] In Sierra Leone there were anti-Lebanese riots in February
1955. In Nigeria, Chief S. L. Akintola moved in April 1955 that the House
of Representatives should request the Council of Ministers to advise the
Governor to set up a committee to probe the activities of the Lebanese
with reference to:

(a) their dealings and interests in real property;
(b) their share in the country's wholesale, retail, import and export
    trade;
(c) their part in the country's transport business;
(d) their interests in the country's mining industry; and
(e) the extent to which these activities have been beneficial or prejudicial
    to the best interests of the indigenous Nigerians.[79]

To Akintola, the 'grabbing and sleek' Lebanese displaced Africans in retail trade and other small-scale activities. Not only did he suggest that immigration controls be used to stop the further entry of the Lebanese, but he also wanted those of them born in Nigeria to be treated as aliens. While the government disagreed with him on the negative consequences of the Lebanese presence, it nevertheless assured him that its policy would be to welcome the Lebanese and other aliens who had concrete and economic and social benefits to offer and who would not compete with Africans. Four months later, another member of the House called for 'some form of retail trade restriction'.[80] The government promised to be vigilant in the implementation of the immigration policy and in protecting the interests of the 'small traders'.[81] Because of further pressure from the nationalists, the government decided in 1956 to amend the Immigration Bill in order to correct some defects, remove anomalies, clarify the provisions on deportation and limit the class of aliens who could be allowed into the country. In December of the same year the government announced that no new alien would be allowed to participate in retail trade unless he could invest a sum of £100,000[82] and prove that his business was of 'exceptional benefit' to the country. Immigration officials were to determine what constituted 'exceptional benefit'. It is not surprising that in the 1940s and 1950s many Lebanese applied for naturalization in the hope that this would enable them to enjoy the rights and privileges of citizenship and protect their businesses.

Yet the Lebanese were able to cope with all the attacks and criticisms. Some migrated to other countries outside West Africa, while some prefered to change their locations within a country, moving to new areas where their activities attracted less antagonism. A few moved into the capital intensive sector, thus reducing their involvement in retail trade.

Conclusion

The Lebanese were successful marginals. They were able to create linkages with power structures, avoided excessive political and social visibility, and knew how to organize resources and to exploit people. And despite the negative picture of them widespread among West Africans, they have made a significant contribution to development in West Africa. This has had three main aspects. First, as Michael Crowder noted, the Lebanese joined other alien and indigenous traders to expand the scope of commercial activity. Second, they provided a model for many Africans to emulate; for instance, the use of lorries, the employment of agents, the sale of cheap and small items, the penetration of small villages, all became part of the strategies of African traders. And like the Lebanese, successful African traders who operated outside of their ethnic base have equally experienced tension and conflicts. For example, Yoruba traders have been criticized in Ivory Coast and expelled from Ghana, while Igbo traders suffered severe victimization and loss of life in Northern Nigeria in 1966 and 1967. Third, the end of colonial rule did not bring an end to Lebanese economic activity. In a 1969 report on Sierra Leone, 1503 Lebanese enterprises were registered, the great majority in general merchandise, and they were scattered throughout the country. What is said of Sierra Leone is true of other places, even if the scope of operations is different. Finally, the Lebanese presence broadened the experience of Africans in relating to foreigners from outside the continent, for instance, Africans inter-married with Lebanese and had to face competition with a more aggressive group. This experience is one of the factors in the vigorous attempts by many African ethnic groups to question some of their economic and political values and practices in order to cope with contemporary changes, crises, and inter-group relations.

Notes

1. M. Crowder, *West Africa Under Colonial Rule*, (London, 5th impression, 1981), pp. 293–8.

2. Ibid., p. 297.

3. The Lebanese were confused with the Syrians in many sources. Most references to the Syrians in West Africa refer to the Lebanese and not to the Syrians whose number was very small. In this chapter we are dealing with the Lebanese, although the analysis for the most part is appropriate for the Syrians. See H. L. van der Laan, 'Syrians or Lebanese: Which name is correct?', *Kroniek van Afrika*, IX 2 (1969), pp. 140–4.

4. See, among others, P. K. Hitti, 'The Impact of the West on Syria and Lebanon in the 19th century', *Journal of World History*, 1954–5; S. M. Haffar, 'The Syrian Emigration Problem', *Elder Dempster Magazine*, June 1938, pp. 32–4; and G. Gayet, 'Les Libanais et les Syriens dans l'Ouest Africain', *Pluralisme ethnique et cultural dans les sociétés intertropicales*, (Brussels: Institut International des Civilisations Différentes, compte rendu de la xxxe Session tenue à Lisbonne, les 15–18 Avril 1957), pp. 161–72.

5. M. Hanna, 'The Lebanese in West Africa', *West Africa*, April 1958, p. 393.

6. Haffar, 'The Syrian Emigration Problem', p. 33.

7. Hanna, 'The Lebanese', *West Africa*, p. 393; E. K. Saadé, *Le Liban dans le Monde: Guide des émigrés Libanis et Syriens en Afrique occidentale et equatoriale*, (Beirut: L'Universelle, 1952).

8. The date when the first set arrived remains a subject of speculation. What is less controversial is that the Lebanese were already in West Africa by the 1880s. See R. B. Winder, 'The Lebanese in West Africa', *Comparative Studies in Society and History*, IV, 3 (1962), p. 298.

9. Hanna, 'The Lebanese', *West Africa*, p. 393.

10. P. Claude Riviere, 'Les Libanais in Guinée', *Kroniek van Afrika*, 6, 3 (1975), p. 267.

11. P. J. Binet, 'Les Libanais en Afrique francophone', *Kroniek van Africa*, 6, 3 (1975), p. 259.

12. D. M. Misra, 'The Lebanese in Nigeria, 1890–1960', unpublished Ph.D. thesis, Calabar, 1985, p. 72.

13. Binet, 'Les Libanais', p. 259.

14. *West Africa*, April 7 1962, p. 375.

15. M. Hanna, 'Lebanese Emigrants in West Africa: Their Effects on the Lebanon and West Africa', unpublished Ph.D. thesis, Oxford, 1958, pp. 82–5.

16. F. I. Khuri, 'Kinship, Emigration and Trade Partnership among the Lebanese of West Africa', *Africa*, XXXV, 4 (1965), p. 385.

17. Winder, 'The Lebanese in West Africa'.

18. Khuri, 'Kinship'.

19. I have drawn my conclusions on the patterns of migrations from the excellent essay by H. L. van der Laan, 'Mobility and Migration of the Lebanese in West Africa, with special reference to Sierra Leone', Leiden, 1975, mimeo.

20. Ibid., p. 18.

21. Crowder, *West Africa*, 298.

22. Laan, 'Syrians or Lebanese'.

23. P. T. Bauer, *West African Trade: a Study of Competition, Oligopoly and Monopoly In A Changing Economy*, (Cambridge, 1954), pp. 158–61.

24. National Archives Ibadan (NAI), *Debates in the House of Representatives*, 13 March, 1954.

25. *Gold Coast Gazette*, February 1949, cited in Bauer, *West African Trade*, p. 158–9n.

26. Anfreville de la Salle, *Notre Vieux Sénégal*, (Paris Challamel, 1909), n.p.

27. M. H. Y. Kaniki, 'Attitudes and Reactions towards the Lebanese in Sierra Leone During the Colonial Period', *Canadian Journal of African Studies*, VII (1973), 111.

28. J. Pedlar, *Economic Geography of West Africa*, (London, 1955), p. 149.

29. H. Deschamps, *Le Sénégal et la Gambie*, (Paris: Presse Universitaires de France, 1964), pp. 71–3; J. Suret-Canale, 'L'Industrie des Oléagineux en A.O.F.', 11 July 1960, pp. 280–1.

30. Rita Cruise O'Brien, *White Society In Black Africa: The French of Senegal*, (London, 1972), pp. 48–50; J. G. Desbordes, *L'Immigration Libano-Syrienne en A.O.F.*, (Poitiers: Imprimerie Moderne, 1938), pp. 18–21.

31. J. S. Hogendorn, *Nigerian Groundnut Exports: Origins and Early Developments*, (Zaria: Ahmadu Bello University, 1978), p. 141.

32. Ibid.

33. Public Record Office (London) CO 658/25, Vol. 9, Ferris George against H. Naselean and Alhassan dan Tata, April 1925.

34. F. Okediji, 'An Economic History of Hausa-Fulani Emirates of Northern Nigeria, 1900–1939', unpublished Ph.D. thesis, Michigan, 1972, pp. 199–206.

35. Ibid.

36. M. Perham (ed) *Mining, Commerce, and Finance in Nigeria*, (London, 1948), p. 56.

37. Ibid.

38. NAI, *Nigeria Cocoa Marketing Board Report 1947–48*.

39. Ibid., 1949–50 and 1950–51; Okediji, 'An Economic History', p. 169.

40. H. L. van der Laan, *The Lebanese Traders in Sierra Leone*, (The Hague/Paris: Mouton.'S Gravenhage, 1975), pp. 66–69, chapter 4.

41. Perham, *Mining*, 278; NAI, Com Col 2010.c18, Lebanese Income Tax; M. Perham, *Native Economies of Nigeria*, (London, 1945), p. 372; Saade, *Le Liban*, p. 372; and Winder, 'The Lebanese', p. 311.

42. *Nigeria Trade Journal*, 4,4, 1956 and 7,2,1959.

43. See for instance, *Nigeria Trade Journal*, 6,4 (1958), 7,4 (1958) and 8,2 (1958).

44. Laan, *The Lebanese Traders*, pp. 141–2.

45. Cf., *Nigeria Trade Journal* 8,1 (1960).

46. *Nigeria Trade Journal*, 2,4 (1954), 5,4 (1957); NAI, Oyo Prof1/3/1674 Lebanese in Ibadan.

47. K. M. Buchanan and J. C. Pugh, *Land and People in Nigeria*, (London, 1955), p. 202.

48. Cf. *Nigeria Trade Journal*, 1,3 (1953), 2,3 (1954).

49. Ibid. 6,3 (1958), 7,4 (1958).

50. Ibid, 2,3, (1954).

51. Laan, *The Lebanese Traders*, chapters 7–9.

52. Ibid., pp. 221–4.

53. Ibid., pp. 224–5.

54. Ibid., pp. 225–6.

55. Ibid., p. 107.

56. W. T. Morril, 'Socio-cultural adaptation in a West African Lebanese Community', *Anthropological Quarterly*, XXXV (1962), pp. 146–55; W. R. Stanley, 'The Lebanese in Sierra Leone: Entrepreneurs Extraordinary', *African Urban Notes*, V,2 (1970), pp. 159–74.

57. National Archives, Enugu, Cal Prof 7/1//1900-Syrian and Lebanese Workers' Union, Calabar Chapter, to the Commissioner of Labour, Lagos, May 1948.

58. Ibid.

59. Ibid.

60. Pierre L. van de Berghe, 'Asian Africans before and after independence', *Kroniek Van Afrika*, 6,3 (1975), pp. 197–205.

61. Ibid.

62. Ibid. p. 200.

63. Haffar, 'The Syrian Emigration Problem'.

64. Winder, 'The Lebanese', pp. 326–7.

65. R. Charbonneau, 'Le probleme Libano-syrien en Afrique noir', *Comptes rendus mensuels der Sciences d'Outre-Mer* (1959), pp. 154–170; and 'Les Libano-Syriens en Afrique noire', *Revue francais d'etudes politiques africaines*, 26 (1968) pp. 56–71.

66. *The Nigerian Daily Times*, 9 August 1928 and 15 August 1928.

67. Hanna, 'The Lebanese', *West Africa*, 17 May 1958, p. 463.

68. *The Nigerian Daily Times*, 4 August 1928.

69. Letter from J. L. Turbé cited in O'Brien, *White Society*, p. 52.

70. An informant quoted in O'Brien, p. 119.

71. See for instance, W. Addison, 'The Syrians in British West Africa: A Plea For Fairness', *African World* (Supplement) 27 July 1925, v.

72. O'Brien, pp. 51–3.

73. A. J. G. Wyse, 'The 1919 Strike and the Syrian Riots: A Krio Plot?', *The Journal of the Historical Society of Sierra Leone*, 3, 1 and 2 (1979).

74. *The Nigerian Daily times*, 19 September 1928; NAI, Oyo Prof 2/3/File c. 56, Syrians in Ife Division.

75. M. H. Y. Kaniki, 'Attitudes and Reactions Towards The Lebanese in Sierra Leone During the Colonial Period', *Canadian Journal of African Studies*, 7, 1973, pp. 97–113.

76. Winder, 'The Lebanese'.

77. *France-Afrique Noire* (1935–37); *Nigerian Daily Times*, 19 August 1928; and *African World*, 6 June, 1928.

78. The best and most interesting source is the weekly *Les Echos de l'Afrique Noire*.

79. NAI, Debates in the House of Representatives, 5 April 1955, p. 921.

80. Ibid, 23 August 1955, p. 231.

81. Ibid.

82. Winder, p. 306.

83. H. van der Laan, 'Lebanese Enterprise in Sierra Leone: A Partial Analysis', *Sierra Leone Geographical Journal*, 13 (1969), pp. 45–50.

47 K. M. Buchanan and J. C. Pugh, *Land and People in Nigeria* (London, 1955) p. 205.

48 Cf. *Nigeria Trade Journal*, I, 3 (1953), 2 (1954).

49 Ibid., 6, 3 (1958), 2, 4 (1958).

50 Ibid., 2, 3 (1954).

51 Leon, *The Lebanese Traders*, op. cit., p. 74.

52 Ibid., pp. 221–4.

53 Ibid., pp. 224–6.

54 Ibid., pp. 235–6.

55 Ibid., p. 107.

56 W. T. Morrill, 'Socio-cultural adaptation in a West African Lebanese Community', *Anthropological Quarterly*, XXXV (1962), pp. 146–56; A. V. P. Stanley, 'The Lebanese in Sierra Leone Entrepreneurs Extraordinary', *African Urban Notes*, V, 2 (1970), pp. 159–74.

57 National Archives, Lagos, Col Prof 7/1, 1900–Syrian and Lebanese Workers Union Cttee, Chairman to the Commissioner of Labour, Lagos, May 1918.

58 Ibid.

59 Ibid.

60 Pierre L. van den Berghe, 'Asian Africans before and after independence', *Kroniek van Afrika*, 6, 3 (1975), pp. 197–205.

61 Ibid.

62 Ibid., p. 200.

63 Hitti, *The Syrians*, *Emigration Problem*.

64 Winder, *The Lebanese*, pp. 385.

65 R. Charbonneau, 'Les problèmes Libano-syrien en Afrique noire', *Cahiers voltaiques, les sciences et l'education* (1979), pp. 129–135; and *Les Libano-Syrien en Afrique noire', Revue française d'études politiques africaines*, 26, (1968) pp. 35–1.

66 *The Nigerian Daily Times*, 9 August 1928 and 15 August 1928.

67 Hitti, 'The Lebanese' (1966) ibid., 17 May 1966, p. 107.

68 *The Nigerian Daily Times*, 9 August 1928.

69 Figure from J. A. Trub, cited in Othman, *Plan Setup*, p. 32.

70 An informant quoted in Othman, p. 113.

71 See for instance A. Adebayo, 'The Syrian in British West Africa & Plea for Fairness', *Sierra Leone Supplement*, 27 July 1925.

72 Othman, pp. 51–2.

73 A. V. P. Vane, 'The 1919 strike and the Syrian Riots: A Kind of Box?', *The Journal of the Colonial African Studies* Leone 3, 2 and 2 (1976).

74 *The Nigerian Daily Times*, 19 September 1928 – PAN, Col Prof 20 of the c. 36 *Streets of the Nigerian*.

75 Abner J. Kamu, 'Attitudes and Reactions Towards the Lebanese in Sierra Leone during the Colonial Period', *Canadian Journal of African Studies*, 7, 1 (1973), pp. 97–112.

76 Winder, 'The Lebanese'.

77 Farhan *African News* (No. 76–9), *Nigeria Daily Times*, 14 August 1928, and *West Africa*, June, 1928.

78 The best and most interesting source is the weekly diary *Israel de l'Afrique*.

79 PAN Debates in the House of Representatives, 5 April 1949, p. 921.

80 Ibid., 23 August 1951, p. 231.

81 Ibid.

82 Winder, 'The Lebanese'.

83 H. van der Laan, 'Electoral Enterprise in Sierra Leone: A Factual Analysis', *Sierra Leone Geographical Journal*, 13 (1969), pp. 15–31.

Chapter Nine

Politics, Families and Freemasonry in the Colonial Gold Coast

AUGUSTUS CASELY-HAYFORD
AND RICHARD RATHBONE

A s the literature on social change in West Africa evolved, the role of voluntary associations was frequently invoked but only rarely spelt out. Their presence and growth from the nineteenth century onwards was seen as evidence of the perceived need to replace or supplement older group affiliations as urban people, in particular, embraced new patterns of trade, western education, literacy and, of course, Christianity.[1] Such associations were explained for the most part in Durkheimian fashion as essentially functional. They mediated the traumatic shifts in values, made rural migrants feel more at home in towns and cut across the ascribed exclusivity of ethnic affiliations.[2] Other scholars with slightly different agendas stressed the latent and sometimes overt politicality of such associations within a colonial environment in which the vast majority of people were *de facto* un-enfranchised.[3] Even if all such associations were not either overtly political or surrogates for political activity, then they were often seen as 'helping to break down the social barriers to nationalism'.[4] Michael Crowder's influential *West Africa under Colonial Rule* embraces a similar approach to that of Kimble.[5]

Membership of such associations, which most authorities on the post-Second World War period insisted was considerable in urban areas,[6] was for the most part assumed to have been inspired by the prospect of material or social gain. Maxwell Owusu insisted[7] '. . .the popularity of the organization. . .was to a very large extent dependent on 'what one gets out of it' in utilitarian and socially symbolic terms. . .participation. . .was instrumental.' Such rugged, no-nonsense materialism has been challenged by a number of writers starting perhaps with Abner Cohen who insisted that 'for a variety

This chapter © Augustus Casely-Hayford and Richard Rathbone 1992

of individual reasons. . .many find intrinsic values in the beliefs, rituals and ceremonies. . .'[8] Our understanding of the rich provenance of motivation has been enormously deepened since the 1970s by works such as those by J.D.Y. Peel,[9] John Dunn and A.F. Robertson[10] and others.[11]

In Ghana at any rate there is no doubt whatever about the extensive nature of a massive number of associations whose generation seems to have been stimulated if not actually caused by the spread of the money economy and the extension of colonial rule. There was an immense variety of such associations and clubs. Many catered for the sporting interests of young men. Busia's delight in discovering football clubs in Sekondi-Takoradi with such splendid names as Heroes, XI Wise, Mighty Councillors, Mighty Poisons, Great Titanics, Simple Winners, Zongo Vipers and Western Wolves is palpable.[12] Alongside such clubs were, however, an extensive network of burial societies, savings associations, debating societies, music circles and choirs and old school associations, all of which are familiar groupings to students of West African towns. In turn such groups co-existed with a vast number of ethnic and regional associations and most importantly of all with a galaxy of religious affiliations. They were and are an important element of what being urban was and is about; they are a vivid proof of the sheer vitality of towns-men and towns-women in West Africa.

The early scholarship from Kenneth Little's pioneering work onwards[13] showed little evidence beyond guess-work about who joined such associations and why. In general it is striking how much more we have learnt about such vital matters in the studies of African churches[14] than we have about more earthly affiliations. In the case of Ghana there is little emulation of research of scholars like Barnes or Cole.[15] Thanks to the work of scholars like Enid Schildkrout and Keith Hart we have learnt a deal about Zongo life and urban Frafra[16] but there is next to no textured social history of Ghana's great coastal towns.

Virtually every scholar who has looked at politics, social life and even demography, mentions voluntary associations. Almost none appears to have talked to association officers or association members. Similarly there seems to have been little attempt to collect data from membership lists, minute books and association correspondence. There is always a doubt about the accessibility of such documentation. But there is a strong assumption that it existed. Hodgkin, for example, insisted that voluntary associations 'have given an important minority valuable experience of modern forms of administration – the keeping of minutes and accounts, the handling of records and correspondence. . .a kind of informal professional training.'[17] As he spent a good deal of time working with people who were members of such associations, it is reasonable to assume that he was not guessing about this.

In fact from Hodgkin's pioneering work onwards a great deal of what is assumed to have been the essence of these associations is based not upon actual research but, rather, upon analogy. Hodgkin, for example, says of them that they: '. . .are an outcome of the "discontent excited by the philosophy of life of which the new town [is] the symbol and expression."'[18] The quotation he used here does not in fact derive from analysis of any African town or any African voluntary association. It comes, rather, from J.L. and B. Hammond's *The Age of the Chartists* and relates, obviously, to observations of another time and another place. The role of analogy is made clearer when Hodgkin stressed that the political education derived from participation in such organizations resembled '. . .the way that Nonconformist and working-class associations trained the new Labour leadership in nineteenth-century Britain.'[19] Hodgkin was not alone in reading into the African data inferences and assumptions derived from British urban experience in the early industrial era. A similar analogy is drawn by Kimble in discussing the apparent instability of many early associations in West Africa.[20] Austin's observations seem similarly to be drawn from an inference about the evolution of voluntary associations into party branches. He writes: '[Elementary school leavers]. . .began to turn to new forms of organization. . .Local scholars' unions, literary and debating clubs, youth movements and improvement societies. . .by 1948–9 each of these little societies was an active nucleus of an anti-chief, anti-colonial movement, quick to acquire new life as a radical commoners' party.'[21]

Comparison is a valuable analytical tool and all of this would be fine and exciting if we we were able to be clearer about what was implicitly being compared with nineteenth-century British experience. It seems clear that a far from random sample of radical or radical-liberal scholars, who were for the most part British, caught up in the heady atmosphere of remarkably rapid change, turned to the most proximate historical experience to hand to explain the vertiginous events unfolding before them. What was at best a makeshift and even rather parochial set of referents[22] began, not unnaturally, to loom rather larger than comparisons should. Ghanaian history in this respect gradually ceased to be seen in its own terms but actually came to be seen as identical to processes which occurred in Bradford or Manchester in the mid-nineteenth-century. Once that accidental substitution of one group of peoples' histories for another had occurred then it followed that there was little need to enquire more deeply into the African reality. Our understanding of many of these processes is the poorer for this.

☆　☆　☆

This essay begins to scratch the surface of the most elusive sector of Ghanaian voluntary associations, those which Ione Acquah calls 'fraternities'.[23] By this it is clear that she means essentially what Cohen later describes as 'secret ritual groups'.[24] By the mid-1950s Acquah was able to list, in Accra, five major international fraternities: the Freemasons, the Ancient Order of Oddfellows, the Order of Gardeners, the Ancient Order of Foresters and the International Order of Good Templars. She also lists some rather less well-known but no less secretive groups: the Gold Triangle, Emmanuel I Am, Dorchett's Occult Circle and the Household of Ruth. By the nature of these things this list was almost certainly not exhaustive. What were and perhaps are these groups? Who joined them and why? What did members or in some cases adepts do at their meetings and what did they do outside them? Such organizations by their very nature do not encourage such enquiries. Part of what defines them and their membership is very precisely this removal from the invasion of public scrutiny. Some, like the Freemasons, with whom this essay is most concerned, are explicitly secretive even if investigative journalism has recently made them insist that such allegations are excessive. Freemasonry was and is perceived by both its members and non-members alike as a 'secret society' and as such extremely difficult to research. We hope to suggest that it has been important in the history of Ghana, and suspect that it probably still is.

Freemasonry was amongst the bags and baggage of both informal and informal empire. By 1895 there were over 50 lodges in the West Indies and over 150 on the Indian sub-continent. Its arrival on the coast of West Africa dates from as early as 1735. In that year Richard Hull was appointed provincial Grand Master for the 'Gambay'. In 1736 David Creighton MD was made Grand Master of the Cape Coast Lodge. These foundations were, it seems, brittle institutions. When the Grand Lodge, the headquarters of Freemasonry in London, re-appraised all Lodge records in 1862, some of those it 'struck off' because they were at best dormant and at worst dead included these early foundations. Amongst those which lost recognition in 1862 were the Torrisinian or Torridzonian Lodge, No. 621, which had been established in Cape Coast Castle in 1810, Cape Coast Lodge No. 599 which had been set up in 1833, the Freetown Lodge of Good Intent, No. 721 founded in 1820 and the Gambia Lodge No. 867 which had been consecrated in 1851. None of these lodges had made the obligatory cash returns to the Grand Lodge for decades and had thus almost by definition ceased to exist.

Without access to hard evidence it is only possible to guess about the fate of these lodges. Clearly the vivacity of lodges depended upon the keenness of individual craftsmen. The staggering death-rates in and around the port towns as well as the ebb and flow of trading must have endowed these lodges with an inherent fragility. Whether or not they had, by any definition, African members in the early stages is impossible to resolve at present. The familiar problem for scholars working on coastal history before the mid-nineteenth century of Africans with European surnames bedevils analysis of this most interesting problem. But we do know that the *Gentleman's Magazine* of the late eighteenth and early nineteenth centuries carried both trade and masonic news which suggests that it was widely used by freemasons. Amongst those to advertize in its pages was William Ansah, a merchant from Anomabu. Ansah had come to school in Britain in 1750 at the expense of the Royal African Company during which time he had been the ward of Lord Halifax. If, as we tentatively infer, Ansah was a craftsman then he seems to have been the first African to have been admitted to freemasonry. Prince Hall, who is usually credited with this, was initiated in North America a full twenty years after Ansah left Britain to return to West Africa. On evidence as thin as this we are in no position to either confirm or deny that these early lodges were segregated on racial lines.

It is however clear that Gold Coast Lodge No. 773 which was founded in 1858 and consecrated in April of the following year was a multi-racial institution. Its sponsors and founders came from both the African and European communities and, as it were, from the communities in between. Freemasonry claims not to discriminate on the basis of race but it is clear that such over-arching policy has been honoured in the breach in specific places and at specific times. Although the evidence is somewhat tangential, it is striking that when the Golden Jubilee of the Grand Lodge of Nigeria was celebrated in 1963, a good deal of space was devoted in the souvenir booklet to self-congratulation about the multi-racial composition of this lodge which its authors contrasted with the history of other West African lodges. It seems clear that there were at certain times specifically African and specifically European lodges as well as multi-racial lodges in West Africa.[25]

Gold Coast Lodge No. 773 became the parent lodge, it seems, of all other lodges in the Gold Coast as only fully-initiated masons may initiate new lodges. It is far from clear where the founders of Lodge 773 were initiated but it could very easily have been in either Sierra Leone or in the United Kingdom as all were prominent and much-travelled men. Once again the racial identity of these founding fathers, in the absence of other biographical details, can be frustratingly unclear. But we do know enough about the brothers Robert and William Hutchinson, the Bannerman brothers and Charles Bartels, who were amongst those named as founders of Lodge 773, to be sure that there were Africans 'on the square'. The Hutchinsons, Bannermans and Bartels were consistently among the foremost coastal families from the mid-nineteenth century up until the Second World War. Though they each had European progenitors, they were all, over generations centrally involved in African movements. The Hutchinsons had been a force in the movement for the establishment of a Cape Coast municipal council, the

Bannermans were involved in the forming of the first newspapers on the coast and the Bartels were major figures in both education and religion. Amongst the European founders of the lodge were two future governors – Ussher and Rowe – and a clutch of the most successful merchants and civil servants.

The consecration of this lodge occurred, perhaps not coincidentally, at a time when other and sometimes rival organizations began to take root on the Gold Coast. In the second half of the nineteenth century we find the establishment of a wide variety of societies: the English Templars, the American Templars, the Christian Guilds, the Knights of Marshall and the Oddfellows. Additionally this period witnessed the burgeoning of the temperance movement. By and large these organizations which were in some senses rivals to freemasonry seem to have had less exacting entry criteria than the older international Order; they were all almost certainly cheaper to join. All of these exciting developments await further study. But by 1900 the *Gold Coast Aborigine* suggested that 'nearly every young person' in the Gold Coast was a member of a friendly society.[26] In a decidedly pre-feminist era, the newspaper meant, of course, nearly every young male person, for like freemasonry for few of these societies admitted women to membership. Many of the societies which came into being in the final quarter of the nineteenth century imitated at least some of the secrecy and rituals of masonry although the organizing principles of these groups was very varied. *The Gold Coast Aborigine* complained that the societies were too dominated by appearance and ritual:

These societies exist more for the display of regalias [sic] and possessions than anything else. . .for you usually find a brother working against a brother, to the very losing of his daily bread.[27]

It was certainly the case that funerals, the Diamond Jubilee celebrations and other formal and not so formal occasions, saw the friendly societies putting on their regalia and marching assertively through the towns in order to impress non-members, young women and, no doubt, one another. Although the press might have cavilled at such parades, the Christian press tended to welcome the growth of such societies as healthy successors to the 'pagan' and frequently very boisterous *asafo* companies. As the *Gold Coast Aborigine* put it:

. . . .the societies are for strengthening of the bond of brotherhood, fostering of that benevolence which in our hearts is an answering glow from the great heart of God our Father; and they are wholly mistaken who join these societies for sinister motives. The great law and doctrine of the Order of Oddfellows, for instance, embodied in the familiar sacred motto, friendship, love, truth are more than just figures of speech.[28]

Inherent in strictures of this sort was a perceived need for 'moralizing leisure time'.[29] A growing urban middle class were beginning to stress the need for social control and urban order. The temperance movement, forcefully advanced by King Ghartey of Winneba, was very much a symptom of this mood. It was, not least, a strong reaction to the proliferation of drinking clubs for young men. At a time when good, fresh drinking water was often in short supply, the *African Times* reported with no little disgust that drinking water could be bought in markets at a greater price than that of gin or rum.[30] A year before that report, the same newspaper had noted the existence of the Tiger Club. This was a collection of young men, who, taking advantage of the low price of hard liquor, had sought to outbid one another by drinking enormous quantities. The club was disbanded in tragic circumstances after two of its members had died while drinking, one by drowning and another from a fall.[31] The press, owned and edited by an essentially burgher group of proprietors and journalists, was always eager to highlight such tragedies. The *Gold Coast People* on 26 October 1891 reported another tragedy after a young man called Aggrey had been 'poisoned' by a 'drunken fellow with who he caroused the previous night. LET YOUNG MEN BE ADMONISHED'. It is no accident that the Temperance Society was responsible for the building of the first street-lighting in the Gold Coast (at Anomabu).

The Temperance Society was initially very much a family affair. Ghartey's brother-in-law, the Revd. J. Parker, was a powerful advocate of total abstention and Parker's half-brother, J.D. Ekem, was the society's secretary. Ekem in turn was extremely well-connected, not least by his success in marrying his six legendarily beautiful daughters to scions of the great coastal families of Abadoo, Amissah, Brew, Ferguson, Fynn and Insaidoo. The society sought every opportunity to denounce the 'accursed drink'. The link between temperance and the urge for civil order was further underlined by the society's construction of a temperance hotel in Winneba as a respectable alternative to the more robust lodging-houses that were springing up in coastal towns towards the end of the nineteenth century. The Temperance movement brings together a number of contemporary concerns. It was strongly evangelical. But it also stressed the notion of family responsibility and by this it meant the nuclear rather than the extended family, for the former was felt by the society's adherents to be somehow more obviously Christian. The ethic of the Christian family was handsomely acted out within Ghartey's close kin. Ghartey's eldest daughter Elizabeth was one of the society's most active members, and, with her father, one of the players of the portable harmonium which accompanied them to all meetings.[32] The society endlessly argued for public decency, civic decency. It was no accident that its most active and important figure was Ghartey himself (d. 1897) who personally entwined considerable merchant wealth with his rule of Winneba.

Ghatey's role in the movement underlines the considerable complexity of urban social life in this era of Ghana's history. We know that in 1893 he joined the Ancient Order of Foresters, Court No. 7423. And at his great state funeral his comrades from the Foresters, in full dress, were in attendance. But so were his brothers and sisters in the Temperance Society. No less part of the cortège were, of course, his wing-chiefs and his court officials. To complete the complex way in which Ghartey was commended to the next world, the funeral procession stopped in front of a Union Jack, flying at half-mast, in the middle of Winneba town where a volley was discharged as a token of the dead king's loyalty to the British Crown.[33] In a striking fashion Ghartey's funeral presents the modern scholar with a massive problem: very simply, how does one socially classify the king of an ancient Fante state who was also a preacher (and, according to some of the contemporary press, also a fine traditional healer and midwife), a novice in the Ancient Order of Foresters and indeed much else besides. Manifestly what he represented to himself as well as to others was far more complicated than 'straddling' the traditional and modern worlds.

The Temperance Society enjoyed no monopoly over abstention. The Rechabites and the American and English Templars all abjured alcohol. Despite the fact that they were frequently at one anothers' throats over who could march where and who should wear which regalia, they came together to share the same church every Temperance Sunday. The Templars seem to have faded in this period. They appear to have outstripped their resources. The proportion of brethren in need of charity to brethren who could proffer it became unbalanced. By the 1920s, the Gold Coast newspapers who had always covered their activities gradually cease paying them any attention. The attachment of English Templars to the Church of England, their encouragement of the establishment of juvenile lodges and the membership of women were, however, very different from the confessional indifference and exclusivity of Gold Coast Freemasonry.

In view of the many attractive alternatives, how did Freemasonry survive? Part of the answer lies in the undoubted fact that a fair proportion of people joined a number of associations at the same time. But Gold Coast Lodge 773 certainly went through serious difficulties in recruiting new members. Its first meetings were held at Dawson Hill, the opulent home of Joseph Dawson. Dawson was amongst the wealthiest of Cape Coast's merchants. He was also an active member of the Temperance movement and, depending on whether one accepts Amissah's or his account of those days, he was either Secretary or Clerk of the Court of the Mankessim Council.[34] It is noteworthy that the Executive Council of the Fante Confederation included J.F. and G. Amissah and J.D. Hayford, all three of whom we can definitely identify as freemasons at this time. Lest this be thought a suggestion of conspiracy and hidden agendas, it is worth pointing out that of the eleven office holders in the Federation seven were active in the Temperance movement as well. Multiple affiliation was clearly the order of the day.

There can be little doubt that the high social standing of at least some of the lodge's brothers was an attraction to the potential member. Membership was, of course, technically secret but craftsmen broke cover with some frequency in order to attend public festivities. They certainly paraded on Queen Victoria's Diamond Jubilee celebrations[35] and did so annually in the Empire Day Parades. The local press recorded Masonic social events and brothers wore their regalia in public from time to time. In these relatively face-to-face societies, it is hardly likely that many freemasons practised their craft in secret. The modern freemasonic convention of concealment was, in any case, far less in evidence in most parts of the world in the nineteenth century. In many parts of Britain, for example, freemasons would join public parades in regalia.

But even if Gold Coast freemasons included some of the most famous men in the colony, we cannot entirely rely on that as an explanation of Freemasonry's success. It is no less clear that the membership of both African and European administrative officers of senior rank was hardly a guarded secret. Even if viewed as distinctly unconspiratorial, Freemasonry then as now, constituted a network, and in the intimate circumstances of these small towns, men with business and professional interests can only have seen initiation as advantageous. If your business centred on imports and exports, then it could do no harm, at least, to be able to regard a senior figure in Customs and Excise as a brother. But Freemasonry was also portrayed very positively in the local press. Most press references we have seen invariably praise the brotherhood for its good works and social conscience. The building of Christ Church in the middle of Cape Coast was facilitated by lodge contributions. And, during the Asante invasion of 1863, one of the lodge's founder members, R. Hutchinson, led his own self-financed force of freemasons into the fray. Tragically he contracted virulent malaria on campaign and died in the field. So Freemasonry was not presented or perceived in the Gold Coast of a century ago in the manner of the more sceptical, even hostile literature on Freemasonry of the late twentieth century.

The inherent respectability of Freemasonry was underlined when Asante again invaded the Coast in 1873. The despatch of Sir Garnet Wolseley to the Gold Coast and the ensuing campaign marked a decisive moment in the history of Gold Coast-British relations. Wolseley was himself a freemason who was not shy of advertizing his affiliation. Within the protectorate at the time Wolseley was regarded as a heroic defender of the Coast's integrity. The fact that he frequently attended meetings at Lodge No. 773 during his period in Cape Coast proclaimed both the respectability and influence of Freemasonry. British military involvement led, of course, to the growth of the colony and the growing numbers of British and West Indian personnel added to the pool of actual or potential craftsmen on the coast. It would be wrong to single out the impact of Britain without underlining the contribution of West Indian troops to voluntary associations. Many West Indian troops stayed on the Coast after the end of hostilities. One of them, Edward Stewart, became a minister of religion and until his death in 1924 actively promoted the American Templar movement on the coast. His success in this direction was considerable and he was credited with the foundation of no less than seven Templar lodges during his career.

By the 1880s, Cape Coast Lodge No. 773 was extremely distinguished. Grand Lodge deemed it to be the Premier Lodge of West Africa which in effect made it the most important regional lodge. The lodge grew and its increased membership necessitated a larger lodge building. In 1878 it moved from Dawson Hill to Fort Gate House on Castle Street. The craftsmen raised more funds and by 1879 a new temple was dedicated. Through lodge fund-raising a large and, by contemporary accounts, magnificent new temple was built in Saltpond in 1892.

Tachie-Menson[36] tells us that some of Cape Coast's most distinguished men were 'on the square'. Sadly this 'insider' account is understandably reticent about naming names. But it is clear that Lodge No. 773 enjoyed the support and brotherhood of several members of the prominent Amissah, Hayford and Plange families and almost certainly of other families. Fathers and uncles seem to have ensured that sons and nephews were initiated. But as we noted above such affiliation was seldom exclusive. On several occasions Grand Lodge recorded its displeasure with the evidence that craftsmen in Lodge No. 773 were simultaneously members of the Templars or the Marshalls.

The attractions of Freemasonry are hard to define.[37] At the practical level, the existence of a benevolent fund to which every freemason is obliged to contribute acted as an informal insurance policy. A craftsman, his widow and orphans, could all petition the lodge for charity. It was safety-net which offered, perhaps, more predictable security than the expectation of assistance from the extended family. Freemasonry also provided, possibly quite providentially, a valuable business network. By the end of the nineteenth century, a craftsman could use that network to contact more than 6 million other craftsmen throughout the world. A whole range of questions emerges from that. To what extent was Freemasonry a factor in contract allocation on the Coast? Did Gold Coast freemasons use their masonic contacts when travelling abroad? Was the masonic connection behind the funding of and hospitality shown to West African businessmen and students in the United Kingdom? And last, but not least, what impact did masonic connections have upon government, given that both prominent and influential Africans and European officials were 'on the square'? It is a matter of great regret that masonic archives are closed to scholars and while we entertain hopes that there may be ways in which other sources might yield further evidence, this absolute closure of records frustrates our understanding of the role of Freemasonry in West Africa.[38]

Cape Coast was, however, a declining town. Accra was the coast's 'pole of growth' and its population was rapidly expanding. In 1891, the Victoria Lodge No. 2392 was consecrated in Accra. For over thirty years the Cape Coast Lodge had been the sole lodge on the Gold Coast and it had been, as we have stressed, a multi-racial lodge. Victoria Lodge and the two other West African lodges consecrated in the 1890s (St. George's, Freetown and St. John's, Lagos) were specifically African lodges. The European population of the Gold Coast was growing and the development of racialism is immediately discernible by the turn of the century. Rather than joining the Victoria Lodge, Europeans instead consecrated three racially segregated lodges of their own in Accra (1904), Sekondi (1905) and Tarkwa (1914). By 1905 in Sekondi, for example, African freemasons belonged to the St. George's and Seccondee Lodge No. 3851 whilst whites were craftsmen of Sekondi Lodge No. 3238. The development of racially-specific lodges is an interesting addition to wide-ranging collection of evidence which demonstrates the increasing racialism in the new colonial situation.

Apart from the attitudinal and structural changes which such segregation signals, what lay behind these developments in local Freemasonry? Black and white merchants were in competition and it is entirely possible that brotherhood compromized the value of trade secrecy at a time of cut-throat competition. Similarly the membership of officials of the growing colonial administration presumably created problems if members of the 'subject race' were craftsmen of the same lodge. Certainly by the turn of the century, Freemasonry seems to have become a more significant aspect of colonialism itself. In 1892, the Grand Lodge's Board of General Purposes had created a special Colonial Board whose membership comprized British freemasons who were either prominent figures in colonial affairs or actually employees of the Colonial Office. The Colonial Board's task was, *inter alia*, to assist the development of burgeoning numbers of lodges in the colonial empire. There is no doubt that many colonial officials and prominent members of the trading communities were freemasons. A member of Accra Lodge No. 3063, the European Lodge, reflected on this in 1904:

Looking through the list of petitioners and founder members we find that they represent a fair cross-section of the European community. . .the Head of Customs, the Treasurer, a Senior Ass't Colonial Secretary, two doctors of the Medical Department, a Captain of the Frontier Force, a technical member of the Education Department, a partner of the leading produce merchants, a railway man, a civil engineer of the Public Works Department. . .[39]

The inter-woven quality of trade and Freemasonry in West Africa makes it hard to come to clear conclusions. There are, however, suggestive hints in the available evidence. For example, the early meetings of the McCarthy Lodge No. 4132 were held in the offices of the Eastern Trading Corporation. Lagos Lodge No. 1171 was housed in the Elder Dempster Building in Lagos. For many years the lighting of Calabar Lodge No. 3434 was supplied by Elder Dempster. Lord Leverhulme was one of Britain's most active freemasons and United Africa Company offices in British West African colonies were used for Freemasonic purposes. At different times, the UAC's premises in both Accra and Lagos were used as masonic temples. The link between trade and Freemasonry, despite the fragmentary nature of the evidence, seems clear.

But that link is only one element of important position of Freemasonry in West Africa. For example, when the foundation stone for Northern Nigeria's first lodge was laid in 1917, it was Brother Sir Frederick Lugard who wielded the trowel. No less emblematic of the relationship between power and Freemasonry was the visit of Freemasonry's Grand Master, His Royal Highness, the Duke of Connaught, to West Africa in 1910. In Freetown he laid the foundation stone for the colony's new law courts. The ceremony was presided over by Sir Philip Crampton Smyly. Smyly was probably the senior freemason in Sierra Leone at the time and went on, in 1911, to be Chief Justice in the Gold Coast. Smyly also presided over a meeting at which Freetown's freemasons presented an address to the Grand Master. The public grandness of Freemasonry was visible to anyone who cared to read the local press.

African Masonic activity was growing in this period. Accra Lodge No. 3063 acted as 'parent Lodge' to a number of Nigerian consecrations. This clear evidence of cross-territorial links is at least suggestive at a period in which pan-West African political activity was becoming more apparent. By 1914 there were five lodges consecrated on the Gold Coast in comparison with three in Nigeria and three in Freetown. Oral testimony suggests that by 1914 such notable figures as the powerful lawyers Thomas Hutton-Mills and J.E. Casely-Hayford were 'on the square'. Tachie-Menson's *History of Freemasonry in the Gold Coast*, which is, as we have said, a cautious 'insider's' work, tells us that the equally socially-and professionally-prominent C.J. Bannerman and

A.B. Quartey-Papafio were also craftsmen. Bannerman was a barrister and from 1921 a member of the Legislative Council. Quartey-Papafio was also a barrister and a scion of one of Accra's most distinguished families.

The evidence which suggests that many of the Gold Coast's 'best and brightest' were freemasons begins to mount. It is particularly striking that the initial Committee of the National Congress of British West Africa should have had freemasons as its President (T. Hutton-Mills), Vice-President (J.E. Casely-Hayford) and as one of its joint treasurers (A.B. Quartey-Papafio). The apparently high number of freemasons to be found in the famous photograph of the members of the inaugural meeting of the NCBWA in 1920 is no less arresting. We can definitely pick out sixteen freemasons out of a total attendance of just over forty members. The scrappy nature of our evidence suggests that this is a significant undercounting.[40] The links between the Freemasonic connection and the NCBWA are assuredly a neglected and possibly important avenue for further research.

To begin with the NCBWA was launched at a conference at the Rodger Club in Accra. The Rodger Club, which was later to become a famous multi-racial venue in the 1940s, was founded in 1904. At the time of the launch of the NCBWA it was often referred to as the Accra Native Club in official circles.[41] The club had strong masonic connections. Masonic social activities were frequently held there and many of its leading members were freemasons. For example some of the Rodger Club's past and future chairmen were at the launching of the NCBWA in 1920; E.C. Quist, who had become the first African Crown Counsel in 1914 and eventually Speaker of Ghana's National Assembly many years later, was a member of Accra Lodge No. 3851. Another member of a distinguished Accra family and confrere at the NCBWA's inaugural meeting was H.R. Ribeiro, a member of St. George's and Seccondee Lodge No. 3851. Hugh Quartey-Papafio, another impeccably connected delegate, was a member of Accra Lodge No. 3065. Akilagpa Sawyerr, one of the founders of the West African Students' Union, was a member of Lodge St. Andrew No. 1299 of the Scottish Constitution of Freemasonry.

Two of the Gold Coast contingent at the historic inauguration of the Congress were possibly not freemasons when the meeting occurred: William Ward-Brew and Henry Van Hein. We derive this from the fact that a short time after the meeting, these two made plans to consecrate a new lodge under the Scottish Constitution. On 5 May, 1921, the Lodge Progressive No. 1261[42] was consecrated in Cape Coast. But it seems that neither of these two were qualified to consecrate the new lodge. They were forced to invite a prominent Sierra Leonean Brother, J.P. Macauley, to perform this task. Ward-Brew was to rise very rapidly through the ranks of that lodge and he eventually became the most senior Freemason in the Gold Coast.

At this early stage of our research we can do little more than point to this evidence of a large proportion of freemasons being connected with this milestone in West African history. We are in no position to go beyond this simple conclusion. Those who wish to see the NCBWA as a cross-territorial masonic connection would be stretching the evidence dangerously. There were assuredly a lot of freemasons at the Rodger Club at the launch of the Congress and, as we have shown, the choice of venue is at least suggestive of Freemasonry being one of the organizational avenues used by the conveners. But being a freemason was only one identity amongst many which that glittering assembly shared. To begin with most of these men were either personally wealthy or were scions of wealthy families.

There is no doubt that Freemasonry was an activity which could be entered into by the elite alone and exclusively by elite males at that. The costs of membership were considerable. By 1915, a prospective craftsman had to find a proposer and seconder and then a guinea for the 'proposition fee'. If he were accepted he needed to find another £5.00 for his initiation fee, 5 shillings as dues to the District Grand Lodge, a further 7 shillings for registration, £2.5s.10d. for admission and an annual subscription of £2.5s. In addition a craftsman would be expected to make contributions to the Benevolent Fund and charities. Entry alone therefore cost £11.9s. approximately. To give some idea of the relative value of this, we may note that by 1915 daily-rated labourers in Accra were earning 2 shillings per day.

Being a freemason was one of things that men of property and position did in the towns of the Gold Coast before the Second World War. Wealth was nothing to be ashamed of. It signalled achievement, hard work, worthiness and in some cases, high birth. All but the last were clearly Christian virtues and were seen as such in the very Christian environment of coastal elite society. Freemasonry might, as we have suggested, have facilitated further wealth creation by its provision of an exclusive but extensive network through which commercial and professional influence could be exerted and by which advantage might be gained. Whether this was real or merely expected we shall probably never know. But there seems to be little doubt that lodge membership was certainly a sign that a brother had 'arrived'.

But many freemasons, as we suggested earlier, had extensive alternative affiliations. Being a freemason was assuredly not an exclusive identity. One can best perceive this through biography. The Revd. I. Sackey was Lodge No. 773's Chaplain. But he was also Minister of Cape Coast's Wesleyan Chapel and a member of the Ratepayer's Association. He was later to be active in the African Methodist Episcopal Zion Church.[43] His wife was the leader of the very successful musical group called Christ's Little Band whose musical endeavours appear to have been an important aspect of Cape Coast's social life. Virtually none of those photographed outside the Rodger Club in 1920 were not formally affiliated to one of the Gold Coast's many churches and some were extremely active as churchwardens, lay preachers or sidesmen. Moreover, seventeen of the Gold Coasters at the launch of the NCBWA were lawyers. Even if we were tempted to see the NCBWA as some kind of political extension of Freemasonry, there would be as much evidential prodding to suggest that the NCBWA was a Christian project, or the West African Bar wearing political hats.

In thinking about alternative and overlapping identities it is even more important to recognize more profound and lasting forms of association. Many of the delegates at the Rodger Club in 1920 and the majority of freemasons also felt the bonds of what had become known as 'tradition' and, even more viscerally, family. In the Gold Coast it is clear that a number of traditional office holders were also freemasons. Men like John Vanderpuije in Accra and B.D. Coker in Cape Coast were both senior divisional chiefs, merchants and freemasons. Hutton-Mills relished his position as *Tufuhin*[44] whilst other freemasons like C.J. Bannerman and Kitson Mills were closely involved, as officials, in the turbulent politics of the Ga stool. J.E. Casely-Hayford as well as being a barrister and freemason was also *Safohin Ahinnana Agyiman* of the No. 3 Asafo company in Cape Coast.[45] He along with his fellow freemasons and kinsmen Mark Christian Hayford and William Ward Brew shared a variety of hereditary responsibilities including the pouring of libation for their matrilineal ancestors every new year.

Freemasonry was in some respects a much less demanding linkage than that of kinship. It incurred fewer obligations and almost certainly less financial cost. Many of the Gold Coast members of the National Congress would have used the appellation 'brother' in their lodges. More importantly, unlike many other freemasons world-wide, they would have used the Twi or Ga word for brother to evoke either genuine or fictive relationships in the Gold Coast. It is interesting, in this connection, to note that Hutton-Mills' speech to the inaugural conference stressed that:

> . . .it is important to note that each one of these delegates is an African, belonging to a distinctive African family and thereby commanding the right of property and other interests either in his own right or in the right of the family to which he belongs. It follows from this that apart from the facts of the Delegates being natural leaders of the people of their several communities, they have in themselves the natural right to appeal to His Majesty's

Government for such constitutional reforms as in their judgement are necessary. . .

We feel that these remarks should be taken more literally than they have been. Most commentary has drawn attention to, and then carped about, the undoubtedly rather arrogant assumption of being 'natural leaders of the people'. Our feeling is that he was expressing, possibly awkwardly, the fact that the Gold Coast network which really mattered by the 1920s centred around inter-and intra-familial relationships and interests. Our suspicion is that Freemasonry and indeed the many other affiliations we have touched on constituted useful over-arching linkages which facilitated, in its broadest sense, 'family-building' and the cementing of relationships between families. Freemasonry and other voluntary associations for that matter need to be more firmly embedded in the social environment in which they prospered or failed.

Notes

1. See, for example, David Kimble, *A Political History of Ghana 1850–1928* (Oxford, 1963) pp. 146–50.
2. For example, Immanuel Wallerstein, 'Ethnicity and national integration in West Africa,' *Cahiers d'Etudes Africaines*. 3 October, 1960. pp. 129–39.
3. The most obvious examples of this kind of reasoning are to be found in the late Thomas Hodgkin's *Nationalism in Colonial Africa* (London, 1956), and especially pp. 84–92.
4. Kimble, *A Political History*, 148.
5. London, 1968.
6. The best examples are K.A. Busia's *A Social Survey of Sekondi-Takoradi.* (Crown Agents, London, 1950), and Ione Acquah's *Accra Survey* (London, 1958).
7. *The uses and abuses of political power*, (Chicago, 1970), p. 117.
8. *Two Dimensional Man*, (London, 1974.) p. 108. We have been greatly stimulated by Cohen's exploration of freemasonry in Freetown which is interestingly developed in his *The Politics of Elite Culture*, (Berkeley, California), 1981. Although there were links between Gold Coast and Sierra Leonean freemasons we suspect that these should be seen within the wider generality of personal, family and business relationships between the English-speaking elites along the coast. Cohen's picture of Freetown freemasonry resembles aspects of that which we have looked at in the Gold Coast. But freemasonry in the Gold Coast appears to have been much less devoted to excluding the *menu peuple*. Although the 'coastal elite' had their own snobberies and exclusivity, they were palpably a more open community than Krio society appears to have been.
9. See his *Aladura: a religious movement among the Yoruba* (London, 1968) and his *Ijeshas and Nigerians: the incorporation of a Yoruba Kingdom 1890s–1970s*, (Cambridge, 1983).
10. *Dependence and Opportunity: political change in Ahafo*, (Cambridge, 1974).
11. We had in mind work like that of Patrick Cole's *Modern and Traditional elites in the politics of Lagos* (Cambridge, 1975) and Max Assimeng's *Social Structure of Ghana* (Accra, 1981).
12. Busia, *Social Survey*, p. 112.
13. See for example his 'The study of social change in the Sierra Leone Protectorate.' in *Africa XXIII*, October, 1953.

14. Most notably in Peel, *Aladura* and *Ijeshas*.

15. S.T. Barnes, *Patrons and Power* (Cambridge, 1986); Cole, *Modern and Traditional Elites*.

16. K. Hart. 'Migrants and entrepreneurs.' Unpublished PhD thesis, University of Cambridge, 1969.

17. Hodgkin, *Nationalism in Colonial Africa*, p. 84.

18. Hodgkin, *Nationalism*, pp. 91–2.

19. Hodgkin, *Nationalism*, pp. 84–5.

20. Kimble, *A Political History*, p. 148.

21. Dennis Austin, *Politics in Ghana. 1946–1960*, (Oxford 1964), pp. 26–7.

22. The analogies are notably Anglocentric. It is fascinating if somewhat idle to speculate on what would have been imposed upon Ghanaian experience had the majority of such scholars been, say, Brazilian or Turkish.

23. Acquah, *Accra Survey*, 1958. p. 151.

24. Cohen, *The Politics of Elite Culture, 1974, p. 106*.

25. An admittedly hostile researcher has recently claimed that in the United States of America, which boasted over 1000 freemasonic lodges, almost none was multi-racial. Freemasonry's predilection for secrecy makes it hard to be sure whether this, and other assertions, are or are not accurate.

26. *Of 3 March, 1900.*

27. *3 March 1900.*

28. *Of 23 July 1898.*

29. A concept borrowed from Professor Tim Couzens who in turn borrowed it from the Revd. Ray Phillips. See Couzens, 'Moralizing leisure time' in Shula Marks and Richard Rathbone (eds.) *Industrialization and social change* (London, 1982), pp. 314–37.

30. 23 November 1863.

31. *The African Times*, 23 December 1862.

32. The Society was admirably equipped for outdoor preaching. In addition to the portable harmonium they also used portable pulpit whose quality was often commented upon by the press.

33. *The Gold Coast Methodist Times*, 31 August 1897.

34. This conflict of evidence is briefly discussed in Kimble, *op. cit.* p. 225. The Mankessim Council met in Mankessim in April 1868 to consider the implications for Fante states of the disequilibrium they feared in the wake of the ambiguous decisions of the 1865 Select Committee's Resolutions and the Anglo–Dutch exchange of Gold Coast territories of 1867. Some Fante rulers and their followers felt threatened by Asante, by Dutch colonial methods and by the evidence of British indifference to their feelings. The Council which fascinatingly considered the future in terms of self-government and paved the way for the Fante Confederation. The most accessible account is to be found in Kimble pp. 222–63.

35. *The Gold Coast Express.* 15 June 1887.

36. *A history of Freemasonry on the Gold Coast.* Accra, 1965.

37. As neither of the authors of this piece is a freemason, this presents us with a particular problem.

38. And of course excites, possibly quite unfairly, speculation about conspiracy and subterfuge.

39. Records of the Accra Lodge, 1905–06. p. 2.

40. Showing whether or not prominent Ghanaians of this period were freemasons is an inexact science. Oral testimony has proved particularly helpful in filling-out a record which is largely and intentionally withheld from the researcher. We have been forced to adopt some more radical and 'high-tech' methods. For example, we were able to enhance a well-known photograph of E.J.P. Brown, a prominent member of both

the Aborigines' Rights Protection Society and a member of the Gold Coast Legislative
Council from 1916–26. Computer enhancement reveals beyond doubt that the left lapel
of his suit sports a Masonic pin.

41. See, for example, Ghana National Archives: ADM 5/4/19. p. 13.

42. The name of the lodge suggests, but only suggests, some kind of connection
between the mood of the meeting in 1920, which was much concerned with progress,
and the name of the new lodge.

43. Founded in the Gold Coast by Bishop B.J. Small in 1898. Small was from the
West Indies and had come first to the Gold Coast as a sergeant in the West India
Regiment in 1874. He subsequently went to the USA to be ordained. Sackey was the
author of the interesting 'Brief history of the A.M.E. Zion Church, West Gold Coast
District' to be found *The Ghana Bulletin of Theology*. 1. no. 3. 1957. For more on the
Gold Coast A.M.E. Zion Church, see Kimble, *op. cit.* pp. 163–4.

44. *Tufuhin* is the head of the Asafo, whose position is both military and political.
During war he supervizes the companies and at times of peace he administers the financial
and legal matters that involve the asafo members.

45. The tensions between Christian, 'burgher' notions of civil order and the sometimes
robust conduct of Asafo companies is an interesting aspect of the construction of these
'moral communities'. The press consistently attacked 'riotous' behaviour and sometimes
accused Asafo companies of being active in fomenting public disorder. *The Gold Coast
Express* of 1 July, 1897 said, for example, that fighting was a logical conclusion of
what it described rather snuffily as 'native dances'. The same paper on 21 September
1897 condemned Asafo company 'fetish dances' implying that they involved, horror of
horrors, nudity. Casely-Hayford's continued attachment to his office was undoubtedly
a strongly-held personal attachment. It was also a token of the fact that although Asafo
companies' power had seemed to decline in the 1870s, it was a crisis they had overcome.
Anyone who wished to exercise any sort of power in the Fante states had, perforce, to
take them seriously.

Chapter Ten

Landscapes of Dissent – Ikale and Ilaje Country 1870–1950

PAUL RICHARDS

Reluctant urbanites

W hen I first began fieldwork in the small Ikale town of Iju Odo in 1968, everywhere I went, when asking about settlement changes, people told me that 'villages' (literally 'farm camps') had been much bigger and more important in the past. Now, like other Yoruba groups, the Ikale live in towns. Iju Odo had even recently undergone a process of 'town planning', with bright blue and neatly-lettered street signs picking out a more-or-less herring-bone street plan to prove it. The main motor road through the centre of the town was called Broad Street. My landlord and protector, who lived on this road, always insisted on an older name, Isowa Street, and required me so to address any letter I wrote to him. It didn't much matter since there was no postal delivery and he had to collect his mail in the district headquarters, Okitipupa. This was just one of the many small ways in which Ikale people would give vent to the feeling that their towns were rather new-fangled and not really proper. People had breathed, and eaten, more freely in the large farm camps of former times. Now there was apocalyptic tension in the air. The great staple of Ikale country, the white yam, everywhere was giving ground to a less palatable alternative, cassava, as soil fertility declined; many cassava farms had been badly attacked by a recent plague of grasshoppers; the pungent smell of a rampant exotic weed, *Chromolaena odorata*, masked the more acceptable aromas normally associated with land in fallow; and Jehovah's Witnesses in Iju Odo were finding ready converts to the idea that the world was due to end in 1975. One humid night, unable to sleep, I sat on the street until late, watching and listening as a prophet in

This chapter © *Paul Richards 1992*

the house opposite, working against the flickering background of a huge bonfire, and with the rhythmic poise of a master drummer, brought his congregation to a state of spiritual exhaltation. Rising in the cool silence of the early morning I met the house swept and bare. The prophet and his followers had quit Babylon at the dead of night: the faint sound of trees being felled in the forest half-a-mile distant indicated where the City of God was to take shape.

It took a fuller acquaintanceship with the archival records on the area for me to realize that these early fieldwork impressions formed part of a broader picture. The Ikale and neighbouring Ilaje people had been engaged in a lively debate about urbanism and its practical and spiritual consequences for close on a hundred years. Peel's study of Ilesha[1] has given us a richly illuminating insight into how one of the established urban polities of the nineteenth-century Yorubaland negotiated the transition from independent city state to full and active membership of the twentieth-century urban hierarchy in southern Nigeria. To follow Ikale and Ilaje debates about urbanism and its consequences over the same period is to glimpse the opposite side of the same coin. This is the story of the folk beyond the pale. Cried down by outsiders as barbarians, but in fact participating in the new regional order as fully as any of the major Yoruba urban centres, the Ikale and Ilaje people pursued settlement strategies that were a conscious rejection of values espoused by neighbours such as the Ijesha. This rejection, I suggest, arose not from cultural or ethnic truculence but because the urbanism of their rivals inclined too much towards the world of the import-export economy, and as such posed a threat to a number of basic values in a peasant food-producing society. In a country grappling with the aftermath of an oil boom this critique still retains its relevance.

The regional setting

The Ikale and Ilaje inhabit the western flank of the Niger Delta, in the southernmost part of Ondo State. For convenience I shall refer to the area as the Okitipupa region, after the small town from which the administrative division is named (Maps 2 and 3). Ikale and Ilaje country are roughly equidistant from Ife to the north, Lagos to the west and Benin to the east, and experienced the impact of all three urban cultures in the pre-colonial period. Ikale ruling houses claim Benin descent, and there are faint traces of an early trade, between this area and the polities of eastern Yoruba country, in salt from the coastal marshes.[2] The historical picture becomes clearer with the opening, in the 1870s, of an important trade route linking Ondo, Ijesha and Ibadan with the creek-side port of Itebu, so allowing traders from these places direct access to Lagos via the coastal creek-and-lagoon system at a time when more direct routes were blockaded by the Egba and Ijebu. Eastwards, the intra-coastal waterway system provided direct access to the Benin river and the trading states of the Niger Delta. The region was thus at the mid-point of waterway network at times open to canoe transport from the mouth of the Volta in the west to the Cross River in the east (Map 2). Late nineteenth-century evidence suggests that canoe transport was up to twelve times cheaper than porterage, the other main means of transportation in the forests of southern Nigeria.[3] Large canoes, some capable of carrying several tons at a time, provided the area with an early entry into the regional foodstuffs trade, as well as the opportunity to participate in overseas trade organized by merchants in Lagos and on the Benin River.

The waterway system was subject to some improvement in the early colonial period. Dredging and sudd clearance permitted the regular passage of launches to creek ports such as Okitipupa, Igbaje and Agbabu. As a consequence, in the early years of the century, the Okitipupa region was better connected to the colonial capital, Lagos, than other parts of eastern Yoruba country. But with the subsequent shift to road transport in the 1930s the region found itself one of the more isolated districts in western Nigeria.[4] Communications with Lagos and the regional capital Ibadan were improved with the opening up, in the 1950s, of a trunk road from Ijebu Ode to Benin across the belt of heavily-forested country separating Okitipupa from Ondo, but much of the southern half of the area still remained without roads and relatively isolated.

Ecologically, the region may be divided (Map 3) into three main zones.

1. *Swamp zone.* This comprises about half the total land area, but contains less than a third of the total population. Settlements are concentrated in two distinct bands, one along the coast and another along the boundary between swamp and mainland. Fishing is the major economic activity in the seaside settlements. The settlements on the mainland margin have a long history of involvement in trade, and the majority of the larger periodic markets in the Okitipupa region are to be found in this boundary zone.[5] Two of these settlements – Igbobini and Arogbo – specialized in the construction of large canoes, exported in the nineteenth century as far afield as Brass in the eastern Delta.[6]

2. *Mainland palm-belt.* North of the swamp is an extensive tract of farming country. Here, sandy loam soils developed from unconsolidated Tertiary and Quaternary sediments are easily worked and well-suited to the cultivation of yams (the main indigenous staple) and cassava (a nineteenth-century introduction).[7] A regional trade in yams and cassava, exchanged for smoked fish, gin, mats and salt in the line of markets along the northern margin of the swamp, was well-established by the second half of the nineteenth century. These foodstuff exports went at least as

far as Makun and Leki on the Lagos lagoon, and may have reached Lagos itself.[8] Regular and intensive food-crop farming created conditions in which secondary forest fallow was colonized rapidly by self-seeded wild oil palms at densities comparable to those of the palm-belt of eastern Nigeria.[9] Palm produce emerged as a major export in the early colonial period. Harvesting and processing was done mainly by Urhobo migrants from the western Delta.[10]

3. *High forest frontier.* In the 1870s an extensive tract of closed-canopy rain forest separated the Okitipupa region from Ondo country to the north. The area was opened up by elephant hunters and prospectors for timber and wild rubber during the 1890s. Farmers soon followed. The local soils, developed over granitic Basement Complex rocks are heavier and more moisture-retentive than those in the palm belt, and suitable for cocoa cultivation. Competition between Okitipupa and Ondo farmers for land in this area intensified with the widespread adoption of cocoa cultivation in eastern Yoruba country in the 1920s.[11] Farm camps have since proliferated along the roads and tracks passing through this zone, but as yet there are no major permanent settlements.

The social geography of the Okitipupa region is complex. Colonial Indirect Rule recognized five basic groupings (Map 3).[12] The largest – the Ikale – occupy much of the mainland palm zone and forest frontier. The Ilaje are the main group in the swamp zone. Both the Ikale and Ilaje speak dialects of Yoruba. The Ijoi-Apoi are a Yoruba-speaking group of Ijo (Izon) origin controlling a strategic section of the swamp-mainland boundary where the Oluwa river, historically an important artery for trade northwards, forms a junction with the east-west creek waterway system. The Ijo-speaking Ijo-Arogbo, and the Edo-speaking people of the 'Bini Federation', occupy further sections of this boundary zone to the south-east. These five main ethnic groupings could be further sub-divided: there are two main sections of the Ilaje, the Mahin and the Ugbo, and the Ikale claim to comprise 'nine tribes', for example. In addition note must be taken of three other social groups: traders, migrant palm cutters and Christians. The activities of Lagos traders were of particular significance (as far as the following account is concerned) in the period 1870–1920. They based their operations in the region on a number of creek-side ports, including Igbo Egunrin and Itebu in the west, Igbobini and Arogbo in central Okitipupa, and Siluko and Iyansan on the border with Benin in the east. The Ekitiparapo Association, a group of Lagos traders of Ijesha origin, established a small colony at Ayesan, a point at which Ijebu, Ondo and Ikale territory meet. Migrant palm cutters of Urhobo origin began to migrate to Ikale country in the first decade of the twentieth century. They comprised an estimated 25 per cent of the population of Ikale country in the 1930s, and 33 per cent by 1952.[13] Ikale and Ilaje country were noted as an early focus of activity by African independent churches. Aladura groups rose to prominence in the region during the 1930s.

The Ondo road and its critics, *c.* 1880

During the 1870s an alliance between the Ijebu and the Egba barred the important Yoruba polities of Ibadan and Oyo from access to the port of Lagos. To circumvent this obstacle to the expansion of overseas trade through Lagos, the colonial administrator, Sir John Glover, sought a new route up-country.[14] One possibility was to follow the lagoon eastward as far as Ilaje, thus skirting Ijebu territory, and then to link up with routes running northwards through Ikale country to Ondo, from where there would be ready access to Ilesha, Ibadan and Oyo. The main obstacle to the opening of this eastern route to traders from Lagos was a long war between Ondo and Ife. Diplomatic intervention by Glover's emissary, Captain Roger Goldsworthy, assisted a settlement of this conflict in May 1872. This was followed by the re-establishment of the long-abandoned site of Ode Ondo as the capital and main trading centre of the Ondo people. The Ondo road was open.[15]

Glover's initiative in securing an eastern road to the interior was given enthusiastic support and practical assistance by a group of African traders (returnees from Sierra Leone and Brazil) with ancestral ties to Ibadan, Oyo and Ilesha, and by those Lagosian chiefs (Baba Isale) who acted as patrons and protectors of interior trading interests using the creek and lagoon waterway system. Equally vigorous opposition to Glover's plans came from the European and Sierra Leonean traders with business and political links with the Egba.[16] Glover was recalled to London soon after Goldsworthy had completed his mission, and Pope Hennessy, Governor-in-Chief for West Africa, sympathetic to the Egba interest, withdrew any further official support for the new route. Despite this setback the Ondo Road, as it was known, began to be used by considerable numbers of Ibadan, Oyo and Ijesha traders, and attracted missionary interest.[17] The route was assessed by Maser and Roper in 1873, and David Hinderer in 1874, resulting in the decision by the Church Missionary Society to establish a small mission, staffed by Sierra Leonean agents, in Ondo.[18]

Apart from the threat of Ijebu patrols on the lagoon the main problems associated with the new route were concentrated in the Okitipupa region. Local trading interests were hesitant to risk alienating their powerful western neighbours, the Ijebu, in order to assist traders and missionaries from Lagos. A Lagos link was not necessary for their participation in the overseas trade. This was as well, if not better, directed through the Benin River.[19] For those involved in supplying foodstuffs to markets in the region the new road was even more problematic, since heavy recruitment of carriers in and around the creekside ports on the Ikale-Ilaje boundary, for the overland journey to Ondo, threatened local sources of agricultural labour. Labour supply had already begun to be a worry to food producers due to the fact that their domestic slaves had only to reach the boundaries of Lagos territory to claim their freedom.[20]

Some local rulers – for example, Manuwa, chief of the small Ilaje town of Itebu – were prepared to gamble on the Lagos connection, trusting that consequent trade and diplomatic advantages would outweigh the price they might have to pay in terms of local opposition.[21] Struggling to free himself from the control of his overlord, Ogubsemoyin, Amapetu of Mahin, Manuwa was deeply compromised by the refusal of the Lagos administration to invest in further diplomatic efforts to sustain the new route. He survived as best he could; first encouraging and then taxing travellers, opening the route at times, closing it at others.[22] The Amapetu meanwhile had his own plans for direct trade with the Europeans, leasing thirteen miles of the Atlantic shore to the Hamburg firm, Gottlieb Leonhard Gaiser,[23] and negotiating with the explorer Nachtigal a Treaty of Protection with the German emperor. Although never ratified, this treaty was a cause of continued factional strife in Ilaje country resulting, in the 1920s, in the deportation of the Olugbo of Ugbo, and the threatened mass migration of his followers.[24]

Ijesha and Ibadan trading interests and supporters of the Ondo mission continued to press Lagos for vigorous diplomatic intervention in the region, backed by military action. They sought government support to strengthen the hand of local rulers, such as Manuwa, who favoured Lagos links. The contradictions of Manuwa's position were little understood, however, and the missionaries, overestimating his power to act on their behalf, were often exasperated by his apparent ambivalence and opportunism. Goldsworthy had the mistaken idea that Ondo was the key to the control of the turbulent Okitipupa region and encouraged the appointment of Edun, an Ondo chief with land at Erinla on the route south to Ikale, as Lisa (the title holder second in seniority to the king). Subsequently the missionaries looked, without much success, to the Lisa, as their main patron in Ondo, to solve problems connected with the route southwards through Ikale, a region in which he had no authority.

Frequent harrassment crossing Ikale country caused the Ondo missionaries and Ijesha traders to consider alternative routes. To begin the Ondo leg of the journey travelling northward via the Oluwa river suffered the disadvantage that the ruler of Igbobini was more interested in maintaining his diplomatic and trading links with delta ports to the east. Accordingly, the missionaries favoured a by-pass around Ikale country, opened in 1877 by Manuwa and the Lisa of Ondo, exploiting a common boundary between Ilaje and Ondo at Araromi Obu, a port once used by the deserted Ondo town of Imorun.[25]

Even at this early date it is apparent that Ikale and some parts of Ilaje were different from surrounding districts. It is clear why the missionaries and traders endeavouring to forge links between Lagos and interior towns such as Ondo and Ilesha had difficulties with rulers of places like Mahin and Igbobini. These men had their own overseas trading aspirations and stood to gain little from becoming tributary to someone else's network. So they fought for their own share of the action. But to that extent they spoke the same 'language' as those with whom they fought, and could be paid off in the same currency. The Ikale chiefs were different. Participating in the local exchange economy as specialist food producers, and not unappreciative of the virtues of commerce, they sensed at the same time a serious threat from trade and urbanism to their agrarian way of life. Several early visitors noted with surprise that the Ikale had fine town houses, but that they only ever inhabited them when urgent market business or diplomatic issues pressed upon them.[26] For the rest of the time they preferred to keep to their country estates, and struggled to keep the number of traders passing through their territory – any traders, not just Lagos traders – under the strictest control. The missionary Maser, visiting the Ikale town of Oke Aye in 1873, noted that 'very good houses' belonging to the Ikale 'are generally quite empty and only occupied on special occasions . . . they live in thick bush on agriculture and change their abode after the land has been exhausted [being] a nation scattered into many fragments having no king to unite them . . .' .[27] Where other local rulers were faced with choosing among rival networks the Ikale chiefs had to come to terms with the entire system of overseas trading links and commerce in foreign ideas. Their suspicion that the values associated with this new system presented a challenge to their way of life proved to be well-founded. The devaluation of role of the food producers has since proved to be a stubbornly durable feature of Nigerian political culture.

Barbarism and civility – some local responses to colonialism

In 1908, with the Okitipupa region now under formal British colonial rule, the Provincial Commissioner and two companies of soldiers marched on Oshoro, the westernmost district of Ikale, to demonstrate the willingness of the Lagos administration to use force to reinstate Nigwo of Igbotako, a local chief sympathetic to British interests deposed by his fellow Ikale chiefs. The *Annual Report* for Southern Nigeria, 1907, describes the Ikale as a 'tribe nearly akin to the Binis' and Nigwo as 'their principal chief'. Ten years after the sack of Benin City the Bini association was in British eyes proof that the Ikale were a 'low and barbarous people'. Nigwo, a Christian convert of the Evangelist's Mission, was considered an enlightened ruler. The mission, a self-supporting off-shoot of the CMS run from Ondo by the Revd. E. Moses Lijadu, drew much of its support from the Okitipupa area. There were sizeable congregations at Igbotako (in Ikale), Igbo Egunrin (in Ilaje) and at Siluko on the border between Ikale country and Benin. All three were important trading towns strategically situated at the meeting place of creek and mainland transportation systems.

After the British show of strength the *Annual Report* 1908, assumed, optimistically, that 'the matter had now been settled, though for a time a commissioner will be stationed in the immediate neighbourhood to assist the Bale Nigwo in the reforms which he is anxious to introduce for the good of his people'. Nigwo was indeed restored to his capital, the burgeoning small town of Igbotako, but opposition continued to flourish in the dispersed farm settlements into which the rest of Oshoro was divided. The dispute between Nigwo and other Ikale chiefs was rooted in the central problem, for the Ikale, of how to relate to the changing regional economic system, with its increased emphasis on overseas commerce, without at the same time undermining the socio-economic fabric of a society specialized in food production.

Authority over the external relations of each of the 'nine tribes' of Ikale was exercized by chiefs known as *oloja* – literally 'owner of the market'. They exercized this authority from special centres set aside for trade and diplomacy known as *ode* (literally, 'outside'). In Oshoro in the late nineteenth century this was a place known as Ode Moribodo, located close to the waterside-mainland junction, and described in a 1937 report as an extensive ruin. To outsiders – missionaries and traders – the *oloja* seemed like paramount rulers and each *ode* a capital. The situation was in fact more complex. Ikale was a federation presided over by a ritually-important ruler, the Abodi.[28] Power over internal and domestic affairs, however, was largely in the hands of title holders of the prestigious Ijamo Society. The office of *oloja* was perhaps closer to minister of foreign affairs than to paramount chief.

Bamido, Nigwo's father, had competed with a man called Ikuyiminu for the position of Oloja of Oshoro. The father failing in his ambition, the battle was continued by the son by other means. Nigwo set himself up as a self-styled Oloja in a new ode, Igbotako, shaping the office and settlement to coincide more closely with outside expectations. In this he was greatly aided by his mother, Dorcas Ogunro, a wealthy trader and convert to Moses Lijadu's Ondo-based mission. Lijadu proved an important ally in the battle for official recognition. Igbotako controlled one of the trade routes through the high forest to Ondo, and Nigwo was a strong proponent of activities of greatest commercial interest to the British. The road from Igbotako into the high forest had been first opened up in the 1890s to supply food to collectors of wild rubber from

Ondo. The immediate cause of the 1907 revolt against Nigwo was a dispute over his disbursement of stumpage royalties collected by the British administration from logging concessionaires working in Ikale forests.

According to Nigwo's own account[29] the conflict really stemmed from his challenge to the authority of the Ijamo Society. Nigwo contested the legitimacy of the heavy funeral levies paid to the society by the children of deceased title holders. He also claimed that Ijamo ritual and legal authority provided support for the continuation of the practice of twin infanticide, and that the society had recently decreed that any runaway wives should be executed. By contrast, in Nigwo's court at Igbotako, women were free to sue for divorce and twins received protection. The British were quite clear that they were supporting Nigwo's cause because he was a progressive ruler. The Ijamo Society, they supposed, was fighting a last-ditch defence of an ancient and outmoded way of life. The contrast between Igbotako, a focus for new trading and export-oriented activities, and the scattered deep-rural hamlets of Nigwo's opponents was a contrast between civility and barbarism. The increasingly urban character of Igbotako as a settlement was one of the pointers to the progress being achieved under Nigwo's enlightened leadership.[30]

The flaw in this view of events was that the Ikale in the nineteenth century had not shown themselves to be especially peripheral or backward. They had participated as strongly as any other group in the mercantile networks of the Nigerian littoral. As already noted, their main interest in supplying this regional system with food, rather than in participating in the overseas trade directly, reflected strong comparative advantage, since there were few other areas so well placed to make good the food deficits of the creek and delta trading communities. That Ikale specialization in food production was not just second-best is shown by the fact that they vigorously expanded their supply to delta towns such as Sapele and Warri, and eventually as far as Lagos, in the early colonial period, when all official efforts were directed towards getting them to participate in the overseas palm produce trade.

In this light, the battle between Nigwo and the Ijamo Society takes on a new significance. The focus appears to have been the struggle to protect and control sources of labour. Yam cultivation is labour-intensive, and heads of Ikale farming households needed to try and limit the outflow of household dependents seeking economic independence in the new centres connected with the rubber and timber trades. Rulers like Nigwo, and centres like Igbotako, were magnets for dissatisfied sons, runaway wives, domestic slaves, and the heavily indebted (who might otherwise have had to pawn themselves as agricultural labourers to meet their obligations). But the more the Ikale chiefs tried to control labour through exercizing their ritual and juridical authority – through, for example, the Ijamo Society's control over marriage, reproduction and the age-grade system[31] – the more scope opponents such as Nigwo had for pinning on them charges of 'backwardness' and 'barbarity'.

In the event, and despite Nigwo's success in enlisting British military assistance to punish his 'unenlightened' opponents, support for the food party in Ikale politics turned out to be surprisingly durable. The Ijamo Society continued to mount opposition to Nigwo until finally proscribed in 1919. Ikuyiminu, accused of involvement in twin infanticide, was deported to Onitsha.[32] Petitions for the society's restoration were answered in the local government reforms of the 1930s, its prestige apparently little diminished in the interim. That strong support for this proposal seems to have come from the large number of Christian converts in Ikale suggests that more was at stake than the continuation of an outmoded subsistence way of life held together by the blind exercize of pagan 'ritual terror' (*pace* Meillassoux).[33] The continued, or evolving, legitimacy of the Ijamo Society is perhaps better understood as a consequence of Ikale determination to stick with food production as an economic speciality. A formative event in this regard seems to have been local experience of the rubber boom in the 1890s. A contemporary commentator, Captain Ambrose, compared Ikale country, with its dense scatter of well-staffed farm estates and abundance of food, with food shortages in Ondo, where the rush for ivory, rubber and timber had fatally disrupted farming activities.[34] These memories, and the lessons to be drawn from them, remained clear to many Ikale, as they observed, from a sceptical distance, first the expansion of the export commodity trade economy in the 1920s, and then its apocalyptic collapse in the following decade.

Palm oil and 'indolent' farmers – Ikale country, *c.* 1920

Not long after the 1908 'show of strength' by the Lagos government it was reported that 'buyers of palm produce . . . had increased sevenfold' in Ikale country.[35] By the 1920s Okitipupa Division exported annually about 5000 tons of oil and a similar weight of kernels, the major part originating in Ikale country (especially the densely-populated Oshoro district).[36] This amounted to about 10 per cent of all palm produce exports from the western provinces of Nigeria.

The specialized work of harvesting the wild palms and preparing oil was undertaken by gangs of migrant labourers from Urhobo country in the western delta. By 1932, according to census estimates, one quarter of the population of Ikale country was of Urhobo origin. Ikale landlords charged the Urhobo a head tax for access to palm groves amounting, according to the market price for palm produce, to between 5 and 20 per cent of each labourer's annual income. The Ikale also sold Urhobo palm cutters their food. Requests from the Urhobo community to rent land for subsistence purposes during the trade recession of the 1930s were steadfastly refused by the Ikale. Food purchases could account for as much as a half to three-quarters of the disposable income of an Urhobo household. In consequence much of the profit from palm export production accrued to Ikale farmers through food crop sales.

The world market price for palm produce was bouyant during the 1920s, but collapsed at the end of 1929. With alternative markets for their foodstuffs in the fishing communities of the swamp zone and, thanks to cheap transport on the creek and lagoon system, in urban centres as far distant as Lagos and Sapele, the Ikale were cushioned against the worst effects of recession.[37] Between August 1929 and August 1931, for example, the decline in prices for palm products was two to three times greater than the corresponding fall in the price of yam in local markets.[38] The colonial administration, concerned that the presence of a large number of migrants would stimulate renewed political unrest in Ikale country, spent much time exhorting local landowners to harvest their own palm trees, in the hope that eventually the Urhobo might be repatriated. The unwillingness of the landowners to oblige was seen as 'indolence' typical of an isolated and backward people stuck in a subsistence rut.[39] It passed unnoticed that the Ikale, as food specialists, had been able to benefit economically from the post-war boom in palm produce exports while passing on a disproportionate share of the risks, now starkly apparent in the aftermath of the 1929 price collapse, to the Urhobo migrant community.

It was not the Urhobo, however, who were responsible for renewed political excitement in the Okitipupa region during the 1920s, but a further round of the kind of economic rivalries and ethical and moral tussles first triggered by the opening of the Ondo Road a half-century earlier. After the deposition of Ikuyiminu, the Oloja of Oshoro, in 1918, the anti-Nigwo faction in Oshoro changed tactics, seemingly deciding on a strategy designed to overtop the appeal to the colonial authorities of Nigwo's town, Igbotako. Abandoning their multiplicity of rural sections, the deposed Ikuyiminu's supporters banded together to build a model town of their own, Ilutitun (literally, 'new town'). This demonstration of defiant loyalty seems to have had the right effect. In 1926, a year after Ikuyiminu's deportation, a government officer described Ilutitun as 'clean and exceptionally well laid out with two good markets . . . in fact it is the nearest approach to a town I have seen in this country'. Given that the site was no more than a mile or two from Igbotako, Nigwo's own model centre for Christian commerce and justice, this must have seemed sweet revenge to the 'barbarians' who built it. Local political discourse had been enriched by a cultural event that was to prove to be of outstanding importance in subsequent years – namely, the ritual of competitive town planning.[40]

Trade and tradition – Ilaje country in the 1920s

Meanwhile, Ilaje country erupted in a fierce feud between the neigh-bouring settlements of Mahin and Ugbo.[41] Early European accounts of Ilaje refer to the people of the swamp region as 'Mahins'. In practice, about half the Ilaje people owed allegiance not to the Amapetu of Umahenge (Mahin) but to the Olugbo, ruler of Ugbo. Mahin and Ugbo are adjacent villages, close to an outlet to the sea from the creek waterway system known to Portuguese sea captains as the Rio Primeiro. This is the only such link between Lagos and the Benin River, and its possible economic significance in the days of the slave trade may help account for the location of Mahin and Ugbo.[42] Whatever their previous significance Mahin and Ugbo were no more than small villages in the 1920s, each with a population of a few hundred. The majority of the Ugbo people lived in a line of sizeable villages along the coast from where they controlled some of the best fishing grounds in the region. Fishing was their major economic interest. The Mahin people were spread far and wide along the creeks of the swamp zone, fishing and farming where they could. Many of them were concerned more with trade and canoe transportation than fishing. As we have seen, an earlier Amapetu encouraged local participation in overseas trade by leasing 'Mahin Beach' to Gaiser, the German trading house, and Mahin sub-chiefs, notably Manuwa, were well-known to Lagos traders using the Ondo Road.

The dispute between the Ugbo and Mahin people had some of the features of that between Nigwo and the Ijamo Society. Approaching from Lagos by way of the Ondo Road colonial officials at first conceived the Amapetu to be the overlord of all Ilaje country. But a large section of the Ilaje people, loyal to the Olugbo, refused to accept the Amapetu's paramountcy, attend his court or pay taxes to Mahin. Olugbo Mafimishebi claimed independence on the basis of his descent from an Ife dynasty deposed by Oduduwa, the putative founder of many Yoruba polities. The Ugbo people, equated with the Igbo of the celebrated legend of Moremi, were said to have settled the creeks as refugees from ancient Ife, thus long pre-dating the in-migration from Warri and Benin of the Mahin, to whom an earlier Olugbo had granted permission to settle. The colonial administration gave no credence to these claims – how would it have been possible for the Mahin people to have settled the greater part of the swamp region if the Amapetu was a mere vassal? In June 1921 a judicial court of enquiry was held into the Olugbo's behaviour and his deportation to Calabar recommended. Mafimishebi subsequently

172

petitioned the Secretary of State for the Colonies, asking that the Oni of Ife, the Oba of Benin and Olu of Warri be approached to testify on his behalf. The Governor, Sir Hugh Clifford, instituting further enquiries, elicited the Oni of Ife's testimony that the Ugbo people were indeed the 'Igbo' celebrated in the Moremi story, but saw no reason to recommend any revision in the original judgement. Ugbo was too small and remote to have been of independent historical significance, and Mafimishebi's claim to overlordship of 'territories which his ancestors could not possibly have controlled' was deemed 'ludicrous'.[43]

The problem between Ugbo and Mahin continued unabated, however, and so intractable did it appear that in 1925 plans were put forward to allow the supporters of the Olugbo to quit their villages and settle further east along the coast. Seemingly as a result of formulating these plans it began to be realized that the Ugbo people were by no means as insignificant, demographically and geographically, as had been supposed hitherto. The Olugbo was allowed to return to Ilaje country in 1927, and the evidence reconsidered. The Intelligence Report for Ilaje District (1931) reversed earlier judgements, concluding that the Ugbo claim to independence of Mahin was plausible.[44] Henceforth, local courts and Native Administration were reorganized to reflect this change in perception.

The colonial administration's initial difficulty seems to have been rather similar to the problem that they had with the Ikale. The bias of British observers towards the world of commodity exports made it difficult for them to conceive that local groups producing foodstuffs (in this case smoked fish) for regional markets might enjoy economic advantages, and ritual prestige and political authority, over groups oriented more towards highly volatile overseas trade. Lack of enthusiasm for the palm oil trade by the Ikale was interpreted as 'indolence' and 'backwardness'. Ugbo enthusiasm for fishing rather than trade was evidence of a subordinate status – proof, if you like, that they must have been the 'hewers of wood and drawers of water' in Ilaje society.

Settlement fission as religious and economic discourse

In the 1880s, disillusioned with Chief Manuwa, the CMS Ondo Mission had transferred its station from Itebu in Ilaje country to Aiyesan on the Ondo border. The Okitipupa region was largely neglected by overseas missions for the next thirty years.[45] Even so, conversion to Christianity was widespread in the first two decades of the twentieth century due to the activities of three independent African churches: the Evangelist's Mission, the United African Church (UNA) and the West African Episcopalian Church (WAE).

The Evangelists' Mission – of which Bale Nigwo and his mother were prominent early members – was first organized by Lijadu as a self-supporting venture within the CMS, but later became independent. The WAE and UNA were Lagos-based organizations; fruits of the Ethiopian movement in Lagos church politics in the latter dacades of the nineteenth century. The UNA was first established in the Okitipupa region by S. Ogunmukomi, an Igbobini man converted to Christianity in Lagos in 1892, who upon returning home brought 8000 adherents into the UNA. Self-reliance was the salient characteristic of the early development of Christianity in Okitipupa, financial independence the bedrock of spiritual freedom. In the case of the UNA self-reliance went even further, for there was no resident minister. Ogunmukomi was made a deacon in 1904, but it was not until 1921 that he was ordained and made superintendant of the district. The 1919 influenza epidemic had resulted in converts dying without the sacraments or Christian burial, and the UNA responded by giving special licence to lay readers.[46]

The influenza epidemic was an unprecedented disaster, engendering an apocalyptic atmosphere in which it is possible to discern the first stirrings of a spiritual excitement that later led to the emergence of the Aladura (praying) churches as a major force in the Okitipupa region. This came about as follows.

The early missionaries in Ondo, Phillips and Lijadu, focused much of their challenge to the old country religions on the issue of wastefully expensive sacrificial rites. The Christian alternative, access to God through prayer, was free to all, including slaves and people heavily in debt. Prayer was a double attack on the power and privileges of groups like the Ijamo Society. It denied them a ritual interlocutory role and the labour and wealth that came as a perquisite of the exercise of that sacrificial role. Not surprisingly, in the early days, this was seen as a straight attack by the missionaries on the likes of the Ijamo Society. By the 1920s the battle lines had changed in subtle and unpredictable ways. As already noted the prestige associated with membership of a title-holding society, such as the Ijamo, did not decline to anything like the extent that might have been expected in a region where a large-scale process of conversion was underway,[47] in part because the regional economy linking the Ilaje and Ikale remained bouyant, even when export trade faltered, and in part because high-handed actions by a remote and uncomprehending colonial regime alienated local opinion, including some influential Christians. One such was Patriarch Campbell of the WAE, a frequent visitor from Lagos (and important in the rise of Aladura Christianity because of his connections with the Garrick Braide movement in the Niger Delta). Campbell interested himself in the Olugbo's cause, and was involved in the moves to petition the Secretary of State for the Colonies against his deportation.[48]

This rather potent alliance of independent Christians and durable traditionalists clearly worried the colonial administration, and they decided they needed to get much closer to the people. This process was well under way even before Governor Cameron's major overhaul of Native Administration in the 1930s, and it drew some of the established Christian leaders in the community into brokerage roles. The turning point was the creation in 1928 of a separate Okitipupa Division, with a new district office in Okitipupa. Formerly the area had been administered, but very lightly, from Ondo, as the Waterside District of Ondo Division. A detailed tax assessment survey was completed in 1933, as a result of which 'the people realize that Government takes a deep interest in their history and customs . . .' .[49] One of these brokers between government and people, with deep knowledge of local history and customs, was none other than Moses Lijadu's son, who offered to help collect taxes for the newly-formed Native Administration. A contemporary report, perhaps conscious of the irony, observes that 'the people he produced were not mainly members of his mission, and the Obas gladly accepted.'[50]

But this new spirit of cooperation between old enemies was not to all tastes. This is where the Aladura Christians take centre stage in the affairs of Okitipupa Division. They were soon being described as 'subversive to law and order', as administered by the new Native Authorities.[51] In particular, the Amapetu of Mahin frequently complained to the colonial administration about members of the Cherubim and Seraphim Society, who (like his Ugbo neighbours fifteen years before) repudiated the authority of his court by 'collectively oppos[ing] the arrest of individual members'.[52] As Aladura groups increased in numbers over the next fifteen years they continued to resist the authority of NA courts, in Ilaje especially, and repeatedly petitioned for some kind of self-governing status (proposing that they should be allowed to pay their tax direct to the colonial government rather than to the Native Administration, for example). British administrators were at a loss to understand the phenomenon, and encouraged local rulers to clamp down hard on the dissidents. In 1945 twenty-five Holy Apostles were jailed for refusing to accept the authority of the Amapetu's court, and for undermining chiefly authority by revealing the secrets of Oro.[53]

Thus far the terms of this dispute would not have been unfamiliar to Phillips and Lijadu fifty years previously. It was the discourse of prayer versus sacrifice. In particular, the Aladura groups charged that the Native Authorities were still secretly condoning twin infanticide. At this point proponents of the 'sacrificial' order added a surprising modern twist to their repertoire – town planning. The 1944 *Annual Report* for Okitipupa Division[54] noted that Oshoro 'long unchallenged as the most progressive and enlightened' district in Ikale 'found a serious rival in Irele'. In January 1944, fire had destroyed a large part of the Ilaje settlement of Atijere, the most famous market in the region, providing the opportunity for it to be replanned 'on modern lines'. Inspired 'by the example of Atijere' the Council and people of Irele embarked on 'a complete scheme of town improvement' in which Ode Irele was 'replanned with a wide main street . . . the former market removed to a proper site' and 'side streets measured out and roads made suitable for motor traffic in anticipation of Irele being connected in the near future with the Ondo–Agbabu main road'. Irele gained an appropriate reward for such initiative when it became for a few years the Divisional Headquarters.

Subsequent reports in the 1940s make frequent reference to the degree of progress in town planning in rival settlements of the Okitipupa region. Improved layouts required the knocking down of houses belonging, often, to some of the most important people in the community. A new form of sacrificial rite had entered the drama of local politics. Power and prestige were now measured by the extent to which leaders were able to reshape or to oppose the reshaping of their settlements. In Arogbo ' . . . the proposed town planning scheme, which involved the removal and re-erection of most of the existing houses, the clearing and levelling of the land for the construction of a sports ground and the re-alignment of the streets, by the voluntary efforts of the people themselves, had not gained the unanimous support of the townsfolk', but in Igbekebo, a town 'built in higgledy-piggledy fashion and suffering from deplorable sanitation, its people seemingly bereft of any civic pride . . . the spontaneous desire voiced by an influential body of townsfolk to replan their town on modern lines came as a pleasant surprise'.[55]

The most spectacular of all these experiments in town planning was then launched by the leadership of the Holy Apostles. Fresh from jail, harrassed by the threat of further court action and convinced that the Ilaje chiefs presiding in these courts still condoned 'pagan sacrifice', the Apostles decamped to the coastal swamps south of Mahin and commenced a tour-de-force of urban politics – the building of a new and advanced settlement, a theocracy-on-stilts, in one of the most peripheral and isolated localities in the entire region. The Holy Apostles had outflanked all the opposition and in one bound passed from the Cameronian world of Indirect Rule to the post-war world of rural development.[56] The settlement, Aiyetoro, was run on communistic lines, and achieved a phenomenal rate of material progress. It was rapidly electrified. The Apostles later acquired fish-freezing and boat-yard facilities, and built and operated a fleet of sea-going fishing vessels. At one stage they were rumoured to be negotiating the purchase of a helicopter. Not surprizingly, this model settlement to surpass all models became a site of national and international pilgrimage for planners and experts in community development. It has remained unique in the degree of technological progress achieved, but Zion Ugbonla, another Aladura-inspired commune established in the vicinity a few years later, became the pattern for numerous Zions established throughout the Okitipupa region in the 1960s and 1970s.

Conclusion

There are a number of general points to be drawn from the story just outlined. First, it reminds us – if such be needed – of the importance and autonomy of cultural factors in political and economic change. Decisions about settlement are not to be explained solely in practical and utilitarian terms. The Okitipupa case brings out the ritual and dramatic potential inherent in choice of settlement location and in the process of town planning. Second, we should not be trapped into seeing the codes associated with these ritual and dramaturgical acts as having a fixed meaning. Unlike, say, the 'red' and 'town' distinctions of Mayer's South African study there is not one style for 'town' and another for 'country'.[57] In fact, there was regular slippage between style and content in this respect, each party trying to outdo its opponent by dressing in clothes borrowed from the other. The farm-camp-orientated food-production party displays its urbanity by building a model New Town. Representatives of an enlightened world of Christian commerce quit town to electrify the wilderness. Traditionalist chiefs embrace 'town planning' as a sacrifice to the spirits of a new age.

Several of my Ikale friends, having developed a critical understanding of the cultural legacy of local factional politics allied to the tenets of millenarian sectarianism, doubted the need to harp on these stylistic and dramatic properties any further. The critique was on record. Their concern now was to tackle directly the problem at the heart of that critique. 'The government does not love farmers', was how one Ikale friend put it in a letter to me in the late 1970s. He wanted above all things for his son to be educated – to take a university degree – but then to come back with his degree and farm the land. 'Where can I send him so that when he has completed his studies he will not be so changed that he rejects food-crop farming as a way of life?' At the time the question was probably unanswerable. There are precious few models anywhere in the world for successfully combining urbanity and the peasant view of the good life. The need to do so in Africa in the 1990s seems as urgent as ever. This is what makes local intellectual legacies of the kind examined in this essay of abiding importance.

Postscript

This essay celebrates a uniquely stimulating intellectual ethos. Its material was compiled in a period when I alternated terms lecturing in the University of Ibadan and vacations in which I was educated in the ways of Ikale agriculture. Colleagues in Ibadan and farming friends in Ikale country would have been equally appalled if they could have forseen the confusion that has arisen in the utilitarian nineties between training and higher education. My Ikale friends wanted their children to become farmer–philosophers, not agro-technicians. Despite Nigeria's poverty, and the fact the country was fighting for its national survival, it never occurred to either party to query the intrinsic value of open-ended speculation on social issues. In those days we knew – none more so than Michael Crowder – that intellectual stimulus was a right and a necessity for the poor, not just a privilege for the rich and over-developed. The present predicament of anglophone universities in West Africa has not been helped by a political climate in Britain and other wealthy countries that, as one commentator has recently put it, pressures the intellectual 'to take out naturalization papers in the kingdom of moral certainty'. But this phase will not last for ever. The day of the West African university will come again, and with it that egalitarian spirit of enquiry so deeply rooted in the African agrarian experience.

> *Why faintest thou? I wandered till I died.*
> *Roam on! The light we sought is shining still.*
> *Dost thou ask proof? Our tree yet crowns the hill,*
> *Our Scholar travels yet the loved hill-side.*

(Matthew Arnold, *Thyrsis*)

Acknowledgement

Even for an academic essay this paper has had an unusually long gestation. At various times Akin Mabogunje, Abner Cohen, Jane Guyer, Murray Last and John Peel have all offered helpful advice. Three Ikale friends also made important contributions: Johnson Ogunji, Chief Tewe and David Akinnusi. The stimulus to persist, however, came from Michael Crowder himself.

Notes

1. J. D. Y. Peel, *Ijeshas and Nigerians*, (Cambridge, 1986).

2. *Intelligence report on Ikale District, Okitipupa Division, Ondo Province* 1934 (NAI CSO 26/29731). According to the Revd. J. A. Maser visiting Arogbo in 1872 Ibadan obtained salt from this place when the Ijebu and Egba roads were closed (CMS CA2/068/142).

3. R. Smith, 'The canoe in West African history' *Journal of African History*. 11, 1970, 515–33. The main determinant of the cost of transport was labour. In March 1877 the

Revd. Charles Phillips, his party and their loads, left Lagos with nine canoe men (six of whom later quit, refusing to risk their lives in Ijo country). But for the overland part of their journey from Agbaje they needed forty carriers, and not all the loads were removed in one day (CMS CA2/078/17). Travelling from Lagos to Ondo in 1891, Phillips paid £3.4s. for the 100 miles or so by canoe to Atijere (canoe hire for nine days, 18s., four canoe men, £2, other expenses, 6s.) and £40 for a similar distance overland to Ondo (NAI CMS (Y) 2/2/4).

    4. P. Richards, *Ideas, environment and agricultural change: a case study from western Nigeria*, Ph.D thesis, University of London, 1977.

    5. Richards, 1977, op. cit.

    6. Maser at Arogbo in December 1873 reported 'The Ijos are very clever at making canoes. There is a regular establishment of shipbuilding as it were on the bank of the river . . . They sell their canoes as far as Brass one of the mouths of the Niger for 60 bags or £30.' (CMS CA2/068/142).

    7. Ambrose, reporting on Ikale, Ondo and Idanre in 1900, states that 'none of the above mentioned peoples excepting a few so-called Portuguese immigrants [i.e. Brazilian ex-slaves of Yoruba extraction] and a few other persons near Iferi, grow cassava, which should be a staple article of food. . . ' (Lagos *Annual Report*, 1900–01). Seventy years later cassava had replaced white yam as the main field crop of the Ikale, much being produced for sale (Richards, 1977, op. cit.).

    8. Maser, arriving at Itebu (Manuwa's town on the Ilaje-Ikale border) on a market day in December 1872 noted that the produce on sale was 'chiefly yams' (CMS CA2/068/142). In 1874 David Hinderer found the markets at Arijan and Atijere 'simply [*sic.*] for vegetable produce such as yams and Indian corn' (CMS CA2/049/74). Phillips to Maser, 2 October 1878, writing from Itebu, concluded that 'the safety of the river to Atijere is necessary for the welfare of Leke because a large portion of food consumed at that place is supplied from these parts' (CMS CA2/078/6). Touring the area in 1900 Capt. Ambrose noted that 'the Ikale people grow a large part of the yams that supply the watery waste between the Benin River and Mahin where nothing can grow' and that the people of this latter region 'catch fish which they exchange for yams and such articles of trade as they require' (Lagos *Annual Report* 1900–01).

    9. Traversing this zone from Araromi Obu to Oke Aye in 1875, David Hinderer observed a landscape in transition. The high forest trees had been replaced by 'monotonous and tangled undergrowth' and an abundance of the 'soft cork tree' (*Musanga cecropioides*, a light-loving species abundant in the first phase of forest clearance), but 'the graceful Palm Tree', dominant in the landscape 50 years later, was as yet conspicuous by its absence (CMS CA2/049/76).

    10. Richards 1977, *op. cit.* In 1900, prior to the arrival of the first Urhobo migrants, Ambrose states that the Ikale harvested palm fruit by felling the trees ('Report on the Eastern District', Lagos *Annual Report*, 1900–01.)

    11. O. Adejuyigbe, *Boundary problems in western Nigeria: a geographical analysis*, (University of Ife Press: Ile-Ife, 1975).

    12. Richards, 1977 op. cit.

    13. Richards, 1977, op. cit. O. Otite, 'Rural migrants as catalysts in rural development', in *Small urban centers in rural development in Africa*, ed. Aidan Southall, African Studies program, (University of Wisconsin: Madison, 1979).

    14. Glover Papers, Bundle 5/4, Library of the Royal Commonwealth Society, London. S. A. Akintoye, *Revolution and power politics in Yorubaland 1840–1893*, (London 1971). S. A. Akintoye 1969 'The Ondo Road eastwards of Lagos *c.* 1870–95'. *Journal of African History*, 10, 581–98.

    15. Strictly speaking it appears that Glover's road was an older route revived. According to Akintoye, 1971 (ibid, 78) Glover first heard of this route 'about 1869'

and after consulting with Ondo people resident in Lagos succeeded in sending an Ijesha man, Awobikun, to Ondo via Igbobini.

16. Willoughby to Earl of Kimberley, Lagos 30 August 1872 (Glover Papers 5/2, Library of the Royal Commonwealth Society, London). P. D. Cole, *Modern and traditional elites in the politics of Lagos*, (Cambridge 1974).

17. Akintoye 1971, ibid.

18. CMS CA2/049 (Hinderer) and CA2/068 (Maser).

19. At first, Hinderer thought any mission in Ondo should be attached to Bishop Crowther and his Niger 'episcopal jurisdiction' on the grounds that he would suit 'Aduwo, chief of Igbo Bini and his neighbours likewise . . . trading to the Delta . . . sooner than anyone connected with and coming from Lagos or Leke' (Hinderer to Wright, 18 May 1875, CMS CA2/049/79).

20. Hinderer, in Leki in December 1874, commented on the numbers of 'runaway slaves from the east' (CMS CA2/049/74) and on first arrival in Araromi Obu in February 1875, found the chief 'out in search of 15 or 20 runaway slaves chiefly owned by Ikale people' (CMS CA2/049/76).

21. In 1874 Hinderer wrote 'I must on no account go to the Igbo Bini country. . .for they would not receive any one from Lagos. . .' (CMS Archives CA2/049/74). Three years later Phillips reported that 'The neighbouring chiefs were bitterly opposed to Manuwa for allowing the white man's agent to stay at Itebu. The reasons alleged for the opposition were that 'the white men would deprive them of their slaves and wives. . .' (CMS CA2/078/2).

22. In 1877 Manuwa was looking for another route than the one passing through Ikale country, because, according to Phillips, he feared free passage of Lagos traders might injure his trade with the Ikales (CMS CA2/078/21).

23. A 'deed of sale' for 'the territory known as the seashore of the Mahin kingdom, commencing at Abejumere and reaching as far as Abetebo' was signed on behalf of Gaiser by 'Herr Eugen Fischer. . .in the presence of the Acting Imperial German Consul. . .' on 29th January, 1885 (*Intelligence Report – Ilaje District*, 1937: NAI ONDOPROF 4/2).

24. The treaty was signed by Nachtigal on 11 March 1885. The Amapetu received a ceremonial staff from the Kaiser, but the treaty was not ratified subsequently, since it failed to meet the conditions of the General Act of the International Colonial Conference of 26 February 1885 concerning effective occupation (*Intelligence Report, Ilaje District*, 1937: NAI ONDOPROF 4/2).

25. 'Though new to us it is really an old road by which the Ondos carried on trade with the Ijebus, but which had been entirely neglected since it became unsafe on account of the wars. . .' (Phillips, CMS CA2/078/18).

26. Captain Ambrose reported in 1900 that the people of Erele (Irele), paying no heed to their Oloja, had 'scattered among their farms . . . every village headman seem[ing] to resent authority. . .' Together with Major Ewart he persuaded them to rebuild their town, which 'they did . . . and straightway left it again'. (Lagos *Annual Report* 1900–01).

27. Revd. J. A. Maser, *Journal*, 1873 (CMS CA2/068/142).

28. The Abodi of Ikale told the District Officer in 1925 that 'there have been nine sections in Ikale country from the earliest days, and the Number Nine has a great meaning to us and of deep impression [sic.]. Eight sections have their different eight Olojas: the Abodi of Ikoya is the head of all. . .' (NAI OKITITDIV 1/1, File 19/1, Ilutitun Affairs). The federal character of Ikale ideas on administration was forcibly restated in the 1950s when the Abodi wished to press 'a claim to the new title of Abodi of Ikaleland' and the other eight *oloja* 'retaliated by declining to acknowledge the Abodi's overlordship and by claiming a station equal to his own' (Okitipupa Division, Annual Report for 1954, NAI OKITIDIV 4/2).

29. NAI ONDOPROF 1/4 *Old records re Ikale affairs from 1905*. Nigwo's account is confirmed by the Abodi of Ikale who wrote in 1925 that the trouble between Nigwo and the Oshoro chiefs arose because of Nigwo and the Igbotako people's friendliness with the 'Government's officials and European merchants' and because of 'the Divorce Law and dowry payment in court by women which Nigwo said it was lawful, the killing of Twins instantly they are born which Nigwo [was] the first to say it is forbidden, [and the] Ijamo company which Nigwo rightly went against for the great Extortion inflicted on children at the burial of such children's relatives . . . running such children into a great debt . . . and for their connection with the twins matter' (NAI OKITIDIV 1/1, File 19/1, Ilutitun Affairs).

30. In the view of the Abodi of Ikale in 1926 'for the introduction of our present . . . civilization into Ikale, Nigwo and the Igbotako people were the means' (NAI OKITIDIV 1/1).

31. The Ijamo Society appears to have had functions similar to that of the Mende Humoi Society in Sierra Leone, in that its officials were responsible for undertaking ritual purification ceremonies after sexual offences such as co-habitation on the bare ground (Chief Tewe, personal communication). Ikale lineage segments were strictly exogamous. The *Ikale Intelligence Report* (1934) suggests this as one of the reasons for settlement fission (each settlement was a lineage segment).

32. According to the *Ikale Intelligence Report* (1934) Ikuyiminu must have been reinstated, because he was deported a second time, to Ilesha, in 1925, and died there in 1926 (NAI CSO 26/29731).

33. C. Meillassoux, *Maidens, meal and money*, (Cambridge, 1981).

34. 'Report on the Eastern District' Lagos *Annual Report* 1900–01.

35. 'Report on a tour in the Ikale Country, December 1908' (unsigned, *Old Records re Ikale Affairs*, NAI ONDOPROF 1/4).

36. Described in the *Annual Report* for Okitipupa Division, 1935 as 'probably one of the richest palm-oil areas in the world' (NAI ONDOPROF 1/2 OP120C). The same report goes on to say that the Ikale 'are too lazy to collect the palm fruit and reap their reward' preferring to live on rents paid by the Urhobo and the farm produce they sell.

37. The *Quarterly Intelligence Report* for September 1929 (NAI OKITIDIV 1/2) records that 'buyers come to Ikale country from Koko and Sapele and elsewhere and buy up large stocks [of yams] from [Ikale] farmers . . . some of the farmers themselves export yams and other farm produce.' Ikale foodstuffs were exported to Lagos through Atijere, an important periodic market to the south-west of Ikale country. This was a major centre for the foodstuffs trade when visited by Hinderer in 1875. Sixty years later the *Annual Report* for Okitipupa Division, 1935 (NAI OKITIDIV 1/2), describes Atijere as 'the centre of a big trade in fish, palm produce, planks, crocodiles, and foodstuffs generally' regularly attended by four native-owned motor launches from Lagos.

38. Richards, 1977, op. cit.

39. The following passage (*Ikale Intelligence Report*, NAI CSO 26/29731) is typical: 'The Ikales are an easy-going and law-abiding race. Though capable of a fairly high standard of intelligence, they have, in consequence of their geographical position and lack of communications, come little in contact with the outside world, with the result that their progress has been in some measure retarded. Their principal failing lies in the fact that they allow themselves to be easily imposed upon by the more progressive stranger communities residing in their midst . . . The people are almost exclusively farmers, their main crops being yams, corn and cassava.'

40. Report of Neil Weir, Assistant District Officer, Waterside District, 19 June 1926 (NAI OKITIDIV 1/1 File 19/1 Ilutitun Affairs).

41. The two principle documentary sources upon which this section draws are the

Intelligence Report – Ilaje District (NAI ONDOPROF 4/2) and a bundle of papers entitled 'Mafimishebi, Olugbo of Ugbo' (NAI CSO 26 06452).

42. For an early nineteenth-century account of Mahin country see Capt. J. Fawckner, *Travels on the coast of Benin*, (1837).

43. Clifford to the Secretary of State for the Colonies, 12 February 1923 (NAI CSO 26/06452).

44. *Intelligence Report – Ilaje District*, 1931, NAI ONDOPROF 4/2.

45. In 1896 Bishop Phillips wrote to the Revd. J. B. Wood of the CMS that 'Our experience in the past moves one to say [that] evangelization of the Mahin people is a hopeless task. After 21 years of labour, we can boast of having baptised only a single adult convert who died last year.' (NAI CMS (Y) 2/2/4).

46. This brief account is based on J. B. Webster *The African churches among the Yoruba, 1888–1922*, (Clarendon Press, Oxford).

47. The *Ikale Intelligence Report*, 1934 (NAI CSO 26/29731) reported that Christians, representing the large majority, 'are strongly in favour of a return to the old [title] system, and quite a number are taking up Ijoye titles today' but that no Christian had yet reached a sufficient age to compete for an Ijamo title.

48. A letter from the Very Reverend J. G. Campbell, March 31 1921 (NAI ONDOPROF 1/4 OC62) argued that the colonial administration's over-estimation of the Amapetu's territorial importance was an artefact of the treaty with Germans – and that this opportunistic treaty was first suggested by one Chief Dogbe of Aboto near Atijere 'a place which is the river way where launches and all pass, and the late Chief Dogbe, being a far seeing chief, seized the advantage and made his overlord sign a Treaty first with the German government and later on with the British Government (for this the late Dogbe received a pension from the British Government until he was fondly (*sic.*) murdered by one of his slaves) . . .'

49. *Quarterly Intelligence Report*, 28 May 1931 (NAI ONDOPROF OKITIDIV 1/2).

50. *Quarterly Intelligence Report*, 5 September 1931 (NAI OKITIDIV 1/2).

51. There was an early disturbance at Obe in Ilaje country in 1930 when members of the Cherubim and Seraphim Association 'apparently carried away by the preaching of a Lagos female called [Josephine] Abiodun' were said to be in 'defiance of the N.A. and Native Courts'. Similar congregations in the area owed their allegiance to Moses Orimolade and to a Revd. Barber. The members of the Revd. Barber's group were described as 'moderately well behaved' and the District Officer requested that Barber visit 'the area controlled by Miss Abiodun and endeavour to put a stop to the nonsense going on, which consist principally of accusing people of witchcraft, taking upon themselves the power of exorcising them by tieing and immersing the accused person in water'. By 1931 it was claimed that the Cherubim and Seraphim Society had 'ousted all other religious bodies' among the Ilaje [Mahin] and Igbo [Ugbo] (*Quarterly Intelligence Reports*, 1930–31, NAI OKITIDIV 1/2). For general accounts of the rise of Aladura Christianity in western Nigeria see J. D. Y. Peel, *Aladura*, (Oxford University Press for the International African Institute 1968, and J. A. Omoyajowo, *Cherubim and Seraphim Church in Nigeria*, Ph.D thesis, University of Ibadan, 1971.

52. *Quarterly Intelligence Report*, 6 September 1930 (NAI OKITIDIV 1/2).

53. The *Annual Report* for Okitipupa Division for 1944 opined that 'the only unsatisfactory feature of the Ilaje area has been the conduct of a number of renegade ex-members of the Order of Cherubim and Seraphim, calling themselves 'Holy Apostles'. These people are mostly illiterate and wander about pretending to preach Christianity but in fact interfering with the lives of ordinary folk and repudiating the authority of the elders. Several of the 'Apostles' have been convicted of revealing the secrets of the 'Oro' juju which is connected with the Ilaje title system.' The 1946 *Annual Report* reported that 'the Holy Apostles of Ilaje area continued to disturb the peace

of the seaside villages, one individual who styled himself 'God' being convicted and imprisoned'.

54. NAI ONDOPROF 1/1.

55. *Annual Report* for Okitipupa Division, 1947 (NAI ONDOPROF 1/1).

56. According to the *Annual Report*, Okitipupa Division, 1951 (NAI ONDOPROF 1/1) 'The Ilaje NA are somewhat perplexed by the progress achieved by some of their religious communities and by the attitude of these communities to authority. The Apostles pay tax promptly and regularly, but refuse to have anything to do with the NA, the Cherubim and Seraphim are reluctant to pay tax and press for exemption, and refuse to allow any of their members to be served with court process unless threatened by extra Court Messengers. 'Oba Jesu' together with his 'Archangel Gabriel' and followers again appeared on the Ilaje scene in November with wild accusations of their oppression by the NA . . . the receipt of tax demands by 'Oba Jesu' and his followers . . . it was [then] discovered that they and six [other] 'angels' had not paid tax for three years. This heavenly host was arrested and held in custody until all their tax arrears . . . were paid up. They have now retired back to the swamps and creeks near Ugbo.' For an account of the social and economic organization of two of these communities see Stanley Barrett's *Two villages on stilts: economic and family change in Nigeria*, (New York, 1974), and *The Rise and fall of an African Utopia*, (Waterloo, Ontario, 1977).

57. P. Mayer, 'The origin and decline of two rural resistance ideologies; in P. Mayer, ed. *Black villagers in an industrial society*, pp. 1–80, (Cape Town, Oxford University Press, 1980).

Acknowledgement is gratefully made to the Church Missionary Society and the archivist of the University of Birmingham, where the CMS archives are now kept, and to Dr. B.S. Benedikz.

Chapter Eleven

Conflict and Collaboration in South-Eastern Namibia: Missionaries, Concessionaires and the Nama's War against German Imperialism, 1880–1908

B. T. MOKOPAKGOSI

The 1960s saw the appearance of numerous published studies and doctoral theses on the colonial history of Namibia. These tended to be either general works on German colonial policy,[1] or studies of African resistance to German rule.[2] Studies of resistance to colonial rule in Namibia, though relatively numerous, are incomplete. These have tended to show either that there is a continuity in the anti-colonial struggle in the country from the German times to the time of the evolution of modern nationalism, or they have paid too much attention to the Herero resistance war of 1904–08.[3] No study of comparable scholarly quality on other communities has appeared.

The south-eastern Nama (the 'Bondelswarts', 'Veldshuhdragers' and 'Swartmodders') are a striking example of this neglect.[4] Yet, the south-eastern Nama fall within the category of those Namibian communities who have maintained a consistent militant posture towards colonial domination. The general war against German colonial rule in 1903 began in South-eastern Namibia. In 1922 the Bondelswarts were again involved in a war, this time against South African occupation. Since the 1960s, the Bondelswarts in particular have tended to support the more militant nationalist movement, the South West Africa Peoples Organisation (SWAPO).

Any examination of the involvement of the South-eastern Nama in the war of 1903–08 must be done against the background of the activities of concessionaires, especially of the Kharaskhoma Syndicate, and later of

This chapter © B. Mokopakgosi 1992

South African Territories Company (SATCO). Such an examination therefore, needs to investigate closely the role of SATCO in attracting capital to the area, acquiring concessions, and compensating the Nama for their loss. Special attention should be given to the ambiguous role of the Rhenish Mission of claiming to have interest in the welfare of the Nama, while at the same time assisting concessionaires to acquire enormous concessions. Some consideration should also be given to the effects of merchant capital against which concession hunting operated. In the final analysis, the decision of the south-eastern Nama to initiate hostilities against the Germans would be seen to have been largely justified.

☆ ☆ ☆

Beginning with the 1820s, several economic, social and political changes occured within the communities of south-eastern Namibia (see Map 4). The main agents of this change were missionaries of the Rhenish Mission Society, the small trader-concessionaires mainly from the Cape, and the Nama Kommandos. The missionaries, because of their long association with merchant capital in the Cape, were received by the Nama chiefs with the hope that they would attract trade to their capitals. The Kommandos had been ruined by the expansion of the Cape agricultural and trade frontiers and crossed the Orange principally to raid for cattle, the main trade item. The principal mode of interaction during the early period, it would appear, was through trade. What is interesting is that this early trade poured into Nama economies non-productive items such as coffee, tobacco and brandy, which smothered their inner capacity to produce themselves, and consequently made them more dependent on trade with the Cape. With the depletion of wildlife and cattle resources, the Nama chiefs and their councils gradually turned to grants of land as exchange commodity. The establishment of the Kharaskhoma Syndicate, forerunner of SATCO, on 5 March 1889[5] was merely to exploit the growing willingness of the Nama to exchange land for European merchandise.

The agents of the syndicate were a new breed of concession hunters. In many ways they were different from the earlier ones, who were associated most closely with the penetration of merchant capital into the area. The post-1880 concessionaires were major speculators closely linked to the sources of big finance capital in Europe and South Africa. They were men who acquired huge concessions with a view to making big profits, not only through the exploitation of their rights, but also by dealing in shares in Johannesburg and London.

The syndicate was organized with a view to acquiring three kinds of concessions in South Africa and Namaland in the area of the Kharasbergs. First, it was to secure a monopoly to search for minerals and start mining in the event of any discoveries. Second, it was to acquire a general concession to construct railways, tramways, canals, telegraph lines, as well as public buildings. Finally, the syndicate was to obtain the exclusive right to acquire property in land and to sell it to raise revenue.[6] It was in order to carry out this task that on 16 November 1889, an expedition under the leadership of Theophilus Hahn, the son of the well-known missionary of Hereroland, Hugo Hahn, arrived in Warmbad, the Bondelswarts' capital.[7]

On arrival in Warmbad Hahn's expedition discovered that the agents of the Great Western syndicate of Johannesburg, Rautenbach and Levi, had been active in the area. They deliberately used brandy to obtain the cooperation of the Bondelswarts' chief Willem Christian to grant them extensive mineral and construction rights in the three territories. Christian was also given £100, much of it in commodities, of which he gave £10 to the upkeep of the mission.[8] In the case of any mining operations being started, the chief was to receive 5 per cent of the net profit.[9] As the concessionaires were operating against the background of frequent financial depression in Europe, and therefore finding it difficult to raise venture capital cheaply from shareholders or money markets, it could take many years before any net profit was realized. But Rautenbach's, and Levi's, use of brandy antagonized a very indispensable force in Nama politics – the Rhenish mission.

Hahn apparently heard of the activities of the Great Western while on his way to Warmbad, but instead of calling off the expedition he planned an offensive.[10] Hahn had several advantages over other concession hunters; he spoke the Nama language and knew several leading figures in south-eastern Namaland, and he clearly intended to exploit that to get a reversal of the Rautenbach/Levi concessions. This was a game he could not afford to lose. For the syndicate was not paying him a salary, but had allocated him 300 shares of £10 each, fully paid up, and failure to acquire the concession would have been a blow to him personally.[11] The expedition brought with it much brandy, guns and ammunition, which Hahn clearly intended to use to achieve his objectives.

Hahn's package addressed one vital issue which instantly tipped the balance in favour of the Kharaskhoma syndicate. He departed from the orthodox methods of earlier concessionaires by proposing transactions where Africans and the mission would ostensibly also benefit. Where the Great Western had offered to pay Christian an annual allowance of £100, the Kharaskhoma doubled it. With respect to royalties on net profits of worked minerals, 7 per cent was to be paid in the case of minerals worked in the Bondelswarts' territory, 5 per cent in the 'Swartmodder' territory, and in the Veldschuhdragers' 2 per cent. Unknown in the many years of contact with European concessionaires, was that the Nama were to be allocated 70 shares, fully paid up, of each £10 in the syndicate.[12] Christian was also to have the right to appoint anyone to examine the accounts of the syndicate on his behalf.

It would be erroneous, however, to conclude from this that the interests of the Nama were well cared for. The chief and his councillors could not have understood British joint-stock company law, nor the business of accounting. Also, the shares to be allocated them were ordinary shares, which would not entitle them to share in the sale of the syndicate's assets in case of liquidation. The real purpose of the arrangement seems to have been to put the Nama in a position where, as shareholders in the syndicate, they would be obliged to protect its interests.

Nevertheless, Christian and his councillors were persuaded. Following some long discussions and several secret night brandy parties, Christian decided in the 'interest of his people' to cancel the Rautenbach-Levi concessions. All the money paid to him by them was repaid and deposited in their bank in Cape Town. Christian then granted the Kharaskhoma Syndicate a general mining concession, the right to construct railways, canals, roads, and to acquire land and transfer property within the 'Bondelswarts' territory. Using his claimed seniority, he assisted the syndicate to secure similar rights in the other two areas. In addition the syndicate secured the right to *dryland* property of 66,750 square kilometres in the area,[13] which was itself revealed to be only 74,671 square kilometres.[14]

The Rhenish mission was also won over. Not only was the mission to share in the annual payments to the Nama, but it was also allocated 20 ordinary shares in the syndicate, given for the upkeep of the church. It is not clear whether the 20 shares were all granted for the above purpose, or part of them was allocated to the missionaries individually for assisting the syndicate during the negotiations. For, the first publication of the list of shareholders on the other hand shows that the missionary Wandres' wife Betha, and Anna Maria, the wife of the missionary Tobias Fenchel, were each allocated 5 shares for unspecified services rendered to the syndicates.[15] The shares could as well have been intended for the mission schools, for both Betha Wandres and Anna Fenchel were teachers, but there is no evidence to sustain this assumption either. Whatever the truth about the ownership of the shares, the vital fact is that the syndicate intended with them to buy the support of the Rhenish missionaries, and they succeeded in doing so.

Once the concessions had been acquired, the syndicate next set off to obtain official recognition of them from the German government. The subsequent conflict over the legitimacy of the concessions belongs to the discussion of Anglo-German relations over Namibia and the scramble, and has been addressed in greater detail elsewhere.[16]

What should be mentioned is that official recognition of the rights of the syndicate had to depend more on changes in German colonial policy than the legitimacy of the acquisitions. In 1890, Bismarck, the architect of company rule in German colonies, was replaced as chancellor. His dismissal, and the failure of chartered company rule in the protectorate, as well as the persistent opposition to financial involvement in the colonies in the Reichstag, caused fundamental changes in the colonial economic policy of the Reich. The German government had come to accept that the retention of the territory depended on the injection of sufficient capital into its economy, be it German or British. All that was required was that concession holders formed companies with sufficient capital resources to exploit their claims. The syndicate immediately reorganized itself into a company on the lines suggested by the German government.

Having satisfied the first condition, the syndicate was granted in 1892, the right to search for and work minerals within the 76,671 square kilometres territory. But, it was also to pay to the treasury a royalty of 2 per cent for precious stones, gold and silver, and of 1 per cent in the case of copper and other mineral ores.[17]

Concerning the land, however, a number of modifications were made, ironically to protect the interests of the Nama people. The syndicate was given the right to select in three installments, 516 farms of 10,000 Cape morgen each, on dryland;[18] therefore, a total of 40,960 square kilometres of freehold farmland. The syndicate had only to demonstrate possession of £10,000 for the first 128 farms to be granted. The second 128 farms were conditional upon the provision of a further £10,000 towards the construction of railway lines, roads and tramways. And the last 256 were to be given after the syndicate had met all its obligations to the government. Therefore, the government allowed to be transferred to the syndicate over 53 per cent of the land belonging to the south-eastern Nama. This arrangement could hardly be seen to have been designed to protect the rights of the African people, especially as the Nama were a nomadic pastoral society requiring extensive grazing land.

☆ ☆ ☆

By the latter part of the century, investment in the colonies was still considered a risky business, though when successful could result in huge dividends. The European public in particular was generally disinclined to invest their money in colonial companies. The smaller firms of the size of the Kharaskhoma syndicate were also not very well connected in Europe or South Africa, and as a result found it extremely difficult to compete for the scarce capital resources with the larger and well established colonial companies. In most cases, the share capital of these smaller companies tended to be watered. The Kharaskhoma syndicate in particular never possessed the necessary capital to exploit its concessions.[19]

The financial difficulties of the syndicate came to a head in September 1895. And in a bid to raise new capital, a new company, the South African

Territories Company (SATCO) was formed to take over the rights of the syndicate.[20] As compensation for the surrender of their concessions to SATCO, the Kharaskhoma Syndicate was allotted 230,000 fully paid up shares of £1 each, and 25,000 debentures of the same value in the new company.[21] The mission and the Nama, as shareholders in the now defunct syndicate were not allotted any shares. The discovery of this share swindle of the syndicate marked the beginning of a prolonged conflict which largely explains why the south-eastern Nama took up arms against German imperialism in 1903.

When the syndicate was transformed into SATCO in 1895, the new company was able to raise new working capital of £33,000, which was, nonetheless, still insufficient for its operations.[22] But with that, preliminary work of tracing the railway line to Luderitzbucht, and some small, though less coordinated, mineral exploration were done. By 1900, the company was again in financial difficulties, and a reorganization was authorized in order to create new capital. But the £3,061 raised fell far short of what SATCO needed.[23] Yet, in spite of its failure to raise sufficient operational capital, SATCO insisted on the granting of the second batch of 128 farms. The company threatened to withhold some proportions of subsidies paid to the Nama if the government refused to release the farms.[24]

SATCO's chronic shortage of capital greatly paralysed the expressed plan to establish good communication system in the south. This, the deputy governor von Lindequist argued, caused two fundamental problems pertinent to the development of the colonial state. In the first instance, the absence of reliable road or rail communication system left the south cut off from the rest of the country, and therefore made administrative and strategic control over the area very difficult. But most importantly, it made the south very unattractive to investment capital and prospective settlers, and in this way, left the area lagging behind the rest of the protectorate in its development.

The undercapitalization of the syndicate, its activities, and later of SATCO, affected the Nama more than the government. Right from the onset, they adopted an approach which was openly confrontational. In May 1893, Henry Gibson, the local director of the syndicate, introduced a plan for the concessionary territory which did not have any provision to survey the farms, or even to get them registered. Even the more crucial question of selling farms to intending settlers was momentarily shoved to the background. Instead, and without the consent of the colonial administration, the syndicate introduced grazing and water licences.[25] The issuing of licenses, as Gibson insincerely explained, was designed to recover, 'a very large amount of money' that the syndicate had already spent in the country. What is disturbing about the strategy of the syndicate is that it was selling water rights, when its farms were not yet selected, which were in any case on dry land. Grazing rights, also, were granted over areas that did not belong to it. This arrogant and neglectful attitude of Gibson and his syndicate in later years created tremendous friction between it and the indigenous people.

Gibson's address to the south-eastern Nama the next day would seek to indicate that he took account of their interests in issuing grazing and water licences.[26] Gibson explained that all foreigners, the white farmers and the Herero, who brought their herds as far as the Kharasbergs, had to be charged for the use of grazing areas and water. He suggested to them that their unused territory could be rented out to white farmers to earn revenue for the communities. At bottom, however, Gibson's address was blatant blackmail – he tied all his proposals to the Nama's participation in the syndicate:

> You must remember you are all interested in the Kharaskhoma syndicate, and that the Captain and Under-Captain and Headmen, as well as the Rhenish mission, on behalf of the station are all shareholders in the syndicate the same as myself, and we are all on the same footing. Therefore, the more valuable we can make the land the more money will you and all of us receive, so it is for your own good . . . to see everything being on proper footing.[27]

Evidently, Gibson's address was an attempt to solicit the cooperation of the Nama chiefs to circumvent the conditions imposed by the agreement with the government. This was the only way the syndicate could raise capital. The syndicate was essentially a speculative venture.

The subsequent years were to witness mounting friction between the colonial administration, the south-eastern Nama, and SATCO. The administration accused the company of holding its land and mineral rights for speculative reasons, and, therefore, hampering economic progress in the south.[28] And the Nama invariably expressed displeasure over the infringement of their rights by SATCO. By the end of 1900, for instance, all the 128 farms had been selected, though not all of them were recognized and registered as company property.[29] Of these, 98 were in the Bondelswarts' territory, and only 38 of them were on arid land. Of the remaining 30 in the area of the Veldschuhdragers, 10 were selected on already existing water places.

☆　☆　☆

The revolt of the south-eastern Nama took place in October 1903, and within three months the Herero had joined. Although several factors such as German racism, and failure to observe their agreements of 'Friendship and Protection', explain why the revolt occurred, it would appear that what was crucial was the transfer of land to Europeans. And nowhere was this practice more widespread than in south-eastern Namaland.

The immediate cause of the revolt in south-eastern Namibia was a near trivial issue which resulted in the chief, Jan Christian, being killed. According to the missionary Wandres, a certain white settler had arranged to buy a sheep from a member of the Bondelswarts' community. Before he paid for it, and for some unexplained reason, the sheep fell into the hands of the chief.[30] Without investigating the matter, the district officer of Warmbad, Lieutenant Jobst, accused the chief of theft, and subsequently tried to arrest him. In the ensuing scuffles, both the chief and Jobst were shot dead. Although it is possible that Christian could have stolen the sheep, the reasons for resisting arrest were much broader. The actions of Jobst were interpreted by Christian and his people as interference in the running of the affairs of the Nama, and were therefore in violation of the agreements of 'Friendship and Protection'.[31] It will become clear below that there were numerous and more important reasons for the rebellion than a mere misunderstanding over a sheep.

But the two factors which significantly contributed to the polarization of relations in south-eastern Namibia were the method used by SATCO to select its farms, and the position of the south-eastern Nama as shareholders in the company. The concessions agreement allowed the syndicate and later SATCO, to select farms on 'dry land', and not on land already used by the indigenous people. But no sooner had the concessions been granted than the syndicate completely ignored this fact. The syndicate and SATCO in later years selected farms and water places already in use, a development which greatly served to alienate Willem Christian from his subjects, as more and more accused him of collaborating with the concessionaires at their expense. But Henry Gibson, the company's local representative, was determined to carry on selecting the best farmland. As he put it: 'The idea that all existing watering places belong solely to the natives, and that we are only entitled to select 'dry' farms, is absurd on the face of it. I myself negotiated our land concessions and there is no restriction of this kind on any of them'.[32]

The attitude of the company's local representatives was also causing serious concern. Publicly they accused the missionaries of inciting the Nama against the company. Secretly, the company was strenuously trying to induce the government to pacify south-eastern Namaland. 'Willem Christian should be dealt with firmly. It is too late for a 'coffee and tobacco policy', and the Bondels have to be kept in order; for if they think they can play false with us, it will not be long before they play false with the government also . . .'[33] But Gibson and his company failed to win the government to their scheme, for among other reasons, the government was also a competitor for farmland in the South-east.

What most worried the government was that the activities of the company were likely to provoke rebellion in the south-eastern area. Governor Leutwein was particularly unhappy about the way the company exploited Christian's weakness as a leader, and his love of brandy, to acquire indisputable public property. A large part of Warmbad, the capital of the Bondelswarts, and several farms in Keetmannshoop were acquired by SATCO in that way. Some of these farms when later examined, were found to be more than 30,000 morgen each, as against the recommended 10,000 morgen per farm. Such transactions were often concluded without the consent of the people of even the *Raad* (Council), and occasionally led to serious outbursts of anger, and at times provoked some low-level militant responses. In October 1894, for instance, the Bondelswarts temporarily captured the syndicate's shop in Warmbad,[34] apparently because the syndicate had fallen behind in the payment of subsidies. A year later, things had deteriorated so much that the governor angrily warned the syndicate that, 'the Germans are not going to fight the syndicate's battles'.[35]

But at the root of the conflict between the south-eastern Nama and SATCO was the failure of the former to get just treatment as shareholders in the company. In parting with their land and mineral rights, the Nama were allotted shares in the syndicate, and were also to receive annual subsidies. In the following years, however, the Nama were to meet with extreme difficulty in trying to get these payments. There were years when these payments were made in part, and others when they were not made at all.[36] The reports of the district officers of Warmbad between 1893 and 1904 contained many instances of the failure of SATCO to pay the subsidies. Even by 1903 when the war begun, SATCO was still in areas.

The troubles of the south-eastern Nama started with the transformation of the syndicate in 1895. First, it took them many months to establish the truth about the transfer of the rights of the syndicate to the new company, yet they were said to be shareholders. When thereafter Christian and the mission requested all relevant papers concerning the transfer, this was strangely enough turned down.[37] It was not until September 1898 that the intentions of SATCO respecting the claims of the Nama and the mission in the new company became known. The board of SATCO informed the German government that it had no legal right to interfere with the liquidation of Kharaskhoma syndicate. And a month later, Wandres was advised that 'the assets of the Kharaskhoma syndicate, when realized, have not proved sufficient to meet the just claims of its creditors, and obviously, therefore, nothing was left for the shareholders'.[38] That meant for the Nama that a land area of over 10,000 square kilometres, and a mining territory of over 70,000 square kilometres had been given to a private company free of charge. The company expressed itself ready to review its position on one condition, that Wandres make an undertaking to further the interests of the company in future.[39] Such cooperation of the mission and the chiefs was never obtained. The hardline attitude of SATCO only made it easier for the Nama to discover that they had been duped, and many of them started to see their progressive impoverishment as being synonymous with the presence of whites in the south-east. The spirit of revolt, therefore, existed. What was missing was the spark provided by shooting of Lieutenant Jobst.

☆　☆　☆

The war in south-eastern Namaland, and in the country as a whole, came to a close at the beginning of 1908. This was a very costly war, in both human and financial resources. The south-eastern Nama lost their livestock and lands, and consequently they were transformed into a labour force with no independent means of existence. In this way the impoverishment of the Nama was accelerated – a process which began with the penetration of merchant capital at the turn of the nineteenth century.

This paper has not completely dismissed the violations of the 'protection' treaties by white settlers, and racial prejudice as factors in the revolt of the south-eastern Nama. It has only emphasized the effects of the operations of concessionaire companies, in our case SATCO, and the attitude of its local representatives, as crucial. For the colonial administration had very few personnel, and therefore those further away from military posts, centres of administration, and areas with high concentration of the settler element, were less affected by the policies of the government than by the operations of the company.

Finally, three generalizations can be made from this essay. First, we can conclude that the revolt was essentially a conservative popular protest intended at recapturing territories lost to SATCO – hence its significance to the subsequent anti-colonial struggle. It had no plans beyond the recapture of the land. Second, the war in south-eastern Namaland provides a suitable analytic tool for the study of resistance in Namibia as a whole, for German colonial policy was based on the granting of rights to concessionaire companies. And third, the war in south-eastern Namaland demonstrates the complexity of Afro-European relations during the early years of colonial conquest, where Europeans of conflicting interests – missionaries and concession hunters – could easily cooperate in the destruction of African societies.

Notes

1. See H. Bley, *South West Africa under German rule, 1884–1914*, (London, 1971); H. Drechsler, *Let Us Die Fighting: The Struggle of the Herero and Nama against German Imperialism, 1884–1915* (London: Zed Press, 1980); G. Sudholt, *Die deutsche Eingeborenenpolitik in Südwestafrika: Von den Anfängen bis 1904* (Hildesheim and New York, 1975).

2. H. Drechsler, *op. cit, Aufstände in Südwestafrika: Der Kampf der Herero und Nama 1904 bis 1907 gegen die deutsche Kolonialherrschaft* (E. Berlin: Dietz Verlag, 1984); see also: P. Katjavivi, *A History of Resistance in Namibia* (London, 1988).

3. See: J. M. Bridgman, *Revolt of the Hereros*, (Berkeley: University of California, 1981); K. Poewe, *The Namibia Herero: A History of their Psychological Disintegration and Survival* (Lewiston and Queenston, 1985).

4. Only two studies have appeared on them. And these have specifically focussed on the military leadership of Jacob Morenga; H. Drechsler, 'Jacob Morenga: A new kind of South West African leader', in W. Markov (ed), *African Studies* (Leipsig: VEB Verlag Enzyklopädie, 1967); U. Tim, *Morenga* (Berlin and Weimar, 1979).

5. B. T. 31:4371/28391: 'The Kharaskhoma Exploring and Prospecting Syndicate Ltd'.

6. Ibid.

7. Reichskolonialamt – Potsdam (RKolA): 1562: Henry Gibson – local director of the Syndicate – to German Foreign Office, London, 23 November 1889.

8. Archiv der Rheinischen Missions – Gesellschaft, Wuppertal – Barmen (ARMG): B/C. II.51/1: Carl Wandres to Missions Inspector, Warmbad, 11 August 1889.

9. Ibid.

10. Ibid.

11. B T 31:4371/28391, op. cit.

12. Zentralbüro des Kaiserliches Gouvernement (ZBU) 1545: R. VII.1.7: Henry Gibson's memo to chancellor v. Caprivi, London, nd.

13. RKolA 1562: H. Gibson to German Foreign Office, Berlin, 23 November 1889.

14. Ibid., H. Gibson to Dr Ernst Goring, Warmbad, August 1890.

15. B T 31: 4371/28391.

16. See; B. T. Mokopakgosi, 'German Colonialism in microcosm: A study of the role of concessionaire companies in the development of the German colonial state in Namibia, 1890–1915', Ph.D. thesis, University of London, 1988.

17. A copy of the agreement is in file: ZBU 1545, R.IV.L.7.

18. Ibid.

19. By 1900 for instance, SATCO had only managed to raise 2,086,480 m (ca. £104,324) of its 10,000,000 m (ca. £500,000) share capital, and only a small fraction of this was spent in south-eastern Namaland: *Kolonialabteilung*, 'Denkschrift über die im südwestafrikanischen Schutzgebiete tätigen Land und Minen - Gesellschaften', Berlin, 28 February 1905.

20. ZBU 1874, U.IV.h.I (Bd.5), 'Indenture between the Kharaskhoma Syndicate and SATCO', London, 13 December 1895.

21. Ibid.

22. M. R. Gerstenhauer, *Die Landfrage in Südwestafrika: Ihre finanzpolitische und ausserpolitische Seite – Ein Beitrag zur der Frage – Wie machen wir Deutch Südwestafrika rentabel?* (Berlin, 1908), p. 18.

23. RKolA 1641: Clipping of *Finanz Chronik*, 6 October 1900.

24. RkolA 1641: Samuel Pope (Chairman of Board of SATCO) to Stuebel (Director of the Colonial Department) London, 15 April 1901.

25. ZBU 1873, U.IV.h.l. (Bd.1). H. Gibson, 'An address by the managing director of the Kharaskhoma Exploring and Prospecting Syndicate Ltd', in 'Provisional Land

Regulations of the Kharaskhoma Exploring and Prospecting Syndicate Ltd'. Warmbad, 22 May. 1893.

26. Ibid., 'Gibson's address to the Nama', Warmbad, 23 May 1893.

27. Ibid.

28. ZBU 1873, U.IV.h.l. (Bd.1): Leutwein to Gibson, Keetmannshoop, 11 April 1894.

29. *DKB*: 'Siedlungsfrage in Südwestafrika', 15 December 1900.

30. Evangelische Lutherische Kirche (ELK), V.35: Gemein-de – Chronik – Warmbad; ARMG: B/c.II,45, T. Fenchel to Missions Inspector, Keetmannshoop, 8 November 1903.

31. ARMG: B/c.II.45, op. cit.

32. RKolA 1566: H. Gibson to I. J. Bashford (British Embassy, Berlin), London, 13 April 1895.

33. Ibid.

34. Bezirksamtmannschaft – Keetmannshoop (BKE) 173, B.II.47c (Bd.1): Gibson to Duft, Vellor, 2 October 1894.

35. Reproduced in RKolA 1566: Niederheitmann (SATCO representative) to SATCO headquarters, Vellor, 5 March 1895.

36. RKolA 1640: Wittrin (officer in Warmbad) to SATCO, Warmbad, 17 Jul. 1899; ARMG, B/c.II,51/l: C. Wandres to Missions Inspector, Warmbad, 16 March 1896.

37. Ibid.

38. RKolA 1640: P. Scratchley to C. Wandres, London, 5 October 1898.

39. Ibid.

Chapter Twelve

Colonel Rey and the Colonial Rulers of Botswana: Mercenary and Missionary Traditions in Administration, 1884–1955

NEIL PARSONS

M ichael Crowder came to the University of Botswana in 1982, as Professor of History, by his own admission feeling academically 'stale'. He left Botswana in 1985 academically very 'fresh' – even if a little 'monomaniac!'[1] The reason for this recovery was the scholarly passion of his remaining years – his discovery of Tshekedi Khama (1905–56) and his determination to write a definitive biography of that African statesman.

Michael was introduced to Tshekedi Khama through the manuscript Bechuanaland Diaries of Sir Charles Rey, and by preparatory work in the Botswana National Archives for a comparative study of Indirect Rule in Nigeria and Bechuanaland. He gave the paper as a lecture at the University of Maiduguri in July 1983. From Maiduguri he reported back to Gaborone:

> I initiated myself as a southern African historian (beginner's grade) yesterday with my lecture on Rey v. Tshekedi . . . The more I read about Rey the more I'm anxious that his diaries should be published . . . And the more I read about Tshekedi Khama, the more I feel that he deserves a major biography. Though I'm rather daunted at the prospect of my undertaking it. A very complex personality.[2]

The sensational aspects of the confrontation between Rey and Tshekedi appealed to Michael's sense of drama. Three days of Michael's last week in Gaborone in 1985 were spent appearing at the National Museum's little theatre in a rumbustious impersonation of Colonel Rey, reading from the diaries which he had helped to edit. It was, he later told me, one of the most enjoyable experiences of his life.[3] He used these histrionic insights to self-conscious effect in his book, *The Flogging of Phinehas McIntosh: a Tale of Colonial Folly and Injustice, Bechuanaland 1933*. It was published in early 1988 as a foretaste of the full biography of Tshekedi Khama, complete with a *dramatis personae* of 'principal actors in the Serowe drama, in alphabetical order', listed before its Prologue. The Rey diaries themselves, including Michael's footnotes, were published in a volume entitled *Monarch of All I Survey*, which came out a month after Michael's death in August 1988.

This paper is in its own way a return to Michael Crowder's agenda of mid-1983 – the comparative study of colonial administration. It takes Colonel Rey's administration of the Bechuanaland Protectorate as its starting point, and seeks to place that administration in the comparative context of Botswana's administrative history and philosophies of colonial administration.[4]

☆　☆　☆

Colonel Rey was incredibly rude about his three predecessors as Resident Commissioner of the Bechuanaland Protectorate, Colonels Macgregor, Ellenberger and Daniel – 'a trinity of the damnedest fools Providence ever produced'.[5] On Daniel in particular,

> I disagree with Daniel on every conceivable subject – he is the damnedest old fool I have ever struck, the most incompetent bungler, and the most pig-headed ass. His mind, or what he refers to in moments of enthusiasm as his mind, works at the slowest rate that any mind could work without stopping altogether; and it invariably works wrong . . . When the Almighty sets to work to create a fool, he certainly turns out a finished article.[6]

Rey despised the three men for their apparent weakness in dealing with African chiefs and for their lack of promotion of 'development'. He was not alone in his criticisms of Bechuanaland Protectorate administration. In 1913 the missionary Haydon Lewis had thought that BP administrators – Jules Ellenberger excepted – 'should be washing clothes instead of Governing nations'; by 1918 he was remarking that the administration's 'chief business' was 'to collect taxes, and receive salaries'. Rey's contemporary Simon Ratshosa (1883–1939), and early Botswana nationalist and polemicist, was scathing about the in-bred nature of the administration: the administrators were, he claimed, 'in many instances replaced by their sons, relatives and friends, that is, their succession is a hereditary one.' A later Resident Commissioner, recalling his tenure in the later 1940s, agreed that the administration had been 'mildly dynastic', and that its recruitment had been too much on the 'office boy' system of promotion through the ranks before the 1930s.[7]

Another of Rey's contemporaries, Leonard Barnes, attributed the BP's 'administrative failure' to its administrative officers being drawn 'for the most part from the police service', so that 'they rejoice, as a group, in the mental habits and range of customary outlook in that walk of life' – including arbitrary use of force and the pocketing of tax monies.[8] Jack Halpern's classic and influential paperback *South Africa's Hostages*, which appeared at the end of the colonial period in 1965, bewailed the 'second-rateness and cheap South African recruitment' which 'bedevilled' Bechuanaland administration.[9]

The idea of the BP administration having been a 'backwater administration' of 'police force and clerical origins', up to the rule of Rey, has been accepted as orthodoxy by modern students of district administration in Botswana, notably by Louis Picard. Recruitment of officers for the administrative service of the High Commission Territories (Basutoland, Bechuanaland Protectorate, and Swaziland) was entirely within the patronage of Britain's High Commissioner in South Africa until 1932, when the first officer was recruited in London as an experiment along the lines of other British colonial service recruits.[10] This became the regular channel for recruitment of administrative officers from 1936–7 onwards, and eventually staffed the senior ranks with an Oxbridge-educated administrative elite. The Picard thesis is essentially that administrative continuity into post-colonial Botswana was achieved smoothly by gradual transfer of power to a compatible local elite headed by Seretse Khama.[11] Seretse was himself an Oxbridge man, who had once been offered (but had declined) an offer of a post within the Colonial Administrative Service (to Jamaica in 1951).

Colonel Rey broke the chain of succession of Resident Commissioners of the Bechuanaland Protectorate. Though he was not an Oxbridge man, he was the first complete outsider without a previous career in Bechuanaland or Basutoland. But it is misleading to see him as completely divorced from the ideologies and administrative practices of his predecessors. This paper will argue that his career and personal predilections can be seen as a restatement, albeit in modernized form, of a 'mercenary tradition' within colonial administration which goes right back to the origins of the Bechuanaland Protectorate itself. This 'mercenary tradition' was in conflict with a 'missionary tradition', and elements of this conflict can be seen in Bechuanaland Protectorate administration from the 1880s through the 1920s into the 1930s.[12]

The 'mercenary tradition' in Bechuanaland administration combined the law-and-order ethos of police origins with service to the colonial interests of capitalism in South Africa. The 'missionary tradition' emphasized imperial trusteeship in protecting and advancing the interests of the indigenous population. It may be argued that the contradiction between imperial protestations of trusteeship and colonial practices of exploitation was inherent in colonialism everywhere. The historian John W.Cell sees two such schools of colonial administration in British Africa, one associated with West Africa and Uganda and the other associated with 'Union-Rhodesia-Kenya', locked in debate and an increasingly dialectical relationship with each other.[13] But rarely can the contrast between them have been so stark as in Bechuanaland, where 'missionary imperialism' and capitalist colonialism were daggers-drawn at the start.[14] The first two commissioners of Bechuanaland were a missionary and a capitalist. Not just a missionary but the Revd. John Mackenzie (1835–99), one of the most articulate spokesmen among Christian missionaries and prime exponent of imperial *protection* of 'native' interests in later nineteenth-century Africa. And not just a capitalist but Cecil Rhodes (1853–1902), the diamond magnate whose name is synonymous with expansion of monopoly capitalism and white settlement in later nineteenth-century Africa.

Mackenzie was Britain's first Deputy Commissioner put in charge of the territory called Bechuanaland in 1884 – meaning the area north of the diamond fields of Cape Colony towards the vicinity of the Molopo river. Mackenzie had been a missionary of the London Missionary Society in Tswana territory since 1858. In 1882 he journeyed to London to campaign for British protection of the 'Bechuana' (Botswana) from the depradations of Boer 'filibusters' from the Transvaal republic. He became the spokesman for a Liberal humanitarian lobby appealing to parliament for justice for the the 'natives' of Bechuanaland combined with peaceful access for British trade through the country to Central Africa. As an exponent of imperial control, he opposed the annexation of Bechuanaland to Cape Colony, and sought to equate the interests of imperialism with those of philanthropy and to distinguish them from those of capitalists based in Cape Colony. He advocated instead a separate Crown Colony to be settled by morally upright farmers from Britain, who would act as the leaven of development in an increasingly integrated society of Africans and Europeans.[15]

Mackenzie took up his position in April 1884 at Kuruman, his old mission station in southern Bechuanaland. But in effect he had been set up as fall-guy by Hercules Robinson (1824-97), the High Commissioner in Cape Town, who favoured annexation by Cape Colony. Mackenzie was given no police or coercive powers to persuade the Boer filibusters to leave the country. Moral suasion failed, and Mackenzie was forced to resign in August 1884. He was duly replaced as acting Deputy Commissioner by Robinson's ally in the Cape, Cecil Rhodes. This was the only time that Rhodes was employed by the British government, albeit on a part-time basis as a diversion from money-making at Kimberley and politicking at Cape Town.

Rhodes appeased the Boer filibusters and proved so enthusiastic in recognizing their land rights that he encouraged more Boers from the Transvaal to make war on the southern Tswana. The sensational murder by Boers of a British agent named Christopher Bethell, at Mafikeng, fed the outcry of Liberal imperialists in Britain. The result was that a military expedition was despatched from England at the end of 1884, equipped with the latest technology of gas balloons and heliographic signalling, its soldiers wearing the newly conceived camouflage of mud-coloured (soon to be called khaki) corduroy rather than red tunics. The expedition was led by Charles Warren (1840–1927), a Welsh relative of Christopher Bethell, who was appointed Special Commissioner for 'Bechuanaland and the Kalahari'. He had served with distinction in the Bechuanaland area during the later 1870s, and was a firm friend of Mackenzie's. A convinced Christian as well as a Liberal, he soon clashed with Rhodes, who was a Tory as well as an agnostic. Rhodes was dismissed as Deputy Commissioner in early 1885.

Warren, with Mackenzie at his side, exceeded his instructions and went north to make treaty arrangements with the northern Tswana states which today lie within the Republic of Botswana. Hercules Robinson, who was by then in Rhodes's pocket, seized the opportunity to have Warren's commission revoked. Back in Britain, Warren attempted to fight the issue as a Liberal parliamentary candidate at Sheffield, but was defeated by a Conservative backed by Rhodes. Warren and Mackenzie wanted the British protectorate over Bechuanaland to stretch from north of Kimberley to the latitude of modern Selebi-Phikwe, as the first step towards a Crown Colony up to the Zambezi entirely separate from Cape Colony. But politicians at the Cape wanted to absorb southern Bechuanaland into Cape Colony, after it had been pacified at imperial expense. Robinson arranged the compromise of dividing administrative responsibilities between a *colony* south of the Molopo, to be called 'British Bechuanaland', and a *protectorate* north of the Molopo which came to be known as 'the Bechuanaland Protectorate'. This division took effect at the end of a financial period on 30 September 1885.

On the next day one person, Sidney Shippard (1837–1902), was appointed to the twin positions of Administrator of British Bechuanaland and Deputy Commissioner of the Bechuanaland Protectorate. His offices were in the colony at Vryburg, the old filibuster capital, a hundred miles south of the protectorate. An old confidant of Cecil Rhodes,[16] he became well known for his partiality to white settler interests in the British Bechuanaland land commission and to Rhodes's mercantile interests in the Bechuanaland Protectorate minerals commission. Shippard was joined at Vryburg by a handful of administrators of like ilk, appointed by the High Commissioner – notably Francis Newton (1857–1948), a barrister turned soldier and Hercules Robinson's former secretary. Shippard was promoted to the title of Resident Commissioner in 1891, when Britain began to assume powers of sovereignty over the Bechuanaland Protectorate in terms of its Foreign Jurisdiction Act of 1890.

The 'mercenary tradition' had clearly triumphed, though a missionary element was partially reasserted after 1887 by the Revd. John Smith Moffat (1835–1918) as Assistant Commissioner for the Bechuanaland Protectorate, resident at Shoshong and Palapye and itinerant to Bulawayo. The only surviving son of the great Robert and Mary Moffat, and brother-in-law of the greater David Livingstone, J.S. Moffat bore the burden of succession to a famous family name. But he was no friend of John Mackenzie or to missionaries in general, and was assiduously courted by the mercantile interests that wished to take hold of Bechuanaland and Matabeleland. He went along with Rhodes's trickery of Lobengula, but had a fit of conscience when Rhodes tried to do the same with Khama. Shippard and Hercules Robinson were delighted to see the back of him in 1895. [17]

All three of Shippard's successors as Resident Commissioner – Francis Newton, Leander Starr Jameson (1853–1917) and Hamilton Goold-Adams (1858–1920) – had been in the pay of Rhodes at some time. Rhodes had bought Newton and Goold-Adams, together with the leading officers of the Bechuanaland Border Police, with free or privileged shares in his British South Africa Company. (Though Goold-Adams was considered sufficiently 'clean' to replace Newton and Jameson, discredited by the failure of the Jameson Raid.) Police troopers formed share syndicates, and the honour-roll of 'Rhodesian pioneers' includes many names of those who founded their fortunes as BBP troopers. [18]

Men of a different mettle began to join the BP administration after 1895, when the Bechuanaland Protectorate gained a separate identity from British Bechuanaland, which was incorporated into Cape Colony. The Bechuanaland Border Police was also disbanded in that year, and was replaced by the Bechuanaland Mounted Police – including a force known as the Protectorate Native Police, which substituted black troopers from Basutoland for the expensive white troopers of the Border Police. The administrative headquarters of the BP were removed from Vryburg to Mafikeng, the main police depot a dozen miles south of the protectorate frontier, at the end of 1895 – probably a temporary expedient until the BP was incorporated into 'Rhodesia', when Salisbury would become its capital. For similar reasons the Mounted Police became a division of the British South Africa Police under the control of Salisbury in August 1898. This arrangement persisted through the South African War, when the Mafikeng headquarters of the BP administration and of Division I of the BSA Police was besieged. It was not until 1902–03 that a new resident commissioner seized the initiative, at a time when the 'Rhodesian' threat of incorporation had lapsed, to reconstitute a separate Bechuanaland Protectorate Police under the command of himself as its honorary lieutenent-colonel. (All resident commissioners up until the 1950s could therefore call themselves 'Colonel', even if, like Rey, they had had no previous military career.)

The man who reconstituted the BP administration after the South African War was Ralph Williams (1848–1927). After arriving in Mafikeng in 1901 he set about police reorganization as his first task. His second task was to institute a central secretariat on bureaucratic principles, rather than the *ad hoc* legal and military lines of his predecessors. This was achieved by the recruitment from Basutoland of an efficient deputy to the Resident Commissioner, Barry May, who took up the new position of Government Secretary in 1904.[19] Williams however failed in his third great self-imposed task, that of trying to win approval for moving the 'capital' from Mafikeng to Lobatse inside the Protectorate.

In many respects Ralph Williams was, like Charles Rey three decades later, a more bureaucratic embodiment of the law–and–order 'mercenary tradition' in colonial administration. But there were also humanitarian elements within Williams's administrative style, which Rey failed to recognize when he hailed Williams as a worthy predecessor. Williams had realized that effective administration by the tiny central secretariat rested on effective cooperation with the chiefs who ran the everyday local administration of 'tribal reserves'. He therefore supported them to the hilt against all comers.[20] Williams's deposition of Chief Sekgoma Letsholathebe in Ngamiland in 1906 was the exception rather than the rule – the rule which Rey was to adopt in deposing so many chiefs.[21] In this regard Williams was more in the Mackenzie tradition of confidence in the potential of African society than in the confrontational tradition of Rhodes, who had even insulted Khama in public to his face.[22]

The foundation of the Union of South Africa in 1907–10 entailed a reconstitution of imperial authority in the region. Britain's High Commissioner in Pretoria became the ceremonial Governor-General of the Union of South Africa (until 1931) as well as continuing to govern the three 'protectorates' of Basutoland, Bechuanaland Protectorate and Swaziland – which now became known as the High Commission Territories, with their own self-contained administrative service. Their separate identity from South Africa, as 'native territories' under direct imperial rule, became reinforced over time with the failure of successive attempts by the Union government to persuade the British government to hand them over.

The move towards political union in South Africa was matched by a move towards ecclesiastical union of Congregational churches in southern Africa, which profoundly affected the missionary churches in Bechuanaland – because the two movements were equated and vigorously resisted by African rulers and their churches. The annual meeting of London Missionary Society missionaries from Bechuanaland and Matabeleland, held at Inyati in April 1910, broke into two warring factions, which voted against each other as two solid blocs on every issue including finance. On the one hand there was the faction which stressed the need for integration into the modern world, for private land tenure and for 'development', and for political unification with South Africa. This faction was also liberal and modernist in its theology. On the other hand there was the faction which pressed for the separation of 'a genuine native church . . . to keep the national life and manners in our Christian communities', protecting and preserving but converting tribal institutions, to be kept apart from the corrupt urban world of white civilization. This faction, which included the women missionaries, was usually conservative and fundamentalist in its theology.[23]

The 'missionary tradition' in colonial administration was undermined and transformed by the triumph of white settler power in the early twentieth century. It lost the classic liberalism of John Mackenzie and the Cape liberal tradition of the nineteenth century. The liberal vocabulary of progress and development had been captured by the advocates of white settlement and white political rights – though they often used the term 'civilized' as a racial synonym for adult white males. The advocates of 'native' rights to land and some degree of political autonomy, notably chiefs and their missionary supporters, were forced to become opponents of progress and development as then conceived. The 'missionary' counter-attack became couched in terms of equitable segregation to protect 'native' rights. The chairman of the 1914–15 Native Reserves Commission in Southern Rhodesia, Robert Coryndon, was therefore obliged to reject the word 'segregation' at this stage, because it implied unacceptable 'native' self-sufficiency. As late as 1927 the missionary Arthur Shearley Cripps was titling a book *An Africa for Africans: a Plea on behalf of Territorial Segregation Areas and of their Freedom in a South African Colony*. However, by that time, 'segregation' had become an unambiguous part of the vocabulary of white settler development in Southern Africa, and the intellectual tide of missionary and secular humanitarian thought was turning back towards classic liberal ideas of integration.[24]

The triumph of the 'mercenary tradition' in Bechuanaland administration can be seen in the 'Jousse trouble' of 1910–16, during the resident commissionerships of Williams's first two successors – one of whom, Edward Garraway (1865–1932), had been a member of Coryndon's 1914–15 commission in Southern Rhodesia which opposed African self-sufficiency in principle.[25] Khama, the most powerful traditional ruler in the Bechuanaland Protectorate, had attempted to modernize his state by setting up a royal trading company (with European managers) which would secure independent state revenue for the future after his death. This received the support and active cooperation of European traders within his country, but was opposed by larger mercantile interests in South Africa and Southern Rhodesia. The BP administration, and the High Commissioner's Office in Pretoria, proved craven to these interests and banned all such investments on the part of chiefs, even as 'sleeping partners'.[26]

The 'missionary tradition' was, however, revived, in its new conservative and tribalistic form, by the accession of two Resident Commissioners between 1917–23 and 1923–7 – James MacGregor (1861–1935) and Jules Ellenberger (1871–1973). Both had intimate connexions with the French and Swiss family network of Protestant (Paris Evangelical Mission) missionaries in Lesotho – the network that provided the High Commission Territories administrative service with some of its most distinguished local recruits.[27] Macgregor was a German-educated Scotsman who had gone to join the the Basutoland Mounted Police from British army service in 1884. Developing great interest in Sesotho language and culture, he married a daughter of the Paris missionary, Revd. D.F. Ellenberger. He transferred to the Bechuanaland service as Government Secretary in 1912 in succession to Barry May. Five years later he was made Resident Commissioner. 'A man created by the Almighty for native interests, a man who keeps his word', was Khama's assessment of Macgregor according to Simon Ratshosa, who added that Macgregor was despised by 'some white men who liked the natives ruined'. (Though this was a somewhat unfair judgement on the left-wing Johannesburg lawyer Emmanuel Gluckmann, father of Max, who was treated by Macgregor as a money-grubber rather than as a serious advocate for oppressed subjects suing Khama.)[28]

Macgregor was succeeded by his brother-in-law Jules Ellenberger. Educated in Cape Colony at multi-racial Lovedale College and in Paris, he joined the BP service as a police clerk and court interpreter at the age of nineteen. He then spent the whole of his working life as a government employee in the Bechuanaland Protectorate, based in Gaborone, Ngamiland and Mafikeng, and rising to Government Secretary in 1916 and Resident Commissioner in 1923. Jules Ellenberger was a fluent linguist thoroughly conversant with Setswana culture who, according to Simon Ratshosa, 'knew natives far better than any other official'.[29]

Jules Ellenberger was the most complete exponent of the 'missionary tradition' in the middle period of Bechuanaland's colonial administration – a tradition obviously compatible with the paternalistic ideas of 'trusteeship' and 'indirect rule' which were being bandied about at the League of Nations and by the British after the First Wold War. Ellenberger supported the chiefs of Bechuanaland in resisting the encroachments of white settler interests intent on colonial development. The chiefs knew full well from experience elsewhere in Southern Africa that 'development' inevitably led to the expropriation of land and to white settlement, thus hastening the incorporation of the Bechuanaland Protectorate into the Union of South Africa. Ellenberger called on his masters in Pretoria and London to abolish all concessions held by expatriate commercial companies in the protectorate. The only way to stop Bechuanaland being absorbed by the Union, he argued, was by a stop on all colonial development as then conceived.[30]

Ellenberger's philosophy appalled Leopold Amery, the new Colonial and Dominions Secretary in London. Privately he accused Ellenberger of keeping 'the natives quiet and happy . . . like a game reserve of wild animals' (or a human Whipsnade) in order to keep them out of the Union. In print Amery was kinder, remarking that Ellenberger was 'a fine specimen of the old type of Protectorate official . . . Steeped in native thought and ways his one concern was for the welfare of his proteges, but suspicious of anything that might upset their accustomed way of life. My heart, but not my head, was with him and I chose, in Colonel (Sir Charles) Rey, an active successor all out to put the Bechuana on their feet economically.'[31]

Charles Rey was therefore deliberately chosen by Amery as a counter-weight against the 'missionary tradition'. Amery's position was that the High Commission Territories should be developed by a dual policy, such as that promoted by Coryndon as Governor of Kenya, promoting both British settler enterprise and the provision of 'native' welfare. This settler-biassed 'dual policy' was an attempt to counter the perceived 'native' bias of Lord Lugard's 'dual mandate', as propagated by the 'indirect rule' theorists of the Colonial Office.[32] Amery had removed the High Commission Territories from the orbit of the Colonial Office in 1925, placing them instead under the newly created Dominions Office, which was responsible for South Africa and the other white settler dominions. He also appointed Rey, as Anthony Kirk-Greene has reminded us, over the heads of two Colonial Office nominees for the position – Philip Mitchell and Granville St John Orde-Browne, both regarded as bright stars in the firmament of 'indirect rule'.[32]

Rey's achievements as an administrator were considerable and should not be demeaned.[33] But his orientation was undoubtedly towards white settler development. He came out of an essentially commercial form of bureaucratic background, in the Board of Trade and the Abyssinian Corporation, with little sympathy for the welfare measures in which he was willy-nilly engaged. This comes out in his attitudes towards British workers and African intellectuals alike, despite being secretary of the Unemployment Grants Committee in London and chairman of the Board of Advice on Native Education at Mafikeng. During his years as Resident Commissioner he also became an enthusiast for the supply of African labour to the Witwatersrand gold mines. By the end of his career, he stood unabashedly on the side of colonial exploitation and settler development, calling for the incorporation of Bechuanaland into the Union of South Africa. (But even Rey found himself dependent on the expertise of BP administrators of the 'missionary tradition'. Jules Ellenberger was called out of retirement and rose steadily in Rey's estimation.)

It is this increasingly 'mercenary' aspect of Rey which helps to explain the dramatic twist in the attitude of a later resident Commissioner, Anthony Sillery (1903–76), when presented with a draft of the Rey Diaries in the 1970s. Sillery himself came out of the trusteeship school of Tanganyika administration, and had devoted many years to writing a biography of the great John Mackenzie. His first response was to be bowled over by the sheer exuberance of the Rey's writing: 'Rey was a distinguished man, a man of energy, ability and perception. His diaries are a faithful report of what he achieved against tremendous odds'. But a month later Sillery wrote back to express an altogether different view:

I have now read the Rey diaries from cover to cover and I am sorry to say that . . . they . . . show Rey as vain, egotistical, contemptuous of people, especially African people, impetuous and totally lacking in patience, and absurdly prone to dramatization. The diaries also contain inaccuracies and I suspect that Rey often raised the tension in order to show himself in a good light. Colonial administration was often a trying & sometimes, tho' rarely, even a dangerous business, but it was not like this . . . least of all in Bechuanaland . . . Much of his writing appears to me to be fantasy, not representing the real man at all.

Sillery concluded with another point, which is all the more telling about the ethos and loyalties of colonial administration: 'Rey does not come out of the diaries as a very attractive type of colonial administrator . . . The world is full of people who seize any opportunity to knock hell out of the Imperial past, and these diaries might, or rather would, furnish another rod for the back of the poor Colonial Service.'[34]

The dominant ethos of colonial administration after Rey was within the 'indirect rule' traditions of British colonial administration – a synthesis of the 'missionary' and the 'mercenary' with an emphasis on trusteeship that became transmuted over time into support for growth of representative institutions of self-rule. But one can still discern among Rey's successors continuing tension between 'missionary' and 'mercenary' tendencies in regard to the primacy of African or of white settler advancement, with a period of fluctuation between repression and encouragement of African advancement brought on by Bechuanaland's political crisis of 1949–56.

'Locally' recruited administrators from the Lesotho missionary network continued to rise to predominance in BP administration after Rey, despite the top senior posts and new junior administrators being recruited through London. Anthony Sillery, an outsider with no previous experience of the Protectorate, appointed as Resident Commissioner in 1946 as an alternative to a job with the British Council, was – by his own admission – heavily dependent on his Government Secretary G.E. Nettelton[35] and on Nettelton's deputy (and brother-in-law) Vivien Ellenberger[36]. Both Nettelton and Vivien Ellenberger (son of Jules) had had lifelong experience of administering the Botswana. They advised Sillery to treat the events following from Seretse Khama's marriage to an English woman in 1948 as 'just another Ngwato row', from which Tshekedi Khama would inevitably emerge the winner. But Nettelton died in 1950, and the 'missionary' star waned. Sillery was peremptorily removed from his position in the same year, as a scapegoat for the failure of British government policy in quietening Bangwato discontent over the exile of Seretse Khama.

The 'soft' Sillery was replaced by the 'hard' Betham Beetham (1905–79), transferred from his post as Resident Commissioner of Swaziland. Beetham would have preferred to take a job with the Colonial Development Corporation. He was backed up by Forbes Mackenzie (1907–80), a Southern Rhodesian who was transferred from the High Commissioner's Office in Pretoria. Mackenzie was first placed as district commissioner at Serowe, centre of the Bangwato troubles, and then went on to succeed Vivien Ellenberger as Government Secretary in 1951.

Forbes Mackenzie and Vivien Ellenberger illustrate the different types of 'mercenary' and 'missionary' officers that could be recruited to the High Commission Territories administrative service from within Southern Africa. The question of officials recruited to the High Commission Territories from white settler societies was one of acute sensitivity for the Commonwealth Relations Office. The question was raised in the House of Commons in London in January 1949. The answer given was that of 600 'European' men and women in High Commission Territories administration, 495 had been recruited from the Union of South Africa. It was, of course, illogical to suppose that all officers recruited in the Union were illiberal. As the High Commissioner remarked, when refusing to supply more exact figures for fear of damaging staff morale: 'in the previous decade there is no doubt that we were drawing men from the liberally-minded section of the South African community. . .It is only in regard to the older school of officers that any unhappiness need be felt.'[37] This failed to distinguish the 'missionary' from the 'mercenary' among older officers, but the essential truth of the statement regarding younger officers was borne out by subsequent events.

The hardening of colonial government attitudes towards the Bangwato led to the unprecedented revolt of the three (assistant) district officers at Serowe in January 1952 – Cardross Grant[38], James Allison[39], and Dennis Atkins[40]. All three were university graduates of South African origin, with extensive military experience in the recent world war, who had been recruited to Bechuanaland via regular Colonial Administrative Service channels in London. They wrote to the Secretary of State in London protesting at British government unwillingness to listen to the views of the Bangwato.[41] There is evidence that younger administrative officers elsewhere in the Protectorate were similarly affronted, and even considered resignation.[42] The affair, highly embarassing in official circles at all levels, was successfully hushed up – two of the three officers being transferred to other districts within the Protectorate. The blame for the district officers' liberal impertinence was put on Jean 'Gerry' Germond, the 'soft' Serowe district commissioner after Mackenzie – one of the last surviving lifelong service officers drawn from the Lesotho Swiss and French missionary network.[43] Also indicted by implication was R.A.R. Bent, the liberal figure acting as Serowe district commissioner while Germond's replacement was awaited.[44] The British authorities became even more determined to settle Bangwato political unrest by the slap of a strong governing hand. When Beetham and Mackenzie were well established, they put a tough new, South African–born district commissioner, P.G. Batho[45], at Serowe. Police reinforcements were shipped in from abroad, provoking the murderous Serowe Kgotla riot of Sunday 1 June 1952.[46]

It is tempting to see 1952 as the last clash between 'missionary' and 'mercenary' tendencies within Bechuanaland administration, but the truth is that High Commission Territories administration had ceased to be *sui generis*. The revolt of the district officers at Serowe showed that the administrative service had become infected with the concerns of British colonial administrative policy as a whole after the Second World War. The Serowe district officers were merely following the logic of the Colonial Office policy towards Africa, that had emerged under the Labour government around 1947 in the light of Indian independence, to develop African capacities for local self-government. On the other hand the Labour government in Britain had developed extra dependence on the Union of South Africa, despite aversion to the newly pronounced doctrine of *apartheid*, for economic and strategic reasons: gold and Simonstown grew in importance because of the dollar crisis and the Cold War. The new Conservative government, which came to power in 1951, had suspended the development of colonial local government in favour of a law-and-order enforcement policy, while maintaining the policy of collaboration with South Africa.[47] The protests of the Serowe district officers reflected new post-war liberal and democratic concern with universal human rights, rather than the old dualistic assumptions of separate racial development evident in the 'missionary tradition'.[48]

Greater wisdom began to prevail after the initial British government response of holding on to tight security reins after Bechuanaland's Bloody Sunday. The Beetham regime was kept in place, and indeed Forbes Mackenzie succeeded him as Resident Commissioner in 1953. But at the same time changes were introduced with the promotion of more conciliatory senior figures in the administration. John Millard, a Tanganyika and former Basutoland officer, who had distinguished himself as a man of 'nerve and judgement' as one of Ralph Furse's assistants on the Colonial Administrative Service Appointments Board in London, was brought into BP administration during 1952. He was made administrative supremo of the northern half of the Protectorate, including Serowe. Millard revived the sort of personal relationship with Tshekedi Khama that Charles Arden-Clarke had had as Resident Commissioner in 1937–42.[49] Meanwhile Germond was promoted into such a position for the southern protectorate. Their status was formalized in 1954 with the creation of the title of Divisional Commissioner for their posts, equivalent to a provincial commissioner in other colonies.

The modernization and liberalization of BP administration was facilitated, despite the appointment of Forbes Mackenzie as Resident Commissioner in 1953, by the appointment of the young and progressive Peter Fawcus as government Secretary in 1954. The High Commissioner's Office pushed for his appointment, despite his relative youth and inexperience, over the heads of older colleagues and two ex-West African officers nominated by the Colonial Office, because 'his ability is outstanding'.[50] Forbes Mackenzie left the country in 1955. The first steps towards economic development were taken in the same year by the appointment of a Development Secretary in central administration. But chiefly and popular resistance to 'development', evident since the 1910s, persisted until the possibilities of autonomous and beneficial development were restored in the later 1950s. There could be no such possibilities so long as Britain maintained its ambiguity over transfer of Bechuanaland to the Union of South Africa, and so long as Seretse Khama remained exiled in deference to the racial prejudice of White South Africa.

British deference to South Africa persisted until 1955–6. By 1954 the Conservative government in Britain had began to pick up where Labour had left off in 1951 on the development of African self-rule. In South Africa the Nationalist government produced its *apartheid* blueprint, the Tomlinson Report, at the end of 1955, and published a summary in

April 1956. The report underlined the ultimate incompatibility between British and South African plans for the High Commission Territories. The anti-black racialism and hostility towards British views expressed in London by the South African prime minister, J.G. Strijdom, at the time of the Commonwealth prime ministers conference of June 1955, showed the Commonwealth Office that no compromise was possible. At this point Tshekedi Khama seized the initiative and flew to London. By October 1956, Seretse Khama was back home.[51] A new era of development, albeit from a very low and neglected economic base, slowly opened up.

John Mackenzie's vision of the potentials of African development with European assistance, without dispossession of Africans from their rights and resources, became possible again in the later 1950s – though really significant achievements in Botswana had to wait until after Independence in 1966. The new synthesis of humanitarian ('missionary') and developmental ('mercenary') concerns was to be based on the collaboration and integration of progressive colonial bureaucrats and emergent indigenous elites. From the later 1950s onwards, the political and economic development of Botswana began to distance itself from other models of development in Southern Africa.[52]

Notes

1. Michael Crowder (Johannesburg) to Neil Parsons, 6 June 1985
2. Michael Crowder (Maiduguri) to Neil Parsons, 5 July 1983. The Maiduguri lecture was not published.
3. The two-night performance was re-enacted and videotaped at very short notice on a Saturday morning, with virtually no audience and inadequate sound. (Mastercopy in Tirelo Setshaba video archive, Gaborone.)
4. Michael Crowder, 'The white chiefs of tropical Africa' in L.H. Gann and P. Duignan (eds.), *Colonialism in Africa 1870–1960, Vol.II The History and Politics of Colonialism 1914–1960* (Cambridge, 1970), excludes the colonial service of Bechuanaland, Basutoland and Swaziland. See also A.H.M. Kirk-Greene, 'The thin white line: the size of the British colonial service in Africa', *African Affairs* (London), 79 (1980) pp. 25–45, which partially makes amends.
5. Sir Charles Rey (eds. Neil Parsons and Michael Crowder), *Monarch of All I Survey: Bechuanaland Diaries 1929–37*, (Gaborone:Botswana Society; London: James Currey; and New York: Lilian Barber Press, 1988), p.22.
6. Rey, Ibid.,9. Rey was in fact an atheist.
7. Rey, Ibid., xvii–xviii
8. Leonard Barnes, *The New Boer War*, (London, 1932), pp. 193–5. The BP Police was descended from the Bechuanaland Border Police, which had ultimate roots in the Cape Mounted Rifles – an irregular cavalry of rough-riders organized along commando lines, disbanded in 1875. The BBP (a.k.a.'Blue-Blooded Police') gained a reputation for recruiting English upper-class misfits. Hence the remark of a visitor to a BBP camp: 'There are several policemen in this camp who do not bear the same names that they did when I knew them at Oxford'. (Hugh Hastings Romilly, *Letters from the Western Pacific and Mashonaland, 1878–1891*, (London, 1893), p. 371. See G. Tylden, 'The Bechuanaland Border Police, 1885–1895', *Journal of the Society for Army Historical Research*,

London, 19,236–46; Q.N. Parsons, 'Botswana Police Centenary' Gaborone: Department of Postal Services, Police Centenary 1885–1895, 5 August 1985.

9. Jack Halpern, *South Africa's Hostages: Basutoland, Bechuanaland and Swaziland*, (Harmondsworth, 1965), p. 264.

10. The first direct recruit from a university to the High Commission Territories administrative service, via Colonial Administrative Service appointment channels, was the Oxford-graduate Edwin Porter Arrowsmith (1909–still living). After Bechuanaland (1933–8) he transferred to the CAS in the Turks and Caicos Islands and then Dominica in the West Indies. Resident Commissioner of Basutoland (1952–6), Governor of the Falkland Islands (1957–64) and High Commissioner of British Antarctic Territories (1962–4). Retired to become director of the Overseas Resettlement Bureau, which helped place ex-C.A.S. officers in civilian jobs.

11. Louis A. Picard, *The Politics of Development in Botswana: a Model for Success?*, (Boulder, Colorado and London, 1987), p. 43 passim.

12. The distinction between 'mercenary' and 'missionary' may have been suggested to me in Gaborone by the slogan on a tee–shirt, worn by Pippa Shillington and admired by Michael Crowder. Under the heading of EXPATRIATE was a check-list consisting of Mercenary?, Missionary?, Misfit? I have hesitated to elaborate on a 'misfit tradition'.

13. John W. Cell, 'Lord Hailey and the making of the African Survey', *African Affairs*,88 (1989), pp. 481–82 and 497.

14. See A.J. Dachs, 'Missionary imperialism – the case of Bechuanaland [*c.*1878–84]', *Journal of African History*, London,13 (1972),647–58; Ake Holmberg, *African Tribes and European Agencies: Colonialism and Humanitarianism in British South and East Africa*, (Stockholm, 1966). The attempt of C.W. de Kiewiet (1937) to equate the whole of the 'imperial factor' with humanitarianism in the 1873–85–period may now be considered discredited – see R.L.Cope, 'C.W. de Kiewiet, The imperial factor, and South African "native policy"', *Journal of Southern African Studies*, (Oxford), 15 (1989), 486–505; and Cope, 'Strategic and socio-economic explanations for Carnarvon's South African confederation policy: the historiography and the evidence', *History in Africa*, (Los Angeles), 13 (1986), N. 13–34. Curiously neither de Kiewiet nor Cope chase up questions of missionary imperialism or humanitarianism among Liberal imperialists.

15. These ideas, which parallel those of David Livingstone referring to Malawi, are indicated in Mackenzie's *Austral Africa* (London: Sampson, Low, 1887), 2 volumes, and in A.J. Dachs (ed.), *Papers of John Mackenzie*, (Johannesburg, 1975). (On the last page of his own book *Ten Years North of the Orange River* (Edinburgh: Edmonston & Douglas, 1871), p. 523, Mackenzie quotes approvingly the vision of Charles Dilke expressed in *Greater Britain*: 'let them intermingle with the whites, living, farming, along with them, intermarrying if possible.' I am grateful to Paul Landau for pointing this out to me.

16. Sidney Shippard, 'Bechuanaland', 46–68 in William Sheowring (introd.) *British Africa*, (London, 1901), pp. 51-2.

17. John Smith Moffat had entered colonial service in 1879–80 as commissioner for the western border during the British occupation of the Transvaal, then transferring to Basutoland in 1881 and British Bechuanaland in 1885. See Robert Unwin Moffat, *John Smith Moffat, Missionary: a Memoir*, (London, 1921). John Moffat was the biographer of his parents. On his relationship with Khama see Quentin Neil Parsons, 'Khama III, the Bamangwato, and the British, 1895–1923.' University of Edinburgh: unpublished Ph.D thesis 1973,chapter 3.

18. Paul Maylam, *Rhodes, the Tswana, and the British: Colonialism, Collaboration, and Conflict in the Bechuanaland Protectorate 1885–1899* (Westport, Connecticut, 1980), pp. 126–32.

19. The Secretariat filing system found in the Botswana National Archives dates

back to 1904, being reorganized by Rey in 1929 (*Monarch*,4) and subsequently indexed by Jules Ellenberger.

20. Williams, *How I Became*, 279. Elsewhere Williams wrote to the missionary Willoughby: 'if we support our weak kings we will not allow Earls of Warwick to trouble us' (Public Record Office, London: CO 417/345, enclosure in Imperial Secretary to C.O., 13 November 1902; draft in Botswana National Archives, Gaborone – S. 178/1).

21. Rey took his cue from reading about the 1906 case in Colonial Office files before he set foot in Bechuanaland – Rey, *Monarch* xxi.

22. Parsons, 'Khama, 87.

23. Parsons, 279–80. The highpoint of the meeting was the clash between Mr Willoughby, the principal of Tiger Kloof institution, and Miss Partridge the head teacher at Molepolole. She spiritedly accused him of teaching his students that there was no Hell, and that Adam and Jonah had not been historical characters. Of course there is a Hell, Willoughby snapped back: 'it will infallibly enter into the experience of persons of orthodox belief who lend themselves to gossiping, scandal-mongering and mischief-making, and . . . sow division in the ranks of those who ought to stand with a solid front united against the armies of heathenism.'

24. See Saul Dubow, *Racial Segregation and the Origins of Apartheid in South Africa, 1919–36*, (Basingstoke, 1989), pp. 26–49.

25. Robin H. Palmer, *Land and Racial Domination in Rhodesia* [1890–1941] (London, 1977).

26. Q.N.Parsons, 'Khama & Co and the Jousse Trouble, 1910–1916', *Journal of African History* (London), 16 (1975), pp. 383–408.

27. On the core of the Lesotho missionary connection, including the Ellenberger, Dutton, Casalis, Germond, How and Nettelton families, see Gordon M. Haliburton, *Historical Dictionary of Lesotho*, (Metuchen,New Jersey, 1977). If the 'missionary' tradition in the High Commission Territories administrative service had its *locus classicus* in Basutoland, the 'mercenary' tradition found its most congenial home in white settler Swaziland. See John J. Grotpeter, *Historical Dictionary of Swaziland*, (Metuchen: Scarecrow Press, 1975), and the biography of its first substantive Resident Commissioner, Robert Coryndon, the former 'apostle' or 'lamb' of Cecil Rhodes who was to formulate the 'dual policy' as Governor of Kenya – Christopher P. Youe, *Robert Thorne Coryndon: Proconsular Imperialism in Southern and Eastern Africa, 1897–1925* (Waterloo, Ontario, 1986); and Peter Duignan, 'Sir Robert Coryndon: a model governor (1870–1925)' in L.H. Gann and P. Duignan (eds.), *African Proconsuls: European Governors in Africa*, (New York, 1978), pp. 313–52.

28. Ratshosa, 'My Book', 167–9; Parsons, 'Khama III' pp. 383–403; Herman Max Gluckman (Gluckmann), 'The tribal area in south and central Africa', in Leo Kuper and M.G. Smith, *Pluralism in Africa* (Berkeley, 1969).

29. Ratshosa, 'My Book', pp. 187–90.

30. Prologue by Parsons in Rey, *Monarch*, p. xix

31. *Ibid* p. xvii; Leopold S. Amery, *My Political Life. Volume Two: War and Peace 1914–1929*, (London, 1953), p. 408.

32. See George Bennett, *Kenya, a Political History: the Colonial Period*, (London, 1963) pp. 54–55. Amery lost his ministerial post after the elections of 1929, but may not have been re-appointed anyway because of political embarrassment over his attempt to undermine the Devonshire Declaration doctrine of 'native paramountcy' in East Africa – Paul Rich, 'British imperial policy, trusteeship and the appeasement of white South African power, 1929–1939' (University of London, Institute of Commonwealth Studies: Commonwealth History/Decolonisation Seminar, 2 February 1989).

32. A.H.M. Kirk-Greene, 'Monarch of all I survey', *African Affairs*, 88 (1989), pp. 449–50. Reference to Mitchell and Orde-Browne appears in Rey, *Monarch* p. xx.

33. See reviews of his published diaries: D.K. Fieldhouse, 'Alien rule, indigenous reaction', *Times Literary Supplement*, (London, 4458, 9–15 September 1988), 994–95; Kevin Shillington, 'I've got the little bugger now', *Southern African Review of Books* (London, 2 December 1988–January 1989),23–24; Kirk-Greene, 'Monarch'; Terence Ranger, 'Monarch of all the surveyed', *Journal of African History* (London), 30 (1989), 345–46; Richard Dale, 'Monarch of all I survey', *International Journal of African Historical Studies* (Boston), 22 (1989), pp. 369–70.

34. Sillery to Richard Brain, Oxford University Press, *c*.6 September and 16 October 1973 – Rhodes House Library, Oxford: Anthony Sillery papers, Mss Afr.s.1611, files 54 and 42. Sillery may have had me in mind as a chief 'knocker'; he had protested to me after *The Times* of London carried a letter of mine referring to colonial neglect of Botswana. The edition of the Rey Diaries referred to here, as compiled by Joslin Landell–Mills, was referred from OUP to the Hoover Institution at Stanford, which made a copy now deposited in its library. Dale, 'Monarch', 369–70, incorrectly states that the Stanford text is a complete copy of the original diaries; the original handwritten diaries and a complete typescript copy are held and owned by the Botswana Society at the National Museum in Gaborone.

35. Gerald Enract Nettelton (1894–1950). Born in Basutoland, and joined BP administration at age 20 after brief service with the Union's Native Affairs Department in the Transvaal. One of his sisters married Vivien Ellenberger; another married a Serowe trader. He married a daughter of the Mafikeng lawyer Spenser Minchin who was the BP government's chief attorney. See Rey, *Monarch* index.

36. Vivien Frederic Ellenberger (1896–1972). Also born in Basutoland, joining the BP administration in the steps of his father in 1915. After retirement in 1952 he lived with his father in Salisbury, Southern Rhodesia. See Rey, *Monarch* index.

37. See Public Records Office, London: DO 35/4 165 ('Bechuanaland Protectorate Administrative Staff: Union Nationals on –').

38. Peter Cardross Grant (1914–87). Educated at Grahamstown in the Eastern Cape Province of South Africa and at Oxford. Joined BP administration in 1937 and served (with interruption of war service 1941–5) until five years after independence, when he retired as District Commissioner of Gaborone.

39. James Anthony Allison (1915–87). Educated in Johannesburg and at Witwatersrand University. Appointed to colonial service in Nigeria 1938, also serving with Nigerian troops in India and Burma 1940–46. Transferred to Dominions Office in London 1946, and then to Bechuanaland administration 1950 and the High Commissioner's Office in Pretoria later in the year. Returning to Bechuanaland in 1951, he was rusticated to the north-west after his Serowe protests, rising to Permanent Secretary Home Affairs in 1965 and retaining that post beyond independence for five years.

40. Dennis A.T.Atkins (1915–still living). Educated in Natal and at Cambridge. After distinguished military service in 1940–5, he joined the BP administration in 1946. Awarded the George Medal for gallantry in the Serowe Kgotla riot of 1952, he remained in the BP until 1963.

41. Public Records Office, London: DO 35/4138 – P. Cardross Grant, James A. Allison, and Dennis Atkins (Serowe) to Secretary of State, 10 January 1952; Minute by W.A.W. Clark, 6 February 1952.

42. Personal conversation with Noel Redmond, London, 8 December 1988.

43. Jean Daniel Arnaud Germond (1904–1967). Joined BP administration in 1925, and served with 'Bechuana' troops around the Mediterranean 1940–6. He then accepted transfer to the Solomon Islands in the Pacific – regarded as a posting only for a superior kind of officer 'with special resources which would enable him to stand up to the strains and stresses of an exceptionally rough and lonely life' (Ralph Furse, *Aucuparius: Recollections of a Recruiting Officer*, (London, 1962), p. 281). Transferred back

to Bechuanaland as an emergency measure in 1950, he identified himself with the interests of common people and continued to clash with Tshekedi Khama as he had done before the war. Described as a 'fascinator. . .Basic trouble he knows what's best for Africans', by Mary Benson – see her 'Background reports so far', 20 May 1961, in Fabian Colonial Bureau papers (Rhodes House Library, Oxford), Mss.Brit.Emp. s.365, box 92, file 4.)

44. Rowland Alan Robertson Bent (1914–still living). Educated in Somerset and at Cambridge, joining BP administration in 1937. War service with 'Bechuana' troops 1941–6 resulted in publication of his *Ten Thousand Men of Africa: the Story of the Bechuanaland Pioneers and Gunners 1941–46* (London: H.M.S.O. for Bechuanaland Government, 1952). While at Serowe in early 1952 he associated himself with educated young Bangwato – see Q.N. Parsons, 'The idea of democracy and the emergence of an educated elite in Botswana, 1931–1960' in University of Edinburgh, Centre of African Studies, *Botswana: Politics, Culture and Education*, in press. In 1953 Bent transferred to the Colonial Office in London and qualified as a barrister in 1954, returning to Bechuanaland to take up the new post of Development Secretary in 1955.

45. Philip Gordon Batho (1909–?). Possibly from one of the many immigrant Cornish miner families on the Witwatersrand, he joined the BP administration in 1934 and transferred to the High Commissioner's Office in Pretoria in 1948. He returned to Bechuanaland in 1950 and left the service abruptly after the Serowe Kgotla riot of 1952. Before he arrived in Serowe, some people assumed he was a Motswana because his Cornish surname is spelt the same as the word for 'people' in Setswana.

46. See Q.N. Parsons, 'The Serowe Kglotla riot of 1952 in colonial Botswana: drink, women, or liberal principles?', in submission to *Past and Present* (Oxford).

47. See Robert Pearce, 'The Colonial Office and planned decolonization in Africa' *African Affairs*, p. 83 (1984), pp. 77–93; Ronald Hyam 'Africa and the Labour government, 1945–51', *Journal of Imperial and Commonwealth History*, (London), 16 (1988); David Goldsworthy, 'Contemplating decolonization: some policy dilemmas of the Churchill and Eden governments, 1951–7' University of London, School of Oriental and African Studies: African History Seminar, 26 October 1988.

48. Parsons, 'Idea of democracy'; Dubow, *Racial Segregation*. The rejection of dualistic assumptions of colonial development in Bechuanaland can be seen in the anthropology of Isaac Schapera from 1929 onwards. But dualistic ideas were revived not only in academic ideas of 'dual economy' and 'dual society' but also in the political ideas of racial partnership developed in Southern Rhodesia and Kenya, and in the political doctrine of *apartheid* developed in South Africa.

49. John Forster Millard (1911–still living), had begun his colonial career in Basutoland in 1934, moving on to Tanganyika in 1937. After war service and serving on the Furse team, he returned to Tanganyika until transfer to Bechuanaland in 1952. See Furse, *Aucuparius*, p. 280; Benson, Tshekedi Khama, opp. cit. 256; Henderson M. Tapela, 'The Tati District of Botswana, 1866–1969' (University of Sussex: unpublished D.Phil Thesis, 1976).

50. Confidential minute by Turnbull, *c.* October/November 1953, in Public Records Office, London: DO 35/4532. Fawcus was serving in the High Commissioner's Office at the time, after being recruited to Basutoland through London.

51. See Public Records Office, London: DO 35/4302 ('Note on the chieftainship of the Bamangwato'), DO 35/4329 ('Transfer: discussions with Strijdom'), DO 35/4381 ('Comparison between native administration in Union and High Commission Territories'), DO 35/4382 ('The Tomlinson report'), PREM 11/1182 (n.b. Home to Eden, 7 September 1956).

52. See Michael Crowder, 'Botswana and the survival of liberal democracy in Africa', pp. 461–76 in Prosser Gifford and William Roger Louis (eds.), *Decolonization and African Independence 1960–80*, (New Haven, 1988), pp. 461–76.

Chapter Thirteen

Gender and Decolonization: A Study of Three Women in West African Public Life[1]

La Ray Denzer

W omen played an important role in the politics of decolonization of West Africa after the Second World War.[2] All mass-based political parties formed parallel women's sections in order to mobilize the support of women at the grassroots. Among the most militant of these women's organizations were those founded by the *Rassemblement démocratique Africain* (RDA) in French West African and the Convention People's Party (CPP) in Ghana, both developed along Marxist-Leninist lines of political organization.[3] Slightly less militant, but nevertheless very active in setting up women's organizations were those parties, like the Action Group (AG) and the National Council of Nigeria and the Cameroons (NCNC) in Nigeria, which advocated ideologies based in part on African socialism.[4] Everywhere women campaigned vigorously, developed a network for the distribution of propaganda, supported boycotts and strikes, and sometimes took part in running political parties when the male leaders were imprisoned. When it came time for the distribution of rewards for loyalty, sacrifice and hard work, however, women found their male colleagues surprisingly obdurate and chauvinistic. Women obtained almost nothing. Few were nominated as party candidates, few were appointed to public office or boards, few received government contracts. The constraints of European patriarchal policy reinforced the patriarchal structures of traditional, and Muslim, African societies, with the result that the wide variety of women's indigenous political institutions were rapidly stripped of their former authority and status.[5] During the phase of decolonization, African male political leaders adopted policies which accelerated this decline.

This chapter © La Ray Denzer 1992

So far feminist scholars have dwelt on this aspect of the decline of female political influence and authority. In their search for an understanding of the female predicament in the world at large, they have emphasized the grand, dynamic failures: the Aba Women's War, the downfall (for two short years) of the Alake of Abeokuta, the march on Grand Bassam. Even Nina Mba, who has analyzed the contribution of women to Nigerian politics, selected for detailed biographical case studies two notable eccentric failures – Adunni Oluwole, an individualist who opposed self-government, and Funmilayo Ransome-Kuti, the famous Abeokuta women's leader who failed in all her attempts to gain regional and national office – rather than the several successful women who appear throughout her work.[6]

Failure was not the whole story. That male leaders did not succeed in their attempt to erase women's influence is due to the emergence of strong-minded, diplomatic and independent women leaders who survived political chicanery and corruption to win elections or to gain appointments to high office. They learnt to play the game of politics. In and out of the office they worked hard to protect women's interests, improve the structure of opportunity available to them, and to raise women's status and civic awareness.

This study focusses on the careers of three such exceptional and largely successful women: Mabel Dove of Ghana, the first woman in West Africa to be elected to a national legislature; Aoua Keita of Mali, the first woman to be elected a deputy to a national assembly in a French-speaking West African territory as well as one of the first to be elected to a national political bureau of the RDA; and Wuraola Adepeju Esan, the first woman appointed as a senator in the federal legislature of Nigeria and the first to be on the federal executive committee of the Action Group. These women have been selected for three reasons. First, their careers illustrate the type of political careers women pursued in three quite different national political arenas: the Gold Coast, the French Sudan (now Mali), and Nigeria. Second, they were in the mainstream of national political life, in the decision-making bodies of their respective political parties and national legislatures. Thus they succeeded in rising above the female ghetto of women's organizations and political auxiliaries, although they remained a part of these activities. Third, among the sources available for the study of these three women are speeches, interviews with colleagues, and two autobiographies, so far an extremely rare occurrence in the source material for the study of African women, which provide very frank and detailed accounts of the genesis of women's political interest, political ideas and goals, personal opponents and interactions with other party members. The main areas in the life histories of these women which will be examined here are: their social background; the development of their political careers; and their role in the national legislature.

218

Social background

An examination of the social backgrounds of these three women reveals the very different colonial situations and cultural *milieux* which shaped their personalities and opportunities for leadership.

Mabel Dove (1905–84) came from an old coastal family of Sierra Leonean origin which had been deeply involved in commerce, colonial politics and law since the late nineteenth century.[7] Her father was Francis Thomas Dove, a prominent lawyer resident in Accra, a very wealthy man who enjoyed luxurious living, and although a Christian Krio, maintained many wives in customary marriage. Dove's mother was Eva Buckman, a Ga businesswoman, who lost her wealth speculating in cocoa during the 1920s.

At the age of six, Dove's father took her to Freetown where she received her primary and secondary school education. She attended the private school run by her paternal aunt, Mrs Lydia Rice (*née* Dove), a widow who was an influential social leader in the colony.[8] When Mrs Rice's school closed, Dove enrolled as a pupil in Annie Walsh Memorial School, the oldest girls' school in Sierra Leone, and still highly regarded. After she obtained her school-leaving certificate from Annie Walsh, her father took her to England for further education, first at the Anglican Convent in Bury St. Edmunds, a school for clergymen's daughters, and then at St. Michael's College in Hurstpierpoint (near Brighton). Towards the end of her training at St. Michael's, she braved her father's displeasure by taking a four-month secretarial course at Gregg Commercial College. For her disobedience she was immediately sent back to Freetown. Moreover, her father refused to allow her to seek employment until she was twenty-one. Reflecting on this in her old age, she wryly observed, '. . . My father was not interested in the higher education for women or something useful, as nursing, he wanted us to acquire what is known as "polish", no doubt to be charming and well-bred and be able to play a good game of tennis.'[9]

While in Freetown she was involved in founding a girls' cricket club, taking part in a local dramatic society, and reading extensively. When she was twenty-one, in 1926, she returned to Accra. Free now to take wage employment, she found a position as a shorthand-typist for Elder Dempster at £7 a month, the only woman typist in the office. Work was for her a liberating and exhilarating experience. After eight years, she transferred to G. B. Ollivant, and in the 1940s to Leventis, where she held the position of manager of the goods and fabrics section.

Simultaneously, she developed a career as a freelance journalist. Some West African newspapers were just beginning to publish a column devoted to women's interests in order to attract a female clientele among the slowly growing group of educated women. J. B. Danquah, charmed by her style of writing letters, asked her in the early 1930s to write a ladies' column for his newly-established *Times of West Africa*, the first daily in the Gold Coast, Hesitant at first, she finally agreed to try her hand. Her column, written under the pen-name Marjorie Mensah, was devoted to women's affairs, male-female relationships, children and morals. It was very popular with readers. After the *Times of West Africa* folded, her columns were much in demand by other West Africa papers. She wrote under a series of pen-names – Eben Alakija (*Nigerian Daily Times*), Dama Dumas (*African Morning Post*), and Akosuah Dzatsui (*Accra Evening News*). Then she wrote only occasionally about politics, but by the 1950s politics had become her major concern. She was one of the principal journalists writing on behalf of the Convention People's Party (CPP).

In 1933 Dove married J. B. Danquah, soon to become a major figure in Gold Coast political and legal circles. They had a son,[10] but it was not a happy marriage, and did not survive Danquah's prolonged absence during the period 1934–36 when he was in England as secretary of the Gold Coast delegation. Despite her married status, Dove (now Mrs Danquah) received and rejected a proposal of marriage from Nnamdi Azikiwe, then editor of the *African Morning Post* in Accra. Shortly after Danquah's return to Accra, the couple separated and neither made any serious effort to seek reconciliation. They were finally divorced in the mid-1940s.

While Mabel Dove came from an established elite family, Aoua Keita (*c.* 1908–1984?), her sister nationalist in the French Sudan, came from the new elite which emerged under French colonial rule.[11] Her father, originally from Kouroussa in Guinea, settled in Bamako after his discharge from the French army, where he took a post as a government health agent. Her mother, one of several wives, distrusted European institutions and ideas, preferring to live according to the traditions of her people.

Keita's father enrolled her in the newly-founded girls' school in Bamako in 1923 which catered mostly for the mulatto daughters of French officials. In doing this he confronted the total opposition of his daughter's mother and the other members of his household, both male and female. Nevertheless he persevered in his decision, partly influenced by his work in the French African civil service and partly because of his concern for the future of Keita's mother who at that time had four daughters but no son to look after her when he died. Keita excelled in elementary school, after which she was sent to the school for midwifery in Dakar. Upon graduation she accepted a post to establish a maternity centre in Gao, again facing much family opposition, but eventually received the blessing of her proud father who had no desire to curb her adventurous spirit.

Exhilarated by her new independence, she quickly proved her professional competence as a midwife and developed a great popularity among the women in the town and surrounding villages which she visited on horseback or a bicycle. Later these families became an important source of political support. At the end of her first year, she petitioned the government for the establishment of a modern maternity hospital, repeating the demand for two more years until one was built in 1934. Aside from her professional activities, she was a member of the local Association des Jeunes du Quartier, composed of junior civil servants, businessmen and students. Soon her house became a lively gathering place where conversation ranged over a wide variety of topics.

In 1935 she married Dr Daouda Diawara, a physician from Gorée, whom she had met while in a midwifery school in Dakar. Keenly interested in local political issues, he introduced his wife to politics, first with regard to the election campaign of Galamsou Diouf in Senegal for election as the overseas delegate to the French National Assembly, and then to colonial politics in general. Like many African intellectuals at the time, her political consiousness was further heightened by a sense of the injustice of the Italian invasion and conquest of Ethiopia. She began to read avidly, especially the Paris newspapers and books of all kinds which exposed her to new ideas. During the Second World War she continued to develop her political ideas as she observed the hardship forced on the people by the Vichy regime.

In many respects the background of Wuraola Adepeju Esan (*née* Ojo) (1909–85)[12] was similar to that of both Dove and Keita. She received the best education available at a time when it was uncommon to educate girls beyond the first few years of elementary school; she undertook a modern profession; she was in the vanguard of young female leaders who developed an early and abiding interest in politics. Unlike either Dove or Keita, she came from a respected traditional family of the local elite in her town, Ibadan.

Esan was born into the well-known Ojo 'Badan family, a prominent Yoruba family in Ibadan which played an important role in town politics. Her mother, the second of eight wives, was Madam Ajitie Ojo (alias Iya Gbogbo, 'Mother of All'), a prosperous trader in kola and alligator pepper, who travelled extensively in southern Nigeria. Esan's father was Chief Thomas Adeogun Ojo (alias Ojo 'Badan), a former Sergeant Major in the Royal West African Frontier Force (WAFF) who had served in the Asante campaign and in the Cameroons during the First World War. After his retirement from the army, he took a post in the civil service as chief manager of the forest reserve in Ibadan. In 1935 he entered the Balogun line of Ibadan chiefs, rising to the position of Ekarun Balogun, fifth in line to the Olubadan. A member of one of Ibadan's earliest Christian families, a devout Baptist, he had no formal education himself, but encouraged his children to get an education. Among his sons was a teacher, a lawyer, and an architect.

Beginning her elementary schooling at Sacred Heart (Calabar) in 1920, she transferred twice before she obtained her Standard VII certificate from Idi Aba Baptist Girls' School (Abeokuta) in 1927. She wanted to become a teacher, the usual career choice then of young elite women. Because of her excellent performance, she was admitted in 1928 to the foundation class of United Missionary College (UMC), the first women's training college in Nigeria, established by the Church Missionary Society (CMS) and Methodist missions in order to meet the growing demand for qualified teachers.[13] In the year of her admission there were only fifty-three girls enrolled in secondary school and forty-three in teacher training courses in the whole of southern Nigeria, about double the number for the previous year.[14] While at UMC she was made prefect of her class, a sign of early leadership qualities.[15] One of her schoolmates recalls an incident when Esan confronted her European teachers to protest a matter which her fellow students felt was unjust. The exact issue has been forgotten, but Esan's audaciousness in taking up the matter made an indelible impression on her school-mates.

Completing her two-year course in 1929, she was appointed as a third class certificated teacher, at a salary of about £30 a year, to the staff of the Girls' Training Centre (Akure), a type of establishment which would today be called an 'alternative' school.[16] It offered domestic science training for girls who were soon to marry and tried as much as possible to replicate local household conditions. Three years later she was transferred to the staff of UMC where Miss Gladys Plummer,[17] just beginning her long career in Nigeria as a lady education officer, noted her competence: 'Miss Ojo has an attractive personality; with added experience and the confidence which is borne of experience she should do well.'[18]

In 1934 she married Victor Owolabi Esan, a member of an influential Christian family in Ibadan, then on the staff of the Public Works Department. The couple moved to Lagos where she taught for a while before the birth of her first child. During this period it seems likely that she continued her involvement with the Nigerian Youth Movement in which she had taken an interst in during school days, but as a young mother, she devoted most of her attention to her household.[19] When her husband went to England in 1944 to study law, she returned with her children to Ibadan. Here, in order to help maintain her family, she founded the Ibadan People's Girls' School, initially a primary school designed to meet the growing demand for girls' education among the ordinary people in Ibadan.[20] The curriculum was somewhat innovative as it offered stenography as well as the usual literary and domestic science subjects. This showed that Esan was among the first to discern the changing structure of opportunities opening to young women. Soundly conceived and financed, the school enrollment rose from 60 to 200 in just two years; today the school is run by the government and has an enrollment of 1026.[21]

This account of the formative years of the three leaders under discussion demonstrates that their social backgrounds had many similarities, but there were also notable differences reflecting variations in wealth, family background and individual personality. All three women came from elite families, but the category of elite differed. All received the highest education then available to girls according to the geographic location and the category of elite that they belonged to. Usually this also meant that they had spent considerable time away from their family home: Keita and Esan in boarding schools; and Dove, removed first to her relatives in Freetown, and then to boarding school in England. This encouraged the development of independence, self-confidence and courage. Dove received a higher level of education than either Keita or Esan because of her family's greater wealth. The determining factor in the education of these three women was the attitude of their fathers. In those days it was very rare for a girl to go to school without the consent and active encouragement of her father. These particular fathers had a western profession or occupation which influenced new ideas about the role and status of women, and two of them were from Christian families already committed to educational attainment. The education the three women received enabled them to take up the 'modern' professions of secretary, journalist, midwife and teacher in which they displayed qualities of professional competence and leadership very early in their careers.

Dove, Keita and Esan enjoyed great popularity. Later this popularity aided their entry into politics and formed a significant component in their base of political support – newspaper readers, patients, pupils and their families.

All married talented men of good families who were to lead distinguished professional and political careers in their respective countries. Of the three women, however, only Esan's marriage flourished, the others ending in separation and divorce. For Dove and Keita this was hardly a tragedy. Freed from the demands of family obligations, they could devote their time to pursuing careers in writing and/or politics, and although Esan's career amply demonstrates that a dedicated politician need not let family demands hamper her activities unduly, they made it more difficult to follow a political career.

Political careers

In the above examination of the social backgrounds of Dove, Keita and Esan, we have seen that the political ideas of these women began to take shape during the 1930s, and probably before then in the case of Dove and Esan, who came from homes in which local politics was a subject of everyday discussion. Their marriages to men involved in community or national politics may have contributed to their thinking – how much is open to debate. Only Keita provides us with a detailed account of her husband's tutelage and encouragement, but it is also clear that he did not so easily accept it when he discovered the extent of her militant organizational activities and when she began to participate actively in political debates.[22] Dove's interest in politics coincided with the time of her marriage, but she does not mention Danquah as being particularly influential in her thinking.[23] Indeed it appears that his progressivism contributed a lot to her decision to marry him in the first place. In the case of Esan, she once confessed to a correspondent in *West Africa* magazine, 'I can't remember any time when I was not interested in politics', which indicates how early her awareness developed and why she opposed her husband's wish that she not participate in politics.[24]

Dove, the first West African woman to be *elected* by popular vote to a colonial legislature, did not become active in party politics until 1950 when she joined the Convention People's Party (CPP), although she had followed the activities and debates of the United Gold Coast Convention from its establishment in 1947.[25] She was attracted to the CPP because of its radical platform and the dynamism of Nkrumah's leadership, Later she explained, 'I was always for action, as against mere words. And I said to myself, THIS is it – action'.[26] Unlike Keita and Esan who were efficient and dedicated organizers at the grassroots level, Dove does not seem to have been involved in organizational work. Her contribution to party work was through promoting CPP ideology through her columns in the *Accra Evening News*, the party newspaper, often writing under the pen-name Akosua Dzatsui. No longer did she write short, witty pieces on women's concerns. Now her writing, sharply worded and full of Biblical allusions, focussed on the need for 'Self-Government Now', the injustices of colonial rule, the heroism of Nkrumah, and the importance of CPP activities.

Nkrumah admired the forcefulness of the Akosua Dzatsui columns which he read while in detention from where he sent her little notes of encouragement on scraps of prison toilet paper.[27] After his release, he confided to her that her writing style had at first convinced him the writer of the columns was a man. Her loyalty, verve and perseverance convinced Nkrumah to appoint her as the editor of the *Evening News* in 1951, one of the first West African women to take complete charge of the publication of a newspaper.[28] She did not remain in the position for long. Independence of mind was another of her qualities and soon she clashed with Nkrumah over editorial policy, resulting in her dismissal after five months. Later she served as a sub-editor of the *Daily Graphic* and continued to contribute to the *Evening News*. Nevertheless Dove remained loyal to the CPP and Nkrumah. Her columns continued to call for wholehearted support and dedication to party objectives, and unstinting support of its leaders.

Women in the Gold Coast had the right to vote at least by 1951. Shortly thereafter the first women candidates began to stand in municipal elections. Early in 1953 the Gold Coast newspapers began debating the question of a woman representative in the legislative assembly.[29] It was generally felt that the time had come for women's viewpoints to be heard in debates. In September of the same year there were three female candidates standing in the Accra Town Council election: Mrs H. Evans Lutterodt and Stella Dorothy Lokko for the Ghana Congress Party (GCP) and Dove for the CPP in ward 16.[30] None succeeded. Dove lost to I. M. Peregrino-Braimah, a popular Muslim leader. The experience, however, convinced Dove that she could stand for national election in the 1954 elections and she asked the party to consider her nomination. According to her autobiography, she made no other effort to gain support and somewhat to her surprise she was nominated as the party's candidate in Ga Rural constituency, the only woman on the national CPP slate.[31] The GCP also named a woman candidate, Nancy Tsiboe, billed as 'the housewife's choice', standing in Kumasi South.[32]

In several respects Dove's nomination seemed very cavalier. The Oshiuman CPP branch in Ga Rural protested against her selection, complaining that she was a foreigner, that they did not know her, that she could not speak Ga.[33] Some important women members, particularly Mary Ardua (alias Mrs Nkrumah) also protested for the same reasons.[34] Everything taken into consideration, Hannah Cudjoe would have seemed the more logical choice for nomination.[35] An Nkrumah loyalist since the time he took over the secretaryship of the UGCC, and the party's indefatigable national propaganda secretary, she had for many years criss-crossed the country disseminating party instructions, organizing women's sections, directing literacy campaigns, and holding child welfare classes. What accounted then for the selection of Dove over Cudjoe?

Dove attributed the party's decision to a promise made to her by Nkrumah while he was in prison, 'Carry on the fight, I know what I will do for you when I return.'[36] While this may have been a factor (Nkrumah was well-known for his personal commitment to certain friends), there were other reasons. Nkrumah's Marxist-Leninist beliefs required building political networks within all sectors of society, including, of course, the women. Dove was perhaps the best-educated and articulate among the female party members and capable of holding her own against her opponents, Nii Amaa Ollenu, a barrister and vice-chairman of the CCP, and I. M. Peregrino-Braimah of the Muslim Association Party (MAP), to whom she had earlier lost the Town Council election. Furthermore, the psychological opportunity represented by running as its candidate the former wife of Danquah, Nkrumah's main opponent, may have been irresistible.

Once nominated, Dove directed an energetic and thoughtful campaign in her constituency of 137 farming and fishing villages. The party provided only a small part of the financing, but her Lebanese brother-in-law and her constituents contributed money and maintenance. She met with constituents and identified the issues they were most concerned about: clean drinking water, good roads, maternity clinics, and the legalization of the production of *akpeteshie* (local gin). Anxious that their sole woman candidate should win, Nkrumah and other CPP leaders campaigned in the area on her behalf. Nkrumah urged the people to vote for her, maintaining that as a woman, she had access to some places that men could not go. Occasionally men would object to a woman candidate on the grounds that women should be subordinate to men, but there was always someone within the meeting, sometimes an elder, who silenced such objections by reminding the people that they all had once depended on their mothers, that their candidate would be their mother in the National Assembly.[37] She won a resounding victory at the polls: 3331 votes to 417 for Ollenu and 266 for Peregrino-Brimah.[38]

In comparison to Dove's experience, Keita's career as a *'femme militante'* in politics in the French Sudan (now Mali) was far more difficult and strenuous. She voted for the first time in 1946 in the metropolitan elections held in Senegal. Female citizens had received the franchise throughout francophone Africa after the reforms instituted by the Brazzaville Conference, partly as a reward for the role they played in the resistance movement during the war.[39] The militant political party, the RDA, was rounded shortly thereafter and established branches in all the French West African colonies. From the beginning, Keita took part in RDA organizational activities in the Sudan. When the Bamako branch was established, of the Union Soudanaise Rassemblement Démocratique Africain (USRDA), in October 1946, she and her husband were among the founder members. They campaigned in the elections for the three RDA Sudanese representatives to the French National Assembly, among them Mamadou Konaté, the leader of the RDA. To show their solidarity with ordinary party members, the Diawaras renounced their French citizenship in the canton elections which took place in January 1947, and voted as ordinary colonial subjects.[40]

While stationed in Niono, Daouda Diawara became secretary-general of the branch political bureau of the RDA. All its meetings took place in their house. Her husband did not allow her to participate in the debates, declaring his position as follows:

You observe [what is going on]. You should be busy in the kitchen with your colleagues from Segu preparing food . . . Already you represent us in the office and you also vote. That already is a great contribution. Avoid in particular talking politics.[41]

Going against his advice, she secretly undertook extensive organizational work among the women, talking to them during her house calls and holding meetings in her maternity clinic in the afternoons and evenings. Very likely her independent politicking, as well as her inability to have children, contributed much to his decision to divorce her in 1949.

Thereafter Keita concentrated on her professional and political activities. Her activities came to the attention of the government authorities who tried to curb them by transferring her from Niono to Gao, considered a punishment posting. This action, however, had the opposite effect. Gao turned out to be highly satisfactory for political mobilization among workers, former slaves and women. Her former patients and their families – a good many of the teenagers aged between thirteen and eighteen had been assisted into the world by her – welcomed her enthusiastically. Helped by young educated people, she organized women's groups which cut across villages, distributed RDA propaganda, contacted the nomads in the desert, and mobilized voters whenever elections were held. She was selected as one of the RDA observers at the polling stations in order to ensure that electoral laws were enforced. So great was her success that the government transferred her away from the Sudan to Bignona (Casamance), much to the anger of her women supporters.[42]

No amount of transfers could stop Keita from taking part in politics wherever she was. Each town, each village had its own special problems which interested her. A natural anthropologist, she made extensive notes of childbirth practices and marriage customs.[43] Each area provided new opportunities to test her ideas for improving women's and children's conditions as well as for political organization. With every transfer, she left behind a network of organizations and a heightened awareness of colonial politics. She rose to influential positions within the local and national RDA hierarchy.

In 1957 she was transferred to Bamako. By this time Konaté had died and her relative, Modibo Keita, had become the leader of the USRDA, which helped to consolidate her position in the party, but created other problems which impeded her organizational work. While working at the maternity hospital at Kati in the vicinity of Bamako, she established a women's union in the face of fierce opposition from their husbands and promoted the establishment of branches of the union in other parts of the country. During the fifth congress of the party in September 1958 she was the only woman elected to the central political bureau. Shortly thereafter, she was appointed as a full member of the constitutional committee of the Sudanese Republic and attached to the staff of the Ministry of Labour and Social Affairs. The following year she was nominated as one of the RDA candidates, the only woman to stand for election for the National Assembly which would usher in independence. She won, but it was not an easy victory; in hostile areas she had campaigned with a loaded pistol in her handbag, and almost had to use it on one occasion.

Keita had to work against tremendous opposition. Social attitudes among the mostly Muslim population did not readily accept the changes she advocated in women's roles and status. Her mother, never easy about the lifestyle of her educated daughter, advised her not to accept the party's nomination as electoral candidate, maintaining that:

> I think that the function of deputy is solely reserved for men. It is too heavy work for a woman. How can you accept it? Your brothers simply want to test you. In your place I would have refused.[44]

Husbands feared her independence and tried to undermine her organizational work among their wives. The wife of Modibo Keita was extremely jealous and used every opportunity to spread dissension and distrust among the leaders of the women's bureaux. Many male leaders, inside and out of the party, bitterly resented her position within the party and her campaign for the office of deputy. A notable instance of this occurred during her campaign in the small town of Fado where the chief refused to let her campaign, declaring:

> Get out of my village, audacious woman! It must be that you are not only daring but full of effrontery to try to measure up to men in accepting a man's place. But you have done nothing. It is the fault of the crazy leaders of the RDA who are insulting the men of our country in making you their equal. Ha! People of Singne, you see this! Koutiala, a country of valiant warriors, great hunters, brave old combatants of the French army, to have a little worthless woman at your head. No! Not possible! If you men of the RDA are mocking us, we know how to make ourselves respected. Myself, Master Sergeant of the French army, who fought the Germans! Am I going to accept being controlled by a woman? Never![45]

Both Dove and Keita have provided us with detailed accounts of their political careers and ideas. For the career of Esan, their counterpart in Nigeria, such richness of detail is sadly lacking although newspaper accounts and a few short biographical accounts provide an outline of the high points of her career.

Esan and her husband were members of the Ibadan Progressive Union and the Egbe Omo Oduduwa, the cultural nationalist organization which spawned the political party, the Action Group (AG). When her husband became the president of the Ibadan Progressive Union in the early 1950s, Esan organized a women's section of that body. Under its auspices, she chaired a reception for Mrs James Aggrey and Mrs Crystal Faucet, two American women visiting Ibadan for the formal opening of the University College. Faucet, a member of the National Association for the Advancement of Coloured People, urged Ibadan women to take part in politics.[46] By that time Esan was interested in the development programme of the Action Group, particularly in the field of education, but she deliberated for a while before she joined its women's wing. Not long after she was one of its main leaders. She conducted tours to organize branches in the western provinces, served on committees, campaigned, earning a reputation for dedication and hard work.

Meanwhile she entered the Iyalode's line of Ibadan chiefs in 1955 when she was made Balogun Iyalode, third in line to the Iyalode, the leader of the women. From the beginning of her career in public life, Esan combined traditional and modern roles to create a solid base of support. She was the proprietor of People's School, an AG women's leader, a traditional chief, an office-holder, member or matron in many organizations, including the Independent Schools Proprietors' Association, the Young Women's Christian Association, the Red Cross, the Ibile Ibadan Irepodun, the Farmers' Council, the Ibadan Descendants' Union, the Oluyole Ladies Club, and several more bodies in the Anglican Church.[47]

The first time that Esan was a candidate for elective office was in 1958 when she was elected to the Ibadan Urban District Council. One of the difficulties faced by Nigerian women interested in politics was that the right to vote devolved in a piecemeal fashion, gained in different places at different times.[48] Port Harcourt women in 1949 and Lagos women in 1950 voted for the first time in their respective Town Council elections. Universal suffrage applied for the first time in the eastern regional elections in 1954, but not in the Western Regional elections until 1959. In the Western Region, only women tax-payers had the right to vote from 1954 to 1958: thus the success of women's earlier protests against taxes (in eastern Nigeria, Lagos, Abeokuta, etc.), so much romanticized in the literature on Nigerian women's history, had serious repercussions in delaying women's entry into national politics on anything but an *ad hoc* basis.

Also in 1958 the AG appointed Esan as one of its female advisers to the constitutional talks taking place in London.[49] That same year she was nominated as a candidate for SW9 ward in Ibadan in the western regional election, although the AG knew that she had little hope of winning and nominated her because the party could find no other candidate willing to stand. In the general election of 1959 the AG again nominated her as a candidate in one of the wards of Ibadan, making her the second woman to stand for national election in Nigeria. As in the Sudan, the campaign was characterized by underhand methods and much violence was employed, but unlike Keita, she avoided trouble.[50] Later she explained how she managed this:

> I have the power of combating those people who want to fight me better than men, because when you smile sweetly when your enemy is coming there will not be any fight. Whenever we have occasion for our opponent to challenge us, I just advise my people to leave me to him. I will go forward and say to him, 'Oh, my dear brother, do you also stay in this village?' We will smile and the battle is won. After three or four visits they will call me 'sister' and even prepare food for me, though I know very well that some of them will not vote for me for certain reasons.[51]

Despite her defeat at the polls, 7169 votes to her opponent's (Oyewole) 9355, she was pleased because her performance was much better than that of Ransome-Kuti, running as an independent in Abeokuta (she had broken with the NCNC on the issue of her nomination), who received only 4665 votes.[52]

Tactful and diplomatic, Esan's continued loyalty and hard work on behalf of the party, convinced the central leadership of the need to reward her services by appointing her a special women's representative in the federal senate to protect women's interest in the government formed to preside over independence. In 1960 she became the only woman senator as well as the only woman to serve on the federal executive committee of the AG, a post she held until she resigned from the party. There was no other woman legislator at the time. The following year, however, Margaret Ekpo and Janet Mokelu won seats in the Eastern Regional Assembly.

The Voice of the Women

Dove, Keita and Esan, token women in their respective country's legislatures, represented 'the voice of the women'. Their original candidacy was the result of their articulateness, their party work, and their social prominence in the era of decolonization. More research must be done on Keita's role in the Malian legislature, but there is every reason to believe that there she would have continued to voice the beliefs, based on the USRDA interpretation of Marxism-Leninism, developed in her campaigns and organizational work among women. These included the need to reform marriage and divorce laws, improve health facilities, promote more education for girls and women, improve the conditions of workers, and to do everything possible to counteract those traditional and Islamic customs which kept the status of women low. From Keita's account of the period 1959–60, it is clear that her main concerns were not those of her constituents, but with broad party policy. She was much more interested in the process of drafting the new constitution and following developments connected with the ill-fated Mali Federation. Indeed she believed her position in the political bureau to be fundamentally more important than that of deputy.[53]

While a member of the National Assembly, Dove divided her attention between the concerns of her constituency – clean water, the legalization of distilling *akpeteshie*, good roads, and dispensaries, banning of immoral movies, better care for beggars and the insane, better housing, more electricity, more education – and those specifically pertaining to women. Girls' education was one of her main concerns and she pointed out that there were few women graduates and only six women in the professions.[54] In 1954 there were no women graduating from the University College: total college enrollment was 418 men and 14 women. 'What is needed,' she maintained, 'is a systematic propaganda campaign for mothers to send their daughters to school.'[55] Furthermore she felt that one way of improving male attitudes towards women would be to have more women teachers in primary schools: 'That would create respect and regard for a woman which would change the present attitude of Gold Coast men to Gold Coast women. At the moment the average man thinks a woman is solely created for his particular need.'[56]

A single term was all that Dove served in the Gold Coast National Assembly and when the country became independent in 1957, there was no woman sitting in the legislature.[57] The CPP did not renominate her as a candidate in the general election of 1956. This was partly because of the growing suspicion among the leadership about her loyalty; not only was she the former wife of Danquah, but her sister, Muriel Odamtten, was married to one of the main opposition leaders, the chairman of the United Party. But more importantly, Dove was naive about political gamesmanship. Having gained the nomination so easily the first time, she ignored Nkrumah's pointed advice not to leave Ghana for a long trip to the United States sponsored by the United States Information Service (USIS) in 1956. In the midst of her journey she learned that Nkrumah had called a general election and that a man, C. T. Nylander, had been nominated for her seat. Reflecting on this in later life, she wrote. 'I felt if I were in Jericho and my Party wanted me to stand, they would sent for me, and if I were in Accra and they wanted to throw me out of the Assembly, they would.' Had she been home, however, she might have been able to counteract her opposition. Furthermore, candidates were required to submit their nomination papers in person.

The truth appears to be that she had become disillusioned with party politics which were hedged with corrupt and unfair practices, even requiring candidates to purchase constituencies, which was way beyond her means.[58] Out of politics she remained loyal to Nkrumah and the CPP, continuing to write political commentary for the party newspapers. However, she was also critical about some of the party's policies and practices, particularly the detention and imprisonment of Danquah, on whose behalf she spoke several times to Nkrumah, but to no avail.[59]

Like Dove, Esan also represented the women's voice in the legislature. She used every opportunity to promote and protect women's interests, but also spoke on matters of general national concern such as the development of policies concerning unemployment, better conditions for workers, agricultural research, education, smuggling, bribery, corruption and tax evasion. In her maiden speech, she declared that women deserved a place in the Senate because of their role as the 'mothers of all those who fought for independence'.[60] As a teacher and a school proprietor, she urged the government to provide more scholarships for girls to study abroad for careers in nursing, pottery, dairy farming, canteen management, and housekeeping.[61] In addition, she called for more instruction in domestic science in the schools. A major concern was the improvement of conditions for market women: the construction of more comfortable markets, better conditions for trading, and equal access with men to loans.

One of the founders of the National Council of Women's Societies, Esan used her position in the Senate in order to campaign for equal rights and raising the status of women. She urged the government to appoint more women to public office, national boards and corporations on merit, noting that 'One or two women are placed on certain statutory boards and corporations because they want us to go and lend colour there, and not because they think us capable of contributing something substantial to the talks being held . . .'[62] Concerning the necessity for female contribution to decision-making, she emphasized how much closer women were to everyday reality:

They [the women] may not be able to say much but little suggestions may come from the experience gathered from the ordinary folks in the streets. Women have ways of finding out things that men cannot do, and it will be profitable to the country if they use this ability. Women have got ability that is specially unique in them and no man can trespass on this ground.[63]

232

Equal rights for women was an issue that Esan constantly raised in the Senate. Of particular concern to her was the fact that northern women did not possess the right to vote. In her maiden speech she pointedly remarked that she hoped that Northern women would soon have full civic rights.[64] Time and again she returned to this issue. During the debate on the subject in August 1962, she replied to one of her Northern colleagues:

A statement was made by both the N.P.C. [Northern People's Congress] in the North and the Northern Region Government to the effect that women would be given the franchise in God's good time. When is the time to come? These women are not given the opportunity to get more experience. So I daresay God's time may never come as far as franchise for women in the North is concerned.[65]

Northern politicians, however, were adamant that the franchise for women went against religious and cultural customs. Northern women finally received the vote from the military government in 1979.

Being the only women among scores of male legislators in their respective legislatures, Dove and Esan shared the experience of ridicule from their male colleagues. Male legislators found any mention at all of women's affairs trivial or a joke or even absurd. Once when Esan was speaking on the need to appoint women to delegations attending international commissions and conferences, she bitterly retorted to a senator's attempt to trivialize the idea, 'I do not see any need for a Senator to turn my contributions in this debate into humour.' Sexual harassment was also a potential hazard.[66] The only woman on a five-member delegation to the Afro-Asian Solidarity Conference in Cairo, Dove was shocked by the aggressive and unwelcome overtures of one of her colleagues.[67]

Epilogue

Few of the West African political regimes that took their countries into independence succeeded in creating a stable government. The post-independence record of struggles for leadership, internal strife, *coups d'état*, and counter-coups is well known. Naturally those women who succeeded in entering mainstream politics suffered the same fate as their male colleagues. Although Dove's career as a parliamentarian did not last long, she continued to write on politics in the Accra papers until her eyesight began to fail. She rushed through the writing of her memoirs against the knowledge that she was going blind. *Coups d'état* in Nigeria in 1966 and in Mali in 1968 interrupted the promising political careers of Esan and Keita. Although Esan had resigned from the AG in 1964 in protest against the party's alliance with the NCNC, she continued to serve in the Senate and supported the Nigerian National Democratic Party government set up by S. L. Akintola. She became an important figure in Ibadan community politics and in 1975 was installed as the Iyalode, a traditional office which still possesses considerable influence in the city. Keita continued to be a prominent figure in international meetings, especially those held in Eastern Europe. She was a major figure in the Women's International Democratic Federation in French-speaking Africa.[68] Notwithstanding the forced retirement from active politics of Dove, Keita and Esan, they achieved notable success as pioneers in opening the way for women in their societies to enter the mainstream of political life. Their careers provided models of courage, independence and professionalism that young women could admire and seek to emulate.

Notes

1. I would like to thank the following: the niece of Mabel Dove, also named Mabel Dove, for permission to use her aunt's manuscript autobiography; Philip Allsworth-Jones and Joyce Kwamena-Poh for their help in translating Aoua Keita's autobiography; and Oluwatoyin Kalifat Alli-Balogun for permission to use the interviews she conducted while doing her B.A. Honours project on Wuraola Esan; and Michael Kwamena-Poh, Glenn Webb and Benson Mojuetan for their comments on an earlier version of this chapter.

2. For an early overview, see La Ray Denzer, 'Towards a Study of the History of the West African Women's Participation in Nationalist Politics: The Early Phase, 1935–1950', *Africana Research Bulletin*, VI(4), 1976, pp. 65–85.

3. Thomas Hodgkin, *African Political Parties*. (London: Penguin, 1961), pp. 120–1; Ruth S. Morgenthau. *Politics in French-speaking West Africa*, (Oxford, 1964), pp. 94, 222, 238.

4. Nina E. Mba, *Nigerian Women Mobilized: Women's Political Activity in Southern Nigeria, 1960–1965*, (Berkeley, California: Institute of International Affairs, University of California, 1982), pp. 235–76.

5. Jean O'Barr, 'African Women in Politics', in Margaret Jean Hay and Sharon Stichter, (eds). *African Women South of the Sahara* (London, 1984), pp. 140–55; and LeBeuf, Annie M. D., 'The Role of Women in the Political Organization of African Societies', in Denise Paulme, (ed.), *Women of Tropical Africa*, (Berkeley, California, 1971), pp. 93–120.

6. Mba, *Nigerian Women Mobilized*, pp. 280–9.

7. This brief biography is based primarily on Mabel Dove's unpublished autobiography. Other sources are K. A. B. Jones-Quartey, 'First Lady of Pen and Parliament – A Portrait', in Ghana Association of Writers, *100 Years International Centenary Evenings with Aggrey of Africa* (Accra: Ghana Association of Writers, 1975); 'Gold Coast's First Assembly Woman', *West African Review*, September 1954, p. 829; and 'Voice of the Women', *West Africa*, 24 July 1954, p. 679.

8. Obituary of Lydia Marion Rice, *Sierra Leone Weekly News*, 14 July 1951.

9. M. Dove, Autobiography, Mss., 25.

10. For a brief biography of Danquah, see L. H. Ofosu-Appiah, 'Danquah, J. B.', *The Encyclopaedia Africana Dictionary of African Biography*, vol. I: *Ethiopia-Ghana* (New York, 1977), pp. 230–33.

11. The following account is based on Keita's extensive autobiography, A. Keita, *Femme d'Afrique: La vie de Aoua Keita racontée par elle-même*, (Paris, 1975).

12. This biographical account is based on Oluwatoyin Kafilat Alli-Balogun, 'A Biography of Chief (Mrs) Wuraola Adepeju Esan (The Iyalode of Ibadan)', B.A. Honours Essay, Department of History, University of Ibadan, June 1987; and 'A Brief History of Chief (Mrs) Wuraola Adepeju Esan Iyalode Ibadan', *Eto Isin Isinku Fun Oloogbe Wuraola Adepeju Esan, Mfr. J. P., Iyalode Ibadan*, Funeral programme, St James Cathedral, Oke-Bola, Ibadan, 19 July 1985.

13. National Archives, Ibadan (hereafter NAI), IBMINED 1/6 LEO 7: list of students in the foundation class.

14. Annual Report, Education Department of Southern Nigeria, 1928, 27.

15. Interview with Mrs E. A. Aboderin, Bodija, Ibadan, 5 January 1987 (conducted by O. K. Alli-Balogun).

16. NAI, IBMINED 1/2 CIW 1109.

17. Gladys Plummer served in the Education Department of Nigeria from 1931 to 1950.

18. NAI, IBMINED 1/1 DDW 539 vol. I: Inspection report of UMC, 3–5 October 1932.

19. 'And Politics, Too', *West Africa*, 6 April 1963, 393.

20. NAI, Oyo Prof 1/4 161.

21. 'Parents Day by Girls School', *Western Echo*, 11 December 1947; M. A. Adeyemi, 'Foreword', *Peoples: A Souvenir Magazine, 21 Years, 1965–1986*, 1.

22. Keita, *Femme d'Afrique*, p. 45.

23. Dove, Autobiography, p. ch. 14.

24. 'And Politics, Too', *West Africa*, 6 April 1963, 373; and Mba, *Nigerian Women Mobilized*, p. 240n.

25. For background on Ghanaian politics, see D. Austin, *Politics in Ghana, 1946–1960*, (London, 1970).

26. Jones-Quartey, 'First Lady of Pen and Parliament'.

27. Dove, Autobiography, p. 119.

28. The first West African woman proprietor and editor was E. Ronke Ajayi who in 1931 founded the *Nigerian Herald* in Lagos. The paper folded after two years of publication.

29. 'Women M.L.As', editorial, *Daily Graphic*, 20 February 1953; 5 October 1953, and *Daily Echo*, 2 February 1954.

30. *Daily Echo*, 27 August and 2 September 1953; *Daily Graphic*, 1 September 1953.

31. Dove, Autobiography, p. 142.

32. 'Election Round-up', *West Africa*, 26 June 1954, p. 588.

33. *Ashanti Pioneer*, 12 May 1954.

34. *Daily Echo*, 12 May 1954.

35. 'Nkrumah Changed Her Career' (profile of Hannah Cudjoe), *West Africa*, 8 August 1953, p. 725.

36. Dove, Autobiography, p. 142.

37. Ibid., 146–147.

38. *Ashanti Pioneer*, 17 June 1954.

39. Morganthau, *Politics in French-speaking Africa*, pp. 38–40.

40. Keita, *Femme d'Afrique*, ch. 3.

41. Ibid., 65.

42. Ibid., ch. 4.

43. See, for example, ibid., ch. 6.

44. Ibid., 386–387.

45. Ibid., 389–390.

46. *Nigerian Tribune*, 20 November 1952.

47. 'A Brief History of Chief (Mrs) Esan', Funeral Programme.

48. Mba, *Nigerian Women Mobilized*, p. 240n.

49. The other two AG women advisers were Mallama Ina Nusa from Zaria and Hannah Otudor from Calabar.

49. Mba, *Nigerian Women Mobilized*, 262.

51. Nigeria. *Senate Debates*, 23 August 1962, col. 777.

52. *Daily Times*, 9 January 1960; 'And Politics, Too', *West Africa*, 6 April 1963.

53. Keita, *Femme d'Afrique*, 387.

54. Dove, Autobiography, p. 169.

55. Ibid.

56. Ibid., 163–4.

57. The CPP rectified this in 1960 when it appointed ten women as special representatives to the National Assembly.

58. Dove, Autobiography, p. 215.

59. Ibid., ch. 57.

60. *Daily Service*, 26 January 1960.

61. Nigeria, *Senate Debates*, 2 April 1960, cols. 197–8.

62. Ibid., 29 April 1960, col. 344.

63. Ibid., 29 April 1960, col. 344.

64. *Daily Service*, 26 January 1960.

65. Nigeria, *Senate Debates*, 20 August 1962, col. 656.

66. In recent series of interviews, Margaret Ekpo, appointed for a brief period to the Eastern Nigerian House of Chiefs in 1954 and in 1961 elected to the Eastern House of Assembly, was very frank about this problem. According to her, some of her colleagues 'tried to molest me' and that 'I wouldn't say that I had no trouble. I had lots and lots of them. But I was very firm! I was very, very firm!'. 'Conversations with Bisi Lawrence. Chief (Mrs) Margaret Ekpo', Episode 3, *Sunday Vanguard*, 8 October 1989.

67. Dove, Autobiography, pp. 225–6.

68. University of Ibadan Library Manuscript Collection, Funmilayo Ransome-Kuti papers, Box 1 (WIDF): Report by Mrs. M. M. Rossi on her trip to Africa, April 18–May 7, 1963, presented to WIDF Bureau Meeting, Moscow, June 18–19, 1963.

Maps

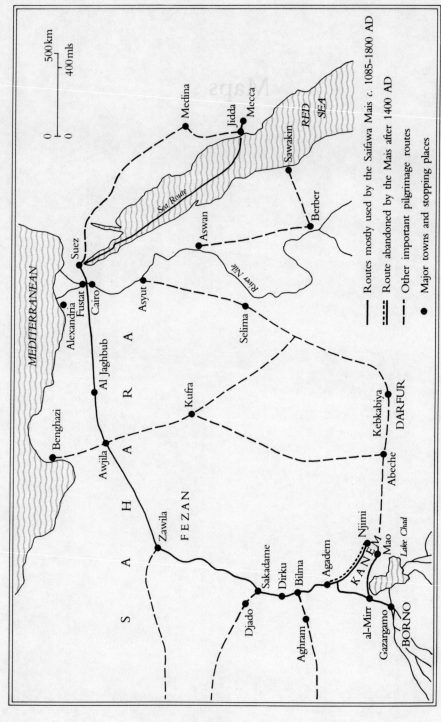

Map 1: Pilgrimage routes used by the Saifawa Mais, *c.* 1086–1800 AD (see Chapter 1)

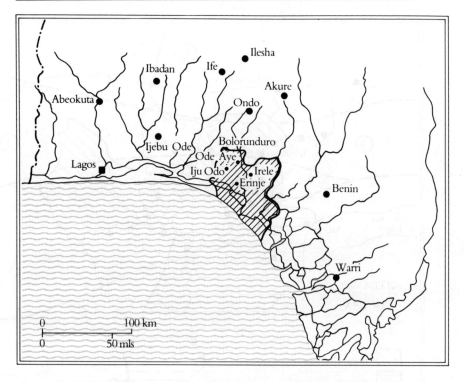

Map 2: Niger Delta: general map showing location of Ikale and Ilaje territories
(see Chapter 10)

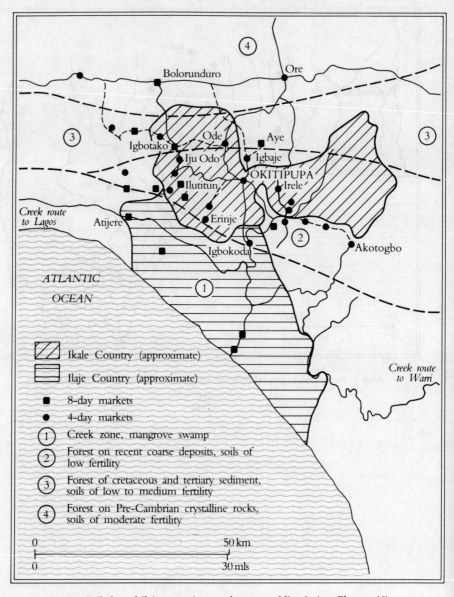

Map 3: Ikale and Ilaje countries, south-western Nigeria (see Chapter 10)

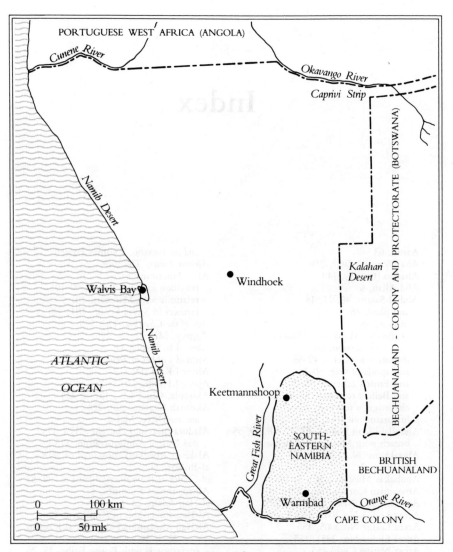

Map 4: Namibia (German South-West Africa) *c.* 1900 (see Chapter 11)

Index